LOTHARINGIA

Simon Winder is the author of the highly praised
The Man Who Saved Britain, *Danubia* and *Germania*.
He works in publishing and lives in
Wandsworth Town.

Also by Simon Winder

The Man Who Saved Britain

Danubia

Germania

AS EDITOR

Night Thoughts

Sea Longing

The Feast

'My Name's Bond . . .'

Simon Winder

LOTHARINGIA

A Personal History of Europe's Lost Country

PICADOR

First published 2019 by Picador
an imprint of Pan Macmillan
20 New Wharf Road, London N1 9RR
Associated companies throughout the world
www.panmacmillan.com

ISBN 978-1-5098-0328-6

1 3 5 7 9 8 6 4 2

A CIP catalogue record for this book is available from the British Library.

Map artwork by Gobal Blended Learning

Typeset in 11.5/14 pt Columbus MT Std by Jouve (UK), Milton Keynes
Printed and bound by CPI Group (UK) Ltd, Croydon, CR0 4YY

Visit **www.picador.com** to read more about all our books
and to buy them. You will also find features, author interviews and
news of any author events, and you can sign up for e-newsletters
so that you're always first to hear about our new releases.

For CMJ

'On the Day of Judgement we shall not be asked what

we have read, but what we have done . . .'

THOMAS À KEMPIS

Contents

Contents

Contents

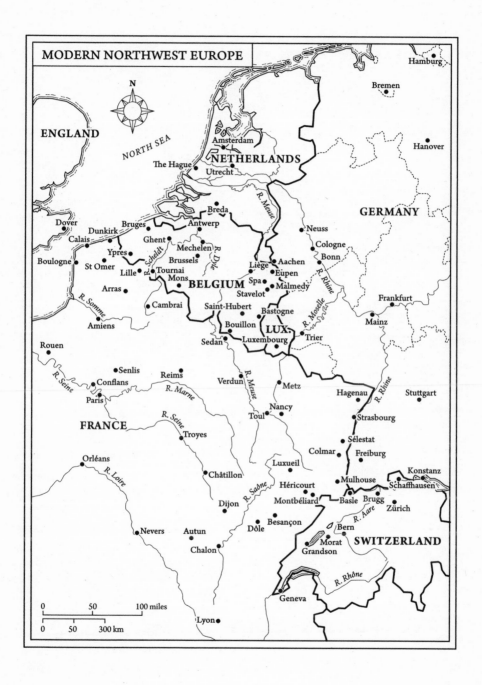

MODERN NORTHWEST EUROPE

N

ENGLAND

NORTH SEA

NETHERLANDS

GERMANY

Amsterdam
The Hague
Utrecht

Dover
Dunkirk   Bruges   Breda
Calais   Antwerp   Neuss
Boulogne   Ypres   Ghent   Mechelen   Cologne
St Omer   Lille   Brussels   Liège   Aachen   Bonn
Arras   Tournai   Mons   Eupen
        BELGIUM   Spa   Malmedy
        Stavelot
Cambrai   Saint-Hubert   Bastogne   Frankfurt
Amiens   Bouillon   LUX.   Mainz
        Sedan   Luxembourg   Trier

Rouen

Senlis   Reims   Verdun   Metz   Hagenau   Stuttgart
Conflans   Nancy   Strasbourg
Paris   Toul
FRANCE   Troyes   Sélestat   Freiburg
Orléans   Châtillon   Colmar   Konstanz
        Luxueil   Schaffhausen
        Héricourt   Mulhouse
Dijon   Montbéliard   Basle   Brugg
Nevers   Autun   Besançon   Zürich
        Dôle   Bern
Chalon   Morat   SWITZERLAND
        Grandson
        Geneva

R. Meuse
R. Dyle
Scheldt
R. Somme
R. Seine
R. Marne
R. Seine
R. Loire
R. Saône
R. Moselle
R. Rhine
R. Rhine
R. Aare
R. Rhône

Hamburg
Bremen
Hanover

0   50   100 miles
0   50   300 km

Lyon

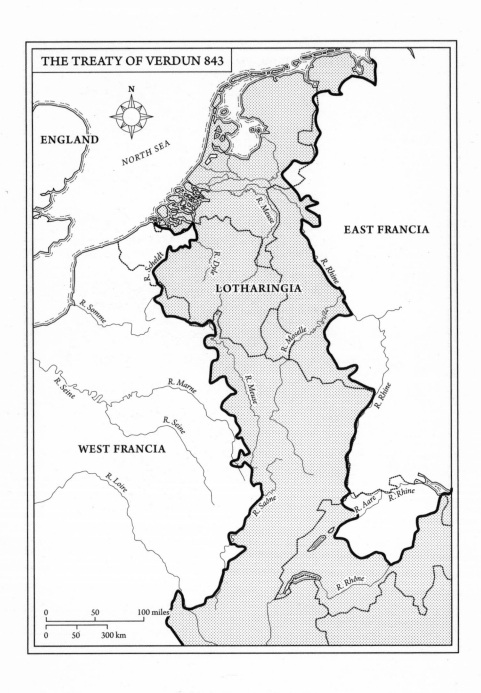

THE TREATY OF VERDUN 843

N

ENGLAND

NORTH SEA

EAST FRANCIA

LOTHARINGIA

R. Scheldt

R. Dyle

R. Meuse

R. Rhine

R. Somme

R. Moselle

R. Seille

R. Marne

R. Meuse

R. Seine

R. Rhine

WEST FRANCIA

R. Seine

R. Loire

R. Saône

R. Aare

R. Rhine

R. Rhône

0   50   100 miles

0   50   300 km

THE LOW COUNTRIES IN THE MIDDLE AGES

N

NORTH SEA

FRIESLAND

UTRECHT

HOLLAND

UTRECHT

GELDERLAND

ZUTPHEN

ZEELAND

KLEVE

R. Meuse

R. Rhine

BRABANT

FLANDERS

R. Scheldt

LOON

R. Dyle

JÜLICH

Tournai
COURTRAI

LIMBURG

PRINCE-
BISHOPRIC
OF LIÈGE

NAMUR

STAVELOT

ARTOIS

HAINAUT

CAMBRAI

R. Somme

LUXEMBURG

BOUILLON

R. Moselle

R. Meuse

0   50   100 miles

0   50   300 km

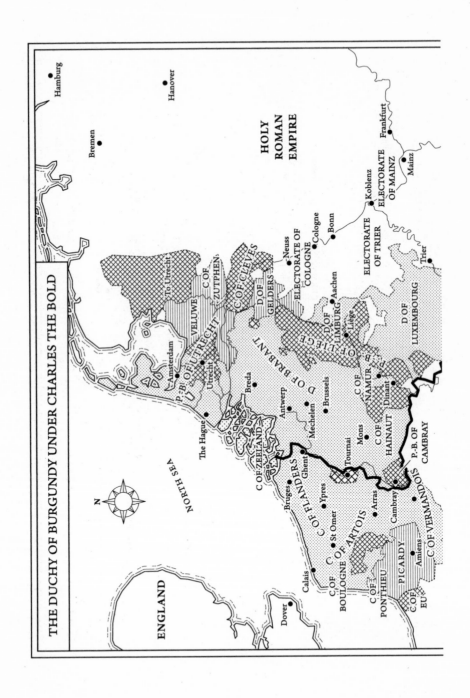

THE DUCHY OF BURGUNDY UNDER CHARLES THE BOLD

ENGLAND

Dover

NORTH SEA

N

Hamburg

Hanover

Bremen

HOLY
ROMAN
EMPIRE

Frankfurt

Mainz

ELECTORATE
OF MAINZ

Koblenz

ELECTORATE
OF TRIER

Trier

ELECTORATE OF
COLOGNE

Bonn

Cologne

Neuss

Aachen

To Utrecht

P.B. OF UTRECHT

Utrecht

Amsterdam

VELUWE

C. OF
ZUTPHEN

C. OF CLEVES

D. OF
GELDERS

D. OF
LIMBURG

D. OF
LUXEMBOURG

C. OF
LIÈGE

Liège

The Hague

Breda

Antwerp

Mechelen

Brussels

D. OF BRABANT

C. OF
ZEELAND

Ghent

Bruges

Ypres

St Omer

C. OF FLANDERS

Calais

C. OF
BOULOGNE OF ARTOIS

Arras

Cambray

C. OF
NAMUR

Dinant

Mons

C. OF
HAINAUT

Tournai

P.-B. OF
CAMBRAY

C. OF VERMANDOIS

PICARDY

Amiens

C. OF
PONTHIEU

C. OF
EU

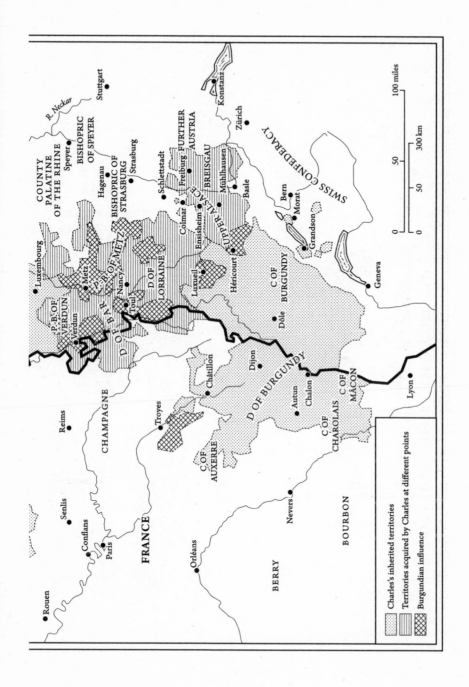

Stuttgart

R. Neckar

COUNTY
PALATINE
OF THE RHINE

Speyer ●
BISHOPRIC
OF SPEYER

BISHOPRIC OF
STRASBURG

Hagenau ●

Strasburg ●

Schlettstadt ●

Freiburg ●
FURTHER
AUSTRIA

Konstanz ●

Zürich ●

Luxembourg

P. B. OF METZ

Metz ●

BAR

D. OF LORRAINE

Colmar ●

BREISGAU

Mühlhausen ●

Ensisheim ●

ALSACE

UPPER

Basle ●

Bern ●

SWISS CONFEDERACY

P. B. OF
VERDUN
Verdun ●

D. OF

Nancy ●

Toul ●

Luxueil ●

Héricourt ●

C. OF
BURGUNDY

Morat ●

Grandson ●

Geneva ●

CHAMPAGNE

Reims ●

Troyes ●

Chatillon ●

Dijon ●

Dôle ●

D. OF BURGUNDY

Autun ●

Chalon ●

C. OF
MÂCON

Lyon ●

C. OF
AUXERRE

C. OF
CHAROLAIS

Senlis ●

Conflans ●

Paris ●

FRANCE

Orléans ●

Nevers ●

BOURBON

BERRY

Rouen ●

0   50   100 miles

0   50   300 km

Charles's inherited territories

Territories acquired by Charles at different points

Burgundian influence

DEPARTMENTS OF THE FRENCH EMPIRE

GREAT BRITAIN

NORTH SEA

N

EMS-ORIENTAL

BOUCHES-DU-WESER

BOUCHES-DE-L'ELBE

FRISE

EMS-OCCIDENTAL

ZUYDERZÉE

BOUCHES-DE-L'YSSEL

EMS-SUPÉRIEUR

YSSEL-SUPÉRIEUR

LIPPE

BOUCHES-DE-LA-MEUSE

BOUCHES-DE-L'ESCAUT

BOUCHES-DU-RHIN

DEUX NÈTHES

ESCAUT

R. Meuse

CONFEDERATION OF THE RHINE

LYS

R. Scheldt

Brussels

DYLE

R. Dyle

MEUSE-INFÉRIEURE

ROER

R. Rhine

PAS-DE-CALAIS

JEMAPPES

NORD

OURTHE

RHIN-ET-MOSELLE

R. Somme

SOMME

SAMBRE-ET-MEUSE

FORÊTS

R. Moselle

SARRE

MONT-TONNERRE

SEINE-INFÉRIEURE

OISE

AISNE

ARDENNES

MOSELLE

R. Meuse

R. Rhine

EURE

R. Seine

Paris

R. Marne

MARNE

MEUSE

MEURTHE

BAS-RHIN

SEINE-ET-OISE

SEINE-ET-MARNE

R. Seine

KINGDOM OF WÜRTTEMBERG

EURE-ET-LOIR

AUBE

VOSGES

LOIRET

YONNE

HAUTE-MARNE

HAUTE-SAÔNE

HAUT-RHIN

R. Rhine

LOIR-ET-CHER

R. Loire

CÔTE-D'OR

R. Saône

DOUBS

CHER

NIÈVRE

NEUCHÂTEL

Bern

SWISS CONFEDERATION

INDRE

SAÔNE-ET-LOIRE

JURA

CREUSE

ALLIER

AIN

LÉMAN

SIMPLON

R. Rhône

0   50   100 miles

0   50   300 km

LOIRE

RHONE

MONT-BLANC

DOIRE

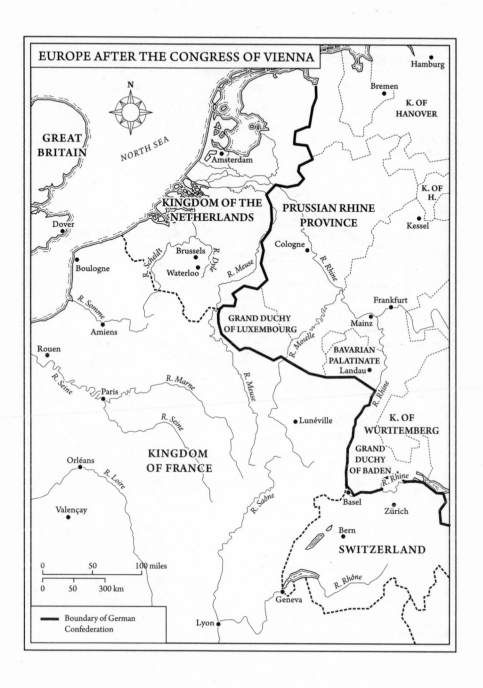

EUROPE AFTER THE CONGRESS OF VIENNA

N

GREAT
BRITAIN

NORTH SEA

Hamburg

Bremen

K. OF
HANOVER

Amsterdam

KINGDOM OF THE
NETHERLANDS

PRUSSIAN RHINE
PROVINCE

K. OF
H.

Dover

Boulogne

R. Scheldt

Brussels

Waterloo

R. Dyle

R. Meuse

Cologne

R. Rhine

Kessel

R. Somme

Amiens

GRAND DUCHY
OF LUXEMBOURG

R. Moselle

Frankfurt

Mainz

BAVARIAN
PALATINATE
Landau

Rouen

R. Seine

Paris

R. Marne

R. Meuse

Lunéville

R. Rhine

K. OF
WÜRTTEMBERG

R. Seine

KINGDOM
OF FRANCE

GRAND
DUCHY
OF BADEN

Orléans

R. Loire

R. Saône

Basel

R. Rhine

Zürich

Valençay

Bern

SWITZERLAND

0   50   100 miles

0   50   300 km

Geneva

R. Rhône

Lyon

■ Boundary of German
    Confederation

WORLD WAR ONE, WESTERN FRONT 1915

N

GREAT
BRITAIN

NORTH SEA

Hamburg

Bremen

Hanover

NETHERLANDS

Amsterdam

The Hague
Utrecht

R. Rhine

Breda

Dover
Calais
Boulogne

Dunkirk
Bruges
Ghent
St Omer
Ypres
Arras

Antwerp
BELGIUM
Mechelen
Brussels
Tournai
Mons

R. Scheldt

R. Dyle

Neuss
Cologne
Bonn

GERMANY

Liége
Spa
Stavelot

Aachen
Eupen
Malmedy

R. Meuse

Cambrai
Saint-Hubert
Bouillon
Sedan

Bastogne

Frankfurt
Mainz

Amiens

R. Somme

Luxembourg

Trier

R. Moselle

Rouen

R. Seine

Senlis
Conflans
Paris

Reims

R. Marne

Verdun

Metz
Nancy
Toul

Hagenau

Strasbourg

R. Rhine

Stuttgart

Troyes

R. Seine

FRANCE

Schlettstadt
Kolmar
Freiburg

Châtillon

Luxueil
Héricourt

Ensisheim
Mühlhausen

Konstanz

Orléans

R. Loire

R. Saône

Basle

Zürich

Nevers
Autun
Chalon

Dijon
Dôle

Besançon

Bern
Morat
Grandson

SWITZERLAND

0   50   100 miles
0   50   300 km

R. Rhône

Geneva

├┼┼┼┤ Trench line in 1915

///// German possession of Alsace-Lorraine

····· Neutral countries

LOTHARINGIA

Introduction

I was in the Ardennes, on a bus travelling from Stavelot to Spa. The bus was filled to bursting with primary- and secondary-school children and I was the only adult, aside from the magnificently stone-faced and imperturbable driver. It was midwinter and the fog was so solid that it looked as though, once outside the bus, you would have to be resigned to washing it out of your hair and brushing strands of it off your coat. The bus was, frankly, a monkey-house on wheels. One child was using a lighter to burn through a plastic handle, another had a phone app which converted a pupil's photo into a demon face. At irregular intervals an inflated condom was fired over our heads to happy cries. The whole atmosphere was hilarious and you almost expected the bus to rock from side to side as it drove along, like in an exuberant cartoon. It made me feel wistful about the long-gone years spent waiting for my own children in various school playgrounds. I had forgotten the magical way in which large groups of children flicker in their moods, managing to be morose, thrilled, exhausted and hyper in perhaps less than a second.

Each stop made by the fog-bound bus was a surprise. As the doors hissed open, a clump of children would gamely launch themselves into what appeared to be a solid form of Milk of Magnesia, with just a roof-angle visible to indicate houses of some kind, and the odd skeletal branch. In all kinds of ways this bus was really in the middle of nowhere – a series of rugged, thinly populated valleys which most Europeans have no need to engage with. From the air you would be able to see each valley filled to the brim with fog. But, like so many places I will write about in this book, it has had its turn as the centre of the world. Most obviously this was where the Battle of the Bulge was fought – the last major attempt by the Germans to defeat the Western Allies. The little town of Stavelot – of which

I had previously been entirely ignorant – was where the battle reached its high-water mark, in December 1944. American troops had kept destroying bridges and blocking the narrow roads by felling thousands of trees, the Germans kept rigging up pontoons and blowing up the obstacles – but at Stavelot they briefly entered the town, massacred dozens of its inhabitants, could not fight their way through, tried to drive round, failed and began the retreat which only stopped with their surrender in May. A small marker in the town states: HERE THE INVADER WAS STOPPED.

I was surrounded by the same fog that had made the initial German attack through the Ardennes so successful, but this was just one part of the region's central role in the twentieth century. It was, famously, the source of the British and French armies' crushing and almost instantaneous defeat in 1940, as thousands of German tanks and troop-lorries secretly wound their way through the same narrow roads. During the First World War, the town of Spa was the German military headquarters in the fighting's later period. A series of photos taken in 1918 show the last weeks of imperial and aristocratic rule in Germany, as Kaiser Wilhelm II, the Crown Prince and various generals stand around hobnobbing in their immaculate uniforms in one of Spa's commandeered assembly rooms. It was in these rooms that the Kaiser, hearing about the revolution breaking out in Berlin, appealed to his generals for support, only to find that they no longer trusted their men and could not even guarantee that they would not attack him. Wilhelm panicked and fled to Holland, abandoning the imperial train in case troops took potshots at it, and ending over eight centuries of Hohenzollern rule. In 1944 the same complex in Spa was in turn the headquarters of the US Army, evacuated during the temporary panic that followed the surprise, fog-bound German offensive.

I had come to Stavelot partly out of contrition and annoyance that I had not heard of the place before. It turns out to have a sensational museum in its sprawling former abbey which showed that in the first half of the twelfth century it was the only place to be. But Stavelot once I was there also showed that I really just had to stop my travelling around for this book. There was effectively *no limit* to the richness and density of a region that is both the dozy back of beyond, *and* central to the fate of humanity. Here I was in a bus filled with the great-grandchildren and great-great-grandchildren of those who had experienced 'historical' events of various, terrible kinds and who were – with their jolly backpacks and untiring ability to laugh helplessly when one of their number farted – happily oblivious. My own children were now adults and I looked back with dismay at the immense amounts of time I had spent away from them, drifting around dozens of Stavelot-like places, face to face with the same question about why European events and ideas have swept through so many places that just wished to be left alone.

I have always wanted to write these words, but they are now true: this book is the completion of a trilogy! *Germania* was a history of German-speakers roughly within the modern Federal Republic of Germany. I tried to make it an evenly spread book, but the locations kept being tugged eastwards as I wallowed shamelessly in the tiny towns of Thuringia and Saxony-Anhalt. I then wrote *Danubia* because I was aware that *Germania* failed to deal with the Germans of Austria or of other points east. Before the twentieth century, German culture had spread into the lands across Central Europe and this opened up several other interests I had, in the nature of competing nationalisms, in the Habsburg family and its many odd-nesses, and the Christian–Muslim frontiers that shaped the whole vast region for centuries. As someone who grew up in the Cold War and was, like everyone, gripped by the discovery of what was for a generation a *new* and previously near inaccessible swathe of ex-communist land, it was easy to take for granted the more familiar, western parts of Europe. Even when writing *Germania* I had a dim sense that I had short-changed and not really engaged fully with perhaps the most important motor of all in Europe's development: the lands to the west. I had not noticed them as they were all just part of the European Union, like the United Kingdom, and simply represented modernity, the present and a sort of ho-hum banality. And yet, even a moment's self-interrogation would have made me realize that the area from the Rhine westwards and the German-speakers' relationship with French-speakers is the least ho-hum subject it is possible to find.

The theme of this book is defined by one of the most important if accidental moments in European history. Charles I 'the Great' (Charlemagne) spent a long and enjoyable career carving out a huge empire across much of north-west mainland Europe. It was very much a personal achievement, however, and after his death in AD 814 the personalities of his successors, new enemies and the sheer, unmanageable size of the Carolingian Empire made it collapse into civil war. Charlemagne's grandsons met at the small town of Wirten (Verdun in French) in 843 and agreed to split the Empire into three chunks, one for each of them. The Franks had often broken up their lands between siblings and there had always been a distinction between the older territory of Austrasia ('eastern land'), on the Rhine, as against the more recent block of Neustria ('new western land') on the Seine, but this new split stuck. Charles II 'the Bald' received the west, which became France. Louis I 'the German' received the east, which became Germany. The big block in the middle, including the great imperial city of Aachen, went to nickname-free Lothair I. Lothair's inheritance stretched from the edges of the North Sea down to central Italy, but was itself impossibly sprawling. On his death it was itself split, with his three sons each taking a bit: one received north Italy, one received Provence and Lothair II received everything north of Provence – a region which was called after him Lotharingia, 'the lands of Lothar'.

Today the area of Lotharingia has reduced, like a small leftover lump of snow – frenchified into the word 'Lorraine' (Lothringen still in German). But the issue of what constitutes Lotharingia has, with innumerable mutations, survived from 843 to the present. Lotharingia has provoked wars in every century and it has been the site of many of the events which have defined European civilization. Sometimes the gap has been sealed up almost completely – indeed it came close to vanishing permanently as early as after Lothair II's death – but its in-between status has never gone away and in 2017 it consists of the kingdoms of Belgium and the Netherlands, the

Grand Duchy of Luxembourg and the northern part of the Swiss Confederation, with the rest of the region shared between the Republic of France and the Federal Republic of Germany. These states are simply the inheritors of a crazy quilt of predecessors and the aim of this book is to give some sense of these and how Lotharingia has proved such a key element in so much of European history.

I have chosen to define Lotharingia for practical purposes as the area from where the Rhine leaves Lake Constance, taking in the banks of the Rhine including the northern Swiss cantons. Once clear of Switzerland, Lotharingia is formed to the east by the banks of the Rhine and to the west by the areas of France which were for many centuries parts of the Holy Roman Empire.

I have had to take one or two sad decisions. The arc of Lake Geneva is the clear southern point, but I have had to leave out Geneva itself as for so much of its history it is part of Savoy and faces south, tangling itself in the affairs of Turin and the rest of Italy. If I had to incorporate Italy too this book would be doomed. On the banks of the Rhine I am fairly strict – so lots of discussion of lands west of it, but on the east not budging much further eastwards to avoid being dragged (by cities such as Frankfurt) into Germany *profonde*. An exception is Heidelberg as so much of the territory under its control, the Palatinate,* is on the Rhine. Once the maze of Rhine branches spreads through the Low Countries I am fairly expansive about what gets included, stopping just short of North Holland. To the south I include the areas of northern France which were also historically contested – down to the old territories of the Counts of Flanders north of the Somme River, the ownership of which has provided soldiers with intermittent pay-packets and constant grief for as long as we have historical records.

* This oddly named Lotharingian territory (Pfalz in German, and surviving still in the name of the province of Rheinland-Pfalz) shows the importance of its ruler as one of the Seven Electors – 'Palatinate' in the sense of 'of the palace'. But it also indicated territory with special, defensive connotations, as in the County Palatine of Chester keeping the Welsh at bay or the County Palatine of Durham doing the same for the Scots. The French word 'paladin' has the same root.

This is an enormous region, but it is strikingly empty of major capital cities. Lotharingia has had a consistent ability to mess up outsiders, but those outsiders have come from states with far greater resources and wider horizons than Lotharingia itself. At different times Paris, London, Amsterdam, Berlin, Vienna, Rome and Madrid have seen both headaches and opportunities here – indeed whole eras have been defined by the headaches, bringing entire dynasties to their knees in rage and frustration. To be consistent with leaving out these interfering external cities I have also left out Bern (or mostly left out – there were one or two things I *had* to mention about Bern) and Dijon (definitely a core part of France, but a principal base for the Dukes of Burgundy during their hundred and twenty magical years of exploiting the Lotharingian seam). I renounced this latter in tears, having to forgo tables loaded up for research purposes with bottles of Nuits-Saint-Georges and plates of parsleyed ham. Amsterdam is the most controversial omission, but just as Geneva heads the reader south into another realm, so Amsterdam moves the story up into the Baltic, Frisia and a variety of other external lures which make it problematic. It is also true I think that, like London or Madrid, say, Amsterdam's interests historically were often far removed from the lands to its south. It always had other fish to fry – or pickle – and is sufficiently north to have almost always been outside the front line, a fact often commented on bitterly by those embroiled in devastating events further south which Amsterdam bankrolled and egged on.

This book requires, like my two previous books, a sort of mind experiment, albeit not one requiring huge forces. Many of the political units in this book existed for centuries and had a robustness and long-term plausibility which gave them an unthinking acceptance. We may now laugh at the Duchy of Bar, which geographically looks like a bowl of spilt breakfast cereal, but we have no evidence that its many generations of inhabitants felt sheepish about its patent unviability – or at least not until the eighteenth century. The Imperial Abbey of Prüm, whose only asset was ownership of a pair of sandals once owned – and rather scuffed up – by Jesus and given to the monks by Charlemagne's father Pippin, kept its semi-independence and attracted an endless stream of pilgrims with surprising success for many centuries, only totally losing its status once Napoleon swept through.

Every period assumes that it represents a rational order and looks back in sorrow at the political idiocy that so defaced earlier, less civilized eras. But, of course, because we grow up with specific arrangements we assume they are natural, whereas even in the twenty-first century 'Lotharingia' remains a mass of seeming illogicality. Just heading from the bottom of the modern region to the top some highlights would include the German exclave of Konstanz, the Swiss exclave of Schaffhausen, the pointless separate bits and pieces of the Canton of Solothurn, the teeny French department of Belfort (maintained in honour of its successful defence – a lone bright spot – in the Franco-Prussian War), the irrationally small German province of Saarland (a side effect of Paris's efforts after both world wars to absorb it into France), the Grand Duchy of Luxembourg (which only exists because France and Prussia could not be bothered to fight over it in the 1860s), the German-speaking districts of Belgium (taken as war booty in 1919 and making no sense as an acquisition then or now), the eccentric Dutch appendix of Maastricht, the eight tiny blocks of Baarle-Hertog (fragments of Belgian territory left inside the Netherlands because of bad-tempered bickering in the 1840s) and ending up with a flourish at the attractively named Dutch territory of Zeelandic Flanders, a chunk of dyked farmland only directly reachable from the rest of the Netherlands by ship and a new car tunnel, left over from the long era of blocking up the River Scheldt to shut the rival port of Antwerp. I am sure there are more (the two pieces of Canadian territory in northern France donated as war memorials for example) but these small or large bits of 'rubble' are wholly characteristic of Lotharingia and represent an almost geological continuity, evidence for the region's strange past, making it quite different from much of the rest of Europe. Even with the ferocious efforts to crush Europe into a single, rational entity after the French Revolution and during the Second World War, somehow these fragmented political units survive, mocking such efforts.

A note on myself and France

The first flight I ever took was when, aged fourteen, I was packed off by my parents to spend three weeks at a farm north-east of Meaux on my own to learn French. My mental state can only be compared to the sort of disregarded small mammals in a zoo that huddle at the back of their cage in soiled straw, ears flat to their heads and eyes blank with permanent terror.

With our own children for years we ran threat variations on the French exchange theme: 'If you don't do your homework, it's six weeks in Clermont-Ferrand for you, eating lamb's brains.' But my parents were serious. My mother had in her late teens worked as an au pair for a French family who we had then visited when my sisters and I were fairly young. Coming from a cheerful 'Home Counties' middle-class background we all found this French family stagger-ingly exotic – with guns and dogs and open-face flans, spiral staircases and Monsieur wearing a long cloak. Their house was a former priory and the wrecked chapel next to it had a baptismal font filled with human skulls – whether this was done as a gesture of *laïque* contempt or just to tidy up we never knew. There was a German student staying with them who had just done his military service and showed us rifle drill using my four-year-old sister, under instructions to stay very rigid, as the firearm. It was an odd few days.

My chief moment of shame happened at a formal lunch featur-ing a seemingly infinite number of strange French adults plus the family and a first course of some very rare slices of beef. My first mouthful simply made my jaws bounce apart and while everyone else was chattering away I felt an excruciating helplessness, almost choking in a failed attempt to swallow just this first leather-like morsel. Help was at hand from a large, strong-smelling schnauzer dog called Clovis. In a reckless attempt to break the meat impasse I started feeding him chunks under the table. This worked very well and soon I had cleared my plate. My thought processes are unclear, but I think as a treat for Clovis being so helpful, I then handed under the table a piece of toasted baguette. This was a disastrous error as the loud crunching sound brought conversation to a halt.

My parents later explained that the resulting chaos came from Clovis being the pride of the house and a very old friend to all, but who was now, toothless and rickety, reduced to a special liquid diet. I went into a sort of dissociative trance of embarrassment and have no further active memory beyond that provided by my parents, who themselves always enjoyed that blend of real and feigned dismay the French so revel in.

I mention this because it was the seemingly infinite family web emanating from this former priory that furnished my sisters and me with French exchanges in coming years. These contacts were to have a deep impact on our lives. One sister ended up taking a modern-language degree, worked in Paris for a while and spent a lot of time in France; the other married a Frenchman and has lived in Brittany for many years, her two children so extraordinarily French that they seem to have been to a deep-immersion pout-and-shrug Gallic acting school.

My own experiences were less happy – mostly because of my incapacity in (and therefore hatred of) foreign languages. It seemed barely credible that I should be sacrificing two weeks of a school holiday to talk, or not talk, French. Even worse, if possible, the 'exchange' element kicked in and these French boys would then turn up at my home, filling up yet more holidays, and, in turn, failing to learn English. My first attempt at writing imaginative literature was sketching the outline of a novel where the French boy hosting an English boy tries to kill him by pushing him off a cliff. Through sheer luck the English boy lands on a ledge and works his way back to safety. The second half would have been about the doomed French boy, knowing his plot had failed, being sent over to England where he is reduced to insanity by dodging an incredible range of man-traps, oil slicks, poisons, out-of-control cars, etc., set up by the stylish and resourceful English boy. Called *Exchange*, I remember this notional novel enjoyably filling up lots of spare mental moments during the wearying hours of playing chess or going round the Tower of London with French boys no more interested in learning English than I had been in learning French.

I need to move on as I am only writing this to introduce my

nervousness about writing French history, not to reel off pages of teen anecdote. Looking back, I can see I was sheltered by the sheer good luck of not having read at the time any books in the rich English tradition in which France was the arena for youthful sexual initiation. If I had known this then, every moment would have been a frenzy of anticipation as I manoeuvred socially through a wilderness of French people all themselves wearily well aware of their ancient duties towards young English house guests. Looking back it is hard not to be slightly cross that such a range of sons and daughters, fathers and mothers must have been appraising me and thinking, 'No, I really don't think so.' Perhaps, when I had left the room, there were family arguments.

My relationship to French is like that of a small dog that can smell the food on a table, but cannot reach it and does not know what it looks like. All these times in France: the money, the collecting from the airport, the polite conversations at each meal – and all to get me a D grade at A-level. I stayed twice with the family who owned a farm north-east of Meaux. This was a remarkable experience. Both parents were impressive, energetic and kind. We went clay-pigeon shooting, drove around the farm in Monsieur's American post-D-Day jeep (the star on its hood still visible), fed chickens, looked through the woods for mushrooms, ate brains-on-toast.

In any event, many hours would go by avoiding speaking French. We were once in the car and one of my exchange's younger brothers said of me: 'He is dumb like an animal,' which I could understand but not reply to. We would go for walks, play ping-pong, pick more mushrooms, watch television – anything to avoid actual talking. I had the over-clever idea of bringing along Gide's *Symphonie Pastorale* because the English translation used the French title, thinking I could get away with reading it with Madame none the wiser. I still remember her look of sad reproach as I came in from ping-pong to find her holding the book. We often took walks along the valley of the Ourcq River with occasional little memorials which I did not pay any attention to at the time, only later realizing that it was in these fields that in September 1914 the Battle of the Marne began, perhaps the most important few days in the twentieth century. I have to stop writing about this stuff – I so admired the family and did so little to make it all worthwhile by actually learning any French.

So now I am in my fifties and still terrible at French. Part of me would like to have a private gold-tooled library of French master-pieces, like Frederick the Great's at Potsdam, where I could succumb to the noble tongue of Racine, but it will never happen. This book is the first time I have come face to face with writing squarely about France and it has been a fun and alarming experience.

A note on place names

British decisions on what to call places are a cheery pick 'n' mix of inconsistency. There are spellings unique to the English language: Basle, Brussels, Antwerp, Ghent, Dunkirk. There are despairing approximations: Flushing for Vlissingen, Brill for Brielle, Dort (tra-ditionally) for Dordrecht. There is the baffling tangle of The Hague for Den Haag – changing the pronunciation to match 'vague' rather than 'aargh'. In Dutch and French it is clear that the city is just called The Hedge, but perhaps English diplomats recoiled from this as being too silly an accredition.

Some names have mutated over time. In the seventeenth century it was still normal to write Ghent as Gaunt (as in John of). Accents on places like Zürich were naturally whipped off, indeed five out of the six letters in the word Zürich are mispronounced in English. Kleve used, of course, to be Cleves (as in Anne of). Calais used to be put through an English wringer and emerge pronounced Kalliss. Some names are just oddly inconsistent – so we have the Frenchi-fied Bruges, but keep Zeebrugge rather than Bruges-sur-Mer. This is just as well as the Flemish form sounds like a rather desolate ferry port (which it is) while the French form erroneously suggests people twirling moustaches and parasols and sipping iced drinks next to a bandstand.

There are a number of towns where how names are pronounced or spelled has sometimes meant a lot. French designs on the

Rhineland led to Mainz, Trier, Aachen, Koblenz and Köln becoming Mayence, Trèves, Aix-la-Chapelle, Coblence and Cologne. In the nineteenth century these were all acceptable English usage, but now only the last has stuck. This may be because the word Köln is just too hard to assimilate in English or because the city is so closely linked with the eau de. In any event while we share the spelling with France, the pronunciation is almost unrelated: French stays close to German, something like *coll-on*, with a linger on the n, whereas in British English it is something like *kerr-loww-n*.

There are obvious daggers-drawn issues around Alsace and Lorraine: Nancy/Nanzig, Strasbourg/Straßburg, Sélestat/Schlettstadt, Lunéville/Lünstadt. Alsatian signpost makers must now look back at their guild dinners with drunken nostalgia for the golden times of 1870 to 1945. There is a similar Walloon–Flemish/Dutch issue: Bruxelles/Brussel, Gant/Gent, Bruges/Brugge, Liège/Luik, Ypres/Ieper, Louvain/Leuven, Courtrai/Kortrijk, Tournai/Doornik. And a related one for French Flanders, although the number of Flemish speakers is now tiny: Lille/Rysel, Dunkerque/Duinkerke. The Swiss move back and forth with bilingual ease: Bâle/Basel; Bern/Berne, Zurich/Zürich, Lucerne/Luzern.

One historical fossil is that Spain's long and vexed rule gave many towns fun, specifically Spanish names: Brujas, Bruselas, Arrás, Lila, Luxembourgo, Mastrique, Gante, Dunquerque, all now sadly extinct. Some place names are so robust that they work in every language: Breda surrenders whether in Spanish, English or Dutch. I had been rather hoping it might be called Brède in French, but it isn't. The Netherlands' most off-putting of all town names, 's-Hertogenbosch ('the Duke's woods') – a wonderful place that would receive many more English-speaking visitors if their eyes did not bounce off the name – is rendered with great elegance in both Spanish and French, as respectively Bolduque and Bois-le-Duc.

In traditional English shorthand the names of the closest bits of the Low Countries are used to cover the whole lot, so the north is just 'Holland' and the south 'Flanders', with all the other counties and duchies (Hainaut, say, or Gelderland) having no real resonance. An even more extreme version was the Victorian tradition in English ships that all European sailors were simply 'Dutchmen' even if they actually came from Sweden or Italy or wherever.

From the late sixteenth century onwards there are a number of ways of referring to the provinces that rebelled against Spanish rule. Those that succeeded coalesced into roughly what is today the Kingdom of the Netherlands. I invariably call the kingdom's predecessor the Dutch Republic, but the United Provinces would have been as good a choice. The modern English names for both Switzerland and the Netherlands attractively bury ancient usages: the inhabitants of the former (particularly as mercenaries) once being 'Switzers' ('Where are my Switzers? Let them guard the door.' *Hamlet*) and 'Nether' for 'Low' as in 'her nether regions' or 'Nether Wallop'. Nobody will ever update these to Swissland or the Lowlands.

Throughout this book I use whatever is the current, most common form in English.

The structure of the book is very simple. It is roughly chronological and follows how at different times different outsiders have tried and failed to get their hands on the wealthy and sophisticated lands of Lotharingia.

When I first started writing this book I printed off a rough outline map of Western Europe and used a yellow marker-pen to highlight Lotharingia, roughly in the form it was when it first came into existence in AD 843. I then adjusted the map by removing the area below Lake Geneva for reasons explained earlier, and adding bits of the Rhine's right bank, as these were also often seen as 'loose' from other nearby territory. After a brief and chaotic separate existence Lotharingia was absorbed into the Holy Roman Empire, but with never-quelled arguments from many of its inhabitants about the zone's separate nature, and from France that this transfer was simply illegitimate.

I then drew on my map what was meant to be a threatening and acquisitive eye for each capital city, looking gloatingly at Lotharingia. As my drawing was so poor, the eye looked in each case like a man on a gate, a Chinese ideogram or a farm animal. In any event, the most important eye is always Paris: as rulers of France and descendants of Charlemagne, the French kings have always seen the lands in between as potentially part of France – this is argued and fought about with varying degrees of success well into the twentieth century. When Louis XIV razed to the ground Frederick Barbarossa's old palace at Haguenau it was to eradicate any further claims of 'Germandom' to the area, but it was only one in any number of acts of eradicatory chauvinism and counter-chauvinism. A further complication for France is that the Duchy of Flanders in the original division of Charlemagne's Empire was made part of 'West Francia', i.e. France, but its counts were often able to maintain a sort of semi-independence. Other eastern parts of Flanders and the territories to its north and east (Brabant, Holland, Gelderland, etc.) were definitely Lotharingian and therefore part of the Holy Roman Empire. But the main part of Flanders was different and vulnerable to Parisian interference – as were the territories to its south: Artois, Boulogne, and at some points in history all the way down to Amiens and the Somme River.

The second eye is London. The security of the coast across from Kent and Sussex has always been crucial. London interferes along the coast whenever it can and its politics can often be expressed by British or mainland exiles skipping back and forth across the Channel, either fleeing disaster or returning home. Friendly Flemish, Zeelandic and Holland ports were as important in the eleventh century as in the twentieth.

The third eye is Amsterdam. This city was founded very late by European standards, not acknowledged as a city until 1300. It has always pursued its own interests as a city state, although it has also always acknowledged that its security requires friendly provinces to the south and as many of them as possible. Other cities in the Netherlands have always relied on Amsterdam's extraordinary resources, but often resentfully, and with a strong sense that Amsterdam would drop them the second they were no longer useful.

The fourth eye is Madrid. From the fifteenth to the eighteenth centuries, for almost quixotically unnecessary dynastic reasons, the

Spanish owned large blocks of Lotharingia, from Holland down to the border with Switzerland. Their efforts to hold this territory, to defeat its unruly inhabitants and fend off other interested parties, generated much of European history until at last, in a welter of expiatory masses and great clouds of incense, they threw in the towel.

The fifth and last eye moves about in ways which wreck the metaphor – but it is broadly a German eye which could be based at some points in Frankfurt, where the Holy Roman Emperor was elected, or Aachen, where he was crowned King of the Germans to match the crowning of the King of the French in Rheims (he only officially became Emperor when crowned by the Pope). As the equally legitimate successor to Charlemagne, the Emperor/King had his own historical explanation for Lotharingia, seeing it all as uncontestably part of the Holy Roman Empire. The Emperor had many tasks, one of which was to defend the western borders against France, but he also had interests in Italy and in the east which frequently distracted him. The question of what did or did not belong to France and what to the Empire was central to everything through to the end of the eighteenth century and fuelled generation after generation of scholars-for-hire. From the point in the early seventeenth century when the Imperial capital becomes near permanent, it is probably fair to place the eye in Vienna. Post-Napoleon Berlin both ultimately inherits the western issue and fights major wars over it until 1945.

The other players are briefer and more minor. The Dukes of Burgundy (with no real capital to stick an eye on) in the fourteenth and fifteenth centuries come close to making much of Lotharingia into their own state and tread very carefully in the spaces between the rival French and German rulers. Bern is also concerned, but generally just for defensive reasons. Most of all however, it is the individual cities which are so important, many Imperial Free Cities within the Empire (Basel, Mulhouse, Aachen), ecclesiastical states which survived for many centuries (Liège, Cologne, Essen) and smaller but durable counties or duchies (Cleve, the Palatinate, Baden). Many of these places have at times been among the great glories of Europe but their wealthy self-sufficiency has meant that the eyes of the nearest major capitals have always viewed them with greed and rapacity.

In 1672 foresters were cutting down some immense old oaks just south of the Rhône near what is now Lyon–Saint-Exupéry Airport. To their consternation their axes hit something very odd and after carefully cutting round the obstruction they found a terrible medley of pieces of metal and human bone which had been dispersed through the trunk and branches as the tree had grown. It was worked out that they must be the remains of an armoured Burgundian soldier who had hidden inside a hollow and either become stuck or been killed there at the Battle of Anthon in 1430, an ambush by French troops which ended the attempt by Louis II, Prince of Orange, to invade the Dauphiné. His troops were massacred and Louis, badly wounded, dashed to freedom on horseback across the Rhône.

Just to warn the potential reader – this book is filled with a lot of this sort of stuff.

CHAPTER ONE

Phalera Regij Equi.

Ice-sheets to Asterix

Almost all of the course of human history in north-west Europe will for ever be a total mystery. We can assume that over thousands of years there were all kinds of heroics, inventions, serio-comic leadership failures, natural disasters and exciting vegetable breakthroughs but their nature will always be opaque. The last Neanderthals (their remains first discovered just outside Düsseldorf in the Neander valley) seem to have died out forty thousand years ago, perhaps destroyed by the ancestors of modern humans. Humans had to coexist with various appalling animals such as European leopards and cave-bears but these, like most humans, were chased away or made extinct by the last ice age, which reduced the region to a polar desert. With the gradual retreat of the ice eighteen thousand years ago a fairly familiar landscape emerged: water levels and temperatures rose and more humans drifted northwards.

The one huge and glaring difference was the hilariously named Doggerland, an area that filled most of what is now the North Sea and into which the Thames, Rhine, Meuse, Seine and Scheldt all flowed as a single monster river, coming out into the sea in what is now the far west of the English Channel. This deeply confusing landscape, filled with the little columns of smoke from villages, wolves, huge deer and proto-oxen grunting and cavorting along the swampy banks of one of the world's biggest rivers, was sadly swept away by rising sea levels and tsunamis by 6500 BC. In one of the most dramatic geological events in Europe's history – which must, among other things, have made an astonishing *noise* – the last, twenty-mile-wide rock-and-mud plug tore loose and Britain became an island. Poor Doggerland was swept away and the English

Channel was born, watched by relieved and appreciative groups of hunter-gatherers lucky enough to happen to be on higher ground in proto-Kent and proto-Pas-de-Calais.

For so much of Europe's history it is impossible not to feel that the heavy lifting is being done elsewhere – by, for example, the north-east Asians resettling the whole of the Americas or, later, such epics as the Bornean settlement of Madagascar. These great ecological adventures are a striking contrast to the quite boring if necessary efforts of small groups of European humans to sort themselves out in a bleak, still tundral environment. There was also an increasingly embarrassing contrast with, for example, the Fertile Crescent, where animals and crops were being domesticated and things such as wheels and writing and cities were being invented. As tens of thousands laboured under a burning sun to build great ziggurats at the whim of gold-clad priests and kings, northern Europeans were still playing about with lumps of bear fat.

At some hard to isolate point in time, north-west Europe, while lacking the increasing sophistication of the eastern Mediterranean, became a far more complex society. The traditional images in museums of circular huts, a worryingly feeble defensive wall made out of something like rushes, a thin wisp of smoke from a central campfire, with everyone resignedly waiting for the Romans to invade and build sewers and proper roads, have long gone. A historian who studied Iron Age Europe once made a head-spinning point to me – that before the Roman invasion of Britain the English Channel would have been crowded with big, complex sailing ships packed with goods, but they would have been filled with sailors and merchants who were entirely illiterate. This is obvious after a few moments' thought – but those few moments, for me at any rate, switched my brain onto different tracks. A highly complex mercantile and military civilization, using ships, systems of barter and drawing on raw and finished goods from all over north-west Europe did not need to write anything down. Indeed the entire course of human history did not, until a certain point, need writing at all. From the angle of our own script-obsessed culture it may be difficult not to feel a bit sorry for such people, with their peculiar gods, animal-pelt clothing and general impenetrability. But vast dramas of emigration, invention, fighting and building went on across many generations, leaving countless, almost entirely mysterious results which once had complex meanings.

The archaeology of this pre-literate Europe has simply added layer upon layer of frustrating mystery. At Glauberg, just outside Frankfurt, there is a sequence of elaborate Iron Age remains, initially excavated just before the Second World War. In later digs an extraordinary figure was found, almost undamaged – a six-foot sandstone statue of an armoured man with a shield, neckerchief and bizarre headgear combining a cap and what look like gigantic flaps almost like rabbit ears. The figure seems to have been carved in around 500 BC and it has an undeniably Roswell alien-invader atmosphere. It may be a prince, a cult object or the much-loved logo of a chain of chariot-repair shops. But we don't know – the statue is both fascinating and boring in a highly unstable mix. With no context and no narrative, I felt almost resentful that this figure had safely stayed underground for two and half millennia just to mess us about now. All we can say is that the north-western Europe which we live in has vast substrata of human achievement about which we can understand next to nothing.

Once the Romans arrive, and particularly once Julius Caesar writes *The Gallic War*, it is as though a huge, Continent-wide curtain has been lifted and what we see – written about by a direct eye-witness, indeed by the man most responsible for messing it up – is a series of highly organized, sophisticated societies, in terms of military technology hard for the Romans to defeat and with large, complex and tough ships designed for the harsh weather of the Atlantic. Reading Caesar's account one immediately feels more confident about the nature of north-western Europe, with the proviso that everyone should nonetheless remain wary: surviving written-down words and more readily understandable remains give an illusion of new solidity and purpose and yet everyone was just as articulate, aggressive, faithless, heroic, haunted and incompetent before some unpleasantly over-militarized Italians arrived.

Perhaps the most striking pre-Roman place in north-west Europe

is on a high hill near Otzenhausen in a wooded area of the Saarland. Fewer locations give a stronger sense of how human life in
much of Europe is dictated by trees. Pine and beech forests were
the great enemies, their seeds creeping forward and within a generation stamping out any areas abandoned by humans. In the
medieval period settlers were given special privileges during the
'mattock' years needed to tear out roots and make farmland: extensive warfare, plague or crop failure might be human disasters, but
they were arboreal opportunities. The Celtic fortified town built up
here over a couple of centuries was enormous. It has been worked
out that in its final form (around the time of Caesar's invasion) it
was made from some thirty-five miles of tree trunks and 315,000
cubic yards of stone (helpfully re-imagined by archaeologists as
some nine thousand railway trucks' worth). This extraordinary need
for wood, both for the structure and for fires, would have meant
that what is now again a convincingly dense region of woodland
would have been largely stripped and its ecology – presumably of
farms and readily visible wide tracks – too different to be imagined.
The town site is protected by a (for me) grimly steep climb to the
top and nourished by a spring at its centre which still flows.

The fort was built by the Treveri to defend themselves against
marauding Suebi. The Treveri were the enemy most respected by
Caesar, repeatedly mentioned in *The Gallic War*, and they caused
him endless problems during nine years of campaigning. The
Romans became so obsessed with their leader, Indutiomarus, that
they adopted the unusual battle strategy of every Roman simply
hacking his way directly towards Indutiomarus to ensure his being
killed regardless of casualties. As the Treveri were always on the
offensive their Saarland base never came into use – or at least is
unmentioned by Caesar. It was abandoned in the same year that a
Roman camp was set up nearby, but there is no evidence either way
as to whether it was abandoned voluntarily or through battle. The
Treveri survive in the name of the city of Trier (more clearly in its
French version as Trèves) and genetically, it can be assumed, all over
the place. All memory of the meaning of the fort was long lost –

and even today it is still known entirely ahistorically as the Ring of the Huns, adding an enjoyable flavour of dark doings.

It is possible to be immobilized by *The Gallic War* as it is such a relief to move on in a flash from second- or third-hand Greek rumours about the nature of north-west Europe mingled with the analysis of bone pits to sudden, brilliant Technicolor. Caesar is nothing if not self-aggrandizing, but he is also just very *interested*, as would his original audience have been. He talks about the region between the Rivers Waal and Meuse as 'the island of the Batavii', which accidentally preserves the sense of the Dutch river system as once being vastly more wide, unruly and isolating. He also talks about the ease with which enemies could flee into the hilly Ardennes or into 'the marshes' – now non-existent but once an almost Amazonian quagmire that spread through the many meanders of the Rhine and Meuse – or onto coastal islands protected by high tides. He discusses the Belgae and the Helvetii, talking about their exceptional bravery and making *The Gallic Wars* the founding document for two modern nationalisms as well as generating a lot of rather mediocre (if richly enjoyable) nineteenth-century town-hall frescoes of people with big moustaches and sandals. He builds the first bridge over the Rhine, probably near Koblenz. Above all, the book is an account of violence – of the superiority of Roman violence over Celtic violence and, when resistance was broken, of massacres and destruction.

My own view of the Romans in Gaul (and of Julius Caesar) is entirely coloured by a lifelong love (happily shared with my sons) of Goscinny and Uderzo's *Asterix* books, set in the aftermath of Caesar's return to Rome from Gaul, so there is no aspect of real Roman culture which is not swamped for me by these books' vivid ridicule. In some moods (and I do not think I am alone in this) I am fairly convinced that *Asterix the Legionary* may be the funniest book ever written, although, in fairness, *Asterix and Cleopatra* can make an equally convincing claim. This adds an interest to visiting the in other ways drearily exhaustive collections of Roman stuff in the museums of places such as Metz, Cologne and Mainz, where anything from a legionary helmet to a toga-clad figure on a tombstone acts merely as a reminder of various hilarious episodes. The roots of the *Asterix* books are complex and deserve more study – they were a response to the Nazi invasion and occupation, a satire on the French army (in which Goscinny served), a response to Goscinny's being Jewish, an attack on Americanization, and so on. But they have also acted more broadly as a sort of wrecking-ball, smashing up through utter derision all traces of fascism, whether of the kind first invented by Mussolini or the variant embraced by Vichy, all of which took deeply seriously the imagined values, discipline, order and frowning gravity of the Roman Empire. The *Asterix* books made it no longer possible to see perfect rows of steel-helmeted troops with their square-jawed officers without them being merely a prelude to some farcical humiliation by the Gallic heroes. As Obelix says in, I think, every one of the books, 'These Romans are crazy.'

The warlord

With his entire cavalcade strongly smelling, as usual, of moustache wax, pricey toilet waters and Brasso, Kaiser Wilhelm II on 11 October 1900 inaugurated one of the funnest things ever to happen to the Taunus hills north of Frankfurt. In a flurry of bizarre hunting caps, badges, special cloaks and sashes he laid the foundation stone to mark the rebuilding of the Roman fort known as the Saalburg.

Kaiser Wilhelm had many failings, but his storybook attitude towards history has left us all in his debt. North-west Europe is dotted with fair-to-middling Roman leftovers but none have the atmosphere of the Saalburg. Tossing aside the usual academic fuss and havering, it was decided to rebuild from scratch the whole thing just as it used to be. This being 1900 one can imagine the complex flavour of the enterprise and the very non-*Asterix* sense of imperial destiny that would have hung in the air even more heavily than the eau de toilette. This was very much a personal project of the Kaiser's, egged on by a handful of toady archaeologists who should have known better. For instance, the Kaiser insisted on a

Temple of Mithras being built, because Mithraism had a soldierly, band-of-brothers, initiation-rite, all-male flavour, although there was literally no evidence whatsoever for its existence at the Saalburg. The inside of the temple is a joy: it has the air of an old-fashioned nightclub long gone out of business, with the ceiling painted blue with stars and a gigantic painted carving of a half-clad youth killing a white bull.

The fort itself is more serious and felt particularly so as I was there mid-winter – and therefore missed all the dressing-up and the reconstructed Roman meals at the taverna. Being there with snow on the ground and skeletal trees was of course ideal for getting some sense of those poor Roman sentries far from home, stuck in a temperature-defective variant of *Beau Geste*, looking wearily into the murk to the east, dreaming of lemon trees and waiting for yet another German attack.

The Saalburg was the furthest point the Romans reached across the Rhine. It must have been a glum posting, but it was protecting a range of Roman towns which still exist, with their names twisted about a bit by time, scattered along the Rhenus (Rhine): Colonia Agrippina (Cologne), Confluentes (the confluence of the Rhine and Mosel: Koblenz), Bonna (Bonn, straightforward enough), Moguntiacum (Mainz), Bingium (Bingen), Novaesium (Neuss).

Once you start walking the ramparts you feel very slightly Roman, blowing into your hands to keep them warm, looking out for the stern-but-fair officer of the watch. The walls do seem a bit low though, whether a reflection of reality or to save Wilhelm money it is unclear – in either event they do suggest an over-reliance by the Romans on Germanic tribes not developing small-ladder technology. The Roman-style storage rooms are used as a museum, packed with the usual ancient things hard-wearing enough not to have rotted – any number of spear-points, votive-oil lamps, figurines, trowels, gutters, pots. It seems unfair that the nature of some Roman materials allows them to survive, while the surrounding wood-and-fibre cultures have largely vanished. There is even a disconcerting little clothing pin with a swastika, a Roman appropriation of an Indian symbol. There is also an excellent display of the size of different Roman military units using Playmobil figures, which catch the mood very well, although probably not as Wilhelm intended. And to bolster the fraudulent temple, there is great stuff on Mithraism, with its wholly mysterious use of stone spheres, and the way that the initiate could move up through the ranks from Lion to Persian to Courier of the Sun (the wonderful word *Heliodromus*) and all the way up to Father – but we do not know, and never will know, how or why. It certainly fits though with the Kaiser's rather redeemingly confused feelings about masculinity.

The organization of the Roman Empire in the north-west changed at various points – but the main units were Germania Inferior, Gallia Belgica and Germania Superior (i.e., superior in the sense of further upstream on the Rhine). Germania Inferior ran through the modern southern Netherlands, its key northern metropolis being Noviomagus (Nijmegen) guarding the split in the Rhine between the southern arm of the Waal and the northern Nederrjin. All points further north, a maze of complex swamps and unrewarding waterways, were shunned. Germania Inferior then continued down the Rhine to Bonn. Gallia Belgica covered what became Flanders and south to the Somme and then ballooned out to the east to cover areas such as Champagne, Luxembourg, Lorraine almost up to the Rhine – it was later split in two parts, one in the west, and the other in the east with its capital at Trier. One curiosity is that the area known as 'Civitas Tungrorum' was moved from Gallia Belgica to Germania Inferior but kept its separate integrity in obscure ways which made it later into the physical territory of Bishopric of Liège – an amazingly persistent, sprawling absurdity on the map which drove all manner of would-be world conquerors mad until at last chucked into the dumpster by Revolutionaries in 1795. The last of the three provinces, Germania Superior, stretched down the Rhine, bulging onto the right bank of which the Saalburg was a notable element, and then down to Lake Zürich and Lake Geneva. Its principal cities were Mainz and Argentum (Strasbourg), with Mainz the main military hub for supplying the forts (result: a particularly numbing museum filled with pots, short swords and spearheads accidentally dropped in the

Rhine on the way across). In the mid-third century waves of attackers and a wider crisis in the empire meant that the Saalburg and other forts were abandoned and the line taken back to the Rhine. Roman rule continued long enough to establish Christianity, from the Emperor Constantine's capital at Trier, to create structures and institutional memories which have existed, albeit sometimes under acute pressure, ever since.

To cap the whole joyous Saalburg experience there is above a statue of Hadrian a stone plaque pronouncing: WILLIAM II, SON OF FREDERICK III, GRANDSON OF WILLIAM THE GREAT IN THE FIFTEENTH YEAR OF HIS REIGN HAS REBUILT THE ROMAN BOUNDARY FORTRESS OF SAALBURG IN HONOURED MEMORY OF HIS PARENTS and then on the statue itself three great names are linked: IMPERATORI ROMANORUM TITO AELIO HADRIANO ANTONINO AUGUSTO PIO (i.e. Emperors Hadrian and Antoninus Pius) GUILELMUS II IMPERATOR GERMANORUM (i.e. our old friend the Kaiser).

From Wilhelm's point of view the most confusing aspect of the Saalburg must have been that all the time, while capering about on the ramparts, pretending to be a deeply professional yet humane Roman commander, staring into the savage-filled murk, waiting for the next attack, he was a German looking in the wrong direction. It was against people like him that the Saalburg had been built.

Bees and buckles

There can be few more damning or more useless terms than 'the Dark Ages'. They sound fun in an orcs-and-elves sort of way and suggest a very low benchmark from which we have since, as a race, raised ourselves up into the light – with the present day using as its soundtrack the last movement of Beethoven's Ninth. But the damage the term does is immense. A simple little mental test is just to quickly imagine a European scene from that era. Now: was the sun shining? Of course not. The default way of thinking about the long, complex era that lasted from the final decades of the Roman

Empire to somewhere around the Battle of Hastings is to assume it all looked like the cover of a heavy metal album.

One problem is that the older the period the more chances there are for its material production to be destroyed. Across Lotharingia there has been century after century of rebuilding (with the re-use of every available piece of old dressed stone) with most evidence of earlier churches and palaces removed in the process. In practical terms one cannot really imagine that the vast, humourless bulk of Cologne Cathedral is merely the latest in a series stretching back to a Roman temple. Many of the great religious buildings of the Rhine have a display table showing somewhat conjectural models of their ancient predecessors, usually starting with a patronizing little wooden block, looking something like a skew-whiff Wendy-house. So great is the weight of 'the Dark Ages' on our shoulders that it is almost impossible not to think of the makers of this wonky church slithering about on the mud floor cursing the way the roof was leaking and how nobody could design a door that shut properly, resigned to the occasional fiasco when the walls would simply fall in on the gurning, fur-clad, battle-axe-wielding communicants. In practice, these now non-existent buildings would have been extremely beautiful – drawing on Roman and Byzantine models, and stuffed with all kinds of wonderful stuff from the Roman Empire which now no longer exists.

This is the related problem suffered by 'the Dark Ages' – our towns often occupy exactly the same sites as they did then (the same river crossing, the same harbour) and are built on top of them, but there have been simply innumerable points at which older material has been destroyed. There is probably some rough mathematical calculation about how each passing century lowers your chance of anything much surviving at all. The famous fat boy of 1666 – who was meant to be watching the baker's oven, but instead gorged on pies, fell asleep and as a result burned down London – is only one of an elite group who caused mayhem through their momentary inattention over the centuries. With every household routinely handling flames in wooden surroundings it is unsurprising that so many towns would often find themselves having to start again from scratch. We know far more about more recent horrors – for example, the gunpowder accident that destroyed much of Delft in 1654 – but any twenty-four-hour period over the centuries was always fraught with some potential fumble-fingered disaster somewhere.

The unrelenting impact of warfare has of course done far more damage, wrecking town after town. There is a lot of warfare in this book, but I have tried to minimize it because it is really quite repetitive if you are a citizen of the southern Netherlands, for example, or the Palatinate. Any breakdown in order or lunge for supremacy ends up with further pyres of the material past. Simply looking at recent disasters, many thousands of ancient records, treasures, histories, valued for centuries by custodians, were destroyed in the 1870 Siege of Strasbourg and the 1914 destruction of much of the Catholic University of Leuven. The true 'dark age', of course, was the early 1940s when, simply as a side effect of industrial killing, great swathes of the past disappeared. One small yet major example – the extraordinary series of paintings of the visions of Hildegard of Bingen, made in the 1170s either by the saint herself or under her supervision, disappeared in the general catastrophe that unfolded in Dresden in early 1945. We only know what they looked like (except from black-and-white photos) through accurate and beautiful copies painted by a group of nuns, by sheer chance, in the 1930s. So these frail little works of disturbing genius survived nearly eight centuries before succumbing, and exist today only through the most ancient form of devotional copying.

This is an over-elaborate way of saying that in as much as the era after the Roman Empire is 'dark' it is because it has been overlaid by many centuries of further things happening – and I have talked only about human agency rather than the terrors of mould, mice, lightning and damp. Our own 'library' at home suffered catastrophic loss from a house-rabbit called Dusty who in his short life ate the spines of innumerable books. My copy of Hermann Hesse's *Narcissus and Goldmund* is cherished, partly because I have owned it for so long, but also because of its memorial teeth marks.

When was the very last beautiful Roman fabric so sun-rotted that it was chucked away? And that is as nothing compared to the

almost totally successful attempts during the early Christian centuries in Europe to erase all trace of native paganism. This last issue
is often overlooked. At the back of our minds when thinking about
the centuries when the Roman Empire mutated into medieval Europe we are unconsciously taking on the spurious guise of specific
communities. We are happy to read about Charlemagne destroying
the Avar Empire and taking all its gold because at some level we
emotionally sneak ourselves into Charlemagne's baggage-train. But
the Avars ruled Central Europe for over two centuries, and it is not
a given that their civilization had no worth and did not represent
a future we would have flourished in. Or earlier, there are the Ale-
manni in what is now south-west Germany and Alsace (and after
whom the French call Germany Allemagne) who were broken by
the Frankish ruler Clovis. Of course, we are the heirs of Christianity, but only in a passive, non-contributive way – to see ourselves
on one specific side in these ancient contests is awkward. I might
hiss at the pagan antics of the Saxons and Vikings, but as someone
part English and part Irish I am much more likely to have their
genes than Frankish ones.

These issues become vivid in the town of Tournai – for centuries a French-ruled enclave squeezed between the County of
Flanders and the County of Hainaut and now part of Belgium, a
classic crossroads through which every army has marched, from the
legionaries of the Roman Empire to Allied troops in 1944. I may
as well say here that Tournai is a fantastic historical palimpsest and
somewhere that always puts a spring in my step. I once found
myself changing trains there late at night and realizing that I had
just enough time to haul my bag up the road through the freezing
dark to look in renewed wonder at the vast, sombre drum – like a
stonebuilt gasometer – of the Henry VIII Tower. In this current
context, however, what makes Tournai so remarkable is the discovery during routine repairs to the Hospice of St Brice in the 1650s
of the tomb of Childeric I. This accidental find catapulted everything back some two hundred and fifty years before Charlemagne,
to the century after the Western Roman Empire had collapsed, a
world which must have still been densely Roman in its appearance,

probably with much smaller populations in towns and more limited trade. Childeric's son, Clovis I, was baptized, united the Frankish tribes and founded the Merovingian dynasty which lasted until Charlemagne's dad put the last of them into a monastery.

The management of Childeric's rediscovered tomb has not exactly been a curatorial model. It started well as by sheer good luck Tournai was then part of the Spanish Netherlands under the benign and intelligent leadership of Archduke Leopold Wilhelm, who as part of his vast expenditure on art objects commissioned a superb book on the tomb from Jean-Jacques Chifflet, an antiquarian from the Spanish-ruled Franche-Comté. This has immaculate pictures of the heaps of extraordinary stuff Childeric was buried with – gold objects of great variety and beauty from a bull's head to coins, buckles, a crystal globe, seal-rings and intricate pieces of cloisonné. It was downhill for the hoard from then on. Leopold Wilhelm took everything back to Vienna when he retired and left it to his nephew the Emperor Leopold I. He gave it to Louis XIV as a present but, in one of the many instances where Louis is so disappointing, he took no interest in the gifts and simply stored them. They survived the Revolution but were stolen in 1831 and dispersed or melted down. The hoard's great aesthetic intervention came from its including dozens of small gold bees (or possibly cicadas), which must have decorated some object which had since rotted away, perhaps a cloak. In his search for an appropriate new symbol for his dynasty (the ancient fleur-de-lys being patently unacceptable to a new era) Napoleon decided to make these bees the imperial motif, scattering them on everything from coats of arms to Josephine's slippers. They cluster all over the decorations of the French Empire and it is one of the sadder aspects of Napoleon's defeat and exile that they then disappear from the decorative arts until their rather wan revival under his nephew Napoleon III.

What remains in Tournai now however (aside from some reproduction bees) is a too-good-to-be-true archaeological museum which lays out everything we can still know about the huge scale of Childeric's tomb and several associated burials. As his son Clovis turned Christian this was the last of the fabulous, full-blown pagan

Frankish affairs, with twenty-one cavalry horses buried nearby in an associated mound and what was clearly a sprawling sacred space with Childeric's body at its centre. An aristocratic woman buried nearby slightly later had objects such as scissors, amber and a wine-strainer which linked her to trade across Europe. Indeed, the more time spent looking at these shield-bosses, necklaces and pins (and not least a debonair and alarming scramasax – a wonderful word for a long knife), the more clear it becomes that this was a highly sophisticated, confident civilization – which just happened to exist a very long time ago and whose achievements were about to be completely disregarded by the new Christian regime of Clovis, who moved his capital from Tournai to Paris. The process by which Childeric's tomb became forgotten is a puzzling one as his dynastic if not his religious significance lasted so long. Somehow, the King of the Salian Franks and his favourite horses, his crystal globe, bees, scramasax and all sank into oblivion, eventually disappearing completely under church buildings, until being summoned back to the surface nearly twelve hundred years later.

The rule of the saints

For reasons I can no longer remember I seem always to have been preoccupied with the poems of the great seventeenth-century religious mystic Henry Vaughan. In the context of this book, I have kept referring to his despairing poem 'Corruption', where he bitterly imagines that somewhere 'in those early days' after the expulsion from the Garden of Eden, man perhaps still

> . . . shin'd a little, and by those weak Rays
> Had some glimpse of his birth.

Vaughan is writing towards the end of the tradition that the present was merely ever further from the time of human happiness. At some much squabbled-over point a bit later some Europeans began to abandon this view and believe in a world they could actively improve and build on: the onward-and-upward feeling about human achievement which we continue to aver despite some overwhelming setbacks.

Wandering around the religious buildings of the Rhine and Low Countries it is hard not to be oppressed by these often huge remains of a great old tradition: that modern humanity is now merely, in Vaughan's terms, 'stone and earth' but was once great. The landscape is encrusted with buildings which express this sense of ancient, constant pleas for mercy. Monks and nuns devoted their lives to intercession on behalf of fallen mankind in a battle between the promise of Jesus's sacrifice and the temptations of the Devil. Humans were doubly fallen though – not just expelled from Eden, but also expelled from the classical ancient world. The medieval rulers of Western Europe were obsessed by a sense that they too were the mere followers of ancient greatness. Their battle tents and palaces were festooned with huge tapestry images of Julius Caesar and Alexander the Great. Monks would routinely have to read out loud at what must have been slightly boring mealtimes page after page of the astonishing activities of Hannibal and Pompey. Again, this tradition only begins to splinter and become silly in the eighteenth century, perhaps with the ever less plausible images of Louis XIV trying to square looking like Scipio with also wearing an absurd wig. To understand most of Europe's history however it has to be seen as in important ways rueful, melancholic and nostalgic – about backsliding, temptation and the struggle to interpret the world almost entirely through biblical and Latin exemplars, handed down to us from an older, more powerful world.

Put in these terms, Europe becomes an ancient, agonized landscape filled with churches and monasteries which remain as sites that most people now ignore, but which were witnesses to centuries of struggle with invaders, earlier heroism and self-sacrifice; and where communities were often forced to rebuild almost from nothing, with their town burned down and much of their population enslaved and dragged away. From the fourth century onwards what became Lotharingia was swept by waves of invaders as Roman power mutated and then fell away. In AD 275 the original Colonia Ulpia Traiana (Xanten) was destroyed by German tribes, and centuries followed in which any number of indignities hit the locals. But these could also be the founding moments for new towns – and so many hundreds of years went by (until, say, the Vikings settled down in the eleventh century) during which each recorded disaster for a given community could have been followed by several generations of unrecorded, normal, steady life.

As soon as you become alert to this ancient past it bristles everywhere. Xanten is a good example. Its cathedral is built around the remains of St Victor, a Roman soldier executed for his Christian faith in the town's arena (enjoyably rebuilt, incidentally, with oddly flabby men dressed up as gladiators play-fighting with plastic weapons – a rough line of work). Indeed, St Victor is just one among many members of the Theban Legion, who in a garbled and confused story were in AD 286 transferred from Egypt to fight in Gaul and on the banks of Lake Geneva refused to abjure their new faith, with the result that they were massacred there (although Victor somehow was also executed in Xanten). The town's very name (from *Sanctos*) means 'Place of the Saints'. The Thebans turn up all over the region – whether killed by Lake Geneva or up in Xanten they populate any number of religious sites. Two survivors from the original massacre, Felix and Regulus, together with their servant, managed to flee but were caught up with at Zürich, where they too were executed – but then picked up their own heads, walked forty paces, prayed and died. The Great Minster was founded in their name.

Very enjoyably, the legionaries feature in the magnificent Trier church of St Paulinus. This ancient foundation was first built in the late fourth century as a shrine to the Theban Legion. It has been through many indignities and was blown up in 1674 by French troops. This had the happy effect of allowing it to be completely rebuilt in the 1740s by, among others, the wonderful Johann Balthazar Neumann, master of late baroque confection. A gigantic ceiling painting seems to show pretty much every individual member of the Theban Legion being martyred in over-ingenious ways. But the real surprise is the crypt, where there are truly weird decorative uses for Theban Legion relics, including a group of three skulls arranged in a tightly packed row, which have a disturbing semblance to a doo-wop trio, with the smallest skull in the middle being that of the cheeky falsetto.

The Legion's equally CinemaScope female equivalent is St Ursula and Her Eleven Thousand Virgins, massacred by the Huns in AD 451. There are various theories about the number eleven thousand, the most plausible being that the original story actually said that Ursula was a virgin who was eleven years old when she was martyred, with subsequent monkish copyists flailing about incompetently until the events emerged from their quills in their final form. Quite possibly even Ursula herself did not exist. In any event, the story became the basis for explaining an unlimited supply of bones when an old Roman graveyard or possibly plague pit was discovered in Cologne. Between them and the Legion there was in some ways rather an oversupply of material, making them the penny candy of the relic world: bits of them turn up all over the place, sometimes (as in the Châlon shrine in Bar-le-Duc) as a sort of sprinkled flavouring over a bigger blend of appropriate saints. The church of St Ursula in Cologne has a whole wall of bones, in gruesome decorative patterns – there is simply not enough room for them all.

These subjects later became some of the classic focuses for Rhineland and Flemish painting, works of extraordinary beauty and strangeness. But by that point these were not only ancient legends but also the foundation of real places and towns perhaps a thousand years old. After a while it becomes a bad habit to look out for these roots. The magical Cathedral of Metz is where it is because during the Hun raid of AD 451 the entire town was destroyed, but one hilltop area where there was a shrine to St Stephen remained miraculously inviolate. As the ambitions of the local church flourished, so the authorities came to curse the restricted site on which the miracle occurred as it required all kinds of very expensive and twisty feats of infilling and buttressing to clear a big enough platform for later versions of the building; hence its hunched up, box-like yet charismatic shape.

The Rhineland particularly needs to be seen as something

equivalent to Angkor Wat – a dense network of churches, cathedrals, monasteries, convents, chapels and shrines with towns, villages and farms attached to service them. For much of its existence its principal role was to generate vast waves of devotional energy in the hope that humanity (or some of it) might be saved. Such atmospheric monsters as Mainz Cathedral could probably fit most of the rest of the medieval town inside their shadowy bulk, with the townsfolk's year ruled by an elaborate zodiac of festivals, penances, processions, masses and prayers linked to specific chapels by guild or family association. A large part of the town worked directly or indirectly for the cathedral and its linked properties, at the most posh level with a job as one of the canons (reserved for the younger brothers of leading aristocrats) down to being a rural church-tied serf, with many monks themselves effectively being just a specialized variety of rural serf denied any involvement with women.

The great shrines had a constant flow of pilgrims from all over Europe, often treating such a journey as the defining moment in the individual's life and with elaborate systems in place for hostels, way-station chapels and simple provisions. Trier, because it was briefly a Roman capital and kept many Roman buildings, was a particularly vigorous focus, including Constantine the Great's old audience hall, which became converted into a church. The Porta Nigra, Trier's intimidatingly gnarled and bulky Roman gateway, only survives because a wandering Greek holy man took up residence there in the early eleventh century and he so impressed the locals that after his death the Porta was turned into a very odd-looking church and monastery. This was impatiently decommissioned by Napoleon and most of the elaborate medieval accretions were pulled off, leaving something again looking fairly Roman. The greatest lure in Trier, however, is the abbey of St Matthias. Awkwardly, I was under the impression I had never visited it before and was walking down the seemingly endless Saarstrasse thinking how the outskirts of all German towns, with their Chinese restaurants and Turkish grocers, look exactly the same, when I reached the abbey with its distinctive cake-icing frontage. I realized that Saarstrasse looked the same because it *was* the same. So as an unintended repeat pilgrim (the most lukewarm possible kind there is) I found myself visiting again the simple stone box tomb of St Matthias, the disciple who replaced Judas. As the only disciple north of the Alps, Matthias seems a long way from home. It was possible his remains came here via Constantine himself. Nobody knows how long pilgrims have been visiting the shrine. A famous route is to walk from Cologne (itself no slouch as a town, having relics of the Three Kings in a dazzling shrine that has somehow stared down every subsequent military, religious and social threat) and the abbey has pilgrim badges going back to the seventeenth century.

This book needs to move on! I have now spent some ten years visiting religious buildings in north-west Europe and feel nowhere near jaded. So often there will be something strange or completely unexpected. Maastricht more than anywhere is the place where, in a parallel existence, I would like to have grown up – it seems a perfect balance of modern and ancient and the ratio of inhabitant to cake shop appears higher than anywhere in the world. But what is truly exceptional about Maastricht is the Basilica of St Servatius. A wandering Armenian holy man, Servatius died in Maastricht at the end of the fourth century, and there still is his tomb, down some steps. Of course the site of the tomb has been fiddled with over the years, but you are encased in a chilly, claustrophobic space with very old stonework and a deep step so ancient it has been worn into a U-shape by centuries of pilgrims. We know, for example, that Charles Martel came to pray here (and was an important patron, giving thanks here after he defeated an Ummayad army at Narbonne in 737 on Servatius's birthday); Charlemagne, Charles V, Philip II, most recently John Paul II. The church above it has been swept aside repeatedly by invaders and accidents, but somehow this tiny, cold space has survived every indignity.

Rhinegold

The *Nibelungenlied* states at the very first mention of its hero, Siegfried, 'Of his best days, when he was young, marvels could be told', but we never hear about them. So already, in one of the greatest works in European literature, there is a crushing sense of melancholy. We will only be told about the actions that end in Siegfried's betrayal and death. If only we *could* know about these 'marvels' – did anybody once know these stories, or were they always just an imagined backdrop of regret? When Richard Wagner ransacked parts of the *Nibelungenlied* to create the four-opera sequence *The Ring of the Nibelung* he also plunged his audience into an after-time: before the action begins, the world was pristine, ruled by the power of Wotan's spear, in the happy days just before his poor management skills led him to pay off some builders by handing them his sister; or before the Rhinemaidens, Europe's most nubile security squad, had through sheer bloody amateurism explained to a megalomaniac dwarf how to steal their gold. I love both versions of the Nibelung story and happily hum *Ring* extracts almost unthinkingly when on the Cologne–Bad Godesberg commuter train or when hiking in the Siebengebirge where, slightly notionally, Brünnhilde once slumbered.

The operas are, of course, very much creatures of the nineteenth century. There is no real dating available for the *Nibelungenlied* itself. The version we have is from the end of the twelfth century but we know nothing about the author except that he probably performed it at courts on the Danube. It incorporates a whole world of far more ancient material, but we will never know what or from where. When introduced, Siegfried is described as being from Xanten. Although barely referred to again – and quite probably meaning just 'somewhere far down the Rhine' – this tiny piece of flavouring has been eagerly battened on to by the modern town of Xanten ('The Pearl of the Rhine') which has streets named after Siegfried, a Siegfried museum and a *Nibelungen-Express* trolleybus for the idle and infirm to be driven around the quite small town centre. The Siegfried museum (like the similar one in Worms) has a seriousness, depth and sense of purpose that embarrass their equivalents on literary subjects in the English-speaking world. When I was there, as a spectacular extra a room had been dedicated to Nazi junior-school textbooks on the 'Wandering Years': the centuries during which various Germanic tribes had settled Europe. The brilliance of the exhibition lay in its trapping the visitors into bracing themselves for some vicious enormity. You pick nervously through all these illustrations of heavily moustached wagon-masters and their womenfolk with elaborate headdresses; through the images of blond young men fighting, building houses or working in a forge: but, of course, there was almost nothing specifically Nazi about them in themselves – it was what the teachers and pupils brought to them, both in conversation and in the assumptions of their gaze, that poisoned the pictures and this cannot be recovered.

The Siegfried story is clearly set somewhere very ancient, even to the teller. Some of it can be linked to real events in the early fifth century, in the last days of the Roman Empire, but it is an unreliable guide as it is also fascinated by magic and epic feats of a purely fictional kind. The idea of there existing a great treasure which was sunk by Hagen in the Rhine could easily be true as so many of the riches of the towns would, as Huns and others roared through, have been hidden and then lost. It is also a curious echo of how, until the Rhine was narrowed, embanked and speeded up in the nineteenth century, it was always a serious source of gold, with many lives devoted to the ghastly work of panning. There is great material in the story on the importance of feuds and the staggering damage they could do to families as layer upon layer of male relatives are swept in and destroyed by some initially trivial insult. The suggestion that some courts – what with feuding, hunting, duelling and war – must have at times consisted mostly of widows and nuns seems not implausible.

Only bits of the story are looted by Wagner but a far more wholehearted appropriation is Fritz Lang's two-part movie epic *Die Nibelungen* (1924), which remains one of the most enjoyable pinnacles of silent cinema and which can be watched with relish almost indefinitely, by me at any rate. The Xanten museum even has a big model of the dragon used for marketing the film in Berlin when it first came out. The actor playing Siegfried looks absurd but he allows the viewer to time-travel close to Victorian traditions of stage ham – and he does look great in the famous movie still with the fatal spear in his back. Setting him aside, *Die Nibelungen* is a miracle of art direction – never have the early Middle Ages looked more early and more Middle Aged: knights, castles, dwarves, boats, dragons, all perfect. Its love of Art Deco geometric patterning means that some scenes have a flapper/cocktail-bar mid-1920s flavour, which does no harm. The spectacular scene where Kriemhild and Brunhild, both claiming to be queen, refuse to give way to one another on the great sweep of steps up to Worms Cathedral and thereby initiate the events that bring down the dynasty and gruesomely destroy almost everyone in the entire film makes the real cathedral's steps (a functional handful) seem deeply disappointing.

After that tangential paragraph promoting a film, I need to return to the era of the Nibelung story. There can be no doubt that in the centuries after the Roman Empire collapsed, populations dropped and economies shrank. But there are amazing continuities – most importantly the clear ascendancy of Christianity, which absorbs and subverts all kinds of woolly invader and keeps its structure throughout. Places such as Cologne never seem to have lost their religious, cult and administrative function. The *lingua romana* diverged across the former Empire and received admixtures from Germanic and Arabic, but in, say, the ninth century Christian Andalusians and Parisians would have still been able to understand each other, one believing the other to be a bit quaint, and the church liturgy in Latin would have sounded very old-fashioned but not presented real difficulties. For various invaders who did not use Latin, it was very easy to snatch some quaking monk prisoner and train him up to become an interlocutor. Germanic was then spoken further south than now and the modern Belgian–French border reflects that, with a messiness which would have been wholly familiar over a millennium ago, when Germanic proto-Flemish was still the language of places such as Boulogne and Dunkirk. Equally *lingua romana* seems to have been spoken extensively in now entirely Germanic places such as Trier, with any number of wars and minor migrations shifting people around to create borders still seriously contested into the 1950s.

Gigantic buildings continued to dot the landscape – Roman baths, palaces, churches. Xanten is a curiously pure example, where the abandoned Roman town is next to the medieval town. Bit by bit the former was dismantled to conjure up the latter – through many mysterious centuries of patient transfer of old stones, which still now fill cellars and foundations. In parallel with this monks were doing a similar work of preservation by the constant writing and rewriting out of Latin texts. These were always rotting away but through copying and recopying across the centuries some of the key documents of the Ancient World kept just ahead of the mould and damp as the scriptoria monks scribbled away. In a sense these monks were labourers as much as those digging the fields. Without their effort nothing would have survived – we would be wholly ignorant of Tacitus and his friends. One curiosity was the role of Irish monks, particularly at Charlemagne's court. When the Irish had been converted to Christianity they had no written language of their own, so took the shaping and purity of letters particularly seriously. On the more slipshod mainland all kinds of bad practices had drifted in, and the Irish were brought in to overhaul writing systems and impose crystalline grammar.

The thread by which we get access to even post-Roman texts is terrifyingly thin. The wonderful *Rule of Saint Benedict*, one of the most humane and thoughtful of all texts, written down in the sixth century, has two variants. The variant I am reading in translation only exists because of a single copy made at Charlemagne's court, just possibly from Benedict's original, which was in turn copied by a monk, whose work is now in the great abbey at St Gallen in Switzerland. Everyone should read every word, once a month or so, and think about their implications. I am always brought up short yet oddly attracted to Benedict's contemptuous description of the magically named 'gyrovagues' – the very worst monks, 'never remaining in the same place, indulging their own desires and caught in the snares of greed'.

The call of the oliphant

German nationalist historians of the nineteenth century were obsessed by a sense of shame that it was the fate of German-speakers to live for centuries in a fractured mass of small and medium states, in shameful contrast to the more powerful and unified states of England and France. Like some endless, morose, post-game pub dissection of a ruinous football match, historians would relentlessly pick over exemplars of past greatness and past failure. What lay at the heart of German disunity? Which emperor, with better follow-through and smarter coaching, could have put Germany at the top of the Premier League? This was in some ways an entirely positive argument. It put particular images on banknotes and specific statues in town squares, led to restored and rebuilt palaces, crypts and castles, and unleashed many weeks' worth of grand opera and many square miles of mural. Each emperor effectively received a final score based on how much new territory in the east he brought under Christian control, how much he tried to centralize and how consciously German he was in his priorities. Figures such as Henry the Fowler, Otto the Great and Frederick Barbarossa loomed large. But even those who were rightly anxious about a unified modern Germany could find heroes – the drunken incapacity of the uncrowned Emperor Wenzel making a terrific contribution to centrifugal German regionalism, for example. But under all circumstances, the greatest hero always remained the same: Charlemagne.

You can get a strong sense of the awe around Charlemagne at the Great Minster in Zürich. This extraordinary church was picked almost clean during the Reformation. The coral-like accretions of religious figures and visual stories were all pulled down, scraped off and destroyed, leaving the church as a model for Zwingli's vision of the believer's direct relationship with God: every intercessor, every pictorial distraction a snare and falsity. The one exception permitted was to keep a gigantic late-medieval statue of Charlemagne – the notional founder of the building.

In an inspired move, during restoration work in the 1930s, it was decided to take down Charlemagne, put up a copy and retire the original to the crypt. The result amounts to a freakish and wholly unexpected cult site. The glowering, ceiling-high statue is a mass of corrosion, pock-marking, ancient lichen and facial repairs. Eaten at by centuries of smoke and guano, nearly killed off by a huge fire in the eighteenth century, this Charlemagne is a figure who demands respect. It seems a shame not to have ritual bowls filled with floating flowers, guttering oil lamps, temple guards in smart outfits, worshippers pressing their foreheads to the cold stone floor – plus a few bits of bunting and perhaps something dreadful involving animals.

Charlemagne, who persuaded the Pope to crown him the new Roman Emperor in a great ceremony on Christmas Day in the propitious year of 800, had such a deep impact on those around him and took such fundamental decisions that we still remain aware of him when all the Chilperics and Carlomans are long forgotten. As Charles I, he and his son Louis I had such cultic resonance that even in the final throes of French kingship in the nineteenth century they were still being invoked by Louis XVIII and Charles X.

By making himself Holy Roman Emperor he was genuinely refounding the earlier empire, the monumental remains from that period still scattered about him, along the Rhine and Mosel. The window of opportunity was small and happenstantial: in the still-continuing Eastern Roman Empire Irene was empress and, as she was a woman, this was interpreted by the Pope and Charles as implying there was a job vacancy. When she died a couple of years later, her successors continued to view themselves rightly as the true Roman emperors and Charlemagne's successors as a barbarian *Goon Show* – but it was too late. This new Western Roman Empire lasted for almost exactly a thousand years and was ended only by Napoleon, who before his own crowning as Emperor of the French came to stand and mull before Charlemagne's throne in Aachen, in the engagingly stagey way at which he excelled. Once Charlemagne was declared Emperor his successors were always Western Europe's most senior ruler, however ragged and embarrassing their real circumstances.

Charlemagne's super-status reflected his bursting the bonds of mere regional chieftaincy. His inheritance was already an extraordinary one. His grandfather Charles Martel had destroyed a serious Muslim invasion of France and was in his lifetime viewed as a great Christian hero. His father, Pepin the Short, had made himself King of the Franks, the Frankish kingdom being an ancient, sprawling and complex entity, directly if stormily linked to Roman Gaul. Charlemagne's birthright included most of modern France, all of the Netherlands and much of what is now western Germany. But by his anti-pagan campaigns in the east, into areas such as Saxony and Carinthia, he initiated a new phase in the campaign to make Europe Christian, and aligned with Rome rather than Constantinople.

It is hair-raising how thin the thread is by which we know about Charlemagne's actions – a handful of chronicles, letters and a couple of biographies (one by the enjoyably named Notker the Stammerer), which are fascinating, but frustratingly without any means by which they can be double-checked. Einhard, who worked closely with Charlemagne for many years, wrote his life so that the events of the present would not be 'condemned to silence and oblivion' – and it is definitely a problem that the many other almost blank reigns of these centuries appear desolate and poorly managed simply because historians have no vivid sources. Even with what we do have about Charlemagne it is often impossible to know if some tall tale, monk's failure of memory or ancient lie has become for ever enshrined in our narrative. Notker is particularly useless as many of his best turns of phrase are simply lifted direct from Roman writers, and he has an anecdote about Charlemagne and cheese so boring it is not worth the vellum it was written on. But some of the stories are vivid and often plausible. There are some great phrases – the Avars are 'that race of iron and diamond' – and Charlemagne comes up with new names for the months: February = 'Mud-month', May = 'Joy-month', etc. In later memory, Charlemagne's position was also made sacrosanct by the popularity of *The Song of Roland* – an epic poem in Old French which found its final form in the eleventh century, where he came to stand for a specific form of ancient greatness. A Norman bard sang about Roland and

Charlemagne at the Battle of Hastings to urge the troops on to heroic deeds, which clearly worked.

The continuity of the office of Emperor over the following ten centuries meant that Charlemagne's principal residence, Aachen, has survived. Despite irregular bouts of being smashed up, extended and redecorated in often poor taste, Charlemagne's chapel and throne are still there. A pedantic but important point is that the ceremonies at Aachen were around being crowned 'King of the Romans', whereupon the lucky winner then had to go to Rome to be made Emperor by the Pope – an arrangement which was some-times not possible, and which would break down completely in the 1500s. In the later split in Charlemagne's former empire which made France a separate place, it was the non-French ruler who remained 'King of the Romans' even if in practice this would now mean 'King of the Speakers of Various German Dialects'.

For anybody even a bit interested in medieval history, it is a struggle not to faint with excitement in the Aachen Treasury. A wonderful advertising print has survived, made in Cologne in 1615, to whip up tourist interest: in a series of little pictures it boasts of the amazing things to be gawped at. The baby clothes of Jesus! The loin cloth worn on the Cross! The cloth John the Baptist's head was placed on! The clothes worn by Mary when Jesus was born! There is also an engraving from a few years later showing a fashionable crowd looking at the displayed relics, which were last shown in 2014 and even then attracted a crowd of some hundred thousand pilgrims. The Big Four are only the start, however – there is also a giant gold hand (which has a debased Buddhist flavour) containing part of Charlemagne's skeleton and such wonders as an early Gospel from the court of Charlemagne or one of his immediate successors, with charming paintings of the Four Evangelists writing away in their togas. I need to stop – but who could not be delighted by a real oliphant? The key moment in *The Song of Roland* revolves around when the oliphant should be sounded. Sadly, later pedants have established that while the one in the treasury is indeed a hunting horn carved from an elephant tusk, it was made in Sicily some two centuries after Charlemagne's death

and cannot be Roland's. But still. Best of all is an ivory book cover
with scenes from the life of Jesus – if not belonging to Charlemagne, certainly made not long after. Each time I see it, there is
something magical in the way that the ivory on the cover is *worn* –
rather like the step at the Maastricht shrine. It is a side effect of
generations of hands holding the prayer book it once protected and
an oddly intimate link between ourselves and the people who stood
in the same place, it feels, really quite recently.

Like most of his family, Charlemagne came from the modern
German–Dutch–Belgian border area. He both inherited a huge
swath of land and extended it through campaigning into the east,
fighting the pagan Saxons in great raids down the Ruhr valley. He
also wrecked the Avar Empire, which had controlled Central Europe
for some two centuries, bringing back to Aachen 'fifteen oxcarts' of
Avar treasure. However, to think of Charlemagne as the acknowledged ruler of everywhere between the Pyrenees and Denmark, the
mountains of Bohemia and central Italy, would be a mistake. Many
of these places must have had a very indirect relationship with him
and we know little about the many aristocrats who would have done
the day-to-day work. But in his extraordinarily long and restless
life he did shift around, imposing his will – sometimes only
temporarily – from Spain to the Baltic. Just as his grandfather
Charles Martel had ended serious Arab incursions into France, so
Charlemagne carved out new Christian areas in Central Europe and
fought back the 'Northmen'. With these last, it gets a bit awkward
as an accidental side effect of his annual campaigns to kill Saxons
meant that, unknown to him, he had wrecked the principal military
organization that had been absorbing the military ambitions of the
Danes. Now that Saxony lay in ruins – with a scattering of anxious
Frankish missionaries trying to buck up handfuls of highly irritable
Saxon survivors with the Good News – the Danish chiefs suddenly
had time on their hands and could lean back on their rough-hewn
stools, wondering whether their berserkers might enjoy going
abroad for a bit. Charlemagne had not been buried long before his
children and grandchildren learned a lot more about these seafaring
tourists.

CHAPTER TWO

The split inheritance

In 2015 an amazingly beautiful Gospel was put up for auction. It is not an elaborate book and is clearly designed for use rather than ostentation. There are some two hundred pages of immaculately written text with some letters in red or green ink. It was created either in Metz or a monastery in Alsace before 835. It had a picturesque fate as one of the many books stolen by the great (in his way) nineteenth-century book thief Guglielmo Libri Carucci dalla Sommaja, who used his position as Inspector of French Libraries to purloin, cut up and sell medieval manuscripts to fund an enjoyable lifestyle. His antics have caused bibliographic mayhem ever since. The Gospel seems to have been lifted from a Dominican monastery, although it may have had further adventures since the French Revolution and was sold intact at Sotheby's in 1859. In 2015 it was sold for three million dollars.

The Gospel is thought to have belonged to Teutberga, one of the great wronged women of the ninth century and someone who stands at the heart of the story of Lotharingia. As mentioned at the beginning of the comparatively cheap book you are currently reading, Lotharingia (initially known as Middle Francia) emerged from the manoeuvres of Charlemagne's grandsons. We probably have more grounds for regretting the fall of the old empire than its inhabitants did. Historians love large political units because they seem more glamorous, but there is no reason to think that an individual living under the control of a firm-but-fair local lord would have had a better or worse time. In any event, after the Treaty of Verdun of 843 had created West Francia (under Charles the Bald), Middle Francia (under Lothair I) and East Francia (under Louis the

German) this proved a permanent if highly unstable set of boundaries until Napoleon scooped the pool some centuries later.

Middle Francia immediately fell into difficulties. Lothair I was the eldest of the three brothers and had once hoped to maintain the old empire whole. In his frantic efforts to ward off his siblings he had even roped in the much contested group called the Stellingabund – the descendants of forcibly converted Saxons, whose rebellion (ferociously put down by Louis the German) based in Speyer was perhaps the last gasp of a memory of paganism in the west. As usual, the records are annoyingly unclear. The damage done by the civil war was made far worse by Viking raids in the north and Saracen ones in the south. Following the Treaty of Verdun, Lothair ruled just Middle Francia, racing back and forth trying to deal both with these predators and with further internal rebellions. When he died the southern reaches of his kingdom (Provence and northern Italy) were split off and disappear from this story, except for the leitmotif of the imperial relationship with the Pope, and the intermittent and generally ruinous attempts by various later emperors to impose themselves on the almost unbelievably annoying and ornery Italian city states.

Lothair's son, Lothair II, took over the new, smaller Middle Francia and it has been known ever since as Lotharingia after him. Teutberga was married to Lothair II (a political match insisted on by his father) and when she was not reading her attractive Gospels she was in the terrible position of not providing an heir, for reasons we have no knowledge of. As a result the new Lothair spent his entire reign twisting and turning to dispose of Teutberga in favour of his mistress Waldrada. There was simply no basis for anybody to agree to this – it was illegal and an annulment would besmirch the Church from the Pope down. His uncles in West Francia and East Francia expressed cheerful concern, both knowing that a childless dead Lothair would offer interesting possibilities for their own expansion. Lothair called his court together, accused Teutberga of every sexual wrongdoing possible and subjected her to trial by ordeal. A stone was put at the bottom of a pot of boiling water and her champion had to pluck it out – if his cooked hand festered then she was guilty. In scenes of operatic excitement (and with Lothair presumably quite confident about what boiling water would do to a hand) the queen's champion plucked out the stone and his hand was unmarked. What would anyone give to have been in that strongly smelling throng of courtly onlookers and join in the general gasp of surprise and consternation! Lothair's reign never really recovered – God had shown his accusations to be lies and Teutberga was faultless. There then followed a series of threats and invasions, helped by his friendly East Francian uncle, Louis the German, who played his cards brilliantly – pretending to be shocked by Lothair's predicament while helping him to burn his bridges with everybody else. Ultimately Lothair went to Rome to appeal to the new Pope (the old one having in a total rage excommunicated all the members of the Rhineland church hierarchy who had taken Lothair's side) but died of fever on the way back. Teutberga then withdrew to a convent in Metz, presumably with her Gospels.

Teutberga's terrible situation raised two issues which would dog Western Europe for centuries. The attempts by the Pope to impose his authority on the divorce marked a major ramping up in his power and prestige and were the origin of the endless, violent disputes between future emperors and popes which, thank goodness, fall outside the scope of this book. Lothair did have a child with Waldrada, Hugh, and he was passed over as Lothair's successor because he was illegitimate – a distinction which had not on the whole been important before. Hugh had a rackety and meanminded career ahead of him, conniving and murdering until he ended up blinded by Charles the Fat and imprisoned in the abbey of Prüm, where his dad was buried.

With Lothair's death his uncles moved in and split Lotharingia between them, Louis the German taking the lion's share. A further fix was made at the Treaty of Ribemont in 880 between their heirs. This was in every way the primal act – most of Lotharingia, from what became Holland down to Burgundy, became attached to East Francia, which would stabilize as the Holy Roman Empire. But cutting up the cake in such a clumsy way made it quite plausible for the ruler of West Francia, the future France, to see rich crumbs and bits of icing that he might nonetheless reach for. Some of the borders established at Ribemont had astonishing longevity. The line of the Scheldt River in Flanders meant that French sovereignty would exist to the west and Imperial sovereignty to the east, a distinction that drove mad many generations of would-be conquerors and which hog-tied the theoretically powerful Counts of Flanders just as much as it did their rich but perennially disloyal and tiresome cities of Bruges and Ghent.

Ribemont also enshrined the incredibly headachy issue of the different Burgundies, with Lower Burgundy falling to the entertainingly named Boso, nephew to the unhappy Teutberga. One historian has counted fifteen different entities over the centuries called 'Burgundy' – post-Ribemont there were four: Boso's Upper Burgundy, based around Lake Geneva and Lake Neuchâtel and taking in a bit of what is now Alpine northern Italy; Lower Burgundy, which was essentially a giant version of Provence; the Duchy of Burgundy, which was linked to West Francia (with its principal town of Dijon); and the County of Burgundy (a bigger version of the future Franche-Comté – the 'free county' – with its principal town of Dole), which was Imperial territory. In practical terms it is only the distinction between the Duchy and the County that will plague readers until chapter six.

The authority issues made particularly vivid by Lothair would become key to Lotharingia's future. The emerging French state would prove able, albeit with innumerable setbacks, to impose its will on most of the counties and duchies of West Francia. The Holy Roman Empire (East Francia) never achieved this. Lotharingia's landscape was a mass of special requirements, legal loopholes and oddities. Neither West nor East Francia were ever aiming to create a unified state of a kind we flatter ourselves we live in today, but over the long term, as the western kingdom came to focus on Paris, there was a logic to trying to subordinate as many surrounding territories as feasible to the royal will.

The eastern empire was structured differently, with no chief city. The Emperor wandered from palace to palace and different territories made different arrangements depending on the ebb and flow of emergencies and personalities. One striking little feature of Xanten today, for example, is that it still has a walled section in its centre called 'The Immunity', in which the town's clerical rulers organized their own business and were not answerable to the Imperial authorities. These immunities were scattered everywhere, honeycombing jurisdictions and creating a parallel ecclesiastical world secular rulers could not do much about – from small monasteries to entire territories along the Rhine, such as the Archbishoprics of Trier (ruler of towns such as Koblenz) and Cologne. Just to wrap this issue up once and for all, in the following centuries special cities were able to do deals with the Emperor to buy themselves out – in return for specific commitments of money and troops they could become Free Imperial Cities. In Lotharingia these were places which took over responsibility for their own legal systems, such as Colmar and Mulhouse, or which managed to wriggle out from ecclesiastical control, such as Basel and Strasbourg.

The result of all this was a map which looked like a jigsaw a dog had tried to swallow and then thrown up. It has nothing in common with the evenly smoothed systems of England or the United States. In both these countries a 'county' was a very simple local administrative unit, albeit with seemingly eccentric boundaries in many English cases. But within Lotharingia 'county' could mean something ranging from the very grand (the County of Holland; the County of the Mark) to a soggy dot (the County of Bentheim) and being count in these places could either be a very serious role or a bit of a joke. Dukedoms were more senior in the hierarchy, but did not necessarily imply more significant territories: the Duke of Bar (on the border with France) or of Fürstenburg (in the Black Forest) had many fewer resources than the major counts.

But that is probably enough obscurantism for one section – the book can return to the western exclaves of the Duke of Württemberg later on. Sticking to the post-Treaty of Ribemont world of 880, this was the last partition of what was still recognizably Charlemagne's inheritance. It enshrined Lotharingia – Middle Francia – as a huge zone which both the French king and German king could equally lay dynastic claim to. The treaty was signed by Louis III for

West Francia and Louis III for East Francia, respectively great-great-grandson and great-grandson of Charlemagne, each named after Charlemagne's first successor Louis I 'the Pious'. Each twist and turn over the coming centuries, as the digits piled up after each further French Louis, would generate much of Western history.

Margraves, landgraves, dukes and counts

It is hard to count the wars that irrupt over the centuries across the ragged line which divided the Empire and France. To describe them all would be numbing to write about and worse to read – specific occasions are well worth discussing, but the general ins and outs of every kingdom, dukedom and county are not. It seems a bit more interesting to think more broadly about the specific tensions that created such a world.

Both France and the Empire had different variants on the same issues of who should be in charge and who should do as they were told. This fluctuation was in itself enough repeatedly to cause mayhem. We have to make a huge effort to take old maps as seriously as new, and not to think of the old ones as mere proto-versions of the more rational current ones. I will try not to make this point again, but Europe's values, behaviour and ideology in the period 1914–45 make it impossible for us to be patronizing about any earlier period's bloodthirstiness, quests for revenge, irrationality. Alternatively, as it sinks into the popular conscience more clearly, the basis on which Europeans maintained their own later overseas empires in the nineteenth and twentieth centuries makes it equally difficult for us to tut-tut about earlier attitudes within Europe towards peasants or non-Christians or any specific group of people who were destroyed because they were in the way.

We still all agree to shudder at the thought of the Mongols, but we have ourselves managed to invade whole continents, kill most of the inhabitants and then entirely repopulate them, to a degree which the Mongols could only dream of. The spread of Christianity eastwards across Europe was achieved over hundreds of years and was achieved by vast resources being drained from France and the Empire. We all instinctively when looking at maps of Otto the Great, the Teutonic Knights and so on follow their route from left to right, putting our brains and sensibilities in their baggage trains, but it is just as interesting an exercise to think of oneself as on the receiving end and see it all from the viewpoint of one of the vanquished. I don't mean this in a particularly hand-wringing way – as a species we seem to value fighting almost as much as we enjoy eating – but there is a tiresome historical narrative where both the writer and the reader mentally become best friends with whoever winds up winning. There is also nationalism of a kind which is patently silly. English enthusiasm for the outcome of the Battle of Waterloo is still valid as we still palpably live in a post-Waterloo world, however many twists and turns since. But there must have been a point at which we rightly became merely mildly interested about, say, the Battle of Agincourt, particularly as we choose to know nothing at all about, say, the Battles of Formigny and Castillon, which threw the English out of France.

As discussed earlier, Charlemagne's inheritors had in West Francia and East Francia created two opposing blocs and in Lotharingia an intermediate bloc linked to East Francia. But Lotharingia was always festooned in legalistic special pleading of a kind that gladdened the hearts of acquisition-minded rulers in West Francia. All the rulers, both large and small, had an equal, increasingly ancient sense of legitimacy. All were potentially distractable by forces outside the bounds of the old Empire (Spain, England, Poland, Italy) but all were keen to gain advantages against each other. At some points Lotharingia appears to be held underwater so long that it must surely drown, but then it bobs up again and ruins everyone's plans. Luxembourg's continuing existence in the twenty-first century as effectively a dynastic and territorial coelacanth is a simply astonishing instance of Lotharingian persistence. So many proud conquerors have held Luxembourg's huge fortress system: but they all, every one, went home.

The principal job of each community across Europe has always been to feed itself successfully and provide security for its inhabitants. In the indeterminate past it was worked out that associations of such communities did this more effectively. Even at the heart of the so-called Dark Ages these networks were so sophisticated that they were breathing in materials from many hundreds of miles away and breathing out their own products. The Treasury of Maastricht includes extraordinarily ancient pieces of cloth from 'Dark Age' Central Asia, Byzantium and Egypt, surviving because they had once wrapped saints' relics. These are pretty and sophisticated in ways which are a confusing reminder that large parts of the world were not 'Dark' at that time, including Maastricht. Sometimes long-distance trade would be interrupted – by raiders, floods, some switch in technology or a forced or otherwise change in allegiance – or trade would go up or down according to the amounts of money in circulation. But it was always elaborate, requiring cooperation, security and broader forces of credit than those of just one isolated town.

The problem has always been the seemingly simple but in practice super-vexed issue of who should most benefit from any specific association. Everybody always assumes that the disappearance of the Roman Empire was a universal disaster, but it could be that for many communities, no longer having to shell out huge taxes and contribute to legions, palaces and the high life in Italy was a fair deal. A great plus must have been no longer having to pretend to like the horrible Roman fermented 'fish sauce'. Experts always claim that the empty clay fish sauce pots that litter the bottom of the Rhine can be dated to show there was a point when trade within the Empire seized up, but it seems just as likely that as soon as the last stern-faced legionary left, the locals joyfully chucked the whole lot off the docks.

In the post-Roman centuries the downward drift in the economy and occasional total erasures by Goths, Saracens, etc. were obviously regrettable, but sufficiently spaced out to be lived with. Many towns from Ghent down to Basel and Konstanz show no sign of ever being unoccupied – they just seem to have kept going, no more nor less vividly for their inhabitants, but invisibly to us through the lack of surviving records. One unhelpful side effect of the nineteenth- and twentieth-century obsession with the Roman Empire was that archaeologists tended – trembling with anticipation and imagining the clatter of chariots across the forum of downtown Noviomagus (Nijmegen) – to chuck away every building layer between the present and the excitement of getting at some Roman heating system or floor mosaic (featuring a dolphin – as usual), with the result that many centuries of dense Frankish and medieval history ended up as landfill without anybody noticing.

Much of the early medieval economy was devoted to the process of staying alive, but that has always been true in almost all of human history in almost all places, with a simple circulation between those who made ploughs and those who used them, or those who churned butter and those who owned chickens. It is amazing the speed at which economies become complicated, even in a fairly small town, and so the need for coins as a symbol of equivalent value. And then, with equal rapidity, some form of external authority is required to guarantee the purity of those coins over longer distances.

Almost all the economy that peeped above the level of subsistence went on spiritual issues – the preparation for the far more serious business of the Afterlife. We are used to seeing major cathedrals in major modern cities: Cologne, say, or Antwerp, where the buildings' size hold their own even as we wade through endless shopping centres and tram stations to reach them. A more striking dip into the past comes from seeing a great cathedral surviving in what has, for many reasons, become or remained a small town. Toul is a perfect example: an ancient Roman Moselle town (Tullum Leucorum) and seat of Christianity, its last great effort before falling into economic irrelevance seems to have been to create its immense cathedral, completed in the fourteenth century, but probably the sixth on the same site (originally that of a Roman temple). As only sixteen thousand people live in Toul now (and it still sits behind its seventeenth-century fortifications), the cathedral remains almost crazily out of scale with its meagre surroundings, like a crashed chunk of one of Darth Vader's Star Destroyers. It looks as though all the other houses in Toul could fit inside. Or there is the sight as the train passes over the bridges at the awe-inspiring Holland Deep of

Dordrecht, with its aptly named Great Church, a structure so huge it appears to be the result of some ancient feet-for-inches mistake in interpreting the plan. Even in earlier versions these churches were also vast – their building and then restless rebuilding would have been for centuries a town's principal non-workaday goal. What we would view as the aim – their completion – was far less important than the process itself, with different parts under temporary roofs coming into use for different generations. To say that they were the 'focus' of life would be too narrow: they were the *point* of life and attracted much of the money that was not devoted to the lower-level business of simply staying alive and in reasonable comfort.

The missing part of this discussion, and where it began, is the role of the ruler. There were never individual, separate communes except in the very remote fringes of Europe. But the nature of the association that would result in security and success has never been resolved, either before or since – effectively, any political discussion about anything in 2017 (when I am writing this paragraph) is merely the latest instalment of something which has gone on for ever. The need for defence (walls, moats, troops) was always very expensive and awkward and as unresolvable as deciding how high a church tower needs to be to look suitably ecstatic and holy and not risk appearing a bit cheap (church towers always being essential also as defensive watch towers, and their bells regulating town-wide military instructions). Everyone understood that pouring cash into vast walls could be more damaging than spending the money on less dull improvements and on trade with neighbouring towns. But equally there was town after town which made a rational decision about cutting back on military training and not bothering to maintain the boring old defensive sluice system, only to find itself burned to the ground. Anybody interested in history is always looking at the big events – the town under siege, the battle down the road – but another way of thinking is to look at the periods of peace in any specific community. If somewhere has been completely tranquil for a couple of generations, who is going to have the courage to suggest that the money for the jolly carnival feast this year really ought to be spent on hiring a few archers just in case?

These interactions have never stopped, but they are poorly recorded. We are still at a loss as to how most of the empire really functioned. The constituent parts of the Frankish Empire were, like all its predecessors big or small, partly enforced at sword-point, but were also partly a sensible scaling-up for protection and mutual aid. In the eleventh century western Europe increasingly became a sort of back country, away from the main external threats, as the Vikings became Christian. The Magyars and the Slavs had ceased to be a problem after the Emperor Otto the Great defeated them at the Battles of Lechfeld and Recknitz in 955. Germanic settlers (which would at this point be taken to mean anyone not speaking *lingua romana* – so including the 'Dutch') moved east, creating many of the towns around which eastern German Christian culture was built, most importantly Otto's foundation at Magdeburg, which became the central focus for a mass movement, using town models first established in the west, and where Otto is buried – a vast jump forward, some three hundred miles east from the old stamping ground at Aachen.

In parallel with Charlemagne's wars with the Saxons and Avars and Otto's further march east in the following century, although with very tangled and widely variegated roots, a modern geography emerged, with regions ruled by counts, margraves or dukes, and which brought its own variants on protection and exploitation. These figures generally owed their supremacy to either the King in Paris or to the peripatetic Emperor in one of his palaces and had shadowy ancestors from the time of the Viking invasions – as local commanders had to deal with the nightmarish world of sea- and river-borne irruption. In the 850s there is a Count of Artois, in the 860s a Margrave of Flanders, in the 880s a Count of Holland. There was the formidable if murky Reginar 'Longneck', who was possibly the Emperor Lothair I's grandson, but in any event accumulated the roles of Duke of Lotharingia, Count of Liège, Duke of Hainaut and Count of Mons and who seems to have been present at all kinds of great if barely recorded events: awkwardly and uncheckably he could have been several people, as Reginar was then a fashionable name. His four children became respectively Duke of Lorraine,

Archbishop of Mainz, Archbishop of Utrecht and Count of Hainaut – in fact his descendants (the 'Reginarids') cascade down through the region's choicest properties (Leuven, Brussels, Limburg) for nearly five hundred years, before at last messing up and, with no males in sight, handing their legacy over to one of the sons of the Duke of Burgundy, just in time for him to be killed at the Battle of Agincourt, in a very different world. Another Reginarid branch went on to rule Hesse until 1918.

It is impossible to repeat too often: the lack of surviving documents does not mean that people were standing around vacantly in the mud, picking their noses and waiting for something to turn up. I have felt this ever since I wandered around the colossal, wholly-illiterate-Treveri-built fortress town discussed earlier: on a mission not to confuse the human trait of happening to write things down with a workable, indeed complex Europe. These rulers, scattered across Lotharingia, from the mouths of the Rhine down to the Swiss Alps, were in some cases secular, in others religious, in some cases pious, in others psychotic. How they managed to rule over their people and how they were ruled over by their sometimes notional and remote, and sometimes frighteningly immediate and focused kings would be the motor which ran European history until the twentieth century.

Imperial grandeur and decay

It would be special pleading on a grand scale to pretend that Christian Western Europe's situation did not become fairly poor during the century after Charlemagne's death. Indeed, it has been convincingly argued that the cult of Charlemagne really only got under way in the ghastly and nostalgic world of the 880s. Notker the Stammerer's extensive if unreliable anecdotes of Charlemagne were written to cheer up the sad, hopeless, ill Emperor Charles III 'the Fat', looking back on a golden world of order and achievement, free both of marauders and of a seemingly limitless supply of mean, disloyal vassals. By 882, in a thoughtful piece of symbolic redecoration, a Viking army had converted Charlemagne's chapel at Aachen into stables.

The Emperor and the Pope and their fates were so entangled that their tumbling prestige dragged everyone down into the swamp, just as when they were both in the ascendant they tended to clash. Christian Western Europe was a very small place, under attack from Muslims and pagans at almost every point and with large areas we now take for granted (Spain and Portugal, much of Britain, all of Scandinavia, Saxony eastwards) non-Christian. Travelling back and forth down the Rhine to Rome was almost the only tourism option available. The bottom of the trough of humiliation was hit by Pope Formosus, whose pontificate was so riven by faction that after his death he was famously dug up, wrapped in papal robes and tied to his throne so he could be put on trial at what became known as the 'Cadaver Synod'. As a rotting corpse clad in gold cloth, he listened as best he could to closing statements from m'learned friend while in other news the brutal Rollo and his Viking (*Normands*) friends were busy devastating West Francia and carving out what became Normandy. This failure of political and religious leadership must have made life grim for most people. The only good news was that the Emperor Arnulf managed in 891 at the Battle of Leuven (the first ever mention of this crucial town) to devastate a Viking army heading south through the Netherlands – an early indicator that for some parts of Europe at least the scourge might be over.

Lotharingia continued to be projected upon by the ambitions of the rulers of West and East Francia. It was a kingdom and therefore grand and important, including at Aachen the core Charlemagne seal of approval. Charles III the Simple of West Francia became King of Lotharingia in 911, but his reign became engulfed in such a welter of fiascos that it is shaming even to sketch these in. Among the many things that go badly for him is the arrival of Henry I the Fowler, King of East Francia, who charges into Lotharingia, ending its independent status and turning it into a major dukedom. Henry is principally known to us today as the bluff, firm-but-fair rugby-coach-like ruler in Wagner's *Lohengrin* (1850), who is rather comically out of his depth with the more mystical, swan-oriented elements in the opera and keen only to get on with persuading the good people of Brabant to help him kill Hungarian raiders. He sings things like 'For German soil the German sword!' which made generations of German nationalist inadequates sob and go bandy-legged, but which now seems odd to us given the squarely Belgian nature of the opera's location.

By the time Henry the Fowler arrived on the scene (and his ascent to power is wholly mysterious, with no surviving record beyond a trite legend), Frankish power in West Francia had retreated to the area around the Île-de-France and in East Francia around the Middle Rhine. Henry began a long period of triumphant expansion, during which both what was now undoubtedly France and 'the Empire' (more poorly defined) became recognizable entities. The hold Henry and his successors had over Lotharingia was crucial as it provided their ever more important cultic link to Aachen (cleaned of Vikings and their horses) and entangled them in the resources and prestige of the three ancient religious territories of Trier, Cologne and Mainz. The Ottonian dynasty (919–1024) and the Salian dynasty (1024–1125) formalized and extended a structure of duchies, counties and margravates (border defence zones – the same word as the English 'marcher') that endured through various twists and turns until 1918, with their ghosts still turning up today in local, harmless forms.

The Ottonians showed a chaotic carelessness in their burial arrangements, winding up in (in order) Quedlinburg, Magdeburg, Rome, Aachen and Bamberg. Nineteenth-century nationalist histor-ians disliked this messiness and were also enraged by Emperors' endless visits to Italy, both as rulers of parts of northern Italy and because it was the Pope in Rome who made them Emperor. This historians' fury fed into German nationalist paranoia about Cathol-icism and the unhappiness that medieval German identity was as much tied to the whim of 'a gentleman living in Rome' as to the swords of Germanic liege-men being beaten on their shields in a *Lohengrin*-like manner.

Some of these historians' and archaeologists' motives may now seem distasteful but it is thanks to their rooting in dirty archives and digging away in mouldering vaults that we know what we do. And many of them were as much motivated by the consistent, attractive localism (not just a Rhineland localism, say, but a *Cologne* localism) that continues to be Germany's great saving grace. Without their obsessive tidying and reorganizing we would not have the superb spectacle provided by descending into the crypt of Speyer Cathedral. This amazing subterranean twenty-foot-high columned hall was built in 1041 and is substantially unchanged – an area that has not seen daylight for almost a millennium. It is the shrine of the Ottonians' successors, the Salian dynasty, from Emperor Conrad II (son of Count Henry of Speyer and Adelaide of Alsace) to Henry V. They are all down here: although two died in Utrecht meaning that their bowels and hearts are separately buried in the cathedral there.* The first great Habsburg, Emperor Rudolf I, is also here, his superb cenotaph statue glowering from a wall. The whole vault was picked over and fixed up just before the First World War and as a result the local museum is filled with sensational stuff: for example, the crowns the Emperors were buried with turned out – reasonably enough given their lack of future wear-and-tear – to be very cheaply made. Or Henry III's cross and orb, or Henry V's spurs. Gisela of Swabia, Conrad II's Empress, was dug up and found to be a mummified blonde. What fun everyone must have had, scrabbling about among these horrors, all beautifully photographed (Philip of Swabia was simply mulch plus a skull). You almost expect on touching the tombs today to find them slightly warm – or to feel uneasy because of some residual hum of power, emanated at a frequency we can only intermittently hear.

---

* Including those of the first of them, Conrad II, the rest of whose body travelled down the Rhine via Cologne, Mainz and Worms in a great cortège that must have been the wonder of the age and in fulfilment of his wish to establish a great cultic and dynastic space at Speyer. All the stuff about bowels and hearts is fun because it is so odd that it shocks us all into seeing that European humans are in practice impossible to differentiate in their hopes, fears and strange habits from those of 'tribes' in other parts of the world beloved of anthropologists.

Accidental fires, deliberate explosions, drastic changes in architectural taste have twisted and turned the extraordinary imperial buildings but they still preserve a powerful sense of purpose and political-military heft. The yawing, cavernous spaces of Mainz, Speyer or Worms cathedrals need to be experienced in all weathers and light conditions. Speyer at night in winter is hard to beat, with isolated pools of electric light and thousands of tons of cold stone somehow held in place above your head.

In a side chapel in Mainz Cathedral is the Udenheimer Crucifix – a simple, painted wooden cross from 1070, with a shockingly direct, almost naive statue of Christ staring down at its latest worshipper across staggering distances of time. The crucifix was made during the reign of Emperor Henry IV. If the 'Cadaver Synod' had marked a nadir for the papacy, then Henry was unlucky enough to live at a time of healthy rebound for that institution. A striking feature of the Empire was the both secular and religious nature of many of its territories. For example, back in the days of Otto the Great, Otto's brother Bruno was simultaneously Duke of Lotharingia and Archbishop of Cologne (where he created the great cathedral which, alas, burned to the ground in 1248, resulting in the embarrassing shambles of stops-and-starts that meant it took six hundred years to replace). Emperors had become used to choosing their own top clerics and indeed relied on them both spiritually and militarily. Henry IV was an effective ruler, battling against recalcitrant Thuringians and Saxons and pagan Slavs in Mecklenburg. In Rome, Pope Gregory VII felt it was completely reasonable that the Church should actually control itself; making its own appointments, operating in parallel to the secular authorities – in other words controlling the 'investiture' of its staff. This was an ancient assertion and the various convulsions it provoked at different times did varying amounts of damage. Gregory's attempts to enforce his views on investiture caused mayhem. Henry held a synod at Worms at which he persuaded 'his' bishops to depose the Pope – Gregory then shook out his entire bag of tricks: threats, fighting, bribes, anti-King Rudolf crowned at Mainz, anti-King Hermann, anti-King Egbert, several invasions of Italy and eventual rebellion by Henry's own son. After Henry died at Liège while handling the latest daft twist in the saga, his body suffered the near unique oddity of being buried *outside* Speyer Cathedral in unconsecrated ground until his excommunication was lifted six years later and he could be moved inside.

Rather like the scenario in one of those science-fiction movies where a universe is only kept in existence through the will of some all-clever being, and shatters if he is even for a moment distracted, the Empire had a tendency to break apart if the Emperor lost concentration. But in common with France and England there were always powers which tended to collude with its rebuilding, who would for familial, mercenary or ideological reasons rally to him. The Investiture Controversy was settled under Henry's son Henry V, who, at the Concordat of Worms in 1122, agreed to papal control over appointments but with steering from himself. It preserved the specific nature of the Empire, where the many religious territories and their countless sprinkled 'immunities' were effectively self-governing in a peculiar mixture of the sacred and profane. This concordat was viewed as the founding shambles by nineteenth-century German historians, the point where Germany went on its own splintered path to weakness and futility while England and France became proper nation states. It embedded the major separate religious territories of Utrecht, Liège, Cologne and the rest, down to tiny but persistent scattered bits of land like those owned by the Abbeys of Stavelot or Prüm. But these German historians were blinded by much later anti-Catholic hatreds inexplicable back in the twelfth century. The vast bulks of the Imperial cathedrals on the Rhine alone show how power lay in a unique tangle between emperors, secular lords and religious lords – but with the sacred underpinning always crucial. Mainz Cathedral was one of the biggest buildings made since the Roman Empire and is still there, while the imperial palaces are all gone and would never have been as grand as the cathedral.

It is undoubtedly true, though, that the Empire that stretched from the mouths of the Rhine and Scheldt to its expanding eastern fighting frontier was structured in a pattern of smaller units – a bit like the hidden matrix structure within the glass of car windscreens – which under stress could break into pieces. Each had its own history, institutions, strengths and weaknesses. As each colonial eastern territory was bashed into shape in the eleventh and twelfth centuries it tended to stay in the same medieval family's grip – with the Hohenzollerns, Habsburgs, Wettins and Mecklenburgs going through many tribulations but grimly holding on until their disgusted subjects finally ejected them in the twentieth century. The older western lands had persistence and strength, setting up rough sets of boundaries and defining who should rule any or all of them. These different entities would either raise up or crush into the dirt any number of conquering heroes in centuries to come.

Boulogne boy makes good

Bouillon is a strange little town. It is entangled in a very small version of the Grand Canyon, its geology created by a river which over millions of years carved a looped meander, leaving a great hump of rock in the middle, and high hills around it. When the first humans arrived, the security this rock gave meant that it was in effect a prefabricated fortress. Ever since, great piles of stone have been dragged up to the top to create layer upon gnarled layer of walls and towers. The town spreads over the surrounding hills, themselves so steep that it feels it would take only a very small earthquake to tumble all the clinging houses down into the river. On the heavily wooded border between Belgium and France it has been fought over often (a wonderfully vainglorious proclamation from Louis XIV has been mockingly left on one of the many castle gateways), and last saw action in the early nineteenth century as one of the Dutch strongholds created to keep post-Napoleonic France from breaking out again. After the Belgian Revolution of 1830 it found itself ruled by Brussels, yet another random outcome for its helpless inhabitants.

Bouillon's fame is over nine hundred years old, through its association with Godefroy of Bouillon, the leader of the homicidal outing later known as the First Crusade. This ascetic knight-pilgrim is everywhere. At one point I lined things up so that I was in a pub drinking Godefroy lager sitting next to a vaguely heavy-metal statue of Godefroy, looking out at the Godefroy Hotel. I could potentially have enjoyed with my lager a Godefroy cigarillo made from Bouillon-region tobacco and a hunk of loaf spread with *pâté de Godefroy*, decorated with red bell-pepper to make it look a bit Levantine. Sadly, Godefroy, however much he might have appreciated a cooling glassful during the rigours of the Battle of Ascalon, lived several centuries too early for lager to exist, and the ingredients of both the cigarillos and pâté were still safely tucked away in the undiscovered Americas. All this fraudulent promotion of the town's hero gives Bouillon an air of daft perfection.

Godefroy is a key nationalist hero both for France and for Belgium. His massive statue is the centrepiece of the royal quarter of Brussels and in the nineteenth century he became the focus of a rather dank Catholic cult, a sort of boy Joan of Arc, but with a colonial conquest flavour. Inside the castle complex there is a statue of him with a large crucifix shape on the floor at his feet that can be filled with candles to create a suitably spiritual-militarist atmosphere. In one of those too-good-to-be-true moments, the local museum has a series of superb 1930s aerial photos of crusader castles, taken by French army flyers, who would have themselves been involved in the ferocious suppression of the Great Syrian Revolt – an undertaking certainly in line with Godefroy's thinking. Sadly though, it is in practice not clear that Godefroy ever even visited Bouillon – he was 'of' quite a lot of things, Bouillon just being one of them.

There are many mysteries around the crusades and why they happened at all. They had a staggering impact on the twelfth, thirteenth and fourteenth centuries – but were in the end a total dud, with the Fall of Acre in 1291 ending the entire fighting-in-the-footsteps-of-Jesus aspect. The years before Pope Urban II gave his great speech in 1095 which launched the whole project had seen successful seaborne invasions of England and Sicily, the growth of Castile, the spread of Italian (Genoese, Pisan, Venetian) naval strength across the Mediterranean and the neutering of the Viking threat. There must have been a general sense of restlessness and enterprise in the air. Many of those who answered Urban's call for a great expedition to take the Holy Places from the Muslims were companions or siblings of those who had made themselves rich and famous from these other recent feats of derring-do. The crusade quite quickly mutated into a general movement to destroy pagan, heretic or Muslim elements across Europe and successfully did this from Lisbon to Riga, becoming an exciting rite of passage for young knights until the final Central European crusades of 1395 and 1443, which resulted in such totally crushing victories for the Ottoman Empire that everyone suddenly remembered that they had something else urgent to do back home instead.

The convulsions that racked Western Europe in the wake of Urban's sermon resulted in tens of thousands of pilgrims and soldiers marching eastwards. North-eastern Europe seemed to empty out much of its population. It was undoubtedly a religious movement, although a fair number of chainmail-clad rascals lurked among the pious. The distances involved were prodigious. A grim start was made by Peter the Hermit, a compelling orator from Amiens, and the sinister visionary Count Emicho, who drew to them a huge mixed bag of pilgrims and set out to glory ahead of the Pope's 'official' crusade. As they passed down through the Rhineland, communities of Jews were massacred at Trier, Mainz, Cologne, Worms and Metz. Exact numbers are unclear, but it seems probable that around eight hundred were killed just at Worms. As these were the very first military actions of the entire crusade movement, they tend to be passed over quickly by historians simply because the rest of the story is so long and complex, but in themselves they were a total catastrophe – the worst single recorded event in these communities, many of which had roots going back to the Roman Empire, until the Holocaust. The Heiliger Sand, the old Jewish cemetery in Worms, was in constant use from at least the eleventh century until it was superseded before the First World War. It is, as one would expect, a powerful place. The disasters of 1096 have left no visible mark – but the oldest identifiable gravestone is for someone called Yaakov ha-bahur, who was buried there in 1076/77. This worn, lichen-pocked stone extraordinarily takes us back to just before the world in which recorded violent anti-Semitism was born. The perpetrators were in fact inadvertently punished: as they marched across Central Europe, many were captured by local rulers and wound up in Balkan slave markets. When the survivors reached Constantinople they rushed across to the Asian side to continue to Jerusalem only to be massacred there by Turkish forces. A chastened Peter the Hermit stayed behind and slunk around in the baggage of the main forces of the First Crusade before disappearing from history.

At the heart of this crusade lay three remarkable brothers – the sons of Eustace II, Count of Boulogne, one of William the Conqueror's companions at the Battle of Hastings and a man who must have created a suitably predatory and devil-may-care atmosphere within the family circle. One of the sons was Godefroy, who was beyond his associations with Bouillon also the Duke of Lower Lotharingia; the second, Eustace, who would inherit his father's lands; the third, Baldwin, who would ultimately scoop the pool, becoming first the ruler of part of Armenia and then, on Godefroy's death, the first King of Jerusalem. An extraordinarily dynamic and brutal figure, without him the kingdom might have been snuffed out before it even began.

The almost unprecedented nature of these brothers' journey is hard to convey: from hanging around Boulogne in a howling gale, watching the seagulls and munching on bits of salted fish, to finding yourself face to face with minarets, bananas and hot sand. Godefroy provided the ascetic, soldier-of-Christ inspiration, Eustace and Baldwin the reckless and ingenious violence. The curious counter-factual about the First Crusade is to think about what would have happened if it had failed. Unknown to the thousands of troops worrying about tummy trouble and being ripped off by Levantine trinket-salesmen, the First Crusade just happened to be marching into a uniquely favourable environment, with their principal adversaries, their bases scattered from Baghdad to Cairo, at odds with one another and therefore defeated one by one. The region of the Holy

Places was significant, but not central to the concerns of these gigantic civilizations based on the Tigris and the Nile. Later crusades never really came close to threatening the cores of these Islamic states.

Baldwin himself, whose luck, relentlessness and relish for his grand position had more or less willed the kingdom into existence, died of disease on a quixotic raid to the mouth of the Nile. One serio-comic shambles (the Fifth Crusade) resulted in the death of innumerable Dutch and Rhineland troops mired in the mouth of the Nile to no great purpose and the shaming of William I, Count of Holland who somehow, unlike most of his men, managed to get back. Given that the crusaders were never strong enough to take these capital cities, it was just a question of time before everything else ended in tears. Even the nearby city of Damascus was impregnable, with King Conrad III of Germany (he was never crowned Emperor by the Pope) and his young nephew, the future Emperor Frederick I Barbarossa, totally humiliated in a failed siege during the Second Crusade. In old age Frederick tried to relaunch the crusading movement by bringing together all his warring vassals to a great ceremony of reconciliation, a 'Feast of Love' at Mainz Cathedral. He then marched an army thought to be some one hundred thousand strong through Hungary and defeated a major Turkish army, but drowned in a Cilician river.

The 'Lotharingian' element in the crusades varied but the initial importance of the three brothers created its own tradition whereby, however disastrous things got, there were always fresh volunteers (sometimes carrying out further pogroms en route down the Rhine), either for the major crusades themselves, or, just as important, contributing to the constant drift of adventurers and the devout as colonists or as members of the new military monastic orders, such as the Templars and the Hospitallers. Throughout the following two centuries it was common for younger sons simply to disappear for years on end and quite often never return. It was a throw of the dice as to whether you ended up wearing perfumed robes in some top new castle, married to an Armenian heiress and tucking into a pomegranate breakfast, or chained up in a Seldjuk atabeg's dungeon trying to lick moisture off the walls.

It is rare for the sources to give a sense of the emotional reality of the crusades – and so much of what we think is in fact shaped by the many hundreds of gigantic, vivid oil paintings, sculptures and frescoes created by nineteenth-century artists for whom these ancient events in the Levant were founding moments in the irrepressible birth of the uniquely (delete as applicable) Belgian, French and German national and religious spirit. Some odd ancient scraps survive that give a sense of the harshness and uncertainty of families parted by the near-lemming-like need for men to head to the Holy Land. The searing text of a song from the Third Crusade has somehow come down to us – a woman lamenting:

> I will sing to comfort my heart,
> For I do not want to die or go mad . . .
> . . . He sent
> me the shirt that he was wearing
> that I might hold it in my arms. At
> night when my love for him torments
> me, I take it into bed and hold it
> close to my naked body to soothe my suffering.

A moving and surprising monument is tucked away in the Museum of Lorraine in Nancy. When Bernard of Clairvaux, the most powerful and prestigious religious figure of his era, marched down the Rhine in 1146, proclaiming what turned out to be the wholly futile Second Crusade, one of those he swept up with his rhetoric was Hugues de Vaudemont, a nobleman who went as part of Louis VII's doomed army. We do not know who commissioned the carving or why, but here is a statue showing a gaunt, bearded Hugues on his return six years later, staff in hand and cross around his neck. He is being embraced by his wife, Aigeline of Burgundy, who wears an elaborate cloak and has a braid hanging down to her waist. He is patently at the end of his tether; she shows relief and pride.

The Cistercians

I had originally planned to start this book by returning to one of my favourite places – the old Cistercian abbey of Altenberg, about twelve miles north-east of Cologne. I saw myself standing, solitary and tiny in the vast building, light pouring through the clear glass, as I contemplated the battered tombs of the once-great counts and the implacable cruelty of passing time. And so, aching with self-consciousness, I arrived there at the beginning of January, the mood of inward rue already a bit messed up after a long chat with a witty and scornful Tunisian taxi driver from Leverkusen.

Everything at my chosen location seemed near ideal to start with: very cold, plenty of snow, stark trees and one of Germany's most beautiful valleys looming above my small inn. Feeling very Caspar-David-Friedrich, I skipped over to the abbey. This was where things began to misfire. The solitude remembered from a previous visit was replaced by a jammed car park and great crowds of people pouring in and out of the abbey, a restaurant and a near-bursting religious knick-knack shop. It was festive and fun, but I was having to recalibrate my own levels of pretension at great speed and entered the abbey somewhat baffled. The crowds were there, it turned out, to see a herculean Nativity scene. It seemed extraordinarily large not least because my own sense of scale was set by having just come from several days' exposure to our own Nativity scene at home, which consists of a tiny set of simplified wooden shapes of the usual suspects but enlivened by the addition of some plastic Asterix characters and a decaying marzipan lamb, bought in Lüneberg many years ago, discussed in my book *Germania* and now looking positively ghoulish with age. It was easy to see why so many people would drive over to see such bravura gigantic angels, oxen and magi, all topped off by great branches of pine needles framing the entire montage.

But it was at this point really everything went wrong. The wistfully disregarded tombs of the family of the Counts of Berg were not there – I had imagined the whole thing. Where were the ascetic Bruno, Gerhard killed in a joust, the long-lived Margaret of

Ravensberg, the fighting Archbishop Friedrich? I panicked that I had got Altenberg mixed up perhaps with Marburg and began wondering if there was some Swiss clinic I could check into where the doctors could draw on many years of experience in cleansing the minds of people whose brains have slid too far into the intricacies of the Holy Roman Empire. The only clue to my continuing sanity was a superb great flag of Berg hanging inside the abbey, just as I remembered, with its blue lion rampant, its tongue and claws red. With a chill of horror the message of the flag suddenly sunk in – it was directly above the Nativity. The platform that supported the weirdly rouged angel, the lugubrious ox, Baby Jesus and their friends was built *on* the tombs of the Counts of Berg, used as mere handy platform supports. Now the original conception for this book's opening collapsed completely: there was too cruel a gulf between the pleasingly Romantic silent reproach of the battered stone tomb boxes in a deserted church, and the active humiliation of their being covered in planks and interlaced with electric flex for fairy lights.

The abbey was built by a Count of Berg as a home for the Cistercians in the twelfth century. Like many such places it has at intervals been severely smashed up and it was finally decommissioned after the French Revolution, being left a ruin until it caught the eye of the mystical Christian Prussian monarch Friedrich Wilhelm IV, who had it renovated in the same spirit that involved him in the building of the spires and nave of Cologne Cathedral.

In some moods I really think that these Cistercian abbeys should lie at the centre of all teaching of European history and that they are far more significant and interesting than most, merely ephemeral political events. We are so used to thinking of the Middle Ages in terms of men covered in sheets of metal clopping about on horses and hitting one another, whereas the true image of the period should be a monk writing. Many suits of armour are still around today just because they are made from a relatively nonreactive metal, but the work of the monks has survived in everything we think, know and believe.

The Cistercian order was founded at the end of the eleventh

century, with their first abbey built in a 'wilderness' outside Dijon. This 'wilderness' is hard to imagine now in a region so closely associated with greedy eating and drinking, but wilderness (like that of John the Baptist, or the Desert Fathers) was then central to the Cistercian ideal. It is essential to recognize the importance over centuries of the Cistercian role in clearing and shaping land across Europe. Each abbey was a polyp of an earlier abbey with monks sent out to a fresh location, ideally Deuteronomy's 'place of horror and vast solitude', to build, work and pray. During the Middle Ages these abbeys marched east, their lay-brothers clearing woods, redirecting streams and generating Christianity, fresh villages, roads and economic change from the Rhine to Poland.

It is odd to think of an area just east of the Rhine as 'wilderness', but even today Altenberg's valley, the Odenthal, is a dank, atmospheric and sullen place with only a scatter of houses. There is an almost ideal walk past the Cistercian fishponds (still there and functioning eight hundred years later), and up onto a ridge where along the horizon as far as the eye can see there is a surreal, continuous wall of distant factories and chimneys glinting in the winter sun. This focus on 'wilderness' allowed the Cistercians to think of themselves as the latest in a direct line from the first Christians and the entire history of the order was a battle to maintain this harshness in a world of temptations, to throw yourself into a lifelong battle to maintain focus on prayer alone: in the words of the greatest Cistercian, St Bernard, to 'leave behind you that tepidity which God vomits from his mouth'.

Altenberg, however beautiful, is a mere shell, with a handful of rebuilt or surviving buildings around it. For the full Cistercian experience the only place to go is the simply astounding Maulbronn, some two hundred miles to the south. One of Europe's greatest building complexes, Maulbronn had the extraordinary luck once it had been shut down during the Reformation of being converted almost immediately into a school by the new owner, the Duke of Württemberg. Despite numerous setbacks it has kept its buildings, even some of its battlements and an atmospheric tower where Faust was supposed to have carried out some unnatural experiments. Hermann Hesse was a pupil there and he used it as the monastery in his spectacular medieval fantasy *Narcissus and Goldmund.* The gigantic, charismatic barn alone shows the monasteries' central role in making the economy work, with Cistercian lay-brothers drying and pickling, weaving and grinding, while the monks themselves devoted themselves to prayer in the solemn, almost unbelievably beautiful church buildings.

As so much of Maulbronn survives it remains as a complete guide to the austerity of the Cistercian vision. There was no room or corridor which in itself did not contribute to a life dedicated entirely to prayer. The monks viewed colour with suspicion (a 'false value' according to St Bernard), with all windows clear, or with a grey tint to reduce direct sunlight. The monks lived in almost total silence, communicating through a narrow range of hand signals and only then on approved occasions. If the abbot needed to talk to a monk then this would be done in a special room, the *auditorium*, in a quiet voice. This silence was all the more striking as it was broken only by prayers, said or sung, in a gruelling sequence beginning in summer at two in the morning and ending just at eight in the evening with sleep. Manual labour began each morning from 4.40. Every year was a relentless round of readings, songs and prayers which ended only with each monk's death. Indeed, one of the most striking aspects of this existence was that it was viewed merely as preparatory: an expiatory and crude limbering up, with the real work to be done by the monks in the Afterlife.

The abbey at Maulbronn has even kept its original structure, with the central church once reserved for the monks, a separate section for the lay-brothers – themselves serious figures but who operated on a lower plane, doing much of the heavy work around the complex – and then the *paradisium*, a covered area outside the church, in itself an almost shockingly beautiful building, to house mere lay onlookers. Over three hundred such locations once formed a dense network covering Europe, each directly linked to a 'mother' monastery, with which there would be frequent contact, and all leading back to the great original Burgundian abbey at Cîteaux (Cistercium), now come a long way from its own 'wilderness' origins.

Each abbey had to deal with the problem of how to maintain its Desert Fathers' inspiration as its economic activities besieged it with worldly temptation. Members of royal families would join specific abbeys (sometimes through compulsion after some entirely secular fiasco, sometimes through genuine inspiration) and needed to be accommodated. In the later Middle Ages many side chapels were built and the monasteries became entangled in the prayers-for-money scandal of unending sequences of pleas to Heaven for specific rich families to reduce their time in Purgatory. Each monk's lifetime was spent navigating through everything from small temptations (was having honey in the refectory a near-Satanic setback?) to wider disasters of sex, backstabbing and loss of vocation. A key part of the charge-sheet of the Reformation was that these abbeys were mere nests of venal hypocrisy, but there seems little genuine evidence for this – every generation was steeped in the same issues and it was always part of Cistercian practice to battle with the commitment to a near-inhuman level of asceticism and to sometimes fail. But these great institutions were for centuries the motor for Europe's spiritual, cultural and economic hopes, places of pilgrimage, guardians of the past and guarantors of the future. Even the most sybaritic lay magnate understood that mere castles, towns and palaces were minor spin-offs. Indeed, it could be that the once-haughty crusading rulers of Berg would be thrilled to know that they have wound up abused as mere platforms for a Christmas crib.

CHAPTER THREE

The Sybil of the Rhine » Some nuts and bolts »
Stories of Wolf Inngrim » Street scenes »
Amiens Cathedral and its aftermath »
Famine, plague and flood » The bold and the mad

The Sybil of the Rhine

I used to make an annual pilgrimage to the Michigan town of Kalamazoo. Each year a large group of medieval historians would meet up at the state university and give papers on their research. I was there during the 1980s as a publisher, looking for interesting book ideas. It was always an enjoyable occasion. Michigan itself, for someone who grew up in England, was a magic place – I could never stop revelling in its sheer inlandness, its weird blackbirds with red feather epaulettes on their shoulders, its vast lakes. I once drove in a loop from Kalamazoo, round the Canadian side of Lake Huron, down through the Upper Peninsula, and back to Kalamazoo – ridiculously happy days with every town having some curious story, from the Finns of Sudbury to the Cornish of the Upper Peninsula, with their mutant, poorly evolved Cornish pasties. The conference itself brought together the most unusual people. There was a group from Toronto who had made a full-size trebuchet, which they glee-fully demonstrated on a sports field, flinging objects vast distances and proving that medieval technology was indeed formidable. Every year, some Trappist monks from the Abbey of Gethsemani, Kentucky would be there, brilliantly expressing their order's suspicion of trivial speech by selling boxes of walnut bourbon fudge. Indeed, the little booths selling icons, rosaries, prayer books, posters and statues made twentieth-century Kalamazoo feel very much like thirteenth-century Bruges, albeit framed by a sports hall.

The conference highlight was always the disco, a complex, deeply awkward event where poor sexual decision-making as a graduate student came back to haunt now-distinguished figures and was in turn renewed. It was always easy to get chatting to someone who could point out who had once grossly betrayed whom and savour the time when so-and-so threw a beaker of mead in so-and-so's face. Once, when the B52s' 'Rock Lobster' was playing (as usual), a whole group in the middle of the dance-floor got down on their hands and knees and were crawling along, bobbing their heads up and down, pretending funly – as I thought – to be rocking lobsters, but it turned out that one of them had just dropped a contact lens.

There were all kinds of papers being given in the intervals between wolfing down monastic candy and frugging, but what was startling, new and exciting then was the sudden emergence of Hildegard von Bingen. This previously obscure mystic from the twelfth-century Rhineland was a dream figure for the 1980s. Hildegard's extraordinary achievements crossed with almost every interesting wave, whether social, feminist, musical, gay or political. Indeed, sometimes she seemed made up, or at least wilfully projected on by her most fervent adherents. She would herself have probably seen the Kalamazoo conference as being emitted by the belching jaws of Hell.

Hildegard was born in a small town near the west bank of the Rhine close to Worms. Her fate stemmed from being a tenth child. Following the universal requirement to 'tithe' – i.e. give a tenth of your goods (money, crops, wine) to the Church – her parents handed her when very young to a monastery. She was walled up as an anchorite with the slightly older Jutta von Sponheim. This ceremony and its consequence sound nightmarish – a religious service which literally treated the young women as in a secular sense no longer living and which culminated in the cell being blocked in. A small window allowed the transfer of necessary items of food and waste, but otherwise the task of the anchorite was simply to spend her entire life praying for human salvation, one cell in the vast hive of prayer across Christendom to redeem humanity. Occasional conversations with the outside world were allowed under strict supervision – but there were elaborate devices to ensure no eye-contact. Hildegard lived like this for over twenty years. Jutta mortified herself in horrific ways – she wrapped chains around her body so that over the years her flesh gradually grew round them; she refused food, cried out and had visions. The practical reality of this life is in some ways mysterious, as their isolation does not seem to have prevented Hildegard from learning to read or play music, but it was undeniably harsh.

In Hildegard's later years it all seems a bit hard lines on poor Jutta as Hildegard moved on, leaving behind the life of the anchorite, founding her own abbey, marching around flanked by an honour guard of young nuns with lavish veils and gold coronets. Hildegard lived to the age of eighty and everything she turned her hand to was remarkable. She was prostrated by searing visions, which she wrote down and which were drawn and illuminated by nuns in her convent at Rupertsberg. The visions are hard to read because they are nonsense, at least in the sense that they could only be valued in a society with values almost unrelated to our own. But as illustrations they are simply astonishing – a golden kite covered in eyes; the three-winged head of God; Lucifer and his followers as black stars thrown into an abyss; the Cosmic Egg; the excrement-covered head of Antichrist emerging from the genitals of defiled Mother Church; an almost Sufic image of Jesus within the gold circle of the Holy Ghost. Everything about Hildegard plunges the unwary into a very peculiar world. She invented her own language with its own alphabet, the point of which remains absolutely mysterious. It includes some wonderful words: kulzphazur for great-great-great-grandfather, zuuenz for saint, limzkil for child. She wrote fascinatingly about medicine, and has become a heroine of New Age healing as a result, with attempts to make practical use of her sometimes outlandish recommendations. There are so many curiosities, but her cure for jaundice by carefully tying a stunned bat to your loins and waiting for it to die seems beyond improvement. She travelled around giving sermons in such cities as Metz, Mainz and Cologne, where she preached against the evils of the emerging Cathar movement. How a woman was able to do this, in a context where only men had any public religious role, is unknown.

In many ways Hildegard's greatness lies in our knowing about her – so many medieval manuscripts are anonymous, but Hildegard's life is documented and her oeuvre is if not comprehensible then certainly finite and manageable. Hildegard is so omni-capable that it is impossible to know at this distance in time what she created herself and what with others. We cannot know, most importantly, if she painted her own visions or whether they were created for her by nuns – we only assume the latter because it just seems too much for one person to have such genius. The music is without doubt her own though and it has a special place both because it is great music, and also because it is possible to focus on it as a specific list of compositions, not (like much of the period's music) as the work, yet again, of Anon. The music's words are visions (towers, spices, jewels, clouds) but with the magical frame of the singing, and often rooted in the Rhineland world – her great songs to St Eucharius, the Bishop of Trier some nine hundred years before Hildegard lived, and to St Ursula and the eleven thousand virgins, whose many bones were unearthed in Cologne during Hildegard's childhood.

Hildegard's rediscovery in the twentieth century began appropriately with her embrace by a new generation of nuns, who republished her work and recopied the paintings of her visions. She has been embraced since by any number of almost unrelated factions – a fantastically more vivid figure than, say, her contemporary Conrad III, about whom even a tiny cabal of specialists can only claim to feel at best lukewarm. Even her recipes continue to be made. I was kindly passed a 'calming cookie' recipe from a north German convent, which had so much nutmeg in it that the cookies seemed to me inedible, but one of the children munched away on one, albeit no calmer as a result. In 2012 she was at last, after centuries of intermittent argument, made a saint, by Pope Benedict XVI, a German helping out another German, only a few years after her beloved St Ursula and the eleven thousand virgins got a very severe downgrade. It is impossible to escape the feeling though that she was in the end a harsh, vexed figure, living in a world crazily remote from our own. We might have taken up her enthusiasm for spelt grain and love her music (played at Ibiza clubs in the 1990s with additional percussion – and almost certainly since at the Kalamazoo disco) but we can at best glance anxiously at most of her output, with its demands for utter, total obedience and a life devoted purely to the life to come. Sometimes she seems to be a twelfth-century Dante in her imagery and vivid strangeness, but then she spins off into a spiritual Outer Space where most of us cannot follow.

Some nuts and bolts

Once Lotharingia had been absorbed into East Francia rather than West Francia, the border between the two sprawling entities became fundamental to the future of Europe – with the allegiance of the major dukes and counts feeding into the networks of what became either the French king or the German king. France was a much thinner, more westerly state than the boxy hexagon it has since become. It diverged from the 'German' lands in having the heavy focus of Paris and its extremely rich surrounding lands of the Île-de-France. The German ruler remained for centuries on the move, shifting from palace to palace, town to town, in a rather King Lear manner. This became a great source of shame to nineteenth-century German historians who saw itinerant monarchy as disgraceful and weak and the root of Germany's misery. They came to focus on the 'strong' emperors, such as Otto the Great or Frederick Barbarossa, and treated the story as a tragedy whereby the failure of such imperially significant cities as Nuremberg, Aachen or Regensburg to become the German Paris doomed the Empire to enfeeblement and abasement. This rather spike-helmeted view of the world has for obvious reasons since been somewhat discredited.

The differences between West and East Francia were substantially those of geography. Whatever setbacks the ruler in Paris had to deal with, he had the confidence of much of his realm being defined by oceans and high mountains while in the east the border with the Empire was also clear. France proved almost impossible to invade, with even the persistent English seen off in the end. East Francia on the other hand was a colonial state, pushing further into Europe against innumerable Slavic, Viking, Magyar and Latinate peoples. In the later Middle Ages, the Emperor then became responsible for an enormous and permanent fighting frontier with Islam which settled the 'capital' (really, just the home town of the Habsburg family) at Vienna as the best place from which to watch the Ottomans – a role it would keep until the eighteenth century. This meant that the Empire (I will now abandon the term East Francia) had a magnetic pull ever further eastwards, with many of the most distinguished soldiers fighting the Ottomans coming from the 'back areas' of Lorraine and the Rhineland. This complex mix of opportunity (the colonizing of 'new' lands in Silesia or Brandenburg) and danger (towns burned flat by Tatar raiders) gave the Empire a destiny almost unrelated to that of France. The Emperor was always obliged to shuttle around dealing with all kinds of emergencies at most points of the compass. He was also obliged to devolve responsibility permanently onto many regional leaders, generally called margraves or dukes, to organize their own regional defence.

This structure became formalized in the fourteenth century, reflecting much earlier practice. The document known as the Golden Bull specified all the steps required to elect each new German king – the somewhat restricted electorate being just seven individuals: the three Rhineland ecclesiastical rulers (Mainz, Cologne, Trier) and four secular rulers (in the west, the Count Palatine; in the east, the King of Bohemia, the Margrave of Brandenburg and the Duke of Saxony). With extremely rare changes, these electors remained in place until Napoleon arrived to sweep the whole lot away. Each election was an exquisite dilemma. It was fun to vote for someone useless because then the electors could do as they wished, but that could also cause a miserable anarchy – so they needed to vote for someone from the tiny handful of families rich enough and with enough land to carry out the job successfully. As with the other major electoral job – the papacy – there was always the lurking danger that some basic disagreement might create kings and anti-kings, but in practice this was rare. Several families (most notably the Staufers and Luxembourgers) provided emperors before Frederick III of the Habsburg family began a sensational run in 1440 that continued, with one brief interruption, until 1806, when the Empire was abolished, and then continued in the reduced but by no means contemptible role of Austrian Emperor until 1918.

The French monarchy was by contrast entirely hereditary. Once Hugh Capet in 987 had been elected King of the Franks his descendants, through some twists and turns, continued to rule France until Louis-Philippe fled into exile in 1848. Both monarchies – all monarchies – shared the usual problems of over-mighty subjects, madness, poor judgement, battlefield humiliation, personal acrimonies, senility, scheming wives and children, putting on weight, too much time spent hawking/fornicating/praying/buying tapestries, and so on. Both monarchies – all monarchies – suffered from 'original sin': in other words nobody coming to the throne ever had a clean slate and a clear head. Within moments of taking the coronation oath, the king may still just keep that glowing aura of religious sanction and secular muscle, but he still cannot get on with his mother and has a younger brother who is a better horseman and who, everyone agrees, is simply more likeable.

The most fundamental inheritance for each monarch was their shifting, complex relationship with each of their major noblemen. In France this became extremely awkward in the twelfth century as the Angevin family, based originally in Anjou, became staggeringly powerful – becoming rulers of almost the entirety of western France and Kings of England. The unhappy Louis VII spent his long reign deluged in humiliations, not only messing up the Second Crusade but having his marriage with his first wife, Eleanor, the era's greatest heiress, annulled. She then married the Angevin Count Henry (the future Henry II of England) and handed him the whole of southwest France, the sprawling Duchy of Aquitaine. This led to the French king holding a mere residual chunk of France, completely boxed in by Angevin holdings. Even at this low point, however, what is striking is that in the medium term the French monarchy always wins. I can imagine some future time when a horrible toy is invented, perhaps a robot teddy-bear, which can have chunks cut off it, which can be flattened, can be set alight, but which, even when reduced to a smouldering piece of scrap by its psychotic child owner, regenerates to the same shape and same warm smile as when it was back in the shop. France seems similar. Louis VII must have died thinking, 'Well, that didn't go brilliantly' – but his son Philip Augustus, with remarkable speed, wrecked the Angevins and reflated the entire kingdom.

The crucial background in all this was the County of Flanders. In the original split between West Francia and Lotharingia, Flanders fell to the west, making the split between itself and its neighbour (the Imperial Duchy of Brabant) a fundamental one. On old maps there is a patch called the Waasland, just west of Antwerp, which is shown as part of Flanders, but which at some point in the eleventh century shifted into Brabant. Historians have given up trying to work out why – the probability was that it was a boggy marsh of so little value that nobody noticed when the Scheldt and Durme Rivers moved their banks. In any event, Waasland issues aside, Flanders became an exceptionally powerful and successful place. It had the immeasurable advantage of a long coast, which (like a mini-version of France) allowed it to focus on defending itself from land attack from only a limited number of compass points. Its cities – Ypres, Bruges and Ghent – became extremely prosperous and were the great conduits for English wool, with a large part of its population engaged in cloth-making. Down the road was the County of Boulogne – a smaller, but also prosperous territory with counts, as with Flanders, importantly involved in the crusades. *But* both of these were only counties and however much they might have behaved independently they could not pretend that they did not owe their allegiance to the King of France. Philip Augustus's reshaping of the French monarchy led him to look north at Flanders. The major attempt to bring Philip down was a grand coalition of the Count of Flanders, the Count of Boulogne, the Emperor Otto IV and, every English schoolchild's favourite, King John, to whose amazing, incompetent faithlessness we all owe so much – not least the wonderful Errol Flynn film *The Adventures of Robin Hood*, which we watch as a family at least twice a year. At the resulting Battle of Bouvines (1214), deep in Flemish territory, Philip Augustus destroyed the Allies. It is a curious example of how national history works that no English schoolchild has ever heard of the Battle of Bouvines, despite its effectively making England once more a separate island state and therefore being responsible for the resulting universal atmosphere of terminal cock-up and dismay leading to Magna Carta.

In his spare time Philip Augustus was busy building Notre-Dame de Paris, the Louvre and Les Halles, but his main achievement was that by the time of his death he could say that the years of French humiliation were over. But it would not be long before the French robot teddy-bear would take another terrible beating.

Stories of Wolf Inngrim

In the High Middle Ages, an era that devotes itself to conjuring up vast churches and palaces and excels at great intellectual and religious movements, it is good to focus first on a couple of small objects. The first is really tiny – a spherical lattice about the size of a Christmas-tree ornament, made in one of the Meuse towns, perhaps Dinant. Made from chiselled brass, it was designed to burn incense. The orb is made up of stylized creatures and foliage, but the note of genius is that there are three tiny people on top, showing eloquent surprise at their situation. These are (in a tumble of charismatic names) Shadrach, Meshach and Abednego, the Jewish men whose faith was tested in the fiery furnace by King Nebuchadnezzar. It seems sad that these tiny characters should be trapped in a museum case in Lille and unable to continue to carry out their witty, nine-century-old role of having perfumed smoke pour upwards and round them. Perhaps somewhere in Lille there is a secret underground movement to liberate them and return them to their true function.

The other, only slightly larger object, that I have also kept coming back to just because it is so mysterious, lurks high on a pillar in Freiburg Minster. This must have once been part of a much larger decorative scheme, long since erased but with these figures kept as a reminder, or – more likely – just because they are so wonderful. The carving shows three human figures engaged with three

massive, terrible-jawed animals, two of these wearing human clothing. An enormous ram's head hovers in space, unrelated to the already confused action, and presumably part of a now missing piece
of the frieze. Round the corner is a sadly worn – but fabulous –
little fragment of Alexander the Great in a griffin-powered flying
machine. I have returned to these monsters over the years, not least
because of the strange way they echo the animal masks of the
Kwakwaka'wakw of the American north-west. I don't say this as
some borderline insane piece of ethnographic showing off, but because my wife's family live on the edge of the Salish Sea and most
summers I rush off at the first chance to admire examples of this
great artistic tradition. The Freiburg monsters also appear strangely
Disney – the humans unperturbed by them, despite the way the
sculptor has given them a terrible sense of muscular power. I had
assumed they were just mysterious grotesques, but this turned out
merely to be my own ignorance. When last in Freiburg somewhat
to my dismay I was cheerfully informed by an official that the figure on the right, seemingly a woman on a monster, was in fact
Samson (the long hair for strength) subduing a lion, while the two
cowled men with the two clothed monsters were telling two different 'frames' from the story of Wolf Inngrim, in which a monk
dresses a wolf up in human clothes and tries to educate him (there
is a little book and pen) but he keeps being distracted by a nearby
sheep. Unable to deny his wolfish nature, he turns from the monk
and leaps on the sheep. A bit upset at this overturning of what I
had lazily assumed was an ancient mystery, I quickly realized that
it made no difference – these were creatures that conveyed brilliantly a universal human dismay and fascination.

The wolves were carved around 1200 in the opening phase
of the building of Freiburg Minster. It was sponsored by Duke
Berthold V, the last of the Zähringer dynasty, fresh from what
would prove the equally lasting triumph of founding the city of
Bern. These sorts of initiatives are characteristic of what was in
many ways one of the most exciting, cheerful and entertaining
periods in all European history. As usual we could tut-tut about life
expectancy, poor hygiene and the relentless grind of agricultural

labour, but this is just to buy into the patronizing and intellectually null idea that, in effect, the entire prior sum of human activity across the planet should be pitied and disregarded for not having had access to broadband.

The founding of Bern is a fine example of medieval mobility and ambition that, so close to old Roman cities such as Basle or Konstanz, could both build on earlier traditions and also start afresh. In 1191 Berthold ordered the clearing of a forested plateau, a previously unnoticed, brilliantly defendable peninsula looped by the River Aare. A series of highly unreliable but charming paintings in Bern, made many years later, show the discovery, the dense mass of trees and the climax – the killing of the bear which would become the heraldic symbol of Bern and would lead to many generations of unhappy animals living in the bear-pits. With Berthold's death in 1218, the already thriving settlement was able to negotiate with the Emperor to become an Imperial Free City. Future generations of the Valois and Habsburg families would thoroughly regret this sequence of events, as well as another key breakthrough of the same decades: the opening up of the Saint Gotthard Pass.

Although the pass remained hair-raising for centuries (with a completely chilling bridge at one point, teetering over a chasm), horses could now travel from northern Europe to Bern to Italy – carrying either soldiers or merchants, but with a certain percentage adding themselves each year to the wind-dried piles already heaped down various gulches. While this would lead in due course to Bern's wealth from long-distance trade, it also released into the wider world the tough, highly self-reliant and until then mercifully shut in mountain-men of Uri, Schwyz and Unterwalden, who would form the nucleus of the future Switzerland. The sense of the Swiss as relentlessly capable, implacable and sitting in a sort of ice fortress has been appropriated by what is now the country's 'northern rim': cheery commercial cities such as Basle, Schaffhausen, Zürich and indeed Bern, southern bits of the Holy Roman Empire, at best sited on steep slopes. It was the genuinely inaccessible Uri, Schwyz and Unterwalden (the original three Forest Cantons) which really began the trouble as trade, men and concepts now fed up and

down through Luzern and along the Saint Gotthard. There is no
way to pinpoint why too precisely, but unlike other regional protection associations which formed across the Empire, the Swiss one
became serious and permanent. The murals of tough guys that fes-
toon the walls of places like the Basle town hall were *not* on the
whole the sort of softies who actually lived in that town. In later
centuries, when the Habsburg family or the Dukes of Burgundy
unwittingly took their armies just a little too far south towards the
Alps they crossed a sort of Swiss tripwire. This activated the real
giant, stone-muscled characters of few words who came down from
the mountains and caused mayhem. I will return to the peculiar
characteristics of Switzerland in relation to the Habsburgs later, but
this shift began in the thirteenth century and had endless repercussions, not least through breaking the duopoly of what had been
just West Francia and East Francia. Forms of independence became
possible in the Alps even if the Imperial authorities responded to it
by simply pretending the Swiss did not exist (the Habsburgs finally
acknowledged them formally only in 1648).

Elsewhere in the Empire there was further awkwardness for
Habsburgs. At the same time as Bern was first being built, at the
far northern end of Lotharingia, in a near featureless wilderness of
mud, sand, frogs and shifting rivers, an equally ghastly future
adversary was coalescing as an enterprising group of fishermen
built a dam on the River Amstel. This is a book only minimally
about Amsterdam but some background is needed. If Bern became
the controlling intelligence for messing up the Habsburgs in the
south, Amsterdam formed its matching pair in the north, and it is
odd that they were founded near simultaneously. Given the glutin-
ous, marshy world from which it emerged, Amsterdam was sited in
an area of little perceived worth or feudal structure and was ignored
by its notional overlord in Utrecht. Its fortune came both from ever
more elaborate management of sluices and from a bolt of religious
good luck – a particularly absurd miracle involving fire-proof
blessed bread turned Amsterdam into a major religious site. It then
brought together fishing, shipping and soap-making in a harshly
industrial combination (in contrast to all the weedy tapestries, fine

gloves and folderol that fuelled the posh southern Low Countries) and became extremely rich.

Somehow, somebody worked out that mixing a little pouch in herrings' stomachs into the barrel in which the fish were packed both preserved them and made them much tastier. In a world of frightening seasonal lurches from plenty to dearth, barrels of herring were a sort of miracle. Amsterdamers also invented special robust ships so the fish could be gutted and packed at sea, the vessels bobbing up and down on the Dogger Bank (a shallow remnant of Doggerland), home to an effective infinity of herring. At the height of the bonanza 200 million herring a year were being caught.

That is enough about Amsterdam, except to say that its origins and interests always lay north and east and in the outer world – in Germany, the Baltic, the North, the New World and the eastern spice islands. Its attitude towards the rest of the Netherlands was, from its own origins onwards, always somewhat aloof. It was part of the County of Holland, but felt a limited affinity for points south. Events, particularly religious and particularly Habsburg, meant that, like Bern, Amsterdam would become an implacable and awful enemy to external interferers, but almost despite itself – and neither city was ever captured by all those who ground their teeth with rage at their very mention, until they both fell at the end of the eighteenth century.

The political chaos of the first half of the thirteenth century turned out to be a boon not just for Bern and Amsterdam, but for many other individual princes and cities. Just as everyone should be grateful for King John's total incompetence leading to Magna Carta, so the Emperor Frederick II's reign waved goodbye to any chance that the Empire might become like France, whose kings spent the century successfully making their realm much warmer and more pleasant by massacring heretics in the south and taking over Provence. Frederick was an attractive figure of extraordinary talent, but his interests became so focused on Italy and the Mediterranean that his German nobles were able to wring concessions that meant individual princes had ever more active, practical independence over their fiefs. While Frederick was off on the Sixth Crusade –

negotiating personally in Arabic for renewed Christian access to Jerusalem – or writing a treatise on falconry in Palermo, where his court was based for many years, or being accused of being the Antichrist, he was *not* helping his German subjects much. There had always been uneasiness between nobles, city councils and the Emperor, but now the result was definitively to make the German lands into a sort of geopolitical rubble, a highly creative one, with each ruler sponsoring state-of-the-art palaces, castles, churches and monasteries in the cheerful pattern that can still be seen today.

The century was marked by exciting news stories – such as the introduction of paper from the Arabic world, partly thanks to Frederick, and its rapid replacement of clumsy vellum. This would have an unfortunate archival effect because of paper's easy destruction, but was in every other way a boon, making written books much cheaper and more widespread. Excitement was caused too by the Mongol invasions of the 1240s, which would be catastrophic for Eastern Europe, but which further west proved merely an exciting frisson when the invasions came to an end as mysteriously as they had begun, having spread the recipe for Chinese gunpowder, the vast implications of which were worked out over coming centuries. There were waves of religious innovation which would have as great an impact, albeit in a different sphere. The Dominicans, Franciscans, Minorites and the institution of beguinage would in their different fields reshape Christianity, all trying to drain what Pope Alexander III had called 'the stinking slurry of heresy'. There were Dominican geniuses such as Meister Eckhart and Thomas Aquinas and startling mystics such as Christine of Saint-Trond, in Brabant, a cowherd who could speak Latin and performed extraordinary feats, spinning like a dervish or clambering up church rafters or to the top of towers in a trance.

Street scenes

I know I am repeating myself in some ways, but it is impossible in many of these towns not to be almost overwhelmed by the sense of walking through an unbelievably ancient continuum of experience, of being merely the latest character to trot through a street-pattern and set of thoughts and needs effectively unchanged from before records exist. This is most palpable in Bruges because the choking-up of its route to the sea around 1500 gradually suffocated its prosperity, leaving a strikingly old-fashioned cityscape. But it is more dynamically felt in Ghent, where despite its becoming a major Victorian industrial city with the buildings updated, the locations have stayed the same, with the tram-tracks and discount shops merely emphasizing these continuities.

So if you walk south from the Castle of the Counts you go past the Fish Market, over the River Leie past the Meat Market and the Vegetable Market, down to the Corn Market. Just behind the western buildings on the Corn Market are the guild houses and just to the south, along the riverbank, the mighty bulk of Het Pand, the former Dominican monastery that still dominates the town centre. Walking east from the Corn Market, the massive Church of St Nicholas gives way to the Poultry Market,* the Cloth Hall, the Belfry and St Bavo's Cathedral – and to the north, by the Butter Market, is the much rebuilt City Hall.

The walk would not have been very different a thousand years ago. The location of some things would have moved around, and there would have been an earlier version of St Bavo's – indeed the entire town of Ghent seems to have sprung from the original monastery dedicated to St Bavo, a Merovingian ne'er-do-well who became an ascetic and lived in a tree, whose relics were for centuries the principal focus for processional life in the city. An earlier version of St Nicholas was built in 1100. The Cloth Hall and Belfry are later. One of the advantages of having done this walk before the eighteenth century would be to avoid the freakish carving then put over the entrance to the city gaol in the basement of City Hall, which features the pointlessly seedy Roman story of Old Cimon, who is imprisoned with no food but stays alive because

---

* An attractive language consonance: Poeljemarkt; Marché des Poulets; Poultry Market.

when his daughter visits him she secretly breastfeeds him. How anyone imagined this was a good topic for a carving I have been unable to discover (I suspect some bewigged and very rich classical pedant) but it could be argued that one of the few benefits of being stuck in the Ghent gaol was no longer having to walk past a picture of Old Cimon slurping away.

This cityscape preserves the complex workings of ancient towns and the elaborate interplay between the secular authorities, the religious and the merchants. Before any surviving records existed, a place like Ghent was still extraordinarily complicated: who belonged, who didn't belong; who had the right to sell chickens, who didn't; who performed which religious function and in return for what. Issues which are modern to us around zoning, permits, hygiene, tax, timetabling, transport, qualifications, security, communication would have been no less heavily scripted and controlled in, say, 1200, or 1500. Each cart of vegetables would have been pinned down to a specific space at specific times, with payments scattered between various religious and secular characters. Weights and measures would have been crucial, a complex source of corruption and anger in any settled society. The belfry both dictated the religious sequence of the day and gave instructions during military emergencies to different troops. Anybody who was within the city walls was there only because they were permitted, and those with day passes had to get back outside before the curfew and the gates being locked. Those staying at an inn needed to be registered and sponsored. Specific levels of official, working for the Count or for the Empire, could have symbols of office which gave them rights of transit or hospitality. Monasteries (such as Het Pand) provided hospitality for everyone from private guests of the abbot to wandering pilgrims.

Ghent was particularly known for its *gebuurten* – neighbourhood associations usually based around a street and its associated alleys. They would organize the night watch, have fire drills (to escape from and to put out any fire) and contribute towards local and citywide festivals (floats, costumes) and the management of funerals, all paid from a central pot. They were key to the lives (now almost lost to official records) of the servants, small shopkeepers and artisans that made places like Ghent work. Many individuals wore uniforms of some kind, sometimes as simple as a ribbon to indicate a specific fraternity, but including of course the different-coloured outfits worn by different grades or types of churchmen, including the immediately distinctive monastic orders.

Obviously, I just love this stuff. My ideal would be to have a bag of coins on my belt, particoloured tights, an Imperial pass and the opportunity to roister or even doister in one of these medieval towns, while at the same time keeping twenty-first-century life expectancy, and having a button to press so I could duck back to the present if things got too rough. Aside from the risk of being burned alive just out of envy and spite at my delirious leg-wear, I would probably have been safe enough. In as much as we can tell, these really were highly regulated places, kept in good order by the elaboration of major religious festivals and the day-in, day-out world of masses and private prayers. The major families, that of the Count of Flanders and all those linked with him, would have had a formidable stranglehold over secular and religious life, supplying key senior functionaries to both and imposing discipline on dependants and their families and associates.

Very early on, Ghent, Bruges and Ypres developed close links to London – the towns are mentioned in the records of Aethelred the Unready in the late tenth century as trading there. England had become the great motor for Flemish prosperity by the twelfth century, with grain, hides, coal and cheese pouring in and the steady growth of what would become a colossal clothing industry, with flock after English flock converted into fabric. Sheep have seldom had such political weight: their numbers remorselessly growing, with countless humans living out their lives in their service: reshaping huge tracts of land to supply them with delicious grass, washing them to make their fleeces bright and curly. They built the great churches of the Cotswolds and East Anglia, an enduring, near-pharaonic reminder many centuries later of a vanished ovine glory. Flemish cloth was on sale in places as far off as Novgorod early in the same century and the whole England–Flanders relationship must have had a dynamism we would associate more with the nine-teenth century.

Flanders was much larger than its size in the modern Belgian state – including more coastal places such as the then insignificant Dunkirk, plus more southern towns such as Lille, Douai and Cassel (Rijsel, Dowaai and Kassel). The genius of cloth was that it created a trans-European industry in stuff which did not perish (unlike food) but which wore out from use and therefore needed replenish-ment. Sheep also paid for all the amazing buildings which still dot these Flemish towns – or their earlier incarnations. The enormous Ypres Cloth Hall of 1304, the interior packed with gallery upon gallery of fabrics, must have looked like a permanent festival of sumptuous clothing. The fabulous hall lasted until its total destruc-tion in the First World War. Bruges revelled in an ever greater proliferation of ingenuity in its state-of-the-art buildings. Origin-ally the halls beneath its huge belfry had been dedicated not just to cloth but to spices and dyestuffs, gloves and mercery. But then one of Europe's great lost buildings was put up – the Water Hall, fully completed in 1366 after some eight decades of refinements. This amazing place was integrated into the canal network, so that barges could simply float under a house-covered bridge and into the building's central space. The interior of the roof was a vast, extraordinarily ingenious cloth-storage area and everywhere there would have been piled fleeces, finished cloths, samples, exotica. Nearby was a massive crane, powered by 'crane children' who walked its circular treadmill and which could land bulk goods from the canal such as wine. All of this has gone – the canal filled in, the Water Hall demolished. Next to the magical Groeninge Museum – with its astounding collection of paintings by van Eyck, van der Weyden, Memling and others whose work was paid for by a later wave of Flemish cloth prosperity – there is a tiny park with two sad little columns standing in it: all that is left of the Water Hall.

I am in a panic as I am running out of space: the entire book could easily just be about Flanders in this period. If I have to choose one last thing, it would be the hospital built in Lille at the orders of Joan, Countess of Flanders, in the 1240s. Joan's dad, Baldwin IX, had a poor time in the Balkans, with his skull turned into a drinking cup. Joan's husband (a luckless Portuguese prince) spent many years in French imprisonment after having fought at the disastrous Battle of Bouvines, freeing her up to rule in her own right. She was a remarkable figure, one of the classical sequence of Flanders counts who split their time between complex water-management and founding monasteries (particularly Cistercian ones) and beguinages. Her hospital in the heart of Lille is entirely made up of later buildings, alas, but still has an unbeatably strange, ancient atmosphere. Run by the Augustinians, it looked after the sick and poor as well as pilgrims passing through. As usual, it was swept away by the French Revolution, becoming a home for orphans and for elderly men until 1939. But, even so, it had a run – interrupted by occasional fires, riots and invasions – of five hundred and fifty years. I was very struck by the way that the hospital enshrined exactly the close links it was possible to feel walking through, say, Ghent today between the everyday and the spiritual – the feeling that the churches and the markets must have once been viewed as aspects of the same thing.

The Hospital of the Countess has a sequence of rooms which make this explicit. The Augustinian nuns shaved their heads, owned nothing and ended their mission only with their own total infirm-ity or death. They took their meals in silence while one read passages from the Bible. They prepared all kinds of remedies, often based on plants they grew themselves and preserved in syrup or ointment jars. They also made the strange mixture known as *théri-aque* ('Venetian treacle'), a potion with an amazing number of ingredients based on a recipe by Galen and which on the face of it had no value whatsoever, except being fun to make, as various bits of fruit, animal, seed, leaf and gum were pounded together. What is so interesting and moving about the nuns was that their activities at the hospital saw no difference at all between nursing someone back to health and someone dying – these were both devotional, religious processes with neither preferred as a better outcome.

Joan's legacy was not to remain part of Flanders for much

longer. Through many generations of sheep and fewer of counts, Flanders never shook off its dependency on France and in the thirteenth century factions formed between those within the cities who were pro-French (the Lilies, after the fleur-de-lys) and anti-French (the Claws, after the claws of the heraldic Lion of Flanders). As part of the general re-expansion of French royal power under Philip IV 'the Fair' – a disturbingly efficient figure – the Count was imprisoned and France put in garrisons across Flanders after a series of brutal, grinding battles. But on the extraordinary night of 18 May 1302, the Claws rose up and slaughtered the French and their sympathizers in Bruges, killing some two thousand people. Philip sent an army to restore order which the Flemish then devastated at the Battle of Kortrijk, using grimly focused infantry armed with pikes and short, heavy spears to destroy the flower of French chivalry. It became known as 'the Battle of the Golden Spurs' after the five hundred or so pairs taken from dead French noblemen and hung in the nearby church of Our Lady (sadly the spurs were not there for long – now there's just a super-morose painting by van Dyck of the Raising of the Cross).

Today Kortrijk has an entire museum devoted to the battle and it has become one of the key days in the Flemish nationalist calendar. At the time its impact was more muted. The initial shock was immense and it was a masterclass in why the hereditary principle was so important to medieval society, as a random cross-section of senior French noblemen were suddenly killed and dozens of dazed inheritors – younger brothers, regents and minors – totally unexpectedly stepped forward to take over a cascade of territories. Philip IV was, however, not lacking resources or determination and crushed the rebellion anyway, in battles which have been less well remembered locally. The epochal Treaty of Athys-sur-Orge of 1305 kept Flanders as a separate and privileged county, but detached the towns of Douai, Bouvines and Lille, making a French-speaking ('gallicant') Flanders which has been a further, tangled and complicating issue ever since.

Lille, like Ghent, is somewhere I have spent a lot of time walking, in both cases with the same feeling of being on streets which are, in the old areas, really just not changed much. They may be lined with newer buildings, but their width is still based on the horse-carriage-width which cars have inherited, still packed with shops with flats tucked above and alluring little signs sticking out into the street of a kind that would have been immediately recognizable centuries ago: boots, pretzels, beer. In many ways they seem to have been no more and no less commercial, busy and 'modern' eight hundred years ago. Now I have finished writing this book and no longer have the excuse to linger in these cities I feel I have myself already become yet another ghost wandering down from the Castle of the Counts to the Fish Market and so to the Butter Market.

Amiens Cathedral and its aftermath

While the vast church buildings of the Middle Ages exude an unbeatable power and longevity, in some moods I feel this is just a bluff: that they are painfully vulnerable to human whim and natural chance. Unable to move an inch in their own defence, these churches rely on our continuing concern and care as much as a cow does in its stall. Warfare, particularly a siege, is the most obvious source of terror, but just as frightening are the freak accidents that are bound to happen given enough time. Aachen's stained glass was in good condition until in the early eighteenth century a monster hail-storm smashed it all in a few moments. In 1857 it was Mainz's turn when, the cathedral having only just been rebuilt after years of use as a French barracks, a tower used to store weapons blew up and the cathedral's glass was sprayed over the town centre. Worms was a victim of the terrible explosion at a factory outside Ludwigshafen in 1921 which killed some five hundred people and, ten miles away, blew out all its glass. The magnificent Great Church at Zwolle once had a high steeple; it was hit by lightning in 1669, was rebuilt and then was totally hammered by lightning in 1682, with one side of the tower collapsing. The same lucky local artist, Jan Grasdorp, was able to paint both disasters with concerned citizens looking on. The consistory mulled these events over and rightly worried that God might be pointing out a certain element of Pride in having such a big spire in such a flat area. It was decided not to rebuild it and to use the site to build a uniquely charming and elegant meeting room instead, with the result that Zwolle is now famous for having a church *without* a spire.

I mention these as just a handful of examples of the sheer physical vulnerability of these seemingly eternal buildings – and that is to set to one side such arbitrary horrors as Louis XIV having the west front of Speyer Cathedral blown up simply from spite. Closely allied to natural disaster is the day-to-day importance for churches of staying engaged with the humans around them – to continue to be needed. For some reason I found myself thinking about this a lot while wandering around Amiens Cathedral, in its sheer charisma, scale and beauty probably one of the greatest buildings in Europe. It is as though an entire quarry had somehow been cut into a single rough cuboid, hauled to the top of a hill, carved into cathedral shape and then hollowed out by an infinite number of men with chisels.

It was begun in 1220 and completed in about half a century and raises awkward questions about the nature of Western civilization: there have of course been many superb buildings created since, but I'm not sure there are any *better*. The idea that such a staggeringly complex, elegant, strange, vast object could have been made so long ago derides our sense of living onward-and-upward. But perhaps more importantly it has continued to be used because it has kept being useful. Amazing events have been held there, featuring the Kings of France, the Dukes of Burgundy and, most famously in the modern period, the huge Allied service of thanksgiving and commemoration at the end of the Great War. But the ideologies that seed and expand in and around the cathedral are a constant threat to the building itself and the thousands of little statues, objects and images it tries to protect. Again, conflict matters (in the Great War the unmovable cathedral treasures were covered in tons of clay-filled bags on steel frames – a single German shell came through the roof, bounced off the floor and failed to explode) but ideas matter more, with the great moments of danger from Protestant iconoclasm and

Revolutionary secularism, the former cleaning out many churches, the latter cleaning them out again and then in some cases destroying them. Enormous, once very famous cathedrals in cities such as Arras and Liège disappeared completely, torn down for their stone over many years in the wake of the French Revolution. France and the areas of the Rhineland and southern Netherlands captured at the height of Revolutionary fervour saw enormous bonfires, disposing of centuries of religious art. Amiens is a spectacular building but much of the interior is filled with sorry, dank and neglected nineteenth-century replacement decorative filler.

I always think about this in the context (moving geographically for a moment) of the spectacularly beautiful Quwwat al-Islam mosque outside Delhi. This was built just before Amiens Cathedral, and is actually made from crushed chunks of Hindu and Jain temples, their decoration patterns still visible. The mosque is now itself a ruin, in a region of India since ruled by Hindus again very briefly, then Muslims again, then Christians and now majority Hindus again. I mention this because the nature of the threat to the mosque's continued existence has been at several points absolute. The battered remnants are all you could now expect. What is odd in much of Western Europe is that there *has* been a continuity of belief: even the most extreme threat of the Revolution proved in Amiens' case superficial, and while church attendance has collapsed today there is no movement either in favour of the building's destruction or one which picks on those who continue to use it. This makes Western Europe very unusual – there are only a handful of places in the rest of the world which have not seen a total turnover in religious and social practices. Whether it is the Mongols in Baghdad or the Spanish in Mexico or the British in Australia, or indeed the Tajiks in Delhi, it has been almost normal for one human culture to attempt to erase another. With the huge exception of terrible, periodic anti-Semitism this has generally not been the experience in Western Europe. Even differences in religious belief within Christianity have created symbolic martyrs on the whole rather than attempted eradication, and the fragmented nature of Western Europe has given most forms of dissent bolt-holes.

The problem that has for many years futilely bugged me around places such as Amiens Cathedral is whether their breathtaking confidence and glamour come from a culture we have directly inherited or from a specifically earlier culture. This is an endlessly argued about and unresolvable issue, but it could certainly be claimed that the disasters that would unfold across much of Europe in the fourteenth century were so extreme that they do put a great ditch between ourselves and the supremely arrogant culture that produced Amiens. The thirteenth century saw a near hysterical impetus for societies to pour their resources into making cathedrals such as Metz, Strasbourg, Cologne – crazily ambitious structures that took centuries to complete and implied a culture which had stability, resources and time on its hands. But then, really everything went wrong.

Famine, plague and flood

Each century has its disasters – these are built into our relations with each other and our planet – but there was a sequence of about a century, from 1315 to 1420, which was peculiarly awful. It is in terms of narrative very strange as it has left no place to visit and no texts to read. It leaves an enormous mark but an invisible one – in the millions of people killed but also, as a result, in the millions not born. To have lived through these years must have been at different times to witness complete breakdowns in European society of a kind hardly experienced since. Of course there were pools of calm and particular generations might be lucky or the inhabitants of a specific village untouched, but there must have been a far wider awareness of cataclysm beyond the mere human agency of an approaching army.

The first blow came in the form of famine across an enormous area of north-western Europe, affecting some thirty million people. Everywhere it was understood that grain needed to be stored against a bad harvest, but for many years harvests had been reasonable and generations had gone by where anybody who had demanded longer-term planning would have been rightly viewed as silly and alarmist. There was also a penalty for storage as grain could so easily rot or be eaten by vermin. The thirteenth century had also seen booming populations fed by farmers converting ever more marginally fertile land. This is a totally needless detail, but in Gelderland a special confection of animal dung, heather roots, forest litter, grass sods and peat was mixed to create an artificial earth ('*plaggen* soiling') which could be laid down and would over many years 'catch' and convert barren land into farmland, though it required patience and good luck. Without realizing it people had become used to good weather and planned accordingly. In 1315 it seems to have never stopped raining – it was as though someone was wildly messing around with the control dial. Fields flooded, rivers broke their banks and most of the crops never even ripened. The dampness was a field-day for smuts, mould, mildew and rusts. Sheep and cattle murrain devastated herds. For liver flukes at least it was a golden age. Already, in what proved to be just the first year, Xanten was holding frantic processions of relics, town-wide prayer sessions and fasting. By 1316 the price of cereals had at some points multiplied by up to eight times. Some people made a fortune – but this only made it worse as speculators shifted scarce supplies to desperate coastal areas where prices had rocketed, ensuring worse dearth inland. Dykes collapsed, the oxen needed for heavy ploughing were dying. Some of the animal sicknesses were highly contagious and completely revolting – I simply cannot bring myself to describe the symptoms. Summer hail beat down the few crops which were close to ripening and the winters were so cold (with ice spreading out into the North Sea) that they killed surviving flocks.

It was the continuing emergency that exhausted all possible help. The figures are all extremely vague but a chronicler in Gelderland called 1315 the year of 'the great death'. A surviving record from Ypres shows that between May and October 1316, in a population of some twenty-five thousand, three thousand died. In Bruges that summer between a hundred and sixteen and a hundred and fifty-six corpses a week were being collected from streets and houses. These towns would have been overwhelmed at this point by refugees, so it is not known whether these were locals or incomers. As all the herds had died, everyone moved on to eating their way through the semi-wild pig population, which had disappeared by 1316. In any event the saltpans, which were needed to preserve food, meat and fish, stopped working as the atmosphere was too wet for the salt to dry – salt prices also shot up. People fled to the east, resettling in the comparatively underpopulated Habsburg and Polish lands (these 'Germans' were in their origin as much Flemish/Dutch as German).

In Flanders somewhere between a tenth and a third of all home-steads were by now abandoned, and monasteries and convents stood empty. Everything that could be eaten had been eaten. Apparently there was no birdsong in northern Europe for several years. It was impossible to plan except for the immediate panic and even quite robust creatures such as geese were eaten rather than kept for their eggs (to the despair of gozzards – at last a context in which this rare and wonderful word can be used). Cities with great financial resources and access to the sea such as Bruges were able to source and pay for grain from south-west France, but further inland it remained catastrophic until, after a last brutally cold winter in 1317/18, things began to recover.

Famine was very rare in Western Europe. A later chronicler in Louvain was able to state clearly (so etched were they in people's minds) that there had been famine in 1146, 1197, 1316 and 1530. There were aftershocks (an Aachen chronicler talks of 'tempests, hailstorms and epidemics' as the flavour of 1322) but recovery seems to have been speedy before the second and completely over-whelming disaster of what came to be called the Black Death. A terrible cocktail of fatal illnesses, this plague was first mentioned in 1333 in China, and reached Sicily in 1346 and France and Germany in 1348. A reasonable estimate is that it killed 45–50 per cent of all Europeans, probably in greater numbers in the Mediter-ranean than further north. There was of course no understanding of how it killed or why.

Aside from God's anger, it was ascribed to the fatal conjunction of three planets. More isolated villages, such as in Switzerland, or more thinly settled parts of the Low Countries, could either get off scot-free or be completely emptied. It seems that some two-thirds of Jewish communities were destroyed. In the summer of 1349 the plague reached Tournai, promptly killing the bishop, followed by a few weeks' lull before it went berserk, killing some 30 per cent of the population. The town council tried to clean up the town morally, with bans on swearing, gambling, working on Sunday, cohabitation – 'everyone from day to day waited on the will of the Lord'. No money was to be spent on mourning dress, no bells were to be rung. In a weird detail, the town's famous dice-manufacturers despaired of custom and instead started carving objects which could be used as aids to prayer.

The social structure seems to have broken down completely. Romani, lepers, pilgrims, foreigners were killed on sight. In 1349 some two thousand Jews were killed in Strasbourg with other massacres later in the summer in Mainz and Cologne. Processions of flagellants were formed and great services held in churches at which, presumably, innumerable parishioners were unwittingly infected. Gradually the plague disappeared. Nobody really knows why, although one plausible idea is that the rats which carried it were themselves all killed by it. Each subsequent outbreak (often devastating locally, but not with the same universal horror as the first) seems to have been from a fresh introduction of rats from Asia. The result was enormously worse even than that of the two world wars of the twentieth century – indeed there is no other yardstick available within Europe for such a catastrophe. The Black Death emptied parts of Europe which did not recover for centuries. Some forty thousand German settlements were still empty a hundred years later.

Just to finish this extremely downbeat section it is important to mention the two St Elizabeth Day floods. The Netherlands has been shaped both by floods and by the attempts to thwart future floods. This creates a landscape in many areas which to me, with no previous experience of it, seems thoroughly frightening. Seeing fields so smooth and flat that they appear like the green or brown (depending on season) surface of a liquid and knowing that these fields are below sea-level is something hard not to be freaked out by. One of the drawbacks of going to one of my favourite places in the world, the mouth of the Scheldt, is – when not rhapsodically hopping about staring at the vast ships – the need to see the little town of Breskens, which is hunkered down in the shadow of a vast dyke, with the threat of the North Sea hanging over its head like a migraine. The dyke obviously works, but I suppose I would just think about living somewhere else.

The scale of the floods that have repeatedly devastated the Netherlands and the massive systems of counterattacks which have channelled and held back sea water and river water form one of the great epics in European history. The Zuiderzee itself is the result of several medieval cataclysms scooping out vast areas of land – indeed Amsterdam exists as a great port because the sea had chewed away to create its site. In the fourteenth century the floods had no upside though and were entirely destructive – in 1375, 1404 and 1421 (the last two oddly both happening on 19 November – hence they are both named after that day's saint, St Elizabeth of Hungary). In a way that must have only made sense through invoking God's judgement they lashed at Flanders, Zeeland and Holland, ignoring some villages and sweeping away others. The second flood was so severe that the islands that had been in the mouth of the Scheldt (left over from Doggerland) were wrenched into the North Sea and disappeared for ever. Duke John the Fearless ordered a dyke built running south from the Scheldt estuary and parts of it are still there (the Duke John Dyke) albeit much cut into and/or upgraded. Nobody really knows how many people were killed – tens of thousands across the three floods without a doubt. The last major Dutch disaster, the floods that hit Zeeland in 1953 and which took advantage of the damage to and neglect of sea defences during the Second World War to kill over fifteen hundred Zeelanders, shows how high the stakes have always been. In a sense, the emphasis that much of the rest of Western Europe gives to fortresses, city walls and so on is merely a pale shadow of the staggering scale of an entire coast fortified against sea water. An almost infinite elaboration of sluices and dykes further and further inland also keeps under control the mouths of Europe's main river systems, which anciently would have whipped around in their courses like snakes held by the tail. I remember being far inland in Zutphen and moaning about how boring the river IJssel looks there, just an overbig gutter, but its boredom is to a very good purpose.

The bold and the mad

Many years ago a selection of family members and I found ourselves in the Burgundian town of Beaune. We had spent an afternoon at the Hospices de Beaune – an astoundingly beautiful fifteenth-century complex endowed by Duke Philip the Good's chancellor, Nicolas Rolin, and his wife Guigone de Salins. Our baby became oddly feverish that evening and we had to go to Beaune general hospital. Once it was clear we were English the hospital staff enjoyed themselves pretending not to understand anything we said, although my sister has a degree in French and had a chunk of her adult life in France. I still remember the odd mixture of anxiety over the purple-faced baby and farce over the mime-artist gestures of the staff (gurns, gawps, slow nods, raised palms) as they picked through the tattered fragments of the language of Racine falling from my sister's lips. Somewhat guiltily though, I remember being furious that it was 1994. We could have had an ill baby at any time between 1443 and 1980 and we would have rushed him to the magical Hospices de Beaune, turning left by Rogier van der Weyden's great *Last Judgement*, passed the door where wimpled nuns were grinding possets and boiling unguents, and into the lovely main hall, with its tiles marked with the marriage motto of the Rolins, 'You alone'. It seemed frustrating to be temporally so near and yet so far – an institution that had lasted many centuries had shut just too early and now we were stuck in this brightly hygienic modern room, as the conversation made its inevitable way round to the beloved French subject of rectal suppositories.

The Hospices are a surprise as so much of the legacy of the Burgundian state has been destroyed. The Emperor Charles V, when he inherited many of the dukes' lands in the sixteenth century, not only had their favourite palace at Hesdin destroyed completely, but moved the entire town several miles away. One of the odder things that can be done in Brussels is to go down into the cellars below the current Royal Palace where the shattered remnants of the old Coudenberg Palace, completely burned down in 1731, have recently been excavated. Duke Philip the Good's Aula Magna, the great banqueting hall which was once the most glamorous building in Europe, is still down there – but reduced to a section of floor-tiling that must have fallen through into the cellars as the whole thing collapsed. Some of the great artworks associated with their reigns still exist, some weapons and some of the much rebuilt civic structures (the town halls of Louvain, Brussels, Middelburg), but their domineering presence has been successfully erased both by their Habsburg successors and wave upon wave of violence and bad luck. And yet their actions accidentally made so much of Europe's future. We still live in a world shaped by their greed, good luck and reckless ambition.

The four dukes – Philip the Bold, John the Fearless, Philip the Good, Charles the Bold – ruled for a little over a century, 1363 to 1477. In many ways they lived in a fool's paradise as their success relied on the weakness of their opposition. An opposition nadir was probably reached in 1398 when Philip the Good was at a meeting in Rheims between Wenzel, the King of the Germans, and Charles VI, King of France, at which Wenzel (whose authority in any event scarcely reached beyond the chair he was sitting on) was drunk and Charles collapsed into another bout of insanity. The dukes' lands insinuated themselves along the length of Lotharingia, stuck together from long strands of territory slipped between the rule of France or of Germany. But in practice they all had fairly clear obediences to one side or the other, and these were only temporarily on hold. The dukes' best strategy could only be to further encourage their rivals in their pursuit of alcoholism or lunacy. The devastation of France by England was also a huge help. When both monarchies recovered, under the Habsburgs in the east and Charles VII and Louis XI in the west, and once the English were kicked out, the dukes' fun was up.

Philip the Bold, the first in the line, was in many ways just a normal French prince, the son of King John II. The superhuman power and grandeur of the French monarchs is easy to state, but hard to believe. They were sanctioned by God and sat at the heart of a vast, intricate web of relationships, secular and religious, that regulated the entire kingdom. The Capetian dynasty, which had reigned since 987, had a single core competence: an ability to have at least one son who lived to adulthood. This gave them an astonishing cumulative heft: they were not ex-Viking pirates like the Norman chancers in London; nor were they mere embarrassing elected officials like the King of the Germans or the Pope. Once Philip II Augustus had crushed all his English, Norman, Flemish and German rivals at the Battle of Bouvines in 1214, he and his descendants switched from being Kings of the Franks (which sounded a bit olden times and tribal) to being Kings of France. How this 'France' should be territorially defined became the issue that has dominated Western European history ever since – perhaps only ending with the Saarland being returned to West Germany in 1957 and Algerian independence in 1962.

The power and prestige of the French monarchy allowed the individual sitting on the throne to be far less important than the role. But after an extraordinary run of son-following-son the Capetian generational engine sputtered when Louis X only managed a son born after his own death in 1316, John I, who then himself died aged five days old. This stalled the succession in the previous generation – with Louis's brother taking over as Philip V and having no sons and, in a final throw, *his* brother then ruled as the also sonless Charles IV. This set of very short reigns (four kings covering less than fourteen years), aside from really cracking through the sacred oil thoughtfully supplied by the Holy Ghost, had a disastrous result. Using plausible arguments on both sides, the next king could either be Philip VI, the closest but not very close male, or it could be the son of the last three kings' sister, Isabella. This, highly unfortunately, was not only a King of England but specifically the teenaged psycho Edward III. This argument over rival legitimacies would be picked up again whenever either side was in the right mood, resulting in the Hundred Years War, a ruined France and in the end with England expelled. The claim that the English king was actually also the French king was only given up in 1802, helpfully.

The opening naval battle of Sluis in 1340, in what is now Zeelandic Flanders, was confusingly held in a great bay which is now solid farmland. It is a uniquely peculiar feeling to bowl along in a bus through field after field trying to imagine where hundreds of castled ships full of crossbowmen once slogged it out. The English victory was so total that it removed any chance of France invading England, with some sixteen thousand or more French sailors and soldiers killed and 190 out of 213 ships destroyed or captured. In manoeuvring around the Somme in 1346 (weirdly echoed in the comparably shattering Battle of Agincourt in 1415) the English and French armies faced each other at Crécy and the latter was destroyed. The Count of Flanders was killed, as was the Duke of Lorraine. Calais fell and became an English base for over two centuries.

Philip the Bold enters the story in 1356, with the matchingly disastrous Battle of Poitiers. In a fresh low, King John II of France was captured at the battle, along with his fourteen-year-old son, Philip. He then accompanied his father as a hostage to London, where he spent the time playing chess with the Black Prince. On his return, after the ruinous Treaty of Brétigny handed the whole of south-west France permanently and completely to England, Philip was made Duke of Burgundy, a large, rich territory based around Dijon. The rest of Philip's life was spent battling with the grim situation of France, ravaged by armed gangs and plague, and with a frightening lack of central authority of which he took full advantage. He was never much of a war leader. Amid serio-comic scenes he was in 1369 put in charge of invading England, gathering a substantial army and arranging for a huge pre-fabricated wooden castle to be made in Normandy (its walls miles long, it was implausibly claimed), but one luckless ship filled with castle was captured by the English in the Channel and the gigantic kit was useless with bits missing. In London, suburbs were being pulled down to give clear fields of fire and a state of emergency was declared. However, the weeks went by. Shivering in the cold and rain at Sluis, facing an ever more stormy and wintry Channel, Philip abandoned the invasion, putting the French on the defensive again for years to come.

Very few people have now heard of Sluis. I grew up in Kent and it is strange to be in what is now a Dutch town which feels so Kentish – the same sort of meandering High Street with people buying little bits of stuff at all hours of the day, stretches of willowed water with ducks, enthusiasm for eating cake. But what is now an inland market town was once the heavily fortified approach to the river which made Bruges one of the world's greatest ports. Now, this seems like a mere crazy assertion as the whole place is so overwhelmingly dozy, with the river's silting up turning it into a literal backwater. Together with Ghent and Ypres, Bruges made Flanders one of the most dynamic parts of Europe. Philip the Bold's great decision was to take advantage of the surprise death of Philip of Rouvres, whose widow Margaret of Flanders, still aged only twelve, would ultimately be heir to Flanders, the County of Burgundy (the Franche-Comté as it will be called from now on), Artois, Nevers and Rethel. As Flanders was part of France, the newly released King John II duly arranged for Philip's marriage to Margaret, beating Edward III's bid to fix her up with one of his own sons, following some dirty work with the Pope.

This was an era of ferocious fighting in Flanders, focused on revolutionary forces in Ghent, which aimed to make itself a city state of a kind familiar across much of Europe (for example among the members of the Hanseatic League – or 'Easterlings' as French chroniclers attractively call them). It was the bad luck of Ghent that it fell geographically just inside France, whereas if it had been the other side of the Scheldt it would have been in the Empire and could have done pretty much what it liked, becoming a Flemish Hamburg. Instead Philip the Bold and his father-in-law Louis of Mâle were able to call on the French army, which chewed through the region, taking Ypres and Poperinghe and threatening Bruges. During fighting in the Waasland, some fleeing Ghent troops were able to escape by using their pikes to vault dykes. As its allies disappeared Ghent had little choice but to fight the sort of pitched battle for which city militia are poorly equipped. Its leaders announced: 'Even if everyone in Flanders was executed, our dried bones would carry on the struggle'. Fighting in thick fog, their army was annihilated at the Battle of West Roosebeke, just north of Passchendaele. Ghent was supported by the English, whose king, wearing his claiming-to-be-King-of-France crown, used this as an opportunity to assert his authority. In 1383 an English army from Calais took Dunkirk and then set about besieging Ypres. The siege was one of the era's great disasters – it was unsuccessful but so ravaged Ypres and its surroundings that they never recovered: from being a major city like Ghent or Bruges, Ypres slumped down to being the mere market town it has been ever since. The English were eventually forced to withdraw because of the usual great leveller and destroyer of plans, the uncontrollable horrors of dysentery. They retreated to Cassel, then to the coast in a wilderness of recrimination and anger. As one rueful English chronicler wrote: 'God struck us in our bottoms'.

CHAPTER FOUR

The fearless and the good » Prayer nuts »
A word of advice from Mehmet the Conqueror »
Poor local decision-making » The bold and the Swiss

The fearless and the good

In many ways the Burgundian state as it developed was like a vast strangler-fig around the borders of France, from the English Channel to the Alps, both crushing France and living off it, using the haziness of Lotharingia to intersperse itself in spaces in between. Both Philip and his son John the Fearless were deeply involved in the unfolding horrors of French politics and clearly saw themselves as French princes trying to intervene to bring stability to Paris in a kingdom ravaged both by the English and, unfortunately, by their own ruthlessness. Enormous sums from the French treasury wound up in Burgundy and the Dukes' personal gain was just one element in the epic looting of what had once been Europe's best-run state.*

John the Fearless was famous when young for his involvement in the catastrophic 1396 crusade – a parody of earlier such expeditions, which had themselves often not been wildly successful, particularly not in the Balkans. As mentioned earlier, one of John the Fearless's distant predecessors as Count of Flanders, Baldwin IX, had been a leader of the Fourth Crusade back in 1204, was crowned Latin Emperor in Constantinople in a vast ceremony at the Hagia Sophia and in the following year wound up being used by the Bulgarian king as a novelty skull drinking vessel. In any event, following alarming Ottoman gains across south-eastern Europe, it was in the grand tradition of Baldwin IX that a large but distinctly

---

* The relationship between the French monarchy and the dukes wobbled about a fair bit. One nadir came when Charles VI besieged John the Fearless in Arras in August 1414 and sent him a letter addressed to 'John, the so-called Duke of Burgundy, raving with the fury of envy and ambition'.

B-team of crusaders marched east to take on the armies of Beyazid the Thunderbolt. The accounts of what happened are frustratingly unclear, presumably because the chroniclers wanted to move on and write about something more uplifting. The crusade seems to have been frivolously managed, with a chaos of different contingents and no clear leadership. At the epochal Battle of Nicopolis, Beyazid (who had enjoyably boasted that he would in due time 'feed his horses on the altar of St Peter's') slaughtered them. The French chronicler Froissart said that the disaster could only be compared to the defeat in *The Song of Roland*. John was captured and obliged to cool his heels in Gallipoli while his father raised the vast ransom of two hundred thousand ducats from his different, presumably unimpressed territories. He also gave Beyazid toadying presents, such as twelve magnificent white chargers with grooms in matching livery. (How did those grooms live out their lives? One of many mysteries.)

John spent the rest of his violent existence entangled both in the affairs of his sprawling inheritance and those of France, whose unhappy but long-lived king Charles VI claimed his name was really George, howled like a wolf and believed himself to be made of glass. France in this period became close to total incoherence as it was torn apart not just by English freebooters but by battles between John's supporters (the Burgundians) and those of the King's uncle, Louis of Bourbon (the Armagnacs). John hired the men who successfully assassinated Louis on the streets of Paris in 1407, an almost unprecedented collapse in standards. The final wrecking ball was the arrival of Henry V, who in part won the Battle of Agincourt in 1415 because John held back his own troops and it was the Armagnacs who were massacred there (although one of John's brothers was also killed). The French Dauphin later organized John's own famous assassination on the Bridge at Montereau, at a meeting disguised as a mere diplomatic exchange of cordialities. It was this sequence of events that made Burgundy a separate state rather than merely a piggy-bank for a French prince. The killing of John the Fearless caused his son and inheritor Philip the Good to recoil completely from France and to ally Burgundy with England.

It was not possible to forgive anyone (including the king) who had connived in the murder, particularly the young Dauphin, who became king as Charles VII in 1422 after his miserable howling father at last died. Unlike his father and grandfather, Philip the Good hardly visited Paris, instead shifting during his long reign between his courts at Bruges, Lille, Dijon, Hesdin, The Hague and – most importantly – Brussels, the capital of Brabant, which he had inherited in 1430.

The longer Philip reigned the more concrete Burgundy became as its own realm. I think he was called 'the Good' because he did a good job, not because he was particularly good in a moral sense. He was involved in ferocious wars and seems in many ways just as mean and sardonic as his father and indeed his son (the future Charles the Bold). He scooped up a number of further territories. Most unchivalric was probably buying the ancient Marquisate of Namur. This was in the hands of another branch of the Dampierre family, whose extinction had handed Flanders to Philip's grandfather. As the ruler of Namur had no descendants he offered simply to sell the place in return for cash payments to fund his extravagant lifestyle until his death, which happened several extremely enjoyable years later. A lot more serious and consequential was Philip's long war with the remarkable Jacqueline of Holland.

In 1417 Count William, ruler of Holland, Zeeland and Hainaut, died of a dog bite. Both John the Fearless and Philip the Good were long and deeply involved in the affairs of these lands. John was married to Count William's sister Margaret; William was married to John's sister, also called Margaret, unhelpfully. The most significant battle of John's reign had been on behalf of her and William's younger brother, John (also unhelpful) of Bavaria, who was Prince-Bishop of Liège (a large separate ecclesiastical territory which cut across the southern Netherlands) and which resulted in the crushing of his rebellious subjects at the Battle of Othée – the secular ring-leaders being executed, the religious ring-leaders drowned, as it was forbidden to spill the blood of churchmen. The uneasy relations between these different siblings could have broken in a number of ways, but were dominated by Margaret's having a son (Philip the

Good) and William only having a daughter, Jacqueline. After William's unlucky encounter with a frothing pet, John of Bavaria dumped being in holy orders, took over as count and quickly married to see if he could come up with an heir himself, but in the event had no children.

Jacqueline of Holland married John IV, the ruler of Brabant, in 1418. Brabant had been the possession of John the Fearless's brother Anthony, who had been killed at Agincourt, and was now inherited by his son John IV, who was unfortunately only fifteen years old and, from the one surviving drawing of him, a total weed. John IV was meant to protect Jacqueline's inheritance but was incapable of doing so. Jacqueline soon lost patience with him and fled with her mother to Brussels, then London and then decided to marry Henry V's younger brother, Humphrey, Duke of Gloucester, having found a helpful, if generally disregarded, anti-Pope short of cash to annul her earlier marriage. None of this reflects well on anyone. John of Bavaria, realizing the game was up and his throwing in the priesthood and marrying had just wasted everyone's time, made Philip the Good his heir. He was shortly thereafter assassinated in The Hague with a poisoned prayer book (yes, really – nothing can beat the fifteenth century). Duke Humphrey and Jacqueline hunkered down in Mons but then, in a scene almost too stupid to be written down, Humphrey fled back to England with one of Jacqueline's ladies-in-waiting under his arm. Jacqueline was put under house arrest in Ghent but, disguising herself as a man, fled to Antwerp and then rallied support in Gouda.

A long, brutal war followed in 1425–8, devastating much of the northern Netherlands, between her own supporters and those of Philip the Good. Individual towns fought on either side, with places such as Rotterdam and Leiden pro-Philip. Eventually Jacqueline retired to private life, keeping her titles but agreeing at the crucial and far-reaching Reconciliation of Delft that Philip could administer the territories and inherit if she had no children. The real Pope then intervened in 1428 to say that Jacqueline's first marriage was still legitimate – but the sorry John IV had died the year before and the main impact this had was to allow Humphrey to marry the lady-in-waiting (who proved to be a sorceress). Jacqueline also remarried, but died still with no heir aged thirty-five having had a quite extraordinarily eventful, concentrated and interesting life.

I apologize for this blur of names and events (which could be presented in theatrical farce form, along the lines of Ray Cooney's *Run for Your Wife* or *Not Now, Darling*), but this sequence, created by the gyrating vagaries of individual lusts, greeds and miscalculations, was carving out future nations. A series of territories which had previously been simply north-westerly elements in the Empire had been wrenched away. Numerous protests by the impotent Emperor Sigismund were ignored by all parties. By the time of Philip's death in 1467 he had torn lands from France (principally Burgundy, Flanders, Artois, Boulogne, Vermandois, Ponthieu and Picardy) and from the Empire (Zeeland, Brabant, Holland, Hainaut, Namur, Limburg, Luxembourg – another coup which I, alas, just cannot also cope with here, but it's really interesting: look it up!* – and the Franche-Comté).

Another great shift was happening further south. This is not the place to get too involved in the Lotharingian vagaries of the Duchy of Bar, but it was split in two parts by the River Meuse – one owning allegiance to France (the enjoyably named 'Barrois mouvant') and the other in the Empire (the 'Barrois non mouvant'). Its relevance here is that in 1412, just a few yards into the French part of Bar, Joan of Arc was born: a woman who would, in an extraordinarily short time, transform the uncrowned Charles VII of France's position. Inspired by a series of visions Joan, in ways now hard to understand, inspired the French army and ruined the Anglo-Burgundian plans to partition France. Taking part in Charles's triumphant coronation she was then captured by Burgundians and

* Actually, that is inhuman – it just can't be left out. Luxembourg was taken by a specialist 'escalader' using a ladder made of silk and hooks to get over the walls. He found a little barred gate unwatched and returned with a hundred shoeless picked men on the darkest night of the year, armed only with daggers and breastplates and carrying a gigantic pair of pincers with handles twelve feet long. These snipped through the gate's bars and locks and the town fell almost without loss of life. There.

handed over to the English who burned her as a witch in 1431, aged nineteen. Like Jacqueline of Holland (who died later in the decade), in the end we know frustratingly little about her. These figures are all in different ways ciphers, living just before the great French writer Philippe de Commynes arrives on the scene to revolutionize the vividness and psychological complexity of the next generation of political actors.

It seems clear from surviving chronicles that Philip the Good and his son Charles the Bold had no real sense of just how unforgiving their enemies the King of France and the Emperor were. They were surrounded by a great, ever-accumulating cloud of animosity which would only in the end be dispelled by the destruction of their dynasty. Philip the Good schemed and flattered to create a series of dynastic delayed-action bombs – arrangements by which, once specific individuals had died, he or his successors would inherit territories which, strictly speaking, were not theirs to own. Now safely back in his reviving capital of Paris, Charles VII, having been given a hard push by Joan of Arc, would take a long view but, with a confidence equal to Philip, was sure he would in the end expel all the outsiders who still squatted in his territories. His son Louis XI, one of the greatest of all French kings, would exercise a malicious cunning in a different league to Philip and Charles. The other bad news for the Burgundians was the new Emperor Frederick III, head of the Habsburg family. He was a figure of sometimes almost dormouse-like inanition, but nonetheless inherited a far more powerful personal base than his helpless predecessor Sigismund. His family links and possessions across the southern Empire and outside it made him hugely more powerful, and he too was looking with cold disfavour on the Burgundians.

The tragedy that now unfolded was not really to do with Charles the Bold, who fully inherited the Burgundian lands in 1467, but with the degree to which he and his predecessors' actions had devastated the autonomy of their northern holdings. John the Fearless's crushing of Liège, repeated Burgundian, French and English ravaging of Flanders and the ending or expulsion of the old regional dynasties meant that those actually living in Ghent or Antwerp,

Leiden or Mons, Luxembourg or Maastricht had lost any semblance of control over their lives. The proud civic worlds of the cloth towns and the same period's frenzy of great city building (such as the town halls of Arras, Leuven and Brussels) would do nothing for people whose fate now entirely rested on the remorseless Charles the Bold's staying alive. But Charles the Bold only had one child, and she was a daughter. It was a shame that Jacqueline of Holland did not live long enough to enjoy the situation.

Prayer nuts

Spiritually I have always been a bit confused. Both my parents were Catholic and I was raised as Catholic. But from an early age I was sent away to very Protestant schools. I cannot swear that I noticed the difference for a long time, but it gradually and dumbly occurred to me that these were two faiths with very different flavours. This quirk in my religious background has pursued me as an adult and inflected my attitude towards history, culture and writing in curious ways. Much of this book is, at the hidden wiring level, about this topic – for the obvious reason that since the Reformation the story of Lotharingia has been its crazy-paving of faith. My own sympathies veer around pathetically, depending on where I am. If I walk into some vast Reformed hall-church in Gelderland, with the only decoration provided by the shapes of the lettering in the prayer book, I recoil as a Catholic: oh, the arrogance of man, the cul-de-sac of mere words, arid and cheerless. If I walk into some baroque Catholic church in the Rhineland, an explosion of whipped-cream stucco, paintings of tortured saints, sobbing Marys, I recoil as a Protestant: emotionalism gone mad, the empty bluster of a picture-book religion, oh but this is practically *Filipino*. Of course, both these responses are infantile, curiously unmediated and not malicious as such. But through an accident of upbringing I find myself equally drawn to and equally repulsed by the great schism that has for five hundred years torn this part of Europe apart – I am as moved by an old Bible in German as by a really splashy Rubens. In the astonishing encounter at Worms between the young Emperor Charles V and Martin Luther I am paralysed by indecision as to which side's colours to wear. The iconoclasm that burns through the Netherlands in the 1560s is at one level a cultural and spiritual catastrophe, at another a welcome bit of tidying.

I am not going to say for a moment that my mental struggles offer me any serious insight into the religious battles that have at irregular intervals ravaged this landscape, but I can at least say that I am oddly inoculated. I am entranced and revolted by both sides and there is no subtext to this book which views the triumph of one or the other as being sought-after, more natural or more progressive. If anything, this is probably an anti-Weber book in that it is Lotharingia that is the home to the great experimental laboratory that disproves any specific link between Protestantism and capitalism: the whole place ends up bristling with purely Catholic smokestacks and industry. And, of course, the chaos of different islands of religious practice is in itself central to the idea that there is a natural and welcome fracturing here which has had a profound effect on Europe's history.

Criss-crossing between different parts of the Low Countries and around the Rhineland it would be hard not to notice that this is a scarred religious landscape – that before the much later overlays of ideological and physical damage there was an era in which the physical nature of the entire townscape, once dominated by religious buildings, was in contention. Coming from England, where many great churches remain but their paintings and fittings were for the most part burnt or melted down during the Reformation, it is hard not to revel in the rich, beautiful chaos of the Continent. Only a few minutes on a train can take you from the whitewashed austerity of Dordrecht to the almost campy excesses of Antwerp. Only a bleak and uninvolving bus journey separates the old Calvinist powerhouse of Heidelberg from the ancient Catholic powerhouse of Speyer.

Being batted back and forth by different religious practices is a stimulating business. Their different geographical areas are a side effect of the most bitter fighting, provoked substantially (but not totally) by the highest stakes: the means of securing the afterlife. The line that can be traced through the region just north of Belgium is either (from a Catholic point of view) the tragic high-water mark in the extirpation of heresy, struggled over for generations before being abandoned for shameful reasons of realpolitik, or (from a Protestant Dutch point of view) the point at which the oozing lava of Rome was, through the triumphant struggle of generations, stopped and the Reformed Church survived.

The formal origins of the Reformation lie further to the east, with Luther's grandstanding. But the continuity of Catholicism has meant that countless treasures have been cherished which would have elsewhere been burned. During an outbreak of iconoclasm in Ghent, the bonfires of paintings, altars, hangings, sculptures, indeed decorations of any kind, were so huge that they could be seen ten miles away. Van Eyck's *Adoration of the Sacred Lamb* was only saved because it was taken apart and hoisted up into the tower. In the face of a second outburst of iconoclasm, the picture had its own armed guard. A very large part of all Western Europe's artistic endeavour throughout its history was destroyed in the space of days.

Areas of the Netherlands which were later forcibly re-Catholicized by the Spanish provided an amazing boon for artists such as Rubens, who had to start again in creating fresh decorations, and this vast repopulation with imagery must have had a profound impact on the economy of the Spanish Netherlands. Some other places were sheltered from having to do this and maintained continuity, even if they lost all kinds of treasures to warfare. We know, for example, almost nothing about the painters of the Cologne school. Various disasters over the centuries have shaken any names loose from their works and there is therefore a frustrating (in art historical terms) lack of narrative or drama – they've no Vasari. The one exception is Stefan Lochner, and we can only link him to specific pictures because of a single mention in Dürer's diary, where he pays a fee for Lochner's triptych in the cathedral to be opened so he can look at it. This one flimsy comment allows an individual to step forward. There is one painting by Lochner which I can never shake off – the *Madonna in a Rose Bower*, painted in the 1440s. It is a tiny

panel that uses such dense, rich colour and such meticulous minia-
turization that it makes merely human eyes smart – it seems designed
for creatures with different optics. Jesus looks a bit like a plastic doll
with moveable limbs, but otherwise everything from Mary's face
and crown to the fruit and musical instruments of her angel attend-
ants is a form of perfection – a kind of art that can go no further.

The picture is so striking because it is so clearly to be used for
private devotion. Everywhere in the region's museums there are
objects such as this which are, of course, Catholic but require no
priest to get in the way. Homes would have been littered with small
shrines, and just a crucifix and somewhere to kneel would have
been available to everybody. The clue in this particular picture is
the rose bower, a private symbolic garden a long way from the
formal, public ceremonial of mass. The most zany extremity of this
intimate form of worship was the brief, early sixteenth-century
enthusiasm for Flemish 'prayer nuts' – wooden spheres the size of
walnuts which opened up to reveal minutely carved crucifixions
teeming with expressive figures the size of rice grains. Both virtuoso and disturbing, the perhaps voluntarily anonymous artists who
created these as the ultimate in portable altars were – again –
aiming at the individual not the community. Indeed, even the
individual could barely see them and it is only with twenty-first-
century digital technology that they really come into their own.

Without heaping up endless examples, my simple point is that
much of the world of prayer was always private and possibly eccentric, certainly personal. Van Eyck's *Madonna of Chancellor Rolin*
seems originally to have been just for Rolin himself to pray
before – so our looking at it in the Louvre is almost a form of
spying. This gap between public ceremony and private prayer has
always been potentially problematic. It is an issue hid in plain sight
in the context of monasteries. Each monastery was a battleground
in which the individual monk was to confront evil and overcome
it both for his own salvation and on behalf of all mankind. This
struggle was expressed through community actions (an unending
round of prayers), but as vigorously through personal devotions.
This is just in brackets, but there remains in London today a very

small convent where the nuns' task is to pray for the safety of Londoners who are out at night. In a very ancient framework therefore, while the ostensible action around Piccadilly Circus is focused on carousing and throwing up, there is a separate invisible spiritual fight still being waged today in the air above.

The rose bower in Lochner's painting is important and the imagery of the garden as a private spiritual space pops up everywhere, explicitly in the cloisters and herbaria of monasteries, but in innumerable similar paintings linking the veneration of Mary to a bower or walled garden planted with symbolic flowers. This in turn was related to the murky origins of the Rosary itself, its use in prayer perhaps beginning in Douai or Zwolle in the late fifteenth century. Nothing could be more Catholic – but this whole world of private spiritual wrestling or invocation was not something that could necessarily be controlled by priests. For centuries the Church seemed able to manage this problem, but in practice it was always there. How the individual monk or priest interpreted his private and direct prayers could not be monitored. One of the most striking and lasting communities of north-west Europe, the institution of beguinage, has left beautiful scatterings of buildings across Belgium and the Netherlands. These were places where men or women could withdraw from the world and without taking holy orders devote the rest of their lives to prayer. The surviving buildings in Breda, for example, or Bruges, enshrine the idea of perfect communities – often, indeed, focused around ideal gardens, providing food, healthy work and flowers linked to specific saints in the Lochner manner. The official Catholic Church tried to ensure doctrinal conformity, indeed that conformity was seen as central to accessing the afterlife. But it was always incomplete, not just in the obvious, vast arena of much of human life as a sort of festival parade of the Seven Deadly Sins, but because private thoughts and ideas simply could not be watched. It was in several Netherland towns that a profound challenge to Catholicism would emerge, long before Luther.

A word of advice from Mehmet the Conqueror

Much of the glamour and style of the Burgundians has been erased by bad luck, vengeance and changing fashion. For example, we know that Philip the Good patronized fifteen different goldsmiths just in Bruges and yet not one example of their work survives. By contrast, many of Philip's manuscripts do survive, presumably because paper can't be melted down for cash. We also know that in 1425 Philip employed one hundred and eighty artists, many of them embroiderers, to create suitably dramatic decorations for his horses and glamorous pavilions in preparation for a planned and then cancelled single combat with Humphrey, Duke of Gloucester – but nothing of this immense and, as it proved, pointless work now exists. None of the automata the dukes delighted in survive and their functioning cannot even be guessed at. More deliberately fleeting were the gigantic snowmen built in the two squares of Arras during the brutal winter of 1434–5 which featured the Seven Sleepers, a Danse Macabre, Joan of Arc and others. Most of the Dukes' northern palaces have been destroyed, except for a fragment at Lille which is a tourist office. The palace at Ghent is still there but so ferociously renovated it looks like a toybox castle – but the empty shell of Philip's audience hall is still inside, now a notably charismatic gift shop. A very elaborate and expensive votive offering from Charles the Bold to St Lambert's Cathedral in Liège still exists, but this is a rare accident as in most of the rest of the Netherlands these things were destroyed by iconoclasts in the sixteenth century. This shows a gold figure of Charles holding a glass vial containing a finger of St Lambert and supported by the gold figure of St George, doffing his hat. With a time-machine one might want to go back to the fifteenth century with Charles's reliquary and see if one could trade it in for something else a bit better as it has a Jeff Koons quality which makes it hard to warm to.

The Dukes loved their palace at Hesdin in Artois. It had wonderful machines to entertain visitors: they could create hidden voices, spray water, sprinkle snow. There was a trapdoor through which visitors would drop onto great piles of feathers; conduits were placed to squirt 'women from below'. There were the mysterious but no doubt beguiling automata. There was a magical room celebrating the story of Jason and the Golden Fleece (to commemorate the chivalric order initiated by Philip the Good), which William Caxton saw while he was working as a printer in Bruges and which he thought 'craftily and curiously depeynted'. The entire palace and its fortifications were razed by the Emperor Charles V and no trace remains. The Burgundian court was once famous for a special dance called the 'moresca', but we have no idea how it was danced, and in any event the music has not survived.

What have survived in quantity are tapestries. These reach a peak of beauty and complexity in this period, becoming – it could be argued – more static and banal thereafter. Tapestries became the quintessential Flemish and Brabantine art. Now often terribly faded, they are massively heavy and therefore rarely worth looting – particularly as the market for individuals wanting to publicly compare themselves to Hercules or Alexander was always a small and clearly defined one. Some beautiful and bizarre pieces fill the Tournai tapestry museum, associated with Philip the Good's tapestry merchant, Pasquier Grenier. In the strange way that they tell an entire story in a single tapestry with no regard for sequence or scale they have an atmosphere lost until twentieth-century modernism. *The Famine and Fall of Jerusalem* shows men bigger than horses, walls which could be easily stepped over; a town is just a tower, an army a handful of men, one starving woman eating a child stands in for many more. This tapestry was obviously meant to remind visitors or supplicants of the fate of disobedient towns. It is particularly appropriate that it should be in Tournai, as the semi-independent enclave politely but nervously shelled out ten thousand francs a year to Charles the Bold to be left alone. There is also a superb *Battle of Roncevalles*, with Roland (his name thoughtfully sewn onto his armour, like on a school PE kit) hideously wounded, his oliphant strapped on his back and a dastardly Muslim in a gold helmet studded with jewels grinning as he stabs a Frank in the neck. Here was Philip associating himself with expiatory chivalry (despite backing out of his single combat with Duke Humphrey), and with the power and glamour of Charlemagne.

It is hard not to wonder whether the Dukes (and indeed other rulers of the period) and their guests got a bit bored with being compared to the same people over and over – there is always a tapestry of Godefroy of Bouillon or Charlemagne. But perhaps the static nature of the iconography was the point: that greatness and legitimacy created a permanent present, where both dynastic heroes and ancient classical examples remained vivid. In 1453 the catastrophic news arrived of the fall of Constantinople to the Ottomans. An elaborate event called the Feast of the Pheasant was held by Philip the Good in Lille, featuring heaps of food and drink, musicians in a giant pie, an elephant, a special lament by Dufay and allegorical figures representing a ravished Constantinople. The Burgundian hierarchy swore to go on crusade but little serious planning was done and Constantinople was quietly forgotten about. With any luck surrounded by his tapestries of classical heroes, Philip the Good received a letter from Mehmet the Conqueror saying to let him know that, by the way, if he was thinking about going on crusade Mehmet'd do to him what his grandfather Bajazet had done to Philip's dad. He signed himself 'the true heir of King Alexander and Hector of Troy, sultan of Babylon, King of Troy'.

Several inventions make the dukes unfairly much more vivid than their predecessors. *At last*, for example, there are good-quality oil-painting portraits and we know what the Dukes and many of their entourage looked like. The same pictures were painted repeatedly and are dotted around the Netherlands, sometimes (as at the Hospice of the Countess in Lille) getting all four dukes in a row, like football cards. Their loyal, long-time Chancellor Nicolas Rolin is one of the best-known faces of the fifteenth century because he was captured both by Jan van Eyck and by Rogier van der Weyden, in two of the greatest pictures ever painted, perhaps both paid for by the enormous bribes we now know he was secretly receiving from the King of France. There are also a mass of accurate drawings from the period. A particularly striking example is Van Eyck's *St Barbara* where in the background a wonderfully elaborate sketch is made of what seems to be Cologne Cathedral under construction, teeming with workmen and featuring the famous giant crane on the belfry which, when work seized up in 1475, would remain one of the Rhineland's most distinctive landmarks for four hundred years.

But most vivid of all is a new form of writing – most notably the astonishing memoirs of Philippe de Commynes. The only comparison that can be made really is between black-and-white film and the arrival of Technicolor. Suddenly, figures who were stiff, hieratic, remote, their motives often mysterious, reported upon only by monastic chroniclers of little percipience, are replaced by living, complex, dithering people. There is not enough room here to do anything other than urge everyone to read Commynes. He served both Louis XI and Charles the Bold for many years, knew them extremely well and wrote candidly about events which were to him contemporary gossip but to us world-historical. He is fascinating on England and the Wars of the Roses and the constant shuttlings back and forth at Calais, with ships full of terrified losers and vengeful victors, depending. Indeed, it becomes clear that the Wars could never have happened without oscillating and patchy Burgundian friendliness nearby. Like Technicolor, Commynes' impact is unfair. His style of writing is perhaps as important as a portal between the 'medieval' and the 'early modern' as any other technical or intellectual change. We can in the end only guess at much of Philip the Bold and his predecessors' personalities, but now here is Commynes giving a brilliantly rounded, complex portrait of Charles the Bold. There is an extraordinary, novelistic moment after the Battle of Montlhéry, where Charles's forces have just defeated Louis, and Commynes describes seeing the thirty-one-year-old Charles on his horse, 'very joyfully on the field, thinking the glory his' – and then Commynes attributes this moment to all Charles's life's disasters: someone who had not thought much about war until Montlhéry now did nothing but fight: 'By it his life was ended and his house destroyed'. The description of that battle itself is something new, catching in all its awfulness the sheer chaos of such occasions and the degree to which nobody had any idea who really was winning or why, as isolated groups panicked here and squads of horsemen galloped away there. Sensibly, Commynes sees all military action as in the hands of God. For a battle to happen both sides must believe they can win, or one would simply surrender beforehand in the hope of mercy. Therefore, the winner is not more skilled but simply divinely favoured: 'This mystery is so great that realms and great lordships sometimes come to an end and desolation whilst others grow or come into existence.'

Poor local decision-making

For any substantial Flemish community in the later Middle Ages it proved over and over again tricky to work out when your aggressive behaviour towards your neighbouring communities might be viewed as appealingly truculent by your overlord or just a bit too sassy. For the leading merchants of a specific town – Dinant is a good example – years might go by without serious interference by their ruler, who could be a minor, or fighting many miles away or simply incompetent or decrepit.

Dinant remains today a geographically very strange place. It is crowded into the tiny area between a huge limestone cliff and the River Meuse. On top of the cliff is a fortress which has for centuries allowed things to be fired at or thrown down at anyone threatening the town. Dinant, in the domains owned by the Bishops of Liège, had a wholly dysfunctional attitude towards the town of Bouvignes, on the other side of the river and owned by the Counts of Namur. At one point a gigantic tower was built just to intimidate Bouvignes and people from both towns – both engaged in making metal drinking vessels and church decorations – seem to have spent much too much time at guild suppers in a lather of scarlet-faced rage at mutual insults going back many generations.

Early in the fifteenth century the County of Namur (and therefore of Bouvignes) was sold to the Burgundians and Dinant found itself with a potentially very tough and aggressive neighbour on the far side of the river. During the complex manoeuvrings in 1465

between the Burgundians and the revived and crafty French monarchy under Louis XI, Dinant made several fatal mistakes, including
launching further violent attacks on Bouvignes. Under the over-
hasty impression that Duke Philip the Good's son, Charles, had
been defeated at the Battle of Montlhéry, someone in Dinant who
should have stuck to making goblets thought it would be a bit of
fun to make a hanged dummy of Charles and dangle it in full view
of Bouvignes. Dinant also laughingly announced that Charles was
a bastard, his father a cuckold and his mother a whore.

In Charles's successful negotiations to end the war with Louis
XI, it was eventually decided by both sides to put Dinant in a special category. Charles marched to Dinant with his state-of-the-art
cannon and in a few days forced the town's surrender. Dinant's
master armourer was thrown from the fortress into the town, hundreds of male inhabitants were tied together and drowned in the
Meuse, the women fled to Liège and the town was looted and
burned to the ground. Charles, in one of his many self-consciously
Ancient Roman gestures, scattered salt on the remains. One of
Europe's wealthiest smaller towns had ceased to exist.

The destruction of Dinant marked the full maturity of Charles
the Bold, who spent the remaining twelve years of his life in a
frenzy of violence, eventually destroying his patrimony and inadvertently reshaping Western Europe. The rebuilt town of Dinant
prefers to dwell on being the birthplace of the inventor of the saxo-
phone rather promote its connection with Charles the Bold. One
curious survival is the local industry that makes and sells the *couque*,
a kind of very hard biscuit made from flour and honey, apparently
invented during Charles's siege from the only ingredients left to the
inhabitants. Or in another version the flour and honey were found
burned together after the conflagration, accidentally making the
delicious *couques* on which the few surviving inhabitants gratefully
survived. Or in another, medieval besiegers were repelled by having
couques thrown at them. As with so much food history, there is a
strong smell of Victorian tourist-industry humbug about these grim
comestibles. They seem useless except perhaps as body armour. The
local way is to snap a bit off and then dump it in your coffee for an

hour or so, or leave one in your mouth until at last it starts to buckle. Mistakenly deciding to buy one, I stood in the queue behind a local couple who were themselves joking about how *couques* were carved from wood. The *couque*-seller's blank expression implied a martyred resignation to hearing such facetiousness at regular intervals. The biscuits are baked in moulds so you have pictures of Dinant on them, baby deer, sheaves of wheat – I settled on one of a sailor-suited boy hugging a dog which, when I got it home, turned out to look more frightening than funny.

Dinant is a curious, pretty town with a grim history – in both world wars it became a momentary focus for attention in ways familiar to Charles the Bold. The Meuse is a river large enough to look like an impressive obstacle on French military maps, but narrow enough to look entirely doable on German military maps. This gloomy fact kept coming back to me as I walked along the river bank from Dinant. A freakish limestone outcrop almost blocks off Dinant from the south, with cars squeezing through a narrow gap. This landscape seemed oddly familiar. This is probably well known to art historians, but I realized quite by accident that this is the biblical landscape visible in the Dinant-born Joachim Patinir's extraordinary painting from about 1520 of Sodom and Gomorrah. Angels usher Lot and his daughters through the limestone cleft, en route to their peculiar drunken sex party. Behind them, a tiny dash of white indicates Lot's wife turned into a pillar of salt, one of the Bible's most cruel and strange moments. The rest of the picture is just flames – a horrible orange reflected in the river, rows of silhouetted burning windmills and even the hills in the far background glowing with heat. Almost all Patinir's surviving paintings have something uncanny about them, but this picture, which reflects the burning Dinant in 1466 and anticipates the burning Dinant in 1914, just seems worse and worse.

The bold and the Swiss

There is a notorious region of Mexico which is rife with quicksand. These terrible dry bogs come and go depending on weather and temperature and can open up at your feet at any time. Apparently quicksand is so awful because it is the way that you instinctively flounder in it that creates the vacuum which drags you under. The only way to survive is to stay quite still and treat it like water: you naturally float in it and can move towards the edge by doing a *very* slow and shallow breast stroke. The problem is that almost nobody has the courage to start to swim – most Mexicans victims know the importance of staying still, but having created that equilib-rium simply cannot bring themselves to take an action which, if misjudged, would, with the slightest flicker of panic, drag them down to an appalling death. As a result the surface of this grim, flat region is dotted with the skulls of unfortunates who ended their lives in a state of total stasis, the skulls still topped by sun-bleached sombreros.

No, well, I don't believe it either. *But* I was told this story so many years ago that I no longer remember who to blame. And it has always struck me as an extremely good historical metaphor. Whenever we are looking at events from the past so many instances come up of actions which to us seem merely a mad lunge, but the alternative would be a form of stasis which simply has no place in human history. There is something about leadership and about the relations of nations that impels action, sometimes harmless, some-times catastrophic. There are almost no instances of a positive immobilism by any ruler. This book is scattered with figures who instead of carefully following coherent policies end up floundering and being destroyed. There is clearly some deep human require-ment *not* to end up as a floating skull in a sombrero.

The late fifteenth century is a particularly fruitful period for seemingly pointless military activism. It is such a relief to get to the sixteenth century, when grand-scale realpolitik, social discord and religious hatreds clear the air – at last people are being killed for a purpose. By contrast it is difficult not to feel that earlier wars are sometimes simply too frivolous to invite analysis. A fine example is provided by the tiny, painfully awkward King of France Charles VIII, who ruled in the 1480s and 1490s. He seems to have been universally disliked, with something about his manner that failed to appear kingly or plausible. On a whim he decided to invade Italy, to make himself King of Naples. Putting together a huge, technologically sophisticated army he proceeded to hammer his way down the peninsula, destroying a sequence of great Renaissance towns with his new artillery, wrecking one of the most prosperous and impressive areas of Europe and initiating a new, horrible era in Italian history that went on for generations.

Having spent a few weeks in Naples, Charles then fought his way back up to France, seemingly not having thought through that Naples' southern location meant that he was entirely reliant on the continuing goodwill, which was not forthcoming, of the towns he had smashed or threatened on the way down. In a further entirely arbitrary twist, back in France, aged only twenty-seven, he smacked his head on a lintel and died. Given how small he was, this suggests that a secret cabal of courtiers had, while he was in Italy, working with fanatical yet discreet carpenters, carefully lowered the height of all the palace doors in the hope this might happen. Or, more plausibly, someone helped his head connect with the lintel. In any event it is impossible to read about Charles VIII and not be amazed by the sheer pointlessness of it all – all those thousands of deaths. Two side effects were that both Parmesan cheese and syphilis were spread across Europe by Charles's returning veterans and in addition the dazzling culture of the Renaissance was squarely implanted in France, inaugurating a new era. But a counter-argument to the last point might be that a similar, but less *Triumph-of-Death* effect could have been achieved by just sending a polite letter to Leonardo da Vinci asking for a few tips.

The other giant instance of the era's military futility springs from the generation before, with the careering shambles of Charles the Bold. In English he is called 'the Bold' just as his great-grandfather was called Philip the Bold. But in French they are different words – 'Téméraire' for Charles and 'Hardi' for Philip, the former with a reckless, dashing edge and the latter with a sense of boldness allied to strategic vision. In his nearly ten years as Duke of Burgundy Charles frittered his inheritance on incoherent and poorly thought-through warmongering. In Lotharingian terms you can see him stepping over a number of boundaries. He unknowingly walked into the infra-red alarm system that separated his territories' French and French-Fleming systems from the squarely German world that lay to its east. What he saw as a rounding off or filling in of his inheritance (which was, as a quick glance at a map would show, a crazy-paving of bits) was seen by others as a mortal threat. Rhinelanders, Swiss and Lorrainers all had reasons to want him dead.

Charles never gave any evidence of being aware of the vast scale of forces accumulating against him. He sneered at the Swiss as mere 'bestial people' and saw all his enemies as just a sequence of military roadblocks to be readily cleared. He also seems to have imagined that he had a best friend in the convulsively tortuous French King Louis XI – little Charles VIII's father – who in practice dreamt of little else except his destruction. The seeming inertia of the long-serving Emperor Frederick III also masked his determination to destroy Charles. At the long, futile Burgundian Siege of the Rhineland fortress of Neuss, Charles discussed with Frederick the possibility of marrying his only child, Mary of Burgundy, to Frederick's eldest son, Maximilian. This conversation, which appeared to strengthen Charles and which also involved Frederick taking seriously Charles's plan to be made King of Burgundy, in the end transferred almost everything that Charles and his ancestors had worked for into the Habsburg pocket.

It is hard to exaggerate the mayhem Charles initiated. During the Siege of Neuss, other Rhineland cities understandably began to panic. We have remarkable detail about Strasbourg's actions in the winter of 1475. Worrying that when Charles had finished with Neuss, he would come for Strasbourg, that city's authorities destroyed five monastery complexes and six hundred and twenty houses to create a belt of empty, defendable ground outside the walls, diverted the course of the Rhine to ring the city and bought enough corn to feed the inhabitants for ten years and three years' worth of salt and wine. There cannot have been a mercenary in the whole of the Western world who wasn't cheerily cleaning his cross-bow, selling himself to the highest bidder and thinking about settling down after the current business was over. Worried rumours reached Bern that Charles planned to kill everyone in the entire city and reduce it to meadowland, with a stone plaque saying, 'Here once there was a town called Bern.'

The ins and outs of Charles the Bold's campaigns are enjoyable, but they are in the end just the actions of Aesop's frog puffing himself up until he explodes. He seemed quite oblivious to Louis's implacable campaign to reunite the bits of France alienated during past humiliations, to the recovery under the Habsburgs of the Holy Roman Empire and to Swiss alarm in the face of his encroach-ments in the far south of Germany. Charles went from being within an inch of becoming King of Burgundy in 1473 to being a naked corpse in the snow, gnawed at by wild animals, at the begin-ning of 1477.

The much rebuilt Grandson Castle in the far west of Switzer-land (just opposite a restaurant offering 'medieval specialities') was where implacable forces began to press in on Charles. The castle itself is a treat – not just featuring a studded and iron-barred toilet door and a comically perfunctory fake torture chamber, but also an eighteenth-century statue of Baby Jesus made from painted lime-wood that at some point has had an apple nailed to its head to convert it into William Tell's brave little son Walter. The Swiss castle garrison surrendered to Charles but were then massacred in grotesque ways in the same manner as Dinant earlier in the hope that this would terrify the Swiss into submission. Instead the out-rage became a defining feature of Swiss nationalism.

Three huge blows now destroyed Charles's army, all thanks to the formidable 'Great League of Upper Germany'. His wealth and reputation and the resources of his many lands made him formidable but at battles outside Grandson (the Swiss urged on by the blaring horns of the men of Uri), by the lake at Murten and outside Nancy, all these were whittled away. Murten was just a slaughter and

Charles's army was never the same. Immense piles of booty filled Swiss dairy towns with jewels, gold and tapestries. As the Dukes did not have a real capital they were obliged to carry much of their most glamorous stuff with them, which presupposed they would not have to flee a battlefield. The silk battle flags have long rotted away but used to be the pride of Bern Cathedral. Basle still has some of its 'Burgundy Booty' – indeed its great city museum's origins lie in its display – such as two huge cannon made in Mechelen and Mons, and a jerkin reinforced with pieces of steel to deflect dagger blows once owned by Charles. This last is the most extraordinary object – a rare piece of clothing surviving for over half a millennium to mock the bad fortune of its one-time wearer. Lucerne once had a special room of which a drawing survives from 1513 with a tantalizing glimpse of robes, a portable altar, a sword, a glamorous chair, some banners, a goblet. Much of what was grabbed simply disappeared into the pockets of nimble-fingered pikemen. Charles's great yellow diamond called 'The Florentine'* was passed down the centuries from hand to hand across Europe, handled by popes, dukes and Habsburgs, vanishing for ever after the First World War.

Having lost much of his artillery, much of his prestige and many of his best men, Charles tried to stop up yet another hole in his collapsing patrimony by besieging Nancy, from which his men had been expelled by forces loyal to the Duke of Lorraine from whom he had taken it. The conditions were horrific, with snow 'half a lance deep', and some four hundred Burgundians frozen to death just on Christmas Eve. One miffed knight said that someone should use a bombard to fire Charles himself over the walls of Nancy, and with a dash of the debonair charm that won him so many friends, Charles had the knight hanged. Lorraine was the territory Charles needed to join together what he and his predecessors had called 'our lands round here' (the north) and 'our lands over there' (the

---

* This diamond was an early example of a revolution begun by the Jewish diamond-cutter Lodewyk van Berken in Antwerp, inventor of the scaif, a machine that transformed the beauty and complexity of diamonds, and of the 'pendeloque' cut. Antwerp remains central to the diamond industry.

south). In a driving snowstorm a joint Lorrainer–Swiss relief force destroyed Charles's army and killed Charles.

There is a highly unhistorical but richly enjoyable painting of the battle by the young Eugène Delacroix in the Museum of Fine Arts in Nancy. It was commissioned by Charles X in 1828 shortly before his own regime collapsed, although – being an old stager on revolutionary matters – he knew, unlike the earlier Charles, how to flee. This spectacular panorama takes full advantage of battle conditions to show a sort of sandwich of yellow-white clouds above and dirty white snow below with the filling provided by a mass of struggling men and a despairing, wild-eyed Charles the Bold staring up at the swaggering, brilliantly armoured young Duke of Lorraine preparing to destroy the dynasty.

During the night soldiers fleeing from the battle reached Metz and, standing on the frozen moat, pleaded with the city watch to let them in. When they explained what had happened the watch simply refused to believe them and thought they were vagabonds trying to trick them into giving them somewhere to sleep for the night. When at last the gates were opened many of the survivors died of frostbite, shock and exposure in the Metz hospitals over the next day or two. The news gradually spread across Europe that Europe's most powerful, haughty and glamorous ruler was dead and that a nineteen-year-old girl was the new ruler of Burgundy.

CHAPTER FIVE

The great inheritance

It is striking how much of France's history is *not* involved with its sea coasts. During various points in the Hundred Years War, France had hardly any access to the Atlantic, with every harbour in English, Breton or Burgundian hands. It was only in the sixteenth century that the great port of Le Havre was founded and it was reckoned that Louis XIV in his entire, interminable reign only ever actually saw the sea himself on three occasions, all his bewigged adventures being played out in purely inland locations. A general theory could be proposed that the sea coasts were simply not vital organs of the French state and that it was a naturally inland power. In the centuries-long struggles between France and England, England won the immediate issue of the security of the English Channel because it was life-and-death for that country, whereas for France the Channel was always something of an optional extra. A matching general theory would be that English armies whenever they were marching inland through France always suffered from a lack of belief back in London and felt less and less convinced by their role with every step they took. Temporary triumphs always seemed to end in a fiasco for the English, even if it might take a few years for the French state to rally itself to throw them out. The two periods of most thrilling possibility, after Crécy and after Agincourt, proved in the end equally ephemeral. Indeed, one of the reasons Agincourt still has such resonance in the memory of the English was that so many years went by with no comparable victory (nearly three centuries, with the Battle of Blenheim). For the English armies there always seems to be another round of rousing speeches and cheers at Calais followed a few months later by everyone dying of starvation, plague or wounds.

In the later fifteenth century a period of extraordinary fluidity and action was played out in the French, Flemish and English Channel ports. Rather like Shakespeare's three *Henry VI* plays there is simply too much of a crush of people rushing on and off stage in a blur of wimples, tabards and plate armour for it to be particularly involving. One of the reasons that Philippe de Commynes' memoirs are so entertaining is that he looks back on his lifetime and shrugs his shoulders in disbelief – the hand of God seems by miles the best answer to every outcome, as one year's proud horseman becomes next year's trampled corpse. Calais is particularly busy ('Say, shipmate, bain't that Margaret of Anjou again?') with a version of the Wars of the Roses which is rather like being confined backstage as everyone jostles and gets ready for their turn in the main story. At one point a nerve-racked Edward IV landed in Calais with his younger brother (the future Richard III) with no cash or further prospects and was forced to pay the ship's captain with his fur-lined coat before heading off to shiver in The Hague as Charles the Bold's indigent guest ('never such a beggarly company', Commynes sniffs). But then Charles packed Edward off to Zeeland, hired him an Easterling escort fleet and he headed back to England and triumphed.

The greatest drama lay entirely in the mind of Louis XI. This extraordinary man, encircled by belligerent opportunists on every side, ended up dishing them all. He is not a figure who has any resonance in the English-speaking world, but is much relished in France as a figure of succulent pantomime horror. In Paris the incomparable waxworks at the Musée Grévin enshrine this very beautifully – with one of its oldest tableaux showing a macabre Louis XI in his tights and furs mocking the despairing Cardinal de la Balue in the hideous crate-like iron cage where he was confined for eleven years. This scene is apparently a little bit untrue, but it has filled generations of Parisian schoolchildren with the right general idea about Louis. More broadly these waxworks have given my own family permanent happiness with photos we have had on a wall for many years of our young sons in cafe conversation with a wax Jean-Paul Sartre and an even waxier Bernard-Henri Lévy.

Louis had an extraordinary ability to frighten people, but also to know when simply to wait – for years if necessary. Each concession he made, surrendering the Somme towns and Amiens to Charles the Bold for example, he viewed as a temporary expedient. His greatest asset was to stay alive, steering France for twenty-two years until its situation was completely transformed. He was someone who loved special prison cages, but also misdirection, secret letters, dropped hints, embassies with false instructions. Commynes was intimate with him and was astounded above all by the sheer, needless complexity of his master's proliferating schemes.

One of Louis's key enemies was his own younger brother, Charles. He was the heir to the throne and in various twists and turns gained tremendous territories, becoming Duke of Berry, Guyenne and Normandy. In conjunction with the Burgundians and Bretons he thought he was running rings around Louis, but was not. Chatting with Commynes one day Charles joked about how 'Instead of the one King there is, I would like there to be six', the credo of all those who relished French disunity. Charles lost his role as heir in 1470 when Louis had a son (the future Charles VIII) and then died in 1472, probably of venereal disease, aged twenty-five, and his three duchies reverted to Louis. The uneasy but real alliance between Edward IV of England and Charles the Bold resulted in 1475 in an enormous English army arriving at Calais, planning to crush Louis for good. This was the result of Edward's rather drunk/ tearful, we're-putting-together-the-old-band wish to reignite the *Henry V* St Crispin's Day magic. It all ended in shameful farce as Louis, instead of obligingly marching out to battle as part of an Agincourt Re-enactment Society, simply offered Edward and his key entourage a huge sum of money to go away. The negotiations outside Amiens were carried out between Edward and Louis on a fun-sounding specially built bridge, with the two halves separated by a lattice (and without a little door of the kind that had resulted in John the Fearless being hacked to death under similar circumstances – everyone was very alert to that story). Charles the Bold had misunderstood the situation and remained distant from Edward's army, never imagining such a treacherous deal could be done. Edward demanded to be made the next King of France ('as usual' says Commynes), but then settled for cash. The busy sailors of the Calais squadron must have allowed themselves some small expressions of irritation as the low-self-esteem but very rich army commanders slunk back on board.

Already at this point Louis had transformed his situation. Having outlived his sullen brother and paid off Edward IV, only Charles the Bold was left. The curious question is whether, if Charles had stopped at some point, he could really have stabilized his lands and in effect recreated Lotharingia. Very briefly there *is* a huge arc, from the reacquired Somme towns all the way round to the Swiss borders. He buys from old Arnold of Egmont the lands which are now the Dutch province of Gelderland (the Duchy of Guelders, the County of Zutphen and the area known as the Veluwe – 'the Wasteland'); he has under his thumb the ecclesiastical lands of Liège and Utrecht (the latter what are now the provinces of Utrecht and Overijssel, plus the then submerged Flevoland); he invades Lorraine and Bar and already has a mortgage from a cash-strapped Habsburg on the medley of lands around the Upper Rhine based around the Sundgau (the 'southern county' – now southern Alsace).

As news of Charles's death at the Battle of Nancy reached Louis he could not really believe his luck. The entire vast inheritance swam before his eyes. Charles's nineteen-year-old sole heir Mary 'the Rich' (as she was now known) stood to get everything. Both Louis and the Emperor had sons who could marry the heiress. Mary herself seems to have been a tough, icy character, ably backed up by her stepmother Margaret of York (Edward IV's sister). (This is just in brackets, but one of the countless wonders of the Aachen Treasury is Margaret of York's crown, a staggeringly beautiful and haughty object, which she wore in Bruges at her wedding celebrations. It is particularly striking because all other English crowns had their jewels plucked out and were then melted down during the English Civil War.) In the blizzard of rumours, messages, threats and horrors that followed Charles's death, Margaret took the key decisions. Louis's formidable messenger system meant that he knew

Charles was dead on 10 January, whereas Margaret and Mary in Ghent were still hoping he might be alive a fortnight later.

The feudal consequences of Charles's death were crucial. Louis XI immediately declared that all the French lands that had been under the control of the Dukes of Burgundy were now returning to his direct control: Picardy, Artois, Flanders and the Duchy of Burgundy itself. Leading his own army he massacred garrisons to frighten others into surrender and bribed local leaders to betray their trust. In a few heady months town after town, from the line of the Somme to Boulogne, was in French hands: Amiens, Arras, Béthune, Lens, the palace of Hesdin, with its chirpy water-squirting devices. French troops invaded the Duchy of Burgundy, ending over a century of alienation and adding it to Guyenne, Berry and Normandy as another huge region in Louis's collection. Every possible alarm bell went off in London as the French looked as though they might engulf Flanders too – but Louis played off Edward IV brilliantly with vague, value-free promises and further bags of money.

The downside to all this violence, as Louis himself later admitted to Commynes, was that it proved less than ideal as a means of wooing little Mary. Margaret of York's brother the Duke of Clarence put himself forward as a suitor and Emperor Frederick III dusted down his earlier discussions with Charles during the Siege of Neuss. Margaret knew that Clarence, her brother-in-law, was a useless character so he was crossed off (he went on to future fame, a few months later, for his murder in a butt of malmsey). Louis also had to deal with the powerful response to his rampages from the elites in the northern Burgundian territories who saw their privileges under sudden and acute threat from the French. In emotional and drastic scenes on 11 February, Margaret and Mary finished negotiating in Ghent the 'Great Privilege', a document that crossed out much of Charles's more oppressive legislation and created a new basis for Mary's rule over Flanders, Brabant and the rest. One clause stated that Dutch would now be used exclusively for the government of the Dutch-speaking provinces, an issue already old and bad-tempered then, but which continues to dog us today. Margaret was appalled by Louis's invasion of the duchy – but in any event Louis's

wish to get Mary and marry her to his own heir Charles was hob-
bled by Charles only being seven years old and Mary nineteen.
Under normal circumstances his age would be a standard bit of royal
grotesquery, but this was an emergency with almost no precedent
and chaos breaking out everywhere: the Duchy of Guelders declared
its independence; French troops moved into the Franche-Comté, an
Imperial territory which was nothing to do with France. A grown-
up man was needed for the job with a lot of resources, not the
strange little dauphin. Frederick III's son Maximilian was only
slightly younger than Mary, and therefore they could quickly have
children at a dynastically very attenuated moment. Maximilian and
Mary were married in Ghent in August, the Habsburgs scooped the
pool and a new era began.

Commynes, writing some twenty years later, looked back on
this whole time with incredulity and dismay. For four reigns the
dukes had extended and managed their domains – and created a
prosperity and security which now seemed like a distant dream. All
this destruction and misery had happened, Commynes said, referring to the tiny dispute which first caused Charles to turn his
attention to the far south of his lands, 'on account of a wagon of
sheepskins which the lord of Romont took from a Swiss, who was
passing through his territory.'

Mary the Rich and the future of the world

The Church of Our Lady in Bruges is in the middle of a complicated
makeover at the moment and is a mass of wires, plastic sheeting,
plywood screens and apologetic signs. Once you battle through to
the choir area, it is poignant to see the church's two most imperious
and distinguished inhabitants – Charles the Bold and Mary the
Rich – lying passively in their tombs and unable even to offer a
mild complaint about all the drills and hammering. Charles used to
unwind in the quiet of the evening before going to bed by having
someone read to him about the great generals of the ancient world
(after Charles's catastrophic defeat at Grandson, his jester called out

to him, riskily, 'My lord, we are well Hannibal'd this time!'). He would certainly not have appreciated this chaos, and even more so he would not have appreciated just how few visitors seem to notice his or his daughter's tombs – everyone photographed Michelangelo's *Madonna* but I didn't see anybody more than glance at the discreetly grand bronze effigies lying on marble coffins, the tombs' sides encrusted with elaborate genealogies.

This was once one of the principal sacred sites in the Low Countries. The two figures are placed side by side to show the transmission belt of legitimacy from the Valois dukes to the Habsburg family. Mary's marriage to Archduke Maximilian shifted the great tangle of Charles's non-French lands across to a family who were not only Holy Roman Emperors but also the great landowners of Central Europe, making the Habsburgs the most powerful figures in European history since the Roman Empire. Their marriage was brief – Mary broke her back in a hunting accident aged only twenty-five, dying only five years after her father's death on the battlefield. It is fair to say that the decisions she took in her short life, in cahoots with her stepmother Margaret of York, directed the history of the world. This was partly negative: if she had married King Louis XI of France, as had been planned, her enormous legacy would have been added to France, making a coherent, readily defended super-state. But by marrying Maximilian she shifted Europe into an era of chaos, with arguments around the future of the Burgundian legacy continuing well into the twentieth century. Of course, the moment you posit a Mary & Louis outcome so many more possible outcomes come into play that it becomes silly to speculate about the events seconds after the betrothal is announced, let alone ten or twenty years later. But it is fair to say that the French now spent three centuries trying to capture the territories to their north: centuries of grinding warfare, bankruptcies, revolution, countless deaths and literally thousands of uninvolving paintings featuring men in wigs on horses, as they battled to get what Louis XI might have had in return for a little civility, a gold ring and a fair-to-middling banquet. I have not been able to find such a quote, but some historically literate officer in the

Revolutionary army, marching *at last* into Amsterdam in 1795, must have surely said something pretty sardonic.

Mary died before most of the Habsburg marriage gambles had come off, but she had nonetheless ensured the future with an efficiency which her father had lacked by having two children: a son and heir, Philip, and a peculiarly impressive and interesting daughter, Margaret, who is discussed later. Mary's father-in-law the Emperor Frederick III at the age of seventy-seven died after she did, disappearing into his strange, marmalade-coloured tomb in Vienna, having bridged in his own person the entire period from the Battle of Agincourt to the discovery of America. Her husband Maximilian had been elected King of the Romans in Frankfurt and crowned in Aachen during Frederick's lifetime specifically to take over most of the running of the Empire from him. In doing so he created a tradition that the Habsburgs followed from now on, ensuring overlapping dynastic stability by having the electoral bit out of the way before the current owner's death, then leaving the Pope's ceremony that made him Emperor until whenever convenient.

I have tried very hard not to make this a book about endless warfare, but the warfare really *is* endless. The disappearance of the Dukes of Burgundy made critical again the line in the north that ran down vertically, splitting the areas which were in practice part of the Empire and those that owed allegiance to France. Brutal fighting between Maximilian and Louis devastated the region north of the Somme. A series of epic sieges and battles wrecked prosperous towns, with each year further reducing the value to the winner of what was left. The awkward complication was that Mary's inheritance went to her son Philip with Maximilian acting only as regent. As someone new to the neighbourhood and with Philip at this point a four-year-old with only sketchy views on enfeoffment, Maximilian had a poor hold on the local nobility. He also had to handle a rebellious Ghent (as usual). He also had to deal with the financial problems that dogged him throughout his life: everybody would be lined up in battle order, properly equipped, with attractive matching banners snapping in the crisp wind, and then word would get out that Maximilian had run out of money again – and the troops would start to drift off home or, even worse, start chatting to the other side. It was all so hopeless that, despite spending years working with Dürer and others on his own tremendous mausoleum at Innsbruck, he wound up completely bankrupt three hundred miles further to the east and was buried in Wiener Neustadt, where he remains today with nobody in the following centuries ever coming up with the funds to cart him back to Innsbruck to lie decently inside his greatest artistic legacy.

After many clashes and false starts the Treaty of Senlis was signed in 1493 between the representatives of two unpleasant teenagers, the now close-to-grown-up Philip (known as Philip the Handsome) and Charles VIII of France, both representing the next and not very impressive generation, but both still under the control of regencies at this point. The treaty confirmed Habsburg ownership of the Franche-Comté, Artois (which had for a time fallen under French control) and the little County of Saint-Pol. The Habsburgs also got to keep the County of Charolais, a small area under the now French-controlled Duchy of Burgundy, which had an unenviable future, knocking about under various lords until finally becoming fully integrated into France in 1760. The Somme towns and Boulogne fell to France in the agreement and stayed that way. As usual, whatever agreement might be made about Flanders, the French monarchy always kept the mental reservation that *really* it was part of France – if it was now under Habsburg control, this was only ever like putting a piece of fruit pie in the fridge with the intention of taking it out again later.

Charles VIII would direct his silly energies elsewhere than northern France and Habsburg control was consolidated. Under the Dukes of Burgundy the area had gradually developed its own identity. It was, for example, invaluable that otherwise rival entities such as the County of Holland and the County of Flanders were obliged to cooperate against the threat from France. Holland had become fundamentally different from other Imperial counties, such as Mark or Lippe, or even quite large territories such as the Palatinate, in that, whatever its special privileges and exceptions, it had been forced into a dynastic frame where it simply could not directly antagonize, say,

Brabant. The bickering that made the rest of the Empire so unmanageable was in the new Habsburg lands much more muted. This came from a habit acquired under the Dukes, but also from anxiety. Places such as Holland knew they had to cling to the other Habsburg possessions or risk a French visit. Maximilian also took over key Burgundian institutions, most notably the Order of the Golden Fleece, which bound together aristocrats and allies and which would always be the most prominent decoration – in both processions and portraits – around the necks of the Habsburg Emperors.

Philip the Handsome, like his mother, died young – possibly poisoned. But, also like Mary, he lived long enough to have a powerful impact on Europe's future. In another sensational agglomerative Habsburg marriage he had wed a daughter of Ferdinand and Isabella and, following a series of surprise deaths, found himself as Philip I, King of Spain. He reigned only briefly before his own death, but he and his wife had six children, including future consorts of the French, Portuguese and Scandinavian kings, the Emperor Charles V, the Emperor Ferdinand I and Mary of Hungary. In terms of playing poker this falls outside the realms of the possible – a super-imperial-royal-cheat flush. It meant that Charles V inherited all the Burgundian, Habsburg and Spanish lands – including of course America, the potential of which was beginning to become apparent under Philip. Nobody had ever ruled so widely and on so rickety a set of chances.

New management at Hawk Castle

German historians of the nineteenth century loved to talk about the five 'tribal duchies' or 'stem duchies', the great chunks of land created by the Frankish eastern conquests: Lotharingia, Saxony, Bavaria, Franconia and Swabia. This sort of stuff, with its flavour of winged helmets, rough fellowship, drooping beer-stained moustaches and warriors beating their swords on their shields to acclaim their chief, was enough to have followers of Wagner in ecstasies. In their different ways the ghosts of these five entities have endured to the present, but with only Bavaria maintaining a steady and substantial political shape. Swabia and Lotharingia detonated into fragments with parts of both coalescing into Switzerland.

This original, galactic event happened in Swabia's case in the chaotic winding-up of the intensely tangled House of Hohenstaufen in the 1250s. The resulting interregnum was long remembered as a terrifying disaster, with the entire Empire reduced to a period of anarchic *sauve-qui-peut*. In the far north of the Empire, this provided the opening for William II, Count of Holland, appointed at one point as a widely unacknowledged 'anti-king', to donate to himself the County of Zeeland, with great future implications, and start setting up a suitably posh court in line with his wobbly new status, creating the Binnenhof and the origins of the city of The Hague. This was characteristic of the shambles: all over the Empire violence, betrayal and uncertainty ruled and its memory would be a key element in the relative (only relative) discipline under which the Empire kept itself once re-united under Rudolf I, the first Habsburg family Emperor, in 1273.

During the anarchy Swabia broke into an amazing medley of different micro-states as everyone turned on everyone else, from individual castles to small groups of confederates for mutual defence – the latter of course readily being converted to the purpose of mutual attack. It was in the fallout that one set of small territories banded together – Uri, Schwyz and Unterwalden – and, uniquely, remained together. The earliest elements in what became Switzerland coalesced partly by default: sheltered by the political incoherence of the rest of Swabia, by the underpopulated County of Burgundy (the Franche-Comté) and by the great spooky belt of the Black Forest – then made even more spooky by its being fronted by a much wider and more turbulent Rhine. But they also clung together to deal with a serious threat.

The cooperation between various valley communities was galvanized by the Emperor Rudolf I, who had his family castle in Swabia (the original Habsburg Castle, where the clan's fortunes began) and extensive entangled lands round about. Each of the

Swiss communities had its own special attribute which belied its small size. For example Uri controlled access to the Gotthard Pass, the keys to which it had managed to buy from the cash-strapped last Hohenstaufen Emperor. As discussed earlier, the opening up of Alpine passes was like a magic wand, comparable to Holland's ability to fill in bits of sea to conjure up farmland. The new trade meant that Luzern, most strikingly, within a few years became almost as large as it would be in its crazy touristic heyday in the nineteenth century. It was the fate of the Habsburg family to find itself endlessly at odds with these ornery and self-sufficient people, both as local landowners and as emperors. If time travel were ever invented (which by definition, sadly, it cannot be as otherwise our history books would be filled with random silver-foil-wrapped busybodies handing out bazookas to King Harold's thegns at the Battle of Hastings, etc.) then the first traveller's job might be to nip back to the later Middle Ages and tip off both the Habsburgs and the Dukes of Burgundy about not messing with the Swiss.

Habsburg Castle is still there, now part of the very Swiss canton of Aargau. An attractive foresty walk away from the town of Brugg, the castle frowns down on the valley of the almost synthetically bright blue River Aare shortly before it hits the more conventionally coloured Rhine. I have spent so many years thinking about and writing about the Habsburg family that it seemed a bit bathetic at last getting to the original 'Castle of the Hawk' after which they named themselves. I almost expected special singing, a rainbow and some sort of commemorative goblet. The castle itself was also a bit low-key, with a little drinks terrace and a handful of instructive information boards.

The interaction between the Habsburgs and the people who became known in the end as the Swiss was crucial to shaping both sides, but positive only for the latter. The Habsburgs were entangled with non-Habsburg interests from the east in the Tyrol, in part with the 'safe space' of Lake Konstanz in the way, and from the north through their ownership of the area around Habsburg Castle and the oddly named (only from a Western European perspective) 'Further Austria', which in the fourteenth century included such places as Belfort, various bits of Alsace and Freiburg-im-Breisgau with its associated 'forest towns' in the Black Forest. The Habsburgs could, even before they permanently became the Holy Roman Emperors from 1452, call on all manner of family friends, neighbours and mercenary troops to take on the Swiss.

These efforts invariably resulted in humiliation. The peculiar ability of 'Lotharingian' particularism to humble the mighty was as powerful in the south as it would prove elsewhere. Generations of clanking, bearded generalissimos must have stared at maps and laughed at the ease with which these small areas could be subjugated. Not so! One cliché about the Swiss is to link their particularly harsh form of Protestantism to its associated sense of discipline and single-mindedness – but almost all the heavy damage they inflicted on Europe was done as good, conventional Catholics in the fourteenth and fifteenth centuries. The Swiss use of the halberd – a very long pole with razor-edged hooked and slicing surfaces at its tip – absolutely confounded the flower of chivalry, with expensive knights slaughtered *en brochette*. As with the French being mown down by English archers, it was odd how long it took for the losing side to react to their technological failing. It must have been after a while quite boring for both sides as yet another Swabian count dolled himself up in steel plates, prettily coloured heraldic festoons, various things made of leather and my lady's favour tied to his sleeve. Trained in sword-play and the handling of a war-charger since childhood, the count galloped towards the Swiss front line. Meanwhile, some Appenzeller rustic finished his delicious cheese sandwich, spat on his hands, gripped his halberd and awaited his inevitable victory. Ultimately the Habsburgs pretty much ran out of motivated Swabian knights and both sides would instead field great mobs of these halberdiers who would engage in horrifying shoving matches, with the first side to falter suddenly run through at random angles. Almost inevitably, a gaggle of mercenaries and feudal levies versus soldier-citizens defending their families and farms tended to result in the former losing motivation first and getting kebabed.

All these Habsburg invasions simply bounced off. There were

always plenty of minor rebellions dealt with successfully elsewhere in the Empire and throughout the whole sequence of conflicts there was incredulity at this specifically Swiss form of resistance and its solidity of purpose. In 1315 Leopold I, Duke of Austria, came galloping in and had his army devastated and then butchered at the Battle of Morgarten. In 1386 it was the turn of Leopold III, Duke of Austria, who brought with him a specialized detachment of scythe-troops to destroy the harvests as they headed south from Brugg. The Swiss killed him, together with a rich selection of local noblemen and most of his troops (including presumably the ones awkwardly carrying only grass-cutting equipment) at the Battle of Sempach. In 1415 the Aargau, including Habsburg Castle, fell to Swiss control, never to be returned. In 1460 the Swiss seized from the Habsburg the Thurgau – the area east of Zürich – leaving the city of Konstanz as the enclave it has remained ever since and giving the Swiss attractive lakefront views. Having in 1477 destroyed Charles the Bold and therefore transformed the entire story of Europe – ironically, elsewhere at least, in the Habsburgs' favour – the Swiss then in 1499 spent an enjoyable six months massacring all the troops that the Habsburg Maximilian I could send their way. After the cataclysmic Battle of Dornach, where even Maximilian's commander was killed, the Habsburgs essentially decided to pretend the Swiss were not there. They acknowledged that that these truculent Swabians were no longer part of the Holy Roman Empire, but only in the sense of their being in a not-to-be-brought-up-in-conversation, haven't-heard-from-them-in-a-while limbo. As a final and crucial element in the northern Swiss story Basle and Schaffhausen also jumped ship after Dornach, taking advantage of Maximilian's exhausted demoralization.

One consistent advantage the Swiss had (and which would later be shared by the Dutch) was that while they were undoubtedly important to the Habsburgs, they tended to be less important than other family concerns. When they became the Empire's serious retributory focus they could defeat the invaders – but often they could rely on Imperial financial exhaustion or the Empire having battles to fight elsewhere. Figures such as Leopold III's son,

Frederick IV 'of the Empty Pockets', were swamped by such a sea of troubles in the 1410s that it was only one humiliation among many when he too lost various bits and bobs to the Swiss. Each one of these blows though was like a lesson in civics for the Swiss themselves – despite moments of murderous disagreement, once their initial alliance had held, it made sense to extend it, with each member aware of its wider responsibility. Oddly it became a tiny version of the Habsburg Empire itself, with micro-acrimonies about which canton should rule over which field, rural areas subject to ruthlessly extractive urban oligarchies and bad blood that could endure for centuries. But what ultimately became known as Switzerland was a fascinating experiment in non-noble, non-royal existence and hung a durable question mark over the management of other European political entities. It also created a thick black line under southern Germany which was not to be crossed. The agreements of 1499 turned out to make this permanent. The following century would present the same agonies and opportunities to another tangle of cities, counties and Church properties at the drastically less mountainous and more watery far northern end of Lotharingia.

'Beware, beware, God sees!'

One of the smaller events of the malevolent year of 1567 was the hunt by special agents of the Duke of Alva for Hieronymus Bosch's *The Garden of Earthly Delights*. Owned and probably commissioned by the Counts of Nassau, it had been removed from the palace at Brussels and concealed from the Spanish invaders. The agents captured the palace's head of household and tortured him nearly to death. Alva himself owned a tapestry version of the picture (the equivalent of a smudged photocopy) and there was clearly something about it that drove people mad. The torture must have worked as the following year the great triptych was on its way to Madrid, where it has been ever since.

Bosch's paintings have always provoked strong feelings. I am probably writing this book because of the accident of working in a bookshop when I was sixteen with a copy of a lavish edition of Bosch's complete works and his imitators near the till. My interest in the Habsburgs came from an amazed first visit to Vienna – but while I would like to claim it was provoked by enthusiasm for Musil and Mahler, what really drove me along was knowing that Bosch's *The Last Judgement* was there, and, not far behind, Brueghel's *Tower of Babel*. It was not until two years ago that I at last made the pilgrimage to 's-Hertogenbosch, and felt almost nervous doing so. My mind has been cluttered for so long with minor details from Bosch's work that I felt his home town must in some way have the same bright, pinnacle-filled and entangling atmosphere – and was worried that it might instead foreground things like traffic lights and kebab shops. After the initial shock (traffic lights and kebab shops) it seemed just right – in other words a real place with a fascinating history. A lot of its old military defences are still standing and a spectacular set of water meadows give a view unchanged since the seventeenth century: it can be seen in a painting of the 1629 siege, which led to 's-Hertogenbosch now being part of the Netherlands rather than Belgium. But as usual with artists, they just *happen* to live somewhere – and their private vision of the world does not mean that in some weird way it would end up tinting or shaping the place itself.

Hieronymus Bosch's real name was Jheronimus von Aken but he gave as his signature a slightly classicized version of his first name and then an abbreviated version of his town's name (still used today: Den Bosch). He could be further anglicized and called Jerry Wood, although in practice that would be silly. The name 's-Hertogenbosch simply means 'The Duke's Woods' and is from its founder, the vigorous and erratic crusader Henry I, Duke of Brabant and Lower Lotharingia, who in the early thirteenth century founded a number of towns to extend and consolidate his dominions.

Bosch died in 1516, only a couple of years before the Emperor Maximilian, in a world filled with communication, bureaucracy, letter-writing, diaries, and yet very little is known about him. He must always have appeared remarkable, but equally he was once surrounded by all kinds of exceptional artists in other media. At the time his pictures were simply one expression of an all-consuming agony about the fall of mankind shown equally in personal prayer, song, processions, sermons, charitable work, the building, mainten-ance and beautifying of churches, prayer circles for family or friends, the mass itself. A woman who decided to live the rest of her life in a community of beguines, helping the sick and reading the Bible, was a living, human equivalent of the canvas, wood and oil paint of Bosch's *The Hay Wain* – but working in a medium that has left no physical trace. Bosch's paintings were not designed to create an aesthetic reaction, but to drive you down onto your knees, to think about your fate in a fallen world.

A lot depends on whether or not Bosch had a sense of humour – were his visions of Hell and its torments supposed to be entertaining or serious? For myself, I realized with a certain amount of self-congratulation, that having reached my fifties I had finally lost interest in the more lip-smacking, heavy-metal elements in Bosch. A naked glutton having his mouth filled from a barrel of ghoul's diar-rhoea *for ever* is undoubtedly a striking image, but Bosch's lasting greatness is not as an inventor of grotesques, but as a painter of the uncannily beautiful – as a visual equivalent to Milton. Just his birds: how could he invent so many little birds, or bird-like creatures? And his plants: where on earth does the egg-like spiked plant come from in *St John in the Wilderness* which so helpfully dispenses both locusts and wild honey? And his visions of Heaven: as a sort of light-filled cone, or as a place from which Lucifer's rebels are expelled, turning into great insects as they fall? He also invented the best ever trum-peting angels, almost invisibly floating above the mayhem of *The Last Judgement*. It is these happy creations that somehow balance entertainment *and* seriousness – hundreds of small details which are almost needlessly bravura but which successfully make the taken-for-granted sensational again. He must almost certainly win the Best Garden of Eden competition too, against some tough local competition.

The one clue to Bosch provided by 's-Hertogenbosch itself is the sprawling, weird and much patched-up St John's Cathedral. The ancient church was being demolished and rebuilt during Bosch's lifetime and the result is a fabulous labyrinth of Gothic oddities. It still dominates the town, but when built it must have lorded it over all human endeavour. This was the whole effort and focus of the town's people: to create a building so big, grand and expensive, so economically debilitating, that no supernatural authority could mis-understand the town's commitment to redemption. As Bosch inscribes on his painting *The Seven Deadly Sins and the Four Last Things*: 'Beware, beware, God sees.' This little phrase would take on a quite different meaning after the Reformation – Luther would send his famous letter containing the *Ninety-five Theses* to the Archbishop of Mainz in 1517, a bit over a year after Bosch's death. Very soon, for the most rigorous reformers, what God saw in the image-and-incense-filled cathedrals was mere magniloquence and grotesque human pride. Rather than investing in a gigantic, tangled *Gesamt-kunstwerk* like St John's, the role of a church building would in the future, at its most radical, be simply to act as 'a rain shelter'. An entire sensibility would soon be under siege.

But during the actual St John's rebuilding this would have been a surreally remote philosophy. Maximilian I held a meeting of the Order of the Golden Fleece there, for which a painted shield sur-vives for Edward IV of England, who sadly did not attend – but on which the calligraphy matches that on Bosch's *The Stone Operation*, which makes clear that there was at least in this instance collabor-ation between Bosch and the shield's painter, Pierre Coustain. Bosch designed floats for the town's Lenten parade which, it must be safe to assume, would have been totally fantastic and perhaps the best floats ever made, but which are completely unrecorded. Particu-larly tantalizing are the cathedral's most famous feature, the dozens of statues of sinners on the roof, clambering upwards in pursuit of Heaven. In an inspired decision, when these much corroded figures were replaced during restoration work by new stone copies, they were put in a small museum next to the cathedral. We can never know whether or not Bosch was involved with these statues – I like to think that Bosch and his anonymous sculptor vied with one other for rival compelling mutant effects in their different media. As with the Charlemagne sculpture in Zürich, there can be few more atmospheric objects than statues designed for high places but now brought down after centuries of erosion and smoke, to be seen close up. The museum is packed with oddities: a 'backwards-tilting man', convulsed in agony with his back arched and his head staring up, mockingly dressed in elegant shoes and a slashed jerkin. There is a winged dragon with a second monster on its back, a unicorn killing a dragon, a monster with large ears scratching itself, a monk creeping on his knees, a devil with a book, a bear with a beehive, a woman chained up by a Wildman, a howling dog, a violin player. And just when you realize that fifteenth-century northern sculpture was just as great as its painting, the museum throws in an ancient statue of Godefroy of Bouillon and a thirteenth-century cow's jaw used as an ice skate – the last one of these giving a permanent moment of enlightenment: you suddenly notice in innumerable Netherlandish ice and snow paintings that indeed the skaters have jaws strapped to their feet.

The museum made me feel as though I was backstage at some chaotically maintained theatre, heaped with discarded props for productions long forgotten and poorly advised about the use of lightweight materials. One of the many oddities of the clambering statues in their proper place on the roof is that they are really very hard to see. Particularly in a world before the telescope their impact is remote. But this is where the past becomes really confusing: the statues were purely religious objects and it was the process of making them and paying for them that was central to their point – indeed large parts of any cathedral have always been invisible, but for the guildsmen working on each pinnacle or choir-stall detail it was the work itself that created the virtue. Bosch would have felt the same about his paintings: the act of making them was a religious one and his unfettered inventiveness a gift from God. Some of the paintings were for public display in churches (although these were often only revealed on specific feast days) but others were for private prayer. Access to *The Garden of Earthly Delights* was only for a handful of friends and guests of the Counts of Nassau. This was a world of rarity and an aesthetic almost wholly alien to our own.

The rarity has been much increased by the passage of five often very rough centuries. There are tantalizing glimpses of lost Bosch paintings. A large and elaborate *Christ Carrying the Cross* was in a church in Ghent and we know it from a drawing made in 1556 by an artist who 'converted' Bosch's figures into a much more fluid, Renaissance style. Nonetheless, you can tell it must have been an astounding object – some thirty figures in elaborate armour, with flags, trumpets and weird spears. It was almost certainly destroyed by Protestant iconoclasts. This may well have been the case too with the large set of paintings of the *Sixth Day of Creation* he created with his elder brother for St John's Cathedral itself. Can you imagine how wonderful they could have been? These have vanished – as has a large *Last Judgement* commissioned by Philip the Fair, who was in town during a war with Guelders. With Philip was his boon companion Henry III, Count of Nassau and Lord of Breda, and it was either him or his uncle and predecessor as count who commissioned *The Garden of Earthly Delights*. This painting passed on his death to his younger brother William the Silent, leader of the Dutch Revolt. Perversely, much more of Bosch's work would probably have been destroyed if it had not been for the swivel-eyed enthusiasm of the Duke of Alva, whose brutal actions opened this section. So many things remain mysterious. The first art historical reference to the painting is in an inventory of 1593, 'A painting of the world's variety, which they call *The Straw-berry*': so even its usual title is a later fabrication and a piece of misdirection.

I imagine that intermittently I will (in common with many others) spend the rest of my life mulling over these mysterious and very beautiful pictures. I have only just noticed how in *The Vaga-bond* there is on a distant hill a brightly coloured crowd gathered around a gallows – but the gallows are to scale at least a couple of hundred feet high and could only be built to hang a giant or a whale. What is going on? We shall never know.

Uses for paper

Just south of Basle there is a wonderfully engaging paper mill, powered by a mossy, thunderous waterwheel. Inside, you can easily
follow the different rotating shafts linked to the wheel as they lift
and drop the hammers which pound the rags into paper: perhaps the
only example of a technical process I have been able to fully understand. Seeing how paper in its liquid form is so closely akin to
pancake batter brought together two of my lifelong priorities in a
way that was uniquely satisfying. The rest of the mill was devoted to
instructive displays about the many uses of paper, but unfortunately
ruined it all with a statement about how Americans and Europeans
use toilet paper in different ways to wipe their bottoms. This may or
may not be true, but I refuse to share the details.

The paper mill is Basle's best shot in the long-running battle
between Mainz, Strasbourg and Basle about who was most important in the invention and diffusion of printing. The details will
always be obscure. It is true that Johannes Gensfleisch, known as
Gutenberg, unhelpfully moved around between Mainz and Strasbourg allowing starchy civic patriots in the nineteenth century to
commission statues for both cities. It is also true that Basle became
an extremely important source of printed books very quickly. But
so did many places. The speed with which printing raced across
Europe from 1440 remains astonishing. In the space of a generation the way in which books were understood was transformed.
From an English point of view, the key figure was William Caxton,
living in Bruges as part of the entourage of Margaret of York. He
seems to have first seen a printing press on a business trip to
Cologne.

Gutenberg's creation was fed by many sources. He was himself a
goldsmith, but the forms of precision needed were common across
many aspects of fifteenth-century life – the fitting of a wagon wheel
(or indeed mill wheel) required precision, albeit on a robust scale; a
suit of armour had many minutely tooled parts. My own hunch, for
which there is no evidence, is that a key spur was the technological
battle across the century for ever more precision in gun-making,

where being fractions of an inch out one way could result in a weapon that squirted burning gasses all over its user or, the other way, made it blow up. Famously, Gutenberg's initial experiments used a wine press, so a key element to the invention already existed.

In everyone's minds there is always a direct line between print-ing and the Reformation: the new technology running rings around the authorities and spreading the Word in forms which simply could not be stopped. The great encounter in April 1521 between the Emperor Charles V and Martin Luther at Worms (in an impos-ing hall next to the cathedral, alas burned down by Louis XIV's troops in 1689) becomes a face-off between hierarchical, medieval Latinate stuffiness and a demotic, modern, populist future; fussy illuminated manuscripts versus cheap, amusing prints showing the Pope being laughed at by devils. This also then becomes the tran-sition between two entire worlds, with everyone wallowing in more than Gothic ignorance on one side and reading attractive novels on the other.

There is no doubt that the future of Europe was indeed played out in the consequence of Charles's decision at Worms to outlaw Luther and that these consequences play out too through Guten-berg's invention and had their most profound impact along the course of the Rhine. But there is much more to what happened than a mere Luther–Pope clash for the future of modernity. We cry out of course for a *Godzilla vs. The Smog Monster* narrative and Protestantism wants this to be true (even as Protestantism itself, of course, shat-tered into pieces), but it never was. In the notionally prelapsarian pre-Worms world Christianity already suffered from severe difficul-ties unrelated to printing presses. Most obviously it was a religion that had always been split. The Western European view (including that of the Pope) was on the whole to pretend that the Eastern Church did not exist, and hum loudly with fingers in ears each time that Constantinople made noises suggesting that Rome was merely its Johnny-come-lately low-comedy offshoot. Much of the elaborate ceremony around the Pope crowning Charlemagne and his succes-sors as Roman Emperor and the elaborate iconography around the Theban Legion martyrs and ancient sites associated with Constantine was to counter the obvious problem that the real Roman Empire had had a continuous existence under a very different management in the East. This had been a key tension during the crusades. Part of these expeditions' failure lay, not just in catastrophes like the crusader sacking of Constantinople in 1204, but in a linked series of fiascos that put an end to the entire realm of eastern Christianity – with Russia disappearing under Mongol rule and the Ottomans engulfing everything to the south, culminating in the final disaster of Constantinople falling in 1453.

While the Pope might have allowed himself a small sherry at this last news, the wider story could only be that Christianity was fading. Both Mongols and Ottomans may have still permitted Christianity, but it was a subjects' faith. In 1529 the Ottomans would try and fail to take Vienna and their failure stabilized the zone of the Pope's domains; but another way of looking at it would be that the Ottomans now ruled a vast area containing many of the key centres of human civilization, from just east of Vienna to the Indian Ocean and Red Sea, whereas if they *were* to successfully fight their way through the Holy Roman Empire there would only be France left before they reached the Atlantic. The dramas of Christian Europe happened in a small space.

This sense of Christianity being penned in, its universalism mocked, was made far worse by the way that there were innumerable forms of heresy even within its heartlands. The Waldensians had survived through countless persecutions, twisting and turning since the twelfth century and suffering a further round of massacres in the late fifteenth century. Most awkwardly, the Kingdom of Bohemia was in the hands of the thoroughly non-papal Hussites, who had successfully fought off several major crusades to get them out.

There was also the degree to which, regardless of Luther, the Pope's authority had been under attack for centuries, at times reducing him to a laughably self-inflated Italian baron. Everyone has their favourite Pope story (it is always worth reading about the Cadaver Synod, obviously) but the Great Schism from 1378, which featured three rival popes, had a ruinous impact on the prestige of the office. This was finally resolved at the Council of Konstanz in

1417, but this did nothing to assuage an elaborate, intellectually powerful view that the Pope should only operate in conjunction with the important men who elected him. Curiously, some of the territories which were most critical of the papacy, particularly the Rhineland, in practice proved most impervious to Luther: in other words, being sceptical of the Pope's special powers was a long, honourable and purely Catholic tradition. The Council of Konstanz was also important because it provided the key, unencouraging precedent for Luther. It was here that Jan Hus came under safe conduct from the Emperor to make the Hussite case, only to end up wearing a paper hat covered in drawings of devils and being burned alive. Hus hung heavily in the air at Worms for both sides – killing him had not ended Hussitism and it had damaged the Emperor's status. But, still, Luther was kind of annoying . . . His being whisked away by his allies, disguised and hidden in a Saxon castle, may well have prevented him from being imprisoned or executed, but it also made him into even more of a European celebrity.

The deepest critiques of Catholicism lay in the lands of the Bishop of Utrecht, a large exclave of territory east of Utrecht itself which since the sixteenth century has been called the Overijssel. Many forms of private devotion were scattered throughout Europe. The great majority of prayers did not involve the structure of a church, but private shrines, pamphlets, images in households, books of hours. There was simply no serious means of regulating any of this activity, with potentially any amount of heresy in just one street of houses. Overijssel turned out to be important as the home of the inward, private world of the Brotherhood of the Common Life and because it was the source of *The Imitation of Christ*, a book attributed to Thomas à Kempis, whose alarmingly scrambled-up bones are now kept in a box in a church in Zwolle together with a charming little painting of him being inspired. One of the most popular books ever written, it is an extraordinarily spiky, strange experience filled with the most crushing direct demands and awkward questions. It is disturbingly self-sufficient and plunges the reader into a world where *The Imitation of Christ* and the Bible are all a poor sinner needs. The Pope's plan to build a glossy new St Peter's Cathedral seems to be happening on a different planet.

The Imitation was a bestseller *in manuscript* – hundreds of copies still survive today. This was, of course, a much smaller circulation than print, but it was also a different habit, with each copy being read by many dozens of individuals before it fell apart. Before Gutenberg there was in other words a very effective, ancient habit of widespread reading, sharing and access. Orthodox Catholics could also embrace à Kempis – it became with the Bible one of the two books always on the desk of Ignatius of Loyola, Superior General of the Jesuits. But it nonetheless was a symptom of a Christianity dangerously (from the Vatican's point of view) unreliant on the Vatican.

I feel I need to make one last, totally unprovable pre-Lutheran and non-Gutenberg assertion, the result of spending two decades wandering the art galleries of the Rhine and Low Countries. There seems to be an absolute explosion of very vivid, high-quality altar paintings from around the 1490s. Fifteenth-century art is often extremely special and high end (van Eyck, van der Weyden) but associated with the court and wealthy donors, whereas now suddenly every small church seems to be getting a picture. They are piled waist-deep in the Frankfurt City Museum, gathered in from countless Hessian villages. Often anonymous, they are works of incredibly direct emotional shock – appalling scenes of the Crown of Thorns being crushed onto Jesus's head (a German speciality as a subject). Even today, to look at them feels like being slapped in the face. They are designed to break the viewer's complacency, a visual version of *The Imitation of Christ*, demanding a direct, unmediated relationship between the emotional extremity of the events painted and the individual looking at them. There is no way of knowing if this is true, of course, but even if printing is set aside, by the time Luther gets to Worms there were already many important ways in which the Church as an institution has been undermined and in which countless Christians felt a direct relationship to the Bible not requiring any more elaborate framework than perhaps a comfy chair. The 'Protest' as it was refined by Luther's followers was meant to provoke the total overhaul of Christianity. This failed: the Protest itself split incoherently and, in a totally unanticipated move, Catholicism itself successfully reformed, broke out of its Western European confines and conquered much of the world. The nature and parameters of that failure would be fought over at the cost of millions of lives for the next hundred and fifty years.

CHAPTER SIX

The New World » Margaret of Austria »
The life and adventures of Charles V » The Oranges »
Rebellion » The Catholic case

Der Alt man.

The New World

In the summer of 1520 my favourite German of all time, Albrecht Dürer, decided to leave his home town of Nuremberg and spend a year with his wife, Agnes Frey, travelling around the Netherlands. The most famous painter, engraver and designer in northern Europe, Dürer was anxious to meet up with the young Charles of Spain, who was coming to Aachen to be crowned King of the Romans, to ensure – perhaps a bit banally – that his imperial pension still got paid. This worked out and the Emperor Charles V's written order to Nuremberg town council to pay Dürer one hundred Rhenish florins a year still exists.

I cannot remember a time when I have not worshipped Dürer – but just through ignorance I had no idea that for the year he stayed in the Rhineland and Netherlands he kept a diary. This extraordinary document seems to have started life as merely a space in which to tally his expenses, and a lot of it is indeed cluttered with the cost of lunch, the payment of tolls and a meticulous record of every tip that he gave. In their way these jottings alone are themselves compelling, conjuring up a whole world of larrikins, vintners, drabs, tapsters and lurky-men in a sneak preview of the scenes of Low Countries drunken chaos which the Brueghels would celebrate a few years later. The expenses themselves sometimes have a strange intimacy. Dürer buys a small human skull in Cologne ('2 white pf.') and in Antwerp he pays a ninety-three-year-old man to sit for him ('3 st.'). The astounding result is his painting of St Jerome, which he sells to a merchant in the Portuguese colony in Antwerp, who sends it back to Lisbon, where it can still be seen today.

Dürer wanders around the Netherlands seeing the most wondrous

new things. He is in the workshop in Antwerp where the triumphal
arch for Charles of Spain's visit to Brussels is being constructed. He
goes to Brussels and watches Raphael's vast tapestries for the Sistine
Chapel being made, presumably using the cartoons which still can
be seen today in the Victoria and Albert Museum in London – the
tapestries themselves being destroyed later in the decade during
the Sack of Rome, one of Charles's biggest cock-ups. He hears a
report that a whale has been washed up on the island of Walcheren and races over to Zeeland for a look, is almost shipwrecked,
but arrives too late as the carcass has been lifted off by the tide. But
now he is on Walcheren he visits the Abbey of the White Canons
in Middelburg and sees Jan Gossaert's triptych – which 'is not
so good in the modelling as in the colour.' We will never know
how perceptive this was as the paintings were destroyed in a fire
four decades later. He goes to the Brussels Town Hall and
admires Rogier van der Weyden's panels of *The Judgement of Trajan*
and *The Judgement of Archimbault* (the latter a made-up ruler of Brabant) – both destroyed in 1695 during the War of the League of
Augsburg.

Not everything is a vanished glory though. Dürer sees Michelangelo's *Madonna and Child* sculpture in the Church of Our Lady in
Bruges, installed four years earlier and still there today. He is shown
van Eyck's *Adoration of the Mystic Lamb* in Ghent and says it is 'a
most precious painting, full of thought, and the Eve, Mary and God
the Father are especially good.' The paintings were then less than
a century old – very roughly in relation to Dürer what Duchamp's
The Bride Stripped Bare by Her Bachelors, Even is to us. So what he saw
was old, but in a tradition he recognized and felt part of – even as
he was, through his own wanderings in the Netherlands, also helping to infect everyone with the Renaissance ideas that would
shortly make van Eyck seem merely naive or, in the much later
crushingly nasty old art-historian term, 'Flemish Primitive'.

The riches of the diary are pretty inexhaustible. One of the
things he makes a note of is when he gives out, sells or swaps some
of his woodcuts and engravings. The idea that he has a satchel
packed with copies of his *St Jerome in His Study*, *The Six Knots*, *Melen-*

colia I and *The Knight, Death and the Devil* I find simply flabbergasting. He is chucking them at friends and colleagues across the Netherlands, some of the greatest works in all northern art – some presumably getting crumpled or having wine spilled on them or being carried off by a dog. Each mention in the diary seems obscurely exciting: these were recent works and one can only assume Dürer was very proud of them. Art historians have enjoyed tracking down the influence of these gifts on subsequent generations of artists, but the occasional borrowing of a profile or a decorative element seems less important than the wonder of sitting in a pub in Antwerp, holding a recently printed-off copy of *Melencolia I* and with its artist awaiting your reaction (I am confident I would have stuttered something deflatingly banal).

Dürer records all kinds of things – his alarm at hearing Luther has been arrested (the Diet of Worms was going on during his trip), fearing that Luther has been killed, although we now know that his abduction was a trick to whisk him to safety. He expresses his overwhelming admiration for Luther and bemoans Erasmus's failure to come out in open support of him – he also pops in on Erasmus himself and does a miraculous drawing of him in old age. He goes to Charles's coronation. All the time he is drawing and these sketches can be precisely linked to his journey: some Irish mercenaries, Livonian women in court dress, the Scheldt waterfront, an African servant. He draws perhaps the most enjoyable little page of sketches ever: a random selection of lions and castles, a baboon and a shaman-like lynx with its eyes closed.

A whole great era in the Netherlands can be seen through Dürer's eyes and the effect is both powerful and frustrating – we will never know more than these few words, the occasional judgements, the arguments about a specific toll. At the heart of the diary though, and which leaps high above its inadequacies, is the way that Dürer quite by accident is standing in the very spot where human history has just changed in the most fundamental and irrevocable way. There are other candidates for this high honour (Barcelona perhaps, with Ferdinand and Isabella meeting Columbus on the palace steps with his parrots and 'Indian' captives) but Antwerp in 1520 has a fair claim to be the sustained point where the Old World and the wider world came together. There are many clues in the text and in Dürer's own sketches. Most famously there is his superb drawing of a walrus, the first in Western art. The animal was dead and a note on the drawing says it was caught in the 'Dutch Sea' (i.e. North Sea), which is unlikely – but it suggests rather that the Dutch were now fishing high in the Arctic. The walrus, with its mournful, doglike eyes, is an unwilling pinniped ambassador from a region previously almost unknown to Western Europeans outside northern Scandinavia.

As pregnant with the future is Dürer's relationship with the Portuguese merchant who bought *St Jerome*. The merchant makes his guest a present of sugar loaves and barley sugar. I was idly wondering where these came from – they were clearly viewed as valuable but Brazil was not up and running yet. Coincidentally I had been in Madeira a couple of years earlier and one of the many remarkable aspects of Madeira is a museum of religious art which features some very battered Flemish sculptures and paintings. In any event, it turns out that Dürer's Portuguese patron, Rodrigo Fernandez d'Almada, imported his sugar from the plantations in Madeira and was *the very man* who had exported these sculptures and paintings to Madeira. I was left astonished. Madeira's pioneering use of Africans as slaves made it a sort of laboratory for the monstrous evil that Europeans were just beginning to spring on West Africa and the New World.

Countless global voyages ended up dumping their stuff in Antwerp. The Scheldt was perfect as it took your ship to a secure anchorage with sophisticated services a long way inland, with easy travel on to all the cities Dürer visits. He himself has an infinite appetite for the exotic, buying 'a wooden weapon from Calicut', an Indian coconut, 'an old Turkish whip', a baboon – in a very few words linking Antwerp to India, the Levant and Africa. But earlier in the year the most astounding cargo of all had been unloaded there as a gift for Charles: the first treasure from Hernán Cortés' invasion of the Aztec Empire. This was now on display in Brussels and Dürer went to see it. Almost no trace of the treasure remains today (the Spanish melted it all down), its greatness undermined both by greed and by religious distaste. All that is left is a beautiful quetzal-feather Mexican object known as Montezuma's Head Dress which was first noted in 1575 in a Habsburg collection in the Tyrol – but it could easily have come from any number of later Spanish bloodbaths in the region.

Dürer is rapt in the face of the things from 'the new land of gold', staring at the clothing, weapons, darts, armour, a huge sun made from gold and a matching moon made of silver: 'All the days of my life I have seen nothing that rejoiced my heart so much as these things, for I saw amongst them wonderful works of art, and I marvelled at the subtle Ingenia of men in foreign lands. Indeed I cannot express all that I thought there.'

Margaret of Austria

There are so many striking things lurking in Dürer's diary that this book could be hopelessly capsized by them. I will restrict myself to one further line from his time in Brussels: 'the King of Denmark gave a great banquet to the Emperor [Charles V], Lady Margaret, and the Queen of Spain, and he bade me in and I dined there also.' This simple report bursts with possibilities. The king was Christian II, chaotic, mercurial and dithering, who was in Brabant with his wife Isabella, the Emperor's younger sister. A superb drawing of him by Dürer still exists, accidentally preserving the odd way that the male fashions of the 1520s – long, pretty hair, a full beard – go underground shortly thereafter until re-emerging again only in about 1967. He would soon return to Denmark, ultimately alienating everyone and ending up imprisoned for the last thirty-six years of his life. The Emperor's being mentioned raises the usual awkwardness that despite the countless banquets he attended he could not, because of his clog-like Habsburg jaw, eat or drink at them as he made so much mess. He seemed to have retreated to a private room to eat, but understandably court records gloss over this issue and I have been thwarted for some years in my attempts to work out how Imperial dignity was maintained on these public occasions, with their elaborate dainties and frequent toasts.

The two really interesting guests of honour though are 'Lady Margaret, and the Queen of Spain'. It is fun to see the latter in town. Formerly pretty Germaine of Foix, she had spent her late teens in the gruesome embraces of the enormously older King Ferdinand of Aragon. A series of deaths meant that Ferdinand, to his horror, had become the last of his dynasty and that on his death the Aragonese throne would fall to the hated Habsburg dynasty via his daughter, Joanna the Mad. Festooned in love potions and urged on by countless high masses and the prayers of the court, each act of intercourse held the hope that this would have preserved Aragon as a separate kingdom. In a nightmarish twist a son was indeed born, but then died a few hours later. The despairing Ferdinand died, meaning that Joanna's son, Charles, therefore scooped the lot, confirming that Spain was now a united kingdom (albeit with fissures which have continued off and on ever since). Germaine, now dowager queen, was through the oddities of her situation Charles's step-grandmother, although only twelve years older. This is a murky topic, but she seems to have welcomed Charles to his Spanish inheritance by having an affair with him which resulted in a mystery daughter. She was married off in 1519 to a minor member of the Hohenzollern family and the two of them would be packed off to Spain to rule Valencia a couple of years after the banquet.

But in this fascinating group, the star turn is definitely 'Lady Margaret'. One of the great figures in early sixteenth-century Europe, Margaret of Austria was Maximilian and Mary the Rich's daughter. She had ruled the Netherlands on Maximilian's behalf, been sacked by Charles on his inheriting the region, but then reinstated as the sprawling and unmanageable nature of his empire became clear. Like Germaine she had had a miserable married existence. She had been raised at the French court with the intention that she would marry the future, deeply unpleasant Charles VIII. After years of toadying from courtiers and elaborate ceremonial she was suddenly dumped as political priorities changed and missed out on weird Charles. Maximilian then shipped her to Spain to marry

Ferdinand and Isabella's son Juan, Prince of Asturias. He then died (creating the crisis that Germaine was meant to fix) and Margaret gave birth to their daughter, who also died. Then, in what was her great piece of luck, she married the dashing and entertaining Philibert II, Duke of Savoy. Detailed accounts exist of their glamorous progress, as the principal towns from Geneva to Chambéry to Turin paid homage to their new Burgundian duchess. As usual it is hard not to feel that the endless allegorical pageants must have worn a bit thin after a while. But who could not have enjoyed the monks who had the surprising idea of building a fountain consisting of a gigantic carved maiden whose breasts squirted streams of wine; or not have felt special when the Turin Shroud was brought over to adorn her personal chapel?

But she had hardly got used to her fun new court when the overheated twenty-four-year-old Philibert, on one of his many boar-hunting expeditions, took the fatal decision to drink from the icy fountain of St Vulbas. As usual the real medical issues are opaque, but for whatever reason he seized up and – despite vows, prayers and the potentially unhelpful decision to dose him with ground-up pearls – he died. This catastrophe was the end of Margaret's peripatetic marriage adventures. Only a few days older than her late husband, she went through a crisis during which she tried to kill herself, cut off her hair and decided to become a nun.

Margaret does seem to have been pursued by bad luck. While she was visiting her father Maximilian in Strasbourg her favourite pet parrot was eaten by a big dog. She also came disturbingly close to being married off to the avaricious old paranoiac Henry VII of England. Her chance for greatness came with a Habsburg family disaster. Two years after Philibert died, her only sibling, King Philip I of Castile, Lord of the Netherlands, Duke of Burgundy (inherited from his mother Mary the Rich) and heir of Aragon (hence Ferdinand and Germaine's activities), suddenly died too. All of Maximilian's plans were under threat, with Philip and Joanna's son, the tiny Charles, needing an absurdly complex set of regency arrangements to ensure he might one day inherit much of the world. Margaret now became invaluable: she had the prestige, immediacy and experience to help patch up a mounting Habsburg fiasco, as Joanna refused to acknowledge her husband's death and descended into insanity. In 1507 Margaret became ruler of the Habsburg Netherlands and, after the period when Charles injudiciously sacked her, was back in the saddle from 1519 to her death in 1530. So when she was sitting round the table talking with Charles, Germaine and Christian II, being looked at by Dürer in 1521, she was the most experienced ruler there, still only in her early forties.

Rather amazingly, the palace from which she ruled the Netherlands, at Mechelen, is still there – or at least its front. This front shows one of her problems, as it preserves her attempt to overhaul the embarrassingly late-medieval building to make it more upscale and Renaissance-friendly but she ran out of money, so it is partly gnarled and turrety and then has a delicate and pretty bit stuck on the end. In a way this accidentally enshrines her virtues – a sense of someone doing their best in a reasonable and thoughtful way rather than going nuts and pouring all the taxes into self-aggrandizement. Her court attracted artists and composers from across the Holy Roman Empire, and, given the Netherlands' central role in northern Europe's trade, many curious characters passed through. During Margaret's first stint as ruler, the young Anne Boleyn was at her court – before going on to her extraordinary role as the catalyst for English Protestantism. Earlier in the summer of 1520 Dürer visited her himself in Mechelen. He records that he showed her his portrait of the Emperor Maximilian. Dürer and Maximilian went back many years and he was deeply entangled in the Emperor's many artistic projects, but this portrait is perhaps the greatest of all Habsburg images – Maximilian as a sort of beak-nosed wizard in furs, holding a pomegranate. It was painted in Augsburg in 1519, just before Maximilian's death. One of Dürer's principal aims for his tour, since even when rolled up the portrait was far from small and not a simple thing to transport, must have been to give it to Margaret. In any event, confronted with this painting of her father, 'she so disliked it that I took it away with me'. In recompense she showed him some of her own collection, which included treasures like van Eyck's

Arnolfini Marriage – which, along with other paintings, Dürer describes simply as 'good', which is a bit disappointing.

Margaret's rule was looked back on with ever greater nostalgia by later generations as life in the Netherlands degenerated into a ferocious nightmare. As an authentic Burgundian, born in Brussels, granddaughter of Charles the Bold, daughter of Mary the Rich, she had her own prestige and made Mechelen a plausible capital. She sheltered her subjects in some measure from their problematic role as small if wealthy elements in a vast, fundamentally absurd dynastic agglomeration. She probably died just in time, as her nephew Charles V staggered along, trying to run everything from Peru to Apulia, and taking or failing to take the fatal decisions that would tear much of Europe to pieces.

The life and adventures of Charles V

Freiburg's Minster is a building so packed with amazing stuff that it seems a bit insulting ever to leave it. I have sometimes wondered whether instead of just floundering around from city to city I could pick up precisely the same wealth of information by standing still. The Minster's chancel would certainly be one place where, with the tiniest investment in footsteps, whole worlds of artistic greatness and historical gravity unfold. Hans Baldung Grien's triptych for the high altar is a sort of summary of and farewell to the German Late Gothic, filled with characteristically weird, startling figures and would continue to be rewarding if looked at continuously for days: a fervent yet wacky series of meditations on the life of Mary, it features, among many other things, the best ever Flight into Egypt, with a grizzled tramping Joseph in an orange pixie hood, an adorable donkey and several putti clowning about in a palm tree. It was painted between 1512 and 1516 and this whole part of the building must have then been a mass of sawing, hammering and shouting as not only was the gigantic triptych being fitted, but also a set of overwhelming stained-glass windows. These were a gift from the Emperor Maximilian extolling the virtues of the Habsburg family.

With the sun in the right position, the emblems of the Holy Roman Empire, even though the Empire ceased to exist two centuries ago, still blaze into the church, above Grien's paintings. In the side chapels behind the Grien a particular moment in Habsburg history is preserved, showing Maximilian I (wearing early designer spectacles), his son Philip the Handsome and his grandsons the future Charles V and Ferdinand I, praying before their respective saints. The saints are far bigger than the Habsburgs but, despite wearing the most tremendous robes and hovering in space, they seem to be trying too hard, like failing genies or unsuccessful candidates to be a department store Father Christmas. They swirl and glower, failing to batter down the insolent self-regard of Europe's most arrogant family.

This ensemble (and countless other carvings and paintings scattered throughout the other chapels) forms just one sensational aspect to a sensational building, but it is striking that these were being fitted during the Reformation – and survived the Reformation unsmashed, with Freiburg remaining a Catholic city today. Places like the Minster show the great vigour and confidence of Catholicism in parallel to the spread of Luther's ideas (initiated far to the east, in Wittenberg, in 1517). Just up the road Matthias Grünewald was creating his *Isenheim Altarpiece* for an Alsatian monastery. The composer Ludwig Senfl, born in Basle and raised in Zürich, was creating his *Missa Paschalis*, one of the most beautiful pieces of music ever written, and turning out fantastic pieces for Maximilian – including as a finale a great lament on his death ('*Howl then, boys; prelates weep; cantors lament, soldiers and nobles bewail it and say: Maximilian rest in peace*'). In Bern and Basle the last two great *Dances of Death* were being created – the former a huge painting by Niklaus Manuel Deutsch, the latter a set of tiny bestselling prints by the young Hans Holbein. These Holbein *Dances* are often seen as satirical as fat abbots and prettily clothed countesses are mocked and led on by a derisive Death, but the overall effect is chilling and levelling: whoever you are (an emperor or a ploughman) you will meet the same fate.

The Reformation tore through the region, but with a surprising range of results. Zürich was cleared of images by 1523, Basle reformed in 1529, with Catholic refugees – including Erasmus – moving to Freiburg for safety. The speed of these changes stunned everyone. Once Luther had established the idea that the Church should be reformed, an explosive burst of entirely contradictory ideas engulfed Western Europe, with Luther ever more furious that his leadership was being so widely ignored. Other reformers popped up everywhere, revealing hidden beliefs, celebrating older strands such as Hussitism, or going completely bananas. It must have been an uncanny period. Strasbourg became a great hub for reform ideas, but this was preceded by the inexplicable episode in 1518 when all together some four hundred people danced themselves to death. No plausible explanation has ever been given for what happened: people simply kept dancing until they had seizures or heart attacks. In 1524–5 much of Germany was engulfed by the Great Peasants' War, which also swept through Freiburg and Alsace and which ended with the massacre of some two hundred thousand peasants by noblemen and their loyal retinues. Luther was horrified when peasants cited his teachings and (in a move that itself helped split reform apart) sided with the princes.

If you were a fan of smashing things up it must have been a brilliant time as acres of stained glass were destroyed and great bonfires of images filled town squares. Of course, Luther's aim was to *reform*, to make the One Church better, but this did not work out. Some rulers switched to reform for the most outrageously cynical reasons, others did so devoutly, others followed Luther's rivals. The Emperor Maximilian, with the sort of chic which defined his whole reign, died just in time to not have to bother with it all, leaving his grandson Charles V to clear up. Just looking at the stained glass of the Habsburgs in Freiburg you can see that there was a less than zero chance that Charles would give five minutes of serious consideration to Protestant riff-raff. The entire structure for his family's rule was supported by Rome. He and his family poured money into artworks, monasteries, great cycles of prayer – Charles stood at the apex of a religio-political frame just as complex and far-reaching as that of

Montezuma in Mexico (whose reign had violently ended thanks to Charles's soldiers a few months before).

One curiosity of Reformation ideas is that they were thoroughly unsuccessful. Much of Europe remained placidly Catholic, given a wash-and-brush-up by the Council of Trent (Trento), which rejigged the Church without reference to Luther. As the century progressed Reformation became a means to end a marriage without the Pope's agreement (England), a way of grabbing a great swathe of property (Prussia), a further expression of localist orneriness (the northern Swiss cities) and a way to sustain an anti-Habsburg identity (the Low Countries). Of course, it was also genuinely, powerfully religious too. In a context where almost all Europeans spent many hours a week preparing for the afterlife, the shattering of unity raised horrific problems: if a specific set of practices, ideas, texts was the route to Heaven, the others *had to be wrong.*

Charles V ruled over the heartland of reform – whether as Emperor or as a duke or count – and he completely mishandled it. In France the state was ravaged by religious issues, but reform was, over several reigns, marginalized and defeated. In Charles's territories in Spain, Portugal, the New World and Italy it never mattered much. But in the Empire itself Charles never successfully imposed his will. Even though he had a clear run from the Diet of Worms onwards, and although he was the most powerful figure to date in Europe's history, with ships full of American treasure and resources undreamed of by his predecessors, he was always hopelessly distracted by some fresh scheme in some other part of the world and turned on the Protestants too late.

There is no good recent biography of Charles and it is easy to see why – his interests spread in every direction, but at some level he was not himself terribly compelling. He left voluminous material on himself, but often seems merely stiff and unimaginative. He inherited Maximilian's semi-comic failings over money but on a cosmic scale. In terms of his reach and ambition, he lived in a dizzyingly different world from his great-grandfather and namesake Charles the Bold. Whereas the latter strained every sinew to besiege just one Rhineland town, the former was as busy with the affairs of Peru as with Tunis. One day his troops were (somewhat unfortunately) sacking Rome, the next they were fighting France. He seems to have never taken any interest at all in the sources of his wealth, viewing lack of money as something that could never hold back a prince from 'heroic action'. At one point he mortgaged the spice island of Ternate to the King of Portugal for 350,000 ducats, but then had his entire campaigning season wrecked by failing to factor in the understandably slow pace at which the Portuguese ducat-laden mule-train was able to get from Lisbon to Barcelona.

His most valuable provinces were Holland, Brabant and Flanders, the most densely urban part of Europe, and he worked to accumulate other provinces around them – taking over Utrecht in 1527–8, conquering Gelderland in 1543 and, by giving this whole block of territory its own identity as the 'Burgundian Circle' within the Empire, unwittingly creating the basis for its later independence. His long-suffering sister Mary of Hungary, who ruled the Habsburg Netherlands in Brussels after her aunt Margaret died, was always having to organize another whip-round for troops and cash, cutting back thriftily on her tapestry purchases only to get a letter from Charles announcing a fun new plan to invade North Africa. Antwerp became the key port linking the Baltic trade to the Mediterranean, taking over from Bruges as the furthest point reachable by Italian galleys (with Anabaptists the increasingly fashionable choice as rowing slaves). The pace of change was extraordinary. For example, Portuguese ships from the Moluccas would now arrive in Antwerp to sell their cargo of spice and then buy copper from Carpathian mines which had been shipped up the Vistula and across the Baltic, which would then be sold in Indian ports en route to the Moluccas again. The sums of money were enormous and their sources glamorous, but irregular and tending to melt away before they got to Charles. Indignities were always lurking. On one ceremonial trip to Speyer his mounted bodyguard simply refused to move until their arrears were paid and several of his huge 'enterprises' went completely wrong, both through money bottlenecks and woeful planning.

By the time he had spent years of action and adventure in various foreign parts, Protestantism was simply too well dug in. He had spent too long ignoring priests who urged him to treat the Protestants as Charlemagne had treated the Saxons: i.e., not well. Following past form, nobody was going to be so stupid as to take on the Swiss, but in the 1540s Charles at last attacked the Schmalkaldic League, an association of proselytizing German territories, allied with France. The League was easily defeated, but there was no serious means any more to dismantle Protestantism and the patchwork religious structure of the Empire was enshrined in agreements that left the Rhine, for example, an absurd theological *grille mixte*.

In their treacherous dealings with France, the Schmalkaldic League had offered a fatal bribe: the territories of 'the Three Bishoprics' (Metz, Tull and Wirten), clearly part of the Empire, but now swallowed by the French and becoming Metz (but pronounced *Mess* to make it sound less German), Toul and Verdun. Charles vowed to get them back and laid siege to Metz in October 1552, late in the season and against all advice. Thousands of his troops were killed by dysentery, typhus and scurvy. In a further instance of his oddness, he remarked to the Duke of Alva, who was standing next to him, that all these dead troops were like mere grasshoppers or caterpillars 'which eat the buds and other good things of the earth'. He felt that 'if they were men of worth they would not be in [my] camp for [a pitiable] six livres a month'. He wearily lifted the siege in January, almost exactly seventy-six years after the traumatized remnants of Charles the Bold's army had stood on Metz's frozen moat pleading to be let in. Exhausted, ill and run ragged, Charles began to consider retirement, a gaunt, battered figure no longer recognizable as the slightly plump, complacent man in the Freiburg stained-glass window. He would leave his boggling piles of debt and religiously mayhemic western empire to his son Philip II and, as it turned out, to the Duke of Alva, who would soon find himself converted from a tough and thoughtful general into one of the greatest of all monsters in the Protestant bestiary.

The Oranges

I had been noodling around online to find out more about Louis II of Chalon-Arlay, victor in 1430 of the Battle of Anthon, which I mention briefly in the introduction – at which a fleeing Burgundian was entombed inside a tree. It is very easy to become a lost soul once plunged into these electronic realms. Too much emphasis has been given to the internet's degradation of life through the access it gives to porn and human horrors, and too little to its fearful role in genealogical tables. It used to be a tortuous and demanding process to trace family trees, let alone find out interesting information. But now there are websites – created through the tireless labour of various anonymous sociopathic dungeon-masters – into which it is possible simply to disappear. The entire course of European history, across a near infinity of noble and royal families, can now be traced up, down and side to side, from the early Middle Ages to the present. The sheer richness of information and the way it proliferates like dandelion seeds ('Oh dear God they had sixteen children') gives it the compulsive flavour of Tetris or Super Mario, with Mario's challenges taking on much of the same flavour as the ins and outs of, for instance, the Princes of Salm-Salm.

Louis of Chalon-Arlay was a typically truculent semi-important ruler who exemplified the way that the borders between Burgundy and France were in a near-permanent state of crumbling. This could weaken either France or Burgundy – but it also created a zone in which figures such as Louis could thrive for a while, whose allegiances could move back and forth between the two super-powers from his own modest power-base in the Franche-Comté. I was interested in him because he was not only Lord of Chalon-Arlay, but also Prince of Orange. How did this title, so closely associated with the Netherlands, move from the hot, dusty world of the French southeast to the altogether soggier landscapes on the North Sea?

The Lords of Chalon-Arlay emerged from the aftermath of the fragmentation of the old Kingdom of Arles. They had the happy luck of many small rulers in having one terrific source of revenue – in this case the major salt works at Salins – as well as a series of castles and towns scattered through the Franche-Comté. Their formidable-sounding founder, John, lived through a huge chunk of the thirteenth century producing industrial numbers of heirs and a dynasty that safely made it through the following century, all its men seemingly named Hugh or John. The enjoyably named Baux-Orange family were less fecund and had run out. Their last member, Marie, married John III of Chalon-Arlay in 1396, splicing her territories with the Chalon-Arlay family, and making her husband John I of Orange, just a tiny principality of a hundred square miles or so in the south of France, but a principality nonetheless, carrying the rank that came with it. Their son was the same turbulent (or truculent) Louis of Chalon-Arlay, who enjoyed himself switching back and forth between the increasingly annoyed French and Burgundians.

Louis's son William then took over, then William's son John. John IV of Chalon-Arlay, who lived through the second half of the fifteenth century, became near-fatally entangled in the revival of the French monarchy under Louis XI and the related implosion of Burgundy. The nadir of his existence was probably being defeated while fighting in Brittany, pretending to be dead on the battlefield and then being unfortunately recognized. It is one of the problems with history that we have no means by which we can measure the perhaps permanent loss of self-esteem generated on such occasions. He had one son, Philibert, but now the sequence of luck which had taken the House of Chalon-Arlay through sons or at worst nephews from 1237 to 1530 (an amazing run) ended. Philibert, aside from being shackled with a borderline comic name, was a leading commander in the chaotic and discreditable Italian Wars of the 1520s, taking part in the Sack of Rome and being killed at the subsequent, ruinous Siege of Florence. His death would have ended the dynasty but fortunately he had a sister, Claudia, who had herself died very young, some years before Philibert, but not before marrying Count Henry III of Nassau-Dillenburg-Dietz and giving birth to one son: René. Claudia's marriage linked the quite separate Chalon-Arlay family into the Counts of Nassau – with Henry, as Lord of Breda, initiating the tombs in the Great Church there, including a sculptural marvel, the memorial to his uncle and predecessor Engelbert II. René inherited on the condition that he pretended to be a Chalon-Arlay, even though he was strictly (i.e. actually) a dynastic member of the Nassau family.

This is really just an opportunity to celebrate my own ignorance – but this René of Chalon-Arlay, to my delight and surprise, turns out to be the same man who is commemorated in Bar-le-Duc by Ligier Richier's astounding Flayed Man monument.* The Flayed Man is mysterious in all kinds of ways – but it marks the end of the *danse macabre* tradition, just as Engelbert II's tomb is squarely Renaissance and new. René's death also marks the end of the house of Chalon-Arlay. René only had a daughter and she died shortly after she was born. He was killed aged twenty-five while commanding an army for the Emperor Charles V (as had Philibert only fourteen years before). The Emperor was at his commander's side as René lay dying, an honour of sorts but also a basis for some posthumous bitter laughter, given René's successors' undying enmity towards Charles's successors. Unknown to anybody present, one of the great wobbles in European history had just happened. As the last member of his dynasty, René left all his titles and lands to his father's brother's son, the young William of Nassau, on the condition that he be raised a Catholic (his family had become Lutheran). The Emperor promised to look after William until he reached his majority. In scenes reminiscent of the end of a *Star Wars*

---

* My first published history essay was about this statue, published under the undemanding editorship of a magazine which I myself edited. Actually going to see it for the first time over thirty years later in Bar-le-Duc was almost too much in its deferred intensity. René is shown as a flayed corpse in a heroic pose, admiring himself in a little mirror with ligaments stretching across his rotting neck. It is just as startling, if smaller, than I had imagined from drawings. The tomb took a beating during the French Revolution, so it was reassembled in 1793 with an awkward box at René's feet filled with tiny bits of other family members picked up off the floor, including Robert the Magnificent, his wife Marie de France, and their son Edward, Duke of Bar, killed at the Battle of Agincourt, having inherited the dukedom after both his brothers were killed at the Battle of Nicopolis.

movie, William is taken under the imperial wing, inheriting René's lands (and therefore becoming Prince William of Orange, soon to be more familiarly known as William the Silent), the rich Nassau territories in Germany and vast expanses of the Netherlands. Once grown up he would proceed to rip apart the Habsburg Empire, create what became a new independent state and found the same Dutch royal family that is still in charge in 2019.

And *that* is the reason that the Netherlands national football team today play wearing an orange shirt.

Rebellion

Tournai is a gift that just goes on giving – endlessly interesting, with museums packed with curiosities left behind by wave after wave of emperors, artists and generals. A French enclave wedged between Flanders and Hainaut, Tournai's territory (the Tournaisis) was only finally conquered by Charles V in 1521 and became part of the Spanish Netherlands. Oddly therefore its great status in early Netherlandish painting, home of both Robert Campin and his pupil Rogier van der Weyden, was as part of France. The stuff it still has though! Just one example: a set of immaculately maintained vestments owned by Thomas Becket and sent to a monastery, with which he had close links, as a keepsake after his murder. Sadly the town's rich historical compost would ultimately allow to flower one of the worst painters of the nineteenth century (a proud claim in a crowded field): Louis Gallait. Gallait created many terrible pictures, with titles such as *Tasso in Prison* and *A Monk Feeding the Poor*, but he was a favourite son of Tournai and has a suitably terrible commemorative statue in the centre of town. What I did not realize was that the small but wonderful Musée des Beaux Arts in Tournai is the last resting place for his gigantic painting *The Abdication of Charles V*, as big as the side of a double-decker bus, but with only a fraction of the bus's aesthetic pleasure.

The painting is often reproduced, as all the contemporary records of Charles's abdication are unsatisfactorily banal – one engraving just shows him standing there before a skimpy little audience, as though he is giving a lecture on some minor but embarrassing aspect of public health. Gallait's painting though, being so sprawling, murky and cluttered, is almost unreadable in shrunken, book reproduction and needs its vast scale. However ham-fisted the treatment, it does dramatize, in an acceptably Verdi-esque way, one of the supreme moments in the history of the Low Countries, with any of the dozens of painted figures seemingly on the verge of breaking into impassioned song. Here in Brussels is the palsied Charles V, leaning on the shoulder of his young protégé William of Orange as he blesses his only legitimate son and successor, Prince Philip. Looking on from a matching throne is the austere figure of Mary of Hungary, Charles's sister and long-time ruler of the Netherlands, who had herself just resigned. In the audience, with varying degrees of historical accuracy, is a guest list of future actors in the disasters that would unfold across the Netherlands: the Counts of Hoorn and Egmont, Granvelle, Alva, Philippe de Croÿ. There too is the young Maria of Austria, Charles's daughter, whose extraordinary future life would entangle her in the politics of much of Europe, with the survivors of her sixteen children defining the later sixteenth century.

Actually, even writing this makes it clear that it is a bit graceless to laugh at Gallait's painting – it may not be very good, but it is a lot better than his egregious and equally vast *The Plague of Tournai in 1095* on the opposite wall about which I would simply rather not elaborate. The virtue of his *Abdication* is that it does enshrine a moment of exceptional drama. Here, in 1555, is perhaps the most powerful man of the sixteenth century voluntarily surrendering power and retiring to spend the rest of his life in a monastery. The following year he will split his lands, among other things handing over the Holy Roman Empire to his younger brother Ferdinand, and the Spanish Empire to his son Philip. For the Low Countries the implications of this were simply staggering. It marked what proved to be the end of a great era: Charles V was born in Ghent, Mary in Brussels; their father Philip I was born in Bruges; Philip's mother, Mary of Burgundy, was also born in Brussels. Like the

Carolingians, they were basically Belgian. Even in retirement at his Spanish monastery, Charles would drink beer, to the horror of his Italian doctors. Prince Philip, however, was born in Spain – he and his descendants would rule from his newly founded imperial capital of Madrid.

Charles's decision to tie the Netherlands inheritance to Spain was an eccentric one and led to untold misery. It would result in an eight-decade-long war between elements in the provinces and the rest of the Spanish empire, fighting broken only by a single long truce. Most of the seventeen provinces were part of the Holy Roman Empire and therefore on the face of it part of Ferdinand's new responsibility. Vienna was a long way off and Ferdinand distracted by possible Turkish annihilation, but then Madrid was hardly close by either. Charles had roped off the provinces by making them a separate 'Burgundian circle' (the empire was split into circles – blocks of territory mixing smaller and bigger for mutual defence) and, through the Pragmatic Sanction of 1549, made them indivisible. Perhaps the best explanation is a Burgundian one – that Charles saw these western lands (including the separate Franche-Comté) as part of a specific dynastic drama associated with his father and with Castile. The provinces' wobbly identity can be seen in many of the figures scattered across Gallait's painting – Granvelle was from the Franche-Comté and became Bishop of Arras, a thoroughly Burgundian figure; William the Silent was from Nassau-Dillenburg; Egmont had married into the Palatinate-Simmern family – only Hoorn is thoroughly Dutch. The process by which the inhabitants of the Burgundian Circle would decide on their loyalties, religion, form of government, language even, would be a nightmarish one that lasted in some ways for over eighty years, but in other ways has continued to be played out ever since.

Philip left for Spain in 1559, saying farewell to his northern inheritance at the port of Vlissingen, never to return. His son, Philip III, and his grandson, Philip IV, would also never visit, although the last of these men would finally see the end of the rebellion. One problem came from the sheer wealth of the Netherlands. Antwerp was one of Europe's greatest ports and countless well-run small and

medium towns churned out everything an empire needed, from battleships to sewing-needles. It is customary to show a map of
Charles's global empire to give a sense of how massive it was – but
much of this was an illusion. The Philippines (named for Philip
while he was still a prince) are always coloured in as Spanish, but
consisted of one or two small stockades filled with glassy-eyed
fever-victims, clutching rosaries and rusty cutlasses and cursing their
careers advisers. The same applied to South America, on which only
a few, small, genuinely Spanish-coloured dabs should be coloured
in. My favourite film, Herzog's *Aguirre, The Wrath of God*, gets this
perfectly – the conquistadors as an insane, dwindling band of fanta-
sists on a raft filled with monkeys. Southern Italy was always a curse
for whoever ruled it, with the hope that in a good year enough tax
would be shaken out of it just to cover its garrison costs. Of course,
immense piles of money were coming out of South America with
countless tons to come – but for a monarch building, scheming and
praying in Madrid, the Netherlands was by a long way the most
reliably taxable and sophisticated part of his entire inheritance and
Philip required its obedience.

The accident of the spread of Calvinism gave an eventual focus
for the rebellion against Spanish high-handedness and provoked
some of Philip's most unfortunate decision-making (e.g. 'The
Council of Blood', which suppressed heresy and treason by executing hundreds) – but there were loads of sincere Catholics who were
also anti-Spanish. The process by which seven of the seventeen
provinces broke off to become the Kingdom of the Netherlands
was a side effect of the high-water mark of Spanish success in the
other ten provinces, with innumerable dramas and horrors in cities
such as Antwerp or Ostend, which ended up in the Spanish Netherlands entirely against their will. Brabant ended up torn in half,
with the north (Breda, 's-Hertogenbosch) in Dutch hands and the
south (Brussels, Leuven) in Spanish. Almost every town has a
monument to the months when it suddenly became the focus of
innumerable hopes and fears, heroism and disaster.

The density of the towns and the era's military technology
stretched the war over generations. A Dutch master-carpenter fight-

ing in Brielle in 1572 broke a sluice with his axe and unleashed what would become the default, unbelievably enraging (for the Spanish) tactic of simply flooding huge areas of land. I had always assumed this was just a reckless throw, with the water engulfing everything, but it had its own art, with the water ideally controlled to be deep enough to be impossible to wade through (and filled with hidden ditches, spikes, etc.) but shallow enough to ground larger boats. Cities bristled with ingenious defences – not just walls and moats but immense thorn hedges (the Twelve Years Truce from 1609 was filled by what were effectively military gardeners maturing these). Maastricht defended itself with some thirty thousand six-foot wooden spikes. Sieges soaked up besiegers, with thousands of men spending months being rained on and convulsing with dysentery. Each epic needed astonishing efforts. The Duke of Parma's Siege of Antwerp required building eight miles of canal and a gigantic fortified bridge to block the entire width of the Scheldt.

As the major southern cities in Flanders and Brabant fell into Spain's grip, the rebels compensated through the crazy growth of the heavily protected and as it proved invulnerable Amsterdam. Behind the fighting, the north was reliably held by the rebels and they could safely train, build and supply themselves. These towns thrived. Whereas the Spanish were frantically trying to get supplies of bullion to their often mutinous garrisons, the Dutch found themselves in a virtuous circle, with the money raised from taxes being re-circulated to other Dutch merchants who were selling breastplates, horses or beer. As one cheerfully admiring London leaflet said: 'What the souldier receives in pay, he payes in drink'. 'Dutch' armies were of course far from being Dutch. The war with Spain brought innumerable mercenaries and adventurers – it became the great training ground for the Thirty Years War, but also a sort of Protestant crusade for Scots, English, Saxons, Swedes.

Every city's drama deserves mention. Leiden, for example, endured a year-long series of horrors with floods and starvation. There is in the town an attractive nineteenth-century statue of Mayor van der Werf, unfortunately not showing his most famous moment, when he rolled up his sleeve and displayed his bare arm to a desperate crowd, saying that if he must die anyway then they should eat him. The city still celebrates the day when flat-bottomed boats full of herring and bread at last arrived. There were lighter moments too, such as when Breda was almost bloodlessly captured in 1590 from the Spanish by a few men slipping in, hidden in a peat barge. The 'Spanish Gate' through which they may have slipped is still there and there is no Dutch museum complete without a jaunty medal or print celebrating this occasion.

My favourite memorial to this era is in Zeeland, now in the Zeeuws Museum in Middelburg. The city fathers were so overwhelmed by the great series of events they had lived through that they decided to commission a set of six huge tapestries. Beautifully looked after and restored, these extraordinary objects have their own room and still make vivid the Battle of the Scheldt, the Siege of Zierikzee and other events that defined Zeeland and made it part of the Dutch Republic rather than the Spanish Netherlands. Minutely detailed Spanish galleys filled with drummers, pikemen and gunners; ships on fire; pennants flying; crews racing up rigging, all captured in the somewhat slow-moving medium of wool and silk. The tapestries have cheery mythological elements too – so William the Silent is shown as Hercules burning off one by one the heads of the Spanish Hydra, although it is impossible not to think that Philip II must have had a matching tapestry put up somewhere in which it is the Dutch who feature as the Hydra.

Through sheer good luck, while I had been sitting staring at these great works for an hour or so, the room suddenly filled with people as part of a Middelburg music festival and a group of Dutch girls sang a cappella. It was hard to think of anything odder or more enjoyable than staring in wonder at woven images of driftwood, billowing sails, fish, waves, smoke and flames while listening to perfect renditions of 'Java Jive' and 'Don't Sit Under the Apple Tree (with Anyone Else But Me)'.

The Catholic case

The Brabant town of Mechelen is overshadowed by the flanking monsters of Brussels and Antwerp, but has had its moments of glory, both as the palatial base for the Margarets of York and of Austria and as a major legal and religious centre, more often known historically under its French name of Malines. Its wonderfully gnarled, battered cathedral has been through a lot. One thing that struck me on my first visit there is that the River Dyle goes through it. This briefly appears as historically important in 1940 when the British and French, after spending over six months creating fortifications for themselves, decided, following the German invasion of what had been neutral Belgium, to abandon their fortifications and move up to the 'Dyle Line'. This was an important element in walking into the very simple trap the Germans had prepared for them. I had always vaguely assumed that the 'Dyle Line' had some heft, but on the basis of its width in Mechelen even the town's tourist board would be hard-pressed to make claims for it as more than anything than a jumpable runnel. I later came across it in Leuven, where it is a sparkling, moss-lined brook, unlikely to hold up Nazi tank commanders except for those particularly interested in herbaceous worts, tansies and celandines.

Shaken by the inadequacies of the Dyle, I found myself walking through the streets north of the cathedral when, strangely, the whole width of road and pavement was blocked by men fixing up the paving. It is a small point, but the geography meant I simply could not proceed to where I wanted to go and had to take a detour that meant accidentally finding myself on a road which contained both the world's first carillon school (founded in the 1920s and still today the carillonneurs' Mecca) and the Church of St John, which was open. I had already been puzzled by the road gang as normally they work on one side of the street and then the other so pedestrians can get by, and once I walked into the church, I was compelled to believe that I had been tricked by members of the Baroque Liberation Front, continuing their army-of-the-shadows campaign to raise awareness of seventeenth-century devotional art.

For myself, I was quite happy to be manipulated in this way and respect their fervour. I had felt them at my elbow in Kortrijk (how else did I come to be standing before van Dyck's lugubrious *Raising of the Cross*?), but here they were, hiding in plain sight.

The Church of St John is where a *lot* of Catholic devotional art has ended up and is so crowded that it feels almost as much an auction house as a religious building. But it is also the home to one of the most astounding paintings by Rubens, himself one of art's greatest wonder-workers. It shows a crowded, magical version of the Three Magi venerating a glowing baby Jesus, seemingly the picture's light source. He is putting his hand in a gold goblet presented by the first of the Magi, who wears a simply staggeringly rich and elaborate gold cloak and lynx muffler. Beyond them are a brilliantly observed gang of bystanders in armour, turbans and fur hats and including a particularly striking African's head. The painting's side panels can be ingeniously flipped two ways. On one side of each there is an upbeat picture of St John baptizing Christ and of St John the Evangelist on Patmos. On the other sides, used for special more glum occasions, the first St John is shown decapitated with a gloating Salome and the second being boiled in oil in the Colosseum (he survived in fact and was such a crowd-pleaser that he immediately converted the entire audience).

I specifically mention these fantastic pictures partly as my fervent evangelical duty to urge anyone in the Mechelen area to go and see them, but also to make a wider, fairly obvious point about the entire conflict from its origins in the 1550s to the final agreement to partition the Netherlands in the 1640s. These extreme, passionate, strange paintings were commissioned from Rubens in 1616 as just one small element in the vast work of rebuilding that followed the consolidation of the Spanish Netherlands during the Twelve Years Truce. The church had been devastated during the wars. Mechelen had been wrecked by a huge gunpowder explosion in 1546, its religious images smashed and burned during Calvinist riots in 1566, it had been captured in 1572 by pro-Orangist forces who were then promptly defeated with attendant massacres by the Duke of Alva's Spanish troops; it was then retaken largely by

English troops in 1580 who carried out further killings, before its final reconquest by Spanish troops in 1585, shortly before the Fall of Antwerp.

For English-speaking readers all sympathy tends to be with the rebels, a tradition begun with the events themselves, which had everyone across the Channel agog. The problem, though, has always been that many inhabitants of the Seventeen Provinces were *not* rebels and it always remained plausible and intellectually decent to stay Catholic. The nightmare for people living in towns such as Mechelen was that, depending on the year, it was fatal to believe either one thing or the other. In the end the great sorting machine of the wars drove Protestants north and Catholics south, but from a Catholic point of view the fighting *saved* ten of the seventeen, just as brutal actions in much of the rest of Europe (in France, in the Austrian Habsburg empire) ensured that, in roughly the span of Rubens' lifetime (1577–1640), Protestantism would become herded just into northern Europe and parts of Switzerland, leaving Catholicism as the genuinely global form of Christianity.

The Black Legend of Spain has so shaped our understanding of the wars that at some level we still do not think of even modern Belgium as an entirely legitimate country. Indeed the very existence of Rubens and the other great Catholic painters of the period in the south who repaired the amazing damage done to the patrimony of the Netherlands has always had an unacceptable, sinister air, certainly to Dutch Calvinists who rejected the very idea of such religious images, but also to British Protestants. It was Charles I's enthusiasm for commissioning paintings by Rubens and his pupil van Dyck that set off alarm bells among Puritans about his being a crypto-Jesuit Trojan horse. Cromwell deliberately made Charles walk to his execution on Whitehall through the Banqueting House, which featured Rubens' vast frothy ceiling paintings he had commissioned, of his father, James I, floating in heaven surrounded by cupids in a thoroughly non-Puritan manner. If Charles glanced up this would have been the last thing he saw before emerging onto the platform, and into a strange form of historical greatness.

The war between Spain and the rebels was carried out through the power of images, and countless paintings and pamphlets now in museums were part of a hysteria-laden propaganda drive by one side or the other. With the Duke of Alva's arrival in 1567 both sides were occupied by a frantic need to appeal for moral and material help. Alva was there, with his ten thousand Spanish troops, not just in response to the spread of Calvinism, but because of the Beeldenstorm ('statue storm'), one of the great cultural catastrophes in Europe's history, where mobs in each province made bonfires of the whole medieval artistic tradition – statues, paintings, robes, flags, carvings in monasteries, convents and churches were hauled out into the street. This had been a factor in Protestant victories across Europe for a generation, from the expunging of images in Zürich to the extraordinary purging of Scotland, which was so effective that almost no traces remain of its Catholic art. For the Spanish it was the last straw, as a confusing swirl of the local, urban, provincial, Burgundian and religious militated against their rule. There were many loyal Catholics who hated the Spanish, but quite rapidly there was not enough room to maintain such a pose. Alva set up what became known to Catholics as the 'Council of the Troubles' and to Protestants as the 'Council of Blood'. It executed some thousand people and pronounced sentence on thousands more who fled north or to friendly German territory and had all their property confiscated. It ruined much of the pre-Alva ruling class – killing most famously the Catholic leaders Hoorn and Egmont. They had known Philip II well, were leaders of the Council, Knights of the Golden Fleece, but this did not save them. Prince William of Orange fled, while Hoorn and Egmont stayed under the impression they could reason with Alva, and this was why it fell to William to become the Revolt's leader.

In the modern Netherlands there is no museum complete without copies of the crude little engravings distributed in their thousands across Protestant Europe, showing Hoorn and Egmont decapitated in the main square of Brussels. This was both a religious and aristocratic outrage and fuelled a loathing for Spain which became fanatical, with volunteers and mercenaries from Scotland, England and the German Protestant states coming to fight. Less well known was that, of course, this also became the great Catholic cause – with equally fervent and articulate fighters from Spain, France and Italy filling the southern provinces, backed up by the intellectual firepower of the Jesuits and with their confidence rebuilt after the reforms of the Council of Trent. It was from this period that the cult of the Virgin Mary became central to Catholicism as Rome realized that Calvin and the others had created a morose, masculine, visually uncompelling (whitewash) and generally unfun creed. Rubens became the premier exponent of this cult of glamour and emotion, wounds and sacrifice. His contribution to the re-Catholicizing of Antwerp Cathedral, paid for by the Guild of the Arquebusiers, is a *Descent from the Cross* of such extremity that it is hard to look at. The painting is a bitter play on the Guild's patron saint being St Christopher, the 'carrier of Christ', who is painted charmingly with the infant on an outer panel as one of Western art's most convincing beefy giants, but in the main image is mirrored by a group of appalled figures who are between them taking the weight of the devastated white corpse of the adult Jesus.

Throughout the fight to suppress the rebellious provinces, the Catholic world poured in money, resources and men to crush the Protestant upstarts. Men such as Alva, Parma and Spinola were heroes, patiently working on the side of God to expunge heresy. Each siege or battle was part of a cosmic conflict – imagined by Rubens in several huge canvases as between St Michael's angels and Satan's demons – which also became confused with the predominantly Catholic battle in Central Europe and the Mediterranean with the Ottoman Empire and, in a wider world, with the battle to extirpate every manner of paganism, from America to Asia.

Needless to say, the Protestants disagreed.

CHAPTER SEVEN

The sufferings of Lady Belge » Life in 'the garden' »
Birds, beasts and flowers » Croissants of crisis »
Whitewash and clear glass

The sufferings of Lady Belge

The English role in sixteenth-century Europe was an unhappy and vulnerable one. Early converted to Protestantism by Henry VIII for reasons of personal convenience, England formally removed itself from the influence of Rome in the 1530s but was buffeted by dynastic accident as three siblings took turns on the throne – Edward VI (the 'godly imp', a convinced but short-lived Protestant), Mary I (an equally convinced Catholic married to Philip II, but who was also short-lived) and Elizabeth I (a Protestant who any number of enemies prayed would also be short-lived). Each one of these reigns was convulsed by the killing or expulsion of those too close to the last regime. The English Channel was filled with the ships of terrified, dispossessed exiles. Douai, in the Spanish Netherlands, became a great centre for English Catholics, with several hundred missionary priests trained there to be infiltrated back into England and spread the word, of whom some one hundred and sixty were hunted down and killed on arrival. England played out its own version of the misery created by having several Christian variant faiths, each claiming absolute authority. Under Mary I, England supported her husband's war with France, which promptly resulted in the humiliating loss of its two-century-old outpost at Calais.

The intimate nature of English links with the nearest Netherlands towns is shown by their having their own English spellings: Flushing, Brill, The Hague, Ghent, Dunkirk. The North Sea was a pooled area of English–Dutch trade and fishing and the vagaries of the wind often meant their ships finding security in each other's ports. With the outbreak of the rebellion against the Spanish, Dutch Watergeuzen ('sea beggars'), a marginal nuisance to the Spanish, used English ports for a while to refit and to sell their booty before Elizabeth kicked them out as too much of a liability. It was their expulsion that forced them into their desperate raid on the coastal South Holland town of Brielle in 1572 which, famously, succeeded – the beginning of a process that would usher in decade after decade of acrimonious correspondence between Madrid and various generalissimi in the Low Countries and a tremendous number of penitential masses.

William the Silent was desperate for allies and there were numerous, inconclusive talks with Protestant states. Elizabeth shared the problem of all European royalty that the Dutch were, however agreeable, just rebels. There was no clear means by which such a novelty could be recognized. The only other case – the Swiss Cantons – was dealt with by pretending they were not there. William's assassination in 1584 removed the closest the Dutch had to a 'real' ruler (a prince) of a kind that could be recognized by other monarchs, but his title of Prince of Orange was now by descent inherited by his estranged Catholic son in Madrid.

Each outrage in the struggle by Spain to impose its authority and scotch the heads of the Protestant Hydra heaped pressure onto Elizabeth. The 'Spanish Fury' in Antwerp in 1576 which killed some eight thousand of its inhabitants and destroyed much of the town was seen by Protestants across Europe as something close to the Apocalypse. Back in rebel hands, Antwerp held out as the capital of the Dutch Revolt until 1585 when, after an epic siege, it finally fell to the Spanish. Thousands of Protestants trudged north and the city was rapidly re-Catholicized. One of the most wealthy and powerful ports in the world was now in ruins. Many of the key figures around Elizabeth – Leicester, Spenser, Sydney, Essex – were whipped up into a frenzy about the awful sufferings of what Spenser called 'Lady Belge'. There had been earlier plans, put forward by William's brother Louis of Nassau, to end the agonies of the Seventeen Provinces by shutting out Spain and giving each of the major adjoining countries a chunk – with England getting Zeeland and Holland, France Flanders and Artois and William the inland provinces and Friesland. This was a very Holy Roman Empire sort of proposal and one which looks wholly alien to us, but was plausible then. But with each year of the rebellion the northern provinces became more clearly a separate and self-conscious entity.

Finally in 1585 Elizabeth cracked, even though she thought the whole thing a 'financial sieve'. At the epochal Treaty of Nonsuch (named after one of Elizabeth's palaces, but in itself having an attractively *Alice in Wonderland* flavour) she agreed to supply thousands of troops and lots of money. Her status remained weird though – plans for her to be made 'Lady and Countess of Holland' fell through and she was never willing to make the jump of claiming full joint sovereignty (a jump eventually made by William III a century later but in the other direction). The Earl of Leicester headed off with Essex and Sydney on the great Protestant adventure – nicely shown on a medal from 1587 with a picture of Elizabeth I and Leicester vanquishing the Beast of the Apocalypse. England took over the sovereignty of the attractively named 'Cautionary Towns' – Brill, Flushing, Fort Remmekens. These re-orientated England further north up the coast from lost Calais and could have become permanent – Sydney was Governor of Flushing, and the Governor of Brill marked his English pride by naming his daughter Brilliana, who went on despite her odd name to have a remarkable and adventurous life. Just to finish up the Cautionary Towns – in a typically unvisionary move they were sold back to the Dutch by James I for cash.

The intervention was a fiasco. Leicester was acclaimed by Puritans as the new Joshua, Moses or Samson depending on which favourite Old Testament hero they wanted to tick. He met up with the new Stadtholder Maurice (William's second son) in The Hague and then did a grand, haughty tour with fireworks, triumphal arches and banquets. These last got out of hand and the English contingent became increasingly contemptible, with disgusting scenes in Amsterdam as drunken, scarlet-faced young noblemen contemptuously tossed sweets from the windows. A small country under siege for decades, with countless battle-deaths, with a religion based on frugal self-examination, filled with impoverished refugees, had scraped together every penny to entertain their seeming saviours, only to find they had invited in, not proud Spartan heroes, but a bunch of vomiting and groping wallies.

Leicester spent his time happily designing cap badges and took a delightful barge to Rotterdam rowed by sailors wearing special blue, red and buff uniforms and 'shag thrummed silk'. Sydney was killed at the woefully useless Battle of Zutphen (there is a small stone marker and a local dining society). If anything, these characters were reducing the Dutch will to resist rather than stiffening it. Philip II, though, had decided to take English intervention very seriously. Appalled at Elizabeth's actions and, as the consort of her late sister, himself a serious claimant to the English throne, he decided to add England to the Habsburg haul. It took years to build, man and victual and had no precedent – a hundred and thirty ships with some twenty-six thousand soldiers and sailors on board – but in 1588 the Armada sailed up the Channel to meet up with a further thirty thousand Spanish troops on the Flemish coast. For a few summer days the whole future of north-west Europe seemed at stake. The English were much helped by the same sort of swaggering, late-sixteenth-century cock-ups which had so dogged their own actions in the Netherlands. The Armada was weirdly unthought-through – a few fewer full-choir-and-incense preparatory masses and a bit more time spent on logistics would have helped. The Dutch had taken the elementary and fun precaution of removing all the seamarks from the terrifyingly dangerous, shifting Flemish shoals and sandbanks. The Spanish army in Dunkirk was separated from the Armada by shallow seas patrolled by aggressive coastal-draft Dutch warships. The English harried the Armada along the Channel and then freaked it out with fireships, which caused many Spanish ships to cut their anchor cables to escape. Once beyond the Flanders coast (and having not picked up the army) the winds meant (as was known to everyone involved – it cannot have been a surprise) that they would only be able to continue by returning home via the seas north of Scotland, for which there were no charts.

Obviously as a patriot I cheer the fate of the Armada, but what a sorry shambles it all was – thousands of corpses dotted around the British Isles, with that terrible, individual privacy that the death of each man on a sea-wreck has. The ships that had lost their anchors off Dunkirk were simply fending off doom by the hour. Some ships that somehow made it into an Irish harbour had their entire surviving crews executed at once. Perhaps ten thousand men returned to Spain, but many of them then died from malnutrition and exhaustion. For the English it was the great founding national victory; for the Dutch Republic it was also an epochal event – but with the additional knowledge that the vast, futile expenditure on the Armada (and its two successors, which were destroyed by storms before even reaching the Channel) could have hired entire mercenary armies for the Spanish. Philip II saw it, as usual, as something to do with God's will rather than just a stupid idea.

I was once in Orkney, hiking around the wonderfully barren, gnarled, 400-million-year-old landscape of the island of Hoy. From the southern settlement of Rackwick you can look out towards Scotland across the Pentland Firth, one of the world's most ghastly stretches of water, littered with hazards, flanked by sheer, implacable sea cliffs and with racing tides that would have made any Armada vessel battling to get back into the Atlantic completely helpless. Soggy and footsore, I staggered into a local community centre. This turned out to be a converted former church with – to my delight – a pulpit made from the oak of an Armada wreck. In itself the pulpit was somewhat disappointing: it was just wood after all, carved in the normal manner of the period. I am not sure how it could realistically look more atmospheric – perhaps if bits of a skeletal Spanish hand were still gripping it. Orkney is virtually treeless so each ship smashing into the shore must have been a total bonanza.

Life in 'the garden'

Following the great Spanish victory over the French army in Picardy at the Battle of St Quentin in 1557, Philip II, who had become king only a few months earlier, took a possibly eccentric decision. In his

Catholic fervour he noticed that the victory had occurred on the day of the feast of St Lawrence, a martyr cooked to death by the Romans on a griddle. As the first monarch of a new Empire, he decided to build a great mausoleum outside his new capital of Madrid, El Escorial ('the Griddle'), which would have a ground plan shaped like that familiar barbecue centrepiece. It was a measure of his power and confidence that his wishes were simply carried out. Nobody seems to have pointed out to Philip that his subjects would have to wait more than two centuries for hot-air balloons to be invented to appreciate from above such an unusual layout – but perhaps it was only meant to be enjoyed by God in Outer Space? The whole monstrous complex took over twenty years to build and in ceremonies that must have filled the entire region with incense his father and mother, Charles V and Isabella of Portugal, were reburied there – as would almost every Spanish monarch be, down to Alfonso XIII in 1980. El Escorial, like all such complexes, was designed to bolster and accrue an overwhelming sense of the royal family's greatness. Philip also built it as a powerhouse of Catholic scholarship – a place where new generations of priests could learn how to spread true doctrine across the Empire and provide the spiritual and intellectual shock-troops to eradicate Protestantism.

While El Escorial was being built, a parallel and very similar project was unfolding in the South Holland city of Leiden. The original Netherlands university was at Leuven, now squarely under Philip's control. In 1575 William the Silent decided, after Leiden had survived its ruinous siege and become more securely part of the north, to build a specifically Protestant university there, which would educate the elite that his new country required. Very oddly and legalistically the original founding document continues to acknowledge Philip II in his role as Count of Holland so, no doubt to his own horror, he technically helped to found this Altar to Moloch.

In my travels over the years I have several times come home to my family with elaborate plans to move to a European town and start life afresh. The children, swinging their legs and eating their beans on toast, gawp with fear, their ears flattened to the sides of their heads, as I explain how we ought to resettle in Bamberg, Novi Sad, Lübeck, Sighișoara. I talk about the languages we could learn, the people we could meet, the different foods, as the children, in mute panic, try to catch the eye of their mother. As I cheerfully sweep from the room, my head filled with the taverns we could run, the embroidered shirts the children could wear and the hikes we could all enjoy, I can hear sounds of whispered reassurance and stifled crying. Sadly, none of these plans have come to anything and the children are old enough now to make withering counter-suggestions as to where I myself might want to go. This is a shame, because it is only now that I can see where we should have settled: Leiden.

Fuelled, like the other northern Dutch towns, by thousands of southern refugees, the university became a rapid success. Its buildings are scattered around the town and give the whole place today an almost ridiculous sense of optimism and interest, helped by the schematic and rational flavour of the canals and bridges, pubs and churches, concert halls and coffee shops that knit together its great urban landscape. Everywhere its late-sixteenth – and seventeenth-century heyday is celebrated. There is the oldest university observatory in the world, started in 1633 (and wonderfully called in Dutch a *Sterrewacht* – a 'Star Watch'). There are buildings associated with the Pilgrims, the sect who settled here, fleeing from England in 1609, before ultimately taking the decision to find religious security and peace in North America. They tried hard to make their austerity work in Leiden but felt let down by constant backsliding and the town's temptations. Just as their arriving and survival in the New World is marked by Thanksgiving Day, I have always thought there should be matching Thanksgivings in places like Leiden, where they lived, Delfshaven, where they sailed from, and Southampton and Plymouth, where they launched themselves into the Atlantic, to celebrate the disappearance of these gloomy folk.*

* One of Barack Obama's ancestors is the beautifully named but no doubt vinegar-faced kill-joy Thomas Blossom.

Leiden's joys just heap up. There is the startling place of execution outside the old palace of the Counts of Holland – a set of pretty, atmospheric buildings including a pillared, covered area for the judges to watch from. Some gardener of genius recently had the brilliant idea of training flattened espaliered trees onto frames facing onto the execution yard so that the branches of each tree stick out on either side like arms spread in horror and dismay – at least, that is my reading of these spindly, Giacometti-esque objects. Just next to them is a former school building, through whose door Rembrandt once used to run.

Then there is the matchless Hortus Botanicus. This extraordinary place was masterminded by Carolus Clusius, born in Arras in 1526, who came to Leiden from Vienna, where he worked on the first ever catalogue of Alpine plants for the genial Habsburg Emperor Maximilian II. Clusius and his generation were perhaps one of the luckiest in Europe's history, flooded with the extraordinary challenges and stimulation of the great trade voyages, alert to the full implications of Europe's religious revolutions, building humanist ideas, but living before the horrors of the Thirty Years War. The Hortus keeps much of its old flavour, with its ranks of strange plants and its mix of academic research and public enjoyment. How many generations have been sickened by the immaculate little tubs of pitcher plants, looking like severed scrotums and filled with a ghastly sweet dew that tricks insects into falling in and then slowly dissolves them alive? There is rank upon rank of the tasty, the poisonous and the weird. An early seventeenth-century engraving shows the Hortus in all its glory, with its collection of strange creatures supplied by Dutch ships coming back from Asia – stuffed monitor lizards, a crocodile, a flying fox, a pufferfish, plus a somewhat random polar bear jaw from Nova Zembla. The gardens were also an early source of bee research, with a famous work on apiary (written as a dialogue between Clusius and his friend, the bee-expert Clutius) published in 1618, and still commemorated in a stack of straw-woven beehives, miniature versions of the ones in Brueghel the Elder's wondrous *The Beekeepers and the Birdnester*.

I will have to come back to the Hortus much later in this book for its huge nineteenth-century role, but I know nowhere that gives a more vivid sense of the excitement of new thinking, new discoveries, new flavours – a world of oranges and durians, of tea as a novelty. Because of the way that the town and university are so entangled you can still sense the degree to which the seventeenth century was filled with people happily wandering between disciplines, both physically and mentally – the sort of promiscuous, chewy intellectual atmosphere that created in the same era in England my own heroes, Sir Thomas Browne, Robert Burton, John Aubrey and Henry Vaughan. Their Dutch equivalents have a similar status in the Netherlands, standing for forms of enquiry that often jump around without the specialization that increasingly clamped down later: figures such as Hugo Grotius and Willebrord Snellius (the latter now with a crater named after him on the Moon, just south of the Sea of Tranquillity). Or the marvellous Simon Stevinus (it is unfortunate that these Latinized names make everyone sound absurd), originally from Bruges, a military engineer and mathematician and heroic dabbler. When not inventing key aspects of the decimal system he added to the joy of nations by building a land-yacht for Prince Maurice, William the Silent's son and successor, which was raced along the beach outside The Hague in 1600. Setting aside the atypical experience of medieval prisoners catapulted into besieged towns to freak out the defenders, the yacht must have achieved the highest human speed (at last outpacing the horse) yet seen on land in Europe.

In fact, more generally that experiment-strewn beach must have been an extremely appealing place. Prince Maurice had his own gun foundry built in The Hague and used to experiment on the beach with different calibres of weapon, battling to match up ideal lightness, range and strength – a perfect example of the sort of practical, mathematical and material fiddling which made the Dutch Republic so remarkable, and which could be seen in every area, from growing tulips to building ships, from drainage windmills to new types of oil-paint. As the Eighty Years War continued, one of the oddities became – as Spain yet again declared bankruptcy or all its ships got sunk – that inside the safety of the region behind the Dutch front line known as 'The Garden' it became more and more fun. This was also true behind the lines in the Spanish southern Netherlands, where the 1598–1621 joint reign of 'the Archdukes' (the Habsburg husband and wife Albert and Isabella) in Brussels saw the blooming of similar arts and gardens and the revival of Antwerp – glassware, jewellery, mirrors, tapestries were churned out and the great printer Christophe Plantin shuttled between Antwerp and Leiden according to the political situation. He printed extraordinary quantities of posters, pamphlets and books (including the works of Clusius), hitting pay dirt with the exclusive contract to supply breviaries and missals to the entire Spanish Empire, a deal which paid for the beautiful house and workshop which survives today in Antwerp.

Between these northern and southern safe zones the war ground on, aside from the Twelve Years Truce, brokered in Antwerp in 1609 between Prince Maurice and Philip III, with hostilities breaking out again at its end and entangling the Spanish–Dutch war with the wider conflict that became the Thirty Years War. For much of this time the Dutch economy boomed, with the ideal efficiency of most tax being recycled into paying Dutch suppliers of armour and guns, food, uniforms, wagons and horses; or most soldiers' wages being then spent on entertainment within Dutch towns, the latter immortalized in countless seventeenth-century genre paintings. These towns came to specialize over generations, turning out vast amounts of stuff – grenades from Utrecht, small arms from Dordrecht, priming matches from Gouda. About 90 per cent of Dutch government revenue went into the war and huge but secure debts were run up, while the Spanish were reduced to prostration, praying for the next treasure ships to arrive from America. In 1628 Admiral Piet Hein (a former galley slave) managed the unique feat of capturing the silver fleet – an event still charmingly sung about by Dutch children today, but presumably prompting another round of flagellation at El Escorial.

Even when things went well for Spain they wound up going badly. The epic of the later part of the war was the Siege of Breda, where Prince Maurice faced the Spanish general Ambrogio Spinola. By this time most Dutch troops were in fact foreign mercenaries and they faced Spanish troops who were mostly not Spanish (and Spinola was Italian). In contrast to the horrifying slog of such sieges as the nightmare at Ostend (some eighty thousand Spanish casualties; sixty thousand Dutch), the Siege of Breda was a triumph. Maurice died before the siege's end and was succeeded by his half-brother Frederick Henry, who now became Stadtholder. With the besiegers was Diego Velázquez, who was close to Spinola, and was inspired to create for his patron Philip IV the astonishing painting *The Lances*, a near sanctification of Spinola as a model of decency and courage, taking the surrender of the town from the Dutch commander Justinus of Nassau (the bastard son of William the Silent). It was a measure of Spanish desperation that by the time Velázquez completed the painting, ten years after the siege's end, it only had two years to be hung on the walls of Philip's Buen Retiro Palace before the Dutch took the town back, leaving a certain tension between the brilliance of the picture's technique and the derisive nature of its continuing presence.

Birds, beasts and flowers

Hopping off a rural train in French Flanders north-west of Lille, it is for a few moments confusing that there are no signs showing the way to the town of Cassel, my planned destination. Almost immediately though it becomes clear that there is no need – Cassel is perched on a hill, the hill, in a region famous for flatness, and squats there alluringly a couple of kilometres away. The surrounding fields look – even for someone as ignorant as myself about farming – almost unbelievably and densely fertile. Ploughs had just turned the soil and each rectangle seemed to be filled with sculpted peaks of soil of a fudge-like richness. Alongside the promise of an infinity of root vegetables, the soil also gave away the region's big problem – that it becomes a nightmarish quagmire in the rain, the soil engulfing boots and wheels, reducing huge animals to floundering helplessness and bringing all movement to a halt. Cassel even has a helpful little tourist information sign pointing out that this quality has encouraged the region's severely introverted localism – it is simply not worth the life-threatening and filthy hassle of visiting the next town. The winter dark in this sparsely populated area also has its terrors, and since earliest times hardly an autumn or winter can have gone by without farmers, travellers or soldiers finding themselves trapped in the mud with the sun rapidly setting and their hooves, feet and wheels starting to freeze in.

This is particularly noticeable walking up the steep hill into Cassel, which must have been a constant adventure for a horse and cart until the roads were fully paved. This hill has a specific cheeriness as it is reputedly the one featured in the folk song 'The Grand Old Duke of York'. It was excellent to feel neither up nor down but halfway up and – therefore – neither up nor down. I had expected the lanes to be blocked with laughing young British families engaged in this improving pastime, singing away, the locals in their cars good-naturedly rolling their eyes waiting for the ruck of brightly coloured Wellington boots and anoraks to clear. But perhaps it was too much of an ask on a cold December morning and this sort of middle-class frenzy only happens in the summer months. There are also pedants who point out that there were several useless Dukes of York who could potentially be derided in the old song, and the one who uselessly scrambled around Flanders during the first of the Revolutionary and Napoleonic Wars is only one candidate, and one undermined by being neither grand nor old at the time.

It was invigorating marching up a hill fuelled by a nursery rhyme nonetheless, an experience nobody should pass up. It was almost as good as what happened next, lunch in a cafe where almost every customer had next to their chair or on their table a bag filled with chicory, presumably just because it was on sale that day in the local market – but seemingly implying a bizarre local uniformity in celebrating that heroic member of the dandelion family's role as the quintessential regional foodstuff.

Cassel's unusual hill has made it the focus of much unwanted military attention. General Foch commanded the French troops in the region from Cassel in the opening phases of the First World War, learning about the unfolding nature of trench warfare and its

horrors, receiving the news of the death of both his son and his
son-in-law on the Lorraine front on the same day and, understandably, praying in the local church at six o'clock every morning.

I had not really done my homework – I was aware there was a
good museum in Cassel but not of what might be showing there.
When I saw a huge banner hanging from the museum entrance
saying ODYSSEY OF THE ANIMALS: FLEMISH ANIMAL PAINTERS
OF THE SEVENTEENTH CENTURY my initial thrill turned to anxiety.
What if this was the like the immortal scene in Disney's *Pinocchio*
where the bad boys are tricked onto Pleasure Island, thinking it is
the most fun place ever, but where they will in fact be turned into
donkeys? Admittedly it seemed an eccentric and over-elaborate use
of funds to create a giant banner specifically to trick just me into
going through the door and then submitting me to some nameless
horror. If someone wanted to abduct me or turn me into a donkey
they could have done so just as readily while I glanced mockingly
at the bags of chicory. Having regained confidence, I trooped into
an exhibition which simply featured everything I like the best. As
I see I've scrawled in my notebook: 'Oh no! Fleming animal painting exhibition!!'

The Flemish obsession with the brightly coloured and exotic
came from Antwerp's continuing role as one of the great entrepôts
for the Spanish Empire. This enthusiasm was matched by the Dutch
in the north, based on their own growing trade with the East Indies
and generation-long rule over the Brazilian north-east (1630–54).
An easy and enjoyable extra source of income for sea captains trading long-distance in sugar or spices was to add a few parrots. A
clamorous need for exotica convulsed the courts of Philip II in his
new capital at Madrid and of his nephew, the Emperor Rudolf II
in Prague. These two men were perhaps the greatest of all collectors, with Philip as enthusiastic about Titian or Bosch as he was
about elephants and rhinos. It is now impossible to reconstruct the
forms of shipboard heroism that safely got these immense creatures
across the oceans and safely unloaded. The Fugger banking family
had a set of cages at the Antwerp docks and were on a constant

lookout, in what must have been an unbelievably exciting time, for previously unimagined exotica.

It is not surprising then that the genre's great painters came from the region. Joris Hoefnagel was born in Antwerp, Peter Paul Rubens (king of the big animal painting, among many other things) moved there in his early teens, Roelant Savery was born in Kortrijk, grew up in Haarlem and settled in Utrecht after a glory period working for Rudolf in Prague. It is Savery who is the star of this exhibition, with a painting, I really believe, that is one of the great justifications for human existence. Called *Noah Thanking God for Saving Creation* (c. 1625), it is a vision of a staggeringly lush, harmonious world filled with friendly animals, and in the far distance, just visible, are the shattered remains of the grounded Ark. All kinds of unlikely creatures seem happy enough next to each other – lions and cassowaries, pelicans and leopards. Chickens peck obliviously alongside a mixed bag of dogs and foxes who do look as though they may be experiencing some inner turmoil on ethical issues. Noah kneels in thanksgiving next to a charismatic elephant, and the picture has the same sense of dreadful tension comparable to Flemish images of the Garden of Eden (filled with animals and illustrating the final happy and harmonious moments, as Eve hands Adam the apple) where everything *seconds later* will be in ruins. This too is a peaceful scene that cannot be preserved – as Noah gets up off his knees the farmyard friends will have to scatter, take to the hills and get reproducing before it is too late.

Most fabulously, in the bottom right of the picture, there is a dodo having a drink. The dodo is this period's quintessential bird. Discovered only a generation before by a Dutch expedition to Mauritius (named after Prince Maurice), there was a flurry of excitement about this bizarre-looking creature. Almost all we know about them comes from a handful of paintings – most in fact by Roelant Savery. Joris Hoefnagel painted one in Prague in 1602, but it is a deeply distressing image as the dodo's blackened head shows it must have already died – it is probably this bird whose partial skull and leg are in the Prague National Museum. Savery himself featured them frequently in his pictures, but also created the painting that everyone knows, now in the Natural History Museum in London, of a jaunty, fat creature, seemingly posing for a seaside saucy photo. This picture, alas, is thoroughly misleading. The first serious attempt in the nineteenth century to rebuild a dodo skeleton found in a Mauritian swamp used Savery's bird as a model and it was only many years later that it became clear the bird was not remotely fat, but quite limber. Savery's painting was copied by Tenniel for his *Alice in Wonderland* dodo and this image of a simple, loopy creature, an innocent almost pre-basted and Bacofoiled treat for sailors, was born. A lucky generation of Dutch sailors did undoubtedly eat a lot of dodos, but it now seems that its extinction came from the usual depressing business of rats and mice jumping off ships and eating all the eggs. There are a handful of other glimpses of dodos – a murky one can be seen rooting about at the back of one of the best-named paintings ever, *Perseus and Andromeda with a Dodo and Seashells*, by Gillis d'Hondecoeter (born in Antwerp), but otherwise the trail goes cold. Somehow Savery intersects by accident with the arrival of perhaps two or three dodos in north-west Europe and happens to paint them before they drift into oblivion.

I am in a quandary with these paintings as I would like to write an entire book about them, but have to move on. Aside from Rudolf, the other great promoters of this genre were the Archduke and Archduchess Albert and Isabella in Brussels, who created a beautiful series of gardens next to the Coudenberg Palace which were immortalized by Jan Breughel the Elder, with Albert and Isabella almost blasphemously prelapsarian in the midst of a crowd of docile birds and deer. It was perhaps unsurprising, in the context of warfare that had persisted for generations, that gardens should become associated, whether in the Spanish Netherlands or the independent north, with specific ideas of peace, grace and privacy. Clusius's Hortus Botanicus in Leiden was part of the same impetus that created Savery's dodo pictures. Dutch ships coming back from the East Indies, the Near East, Brazil, the West Indies, Mauritius and the Cape of Good Hope would load up with exotica and then these could be planted and studied in the chilly air of Leiden University. Clusius's whole career, uneasily weaving between Catholic and Protestant environments, shows that the barriers were far from absolute between the two. But Clusius will for ever be associated with making one of the most important of all interventions in Dutch society. While in Vienna with Maximilian he had experimented with Turkish plants in the gardens there and had since studied them intensively. In 1593, the year he arrived at Leiden he planted the first of these, flowering the following year. The tulip had arrived.

Croissants of crisis

The Anglo-American polemicist Alexander Coburn once wrote an essay deriding the imaginary patterns Pentagon strategists in the Cold War would come up with to link countries in practice separated by mountains, religion, language and history into some unified 'crescent of crisis'. A variant on the domino theory, this allowed alarming lines on maps to link bits of Latin America or South-east Asia in a way that sounded dynamic and plausible, with the leftist bacteria relentlessly creeping round the crescent. But why did it always have to be a crescent? Cockburn suggested it was in practice no more plausible than if they called it a 'croissant of crisis'. Indeed, he suggested, you could muck about with marker pens on maps and come up with pretty much any shape and claim it as an alarming one – a 'bagel of Bolshevism', or a hair-raising 'crumpet of catastrophe' in which 'holes of subversion' sat in the solid 'crumpet base' of Moscow.

In the early seventeenth century the key strategic baked goods were scattered around the area of the north-west where the Rhine split in two – the chunkier (the Waal) heading west to Nijmegen and the lesser (the Nether Rhine) north to Arnhem. All over Europe hungry eyes with rival maps stared at the area, waiting and waiting for Johann Wilhelm, its mad, childless duke, to die, which he finally did in 1609. He owned the Duchies of Kleve, Jülich and Berg, the County of Ravensberg and the tiny enclave within the Dutch

Republic of Ravenstein, to which we will not refer again. Kleve was an important place – it controlled the split in the Rhine and was made up in part of former floodplain which had been converted to particularly lush, dense agricultural land. Hiking west of Kleve today it is still an astonishing sight – deliriously packed and fecund, with every ledge generating peas and carrots without end. It briefly bobs into English history as the home of the unhappy Anne of Cleves (aunt of the last duke), and the duchy used to be known in English, enjoyably, as Cleveland.

Strategically it was important – but only in the way that everywhere is strategically important if you feel that way. The problem was the timing of the duke's death, as Europe's political and religious situation rotted around him. The Dutch needed a friendly Kleve on their eastern borders; the Spanish equally saw the pleasure to be had in placing an ally there to damage their enemy's strategic position. As a half-dozen or so dynastically concerned aristocrats paid rare visits to their bandy-legged court librarians to give instructions to dust off various old forged pedigrees, the key figure became the wife of the Elector of distant Brandenburg. In a development of tremendous significance for the future of European history, the clever and forceful Anna of Prussia stood at the intersection of two great dynastic claims. Her father was the mad Albert Frederick, Duke of Prussia, who had outlived both his sons, making Anna's husband his heir. Anna's mother was the sister of the earlier-mentioned other mad duke, the childless ruler of Kleve-Jülich, and through her Anna became the route to her husband's claim there as well.

For the first and last time everybody was interested in Kleve. The Elector of Brandenburg was absurdly far away in his tiny and impoverished capital of Berlin. His ancestors had bought the land and title of Elector two centuries before from the flailing, low-rent Emperor Sigismund, which made them automatically important, but without the resources for much glamour or many troops. The Kleve-Jülich inheritance was a rich one and it would give the Elector a western base, but he needed allies. Normally the issue would have been resolved through the Emperor – but these were the last days of the chaotic necromancer and melancholic Rudolf II, alone with his dodo sketches. At the highest levels Rudolf's court was wrecked by in-fighting and a fervid Catholic resurgence which was very bad news for Protestant states such as Brandenburg.

This incapacity at the centre encouraged local military solutions. In a fateful move, a Protestant Union had been set up – a military alliance between Berlin, the Palatinate and the Dutch Republic to impose Anna and the Elector on the disputed territories against the five or six other claimants. The Emperor then shook himself awake and responded by allying with Bavaria in a Catholic League. Spanish troops marched towards Jülich and a general war seemed to be threatened. King Henry IV of France (genial, informal, not mad: perhaps the only French monarch it would have been fun to have had dinner with) also decided that the dispute provided an opportunity to take on the Spanish and prepared to march towards the duchies. The entire operation ground to a halt when a Catholic fanatic, Ravaillac, assassinated Henry, creating a trauma that knocked France out of the international arena for many years (Ravaillac was pulled in four bits by horses and his very surname abolished).

In the end the crisis fizzled out, not least because of France's implosion. At the Treaty of Xanten in 1614, the Brandenburgers split the territories with another claimant, the Count Palatine of Neuburg. This was meant to be temporary, but later, overwhelming events froze the arrangement. And so distant Berlin came to rule Kleve and became a Western European power, of a constrained kind. Kleve was never a great asset. It was a classic mini-state of the type that made its money off extortion from ships unfortunate enough to want to trade up the river it controlled. Each riparian entity charged a toll and straightforward goods which were worth a sensible sum up-river in Basle became worth a king's ransom by the time they got to Rotterdam. Understandably most Rhine trade therefore remained local. Kleve never bought into Brandenburg's (later Prussia's) 'Spartan' military aesthetic either. A typically batty, parochial gang of local worthies sabotaged Berlin's rule at every turn and when troops were demanded to be sent east, they deliberately sent 'limp and soft' young men who blubbed with homesickness. But it nonetheless established remote Prussia as a country with western interests and these would play out over the coming centuries in ways undreamed of in the early seventeenth century.

This was a good example of a croissant of crisis, and it was very unfortunate that the Rhine was scattered with similarly flaky and tempting items. There were rival claims, rival families, religious differences which could lead individuals to see continued accommodation with a rival brand as blasphemous. You could join up any number of lines and create sinister linkages, through the Spanish Road which took troops up from Italy to the Netherlands, through marriage arrangements, specific patches of wealth, the Calvinist International. The Kleve Crisis was resolved in part through mediation by France and England. But there was, despite the truce between Spain and the Dutch Republic, an increasing sense in the 1610s that Europe was running out of such mediators and that the grown-ups had left.

Whitewash and clear glass

In the interests of full disclosure I have to admit that my own religious views have never really recovered from watching Federico Fellini's film *Roma* (1972) at a vulnerable age. I never tire of watching Fellini – even his objectively fairly terrible later films you know will sooner or later include some lovely piece of Catholic travesty. There are many scenes in *Roma* which occupy key places in my personal mythology, but the place of honour belongs to the ecclesiastical fashion-show sequence: serving boys roller-skate down the catwalk swinging censers, bishops parade in glowing, flashing neon vestments and the relic skeletons of saints hang at jaunty angles from the sides of jeeps in the manner of the Andrews Sisters.

I mention this partly from missionary zeal to spread the word about Fellini's greatness, but more importantly because I can never hear the words 'modernization' or 'renewal' in a Catholic context without an immediate flashback to *Roma*'s nuns in giant wimples. This issue preoccupied me when spending some time in various

southern Dutch towns where the scars left by layers of 'renewal'
can still be seen. With every brand of Catholic and non-Catholic
Christianity proclaiming renewal, in an atmosphere of poisonous,
frenzied violence, there would, at last, be ushered in, after much
agony, a revolutionary new world of genuine indifference.

In around 1630 the tangled, spotty map of Dutch religious
belief at last froze and has been little changed since, but this was a
result that would have then appalled everybody. By definition a
religion can only be so tolerant before it makes its own message
entirely unconvincing. The many decades of fighting before 1630
forced onto all inhabitants of the Low Countries, outside the
impregnable fortresses of Amsterdam and the north, an acute series
of choices about their beliefs and how far they would go to protect
them. A city like Breda is one of many examples: occupied with a
general massacre by Spanish troops in 1581, retaken by Dutch
troops in 1590, taken after an epic siege by the Spanish again in
1625 and taken again by the Dutch in 1637, its surviving inhabitants were subjected to a nightmare which engulfed several
generations. The nature of the fighting meant that religious identity
was a killer – ownership of a specific book, of some beads, of a
statue, or where and how you buried your dead were issues which
could result in execution, imprisonment, forced enrolment in work
gangs, confiscation of property. Each successful siege created a miserable outflux of those whose only safety lay in entangling their
wagons with those of the defeated army. Dutch towns became used
to dealing with traumatized Protestants from the south heading
north. The Troy-like epic of the Siege of Ostend (1601–4) resulted
in the town and its population having to be rebuilt from scratch,
its few surviving Protestant civilians fleeing to Sluis and Flushing.
The relentlessly Catholic nature of Belgium is the result of any
number of treks northwards by defeated people who had never
imagined they would be leaving their homes for ever (or, in some
cases, until the next successful counter-siege).

The issue of belief is permanently dramatized in the town of
Dordrecht. It may have just been an accident of timing, but when
I was wandering around it there seemed throughout its streets to

be nothing but workmen fixing roads, roofs, doorways and quay-sides. It was as though the lopsided, ancient nature of much of the town meant that its inhabitants were in a permanent rear-guard action to prevent the whole wonky ensemble from falling into the Old Maas River. The town's odd ancientness was summed up by a higgledy-piggledy house with patched-on classical features – little Corinthian pilasters and a design in the entablature featuring a beaver, some fruit and a very strange emblem of two burly mermen with their suffused and muscular tails intertwined. It was completely impossible not to see this as an early-modern thumbs-up for male love, albeit of a specialized kind, but I fear it may just have been some tedious allegory of different rivers joining their courses in the town.

In any event, Dordrecht is famous for its painters and for its bogglingly large, oil-tanker of a church which looms over the town like some permanent, ancient moral reproach. It was near this church in 1618, at the wonderfully named Arquebusiers' Shooting Range, that an international congress was opened, the Synod of Dort as it is known in English, to define and confirm the nature of Protestantism. It was held during the Twelve Years Truce and there were high hopes that with sufficient prayerfulness and intellectual rigour a united Protestant position could at last be found. There was great anxiety that the Catholic Council of Trent (1545–63) had, through agreement on doctrine and discipline, successfully re-launched Catholicism. Newspapers and sermons were full of horror stories about, for example, the successful sweeping away of Protestants from much of Austria by the resurgent Habsburgs: churches blown up, books burned and the corpses of those buried as heretics dug up and thrown into the streets.

The Dordrecht church remains as a sort of enormous bell jar preserving the atmosphere of that synod. Its whitewashed walls and mostly clear glass express a sober aesthetic which would have been matched by the relentlessly black-and-white clothing of the delegates (in contrast to the Fellini-esque Council of Trent, where it must have been sometimes hard to hear yourself speak over the sound of swishing silks). The synod was made up of ten colleges –

one for each Dutch province, one for theology faculties and one for
the Walloon church, meaning French-speaking Protestant refugees
from the south. There were representatives from England, Scotland,
Hesse, Bremen and the Palatinate (the last a Calvinist bastion that
would be shortly torn to pieces in the Thirty Years War). Louis XIII
would not allow French Protestants (Huguenots) to attend so their
bench was left symbolically empty.

The tragedy of the synod lay in the nature of Protestantism.
Inspired by Calvin, the attendees felt as much scorn for Luther as
for the Pope – and this split implied (or made explicit really) the
likelihood of further splits, potentially limitless splits. For the synod
the persecution of Lutherans was almost as significant as that of
Catholics. Indeed, once the Universal Church was broken, Western
Europe stepped into a world painfully lacking any sort of playground monitor – or rather one featuring several rival playground
monitors who were intent on killing one another. The Netherlands
was already a mass of forcibly discarded beliefs. In many ways the
long period in which Dutch forms of Protestantism had developed,
generally in wartime and accompanied by waves of many thousands
of refugees, had destroyed Catholicism, but not necessarily replaced
it with anything else. There was a horror at the idea that the expulsion of the Pope had led just to forms of indifferentism rather than
to true, reformed black-and-white fervour. In the 1590s, it was
reckoned that of Utrecht's thirty churches only three were now in
use. The Truce had allowed a Cologne-based Catholic mission to
be set up which trained courageous priests to re-infiltrate the Netherlands, in the same way that the English College in Douai
smuggled priests into England. The Truce also allowed Catholics in
the eastern borderlands of Gelderland and Overijssel simply to
walk east into Kleve and Münster where they could worship as they
wished.

The stakes at the synod were therefore high, but with the
chance of compromise limited by the nature of intellectual religious
belief, where compromise simply meant failure and the destruction
of the soul. Several delegates made clear they would only attend on
the basis that their own beliefs would be confirmed. At the heart

of the synod's problems lay what proved to be a cataclysmic split between two views on predestination: one in which there was no human action that could alter the nature of punishment or reward in the afterlife – the idea, rather wonderfully, that the Last Judgement was not a future event, but a *timeless process*; the other that there were indeed actions in this life that could influence whether, later on, one was damned or saved. This split was named, after their most articulate spokesmen, Gomarism and Arminianism, and came near to destroying the Republic.

The Great Church preserves a lovely nineteenth-century model of the synod, a simplified interior filled with six-inch-high dolls in white ruffs with individually designed beards. The one epochal, positive decision taken by the life-size versions was to create a new Bible in Dutch, to be re-translated directly from the Hebrew, Aramaic and Greek. The form of Dutch to be used would take elements of Brabants and Hollands and was instrumental in creating a standardized written Dutch which moved it decisively further away from German. These biblical projects were more than purely religious in their impact – creating skills, interests and habits of mind which could be applied to translating any other language as well, with crucial intellectual, trade and colonial implications.

In the end, while everyone could agree on the whitewash and plain glass, they could not agree on the nature of our fate as humans. The Arminians were allowed to make their case at the synod but were derided. The political implications were huge, as Arminianism was embraced by van Oldenbarnevelt, architect of the Truce, and many of the 'regents', effectively the civic ruling class. On the face of it the Truce should have been popular, but many observers made the point that it was a betrayal of all those still crushed beneath the heel of Catholic Spain and, while it allowed a breathing space for the Dutch to prepare for a renewal of the fighting, it also did so for the Spanish. What was meant to be an intelligent response to a nightmare conflict that had already gone for over forty years turned in the view of many into a period of rot and lethargy. The Arminians at the synod were forced to agree to desist from preaching or writing. In response van Oldenbarnevelt tried to create a militia to defend Holland. The Stadtholder Maurice – who in his personal life acknowledged his own adherence to the doctrine of 'total depravity' with a cheerfulness that appalled the austere Gomarists – nonetheless supported them and ended the stalemate by marching through Utrecht and arresting and then executing van Oldenbarnevelt at The Hague. This bloodthirsty spasm made the Dutch Reformed Church in the form understood at Dordrecht into the national religion. It was also one of several moments in 1618–19 which signalled a new and terrible recklessness. The Reformation, it could be argued, had failed. Most of Europe remained Catholic and any religion based on a fervent sense of its own truth cannot live with such failure – it cannot be both true and almost completely unsuccessful. The actions at Dordrecht and The Hague proved to be part of a far wider and, as it proved, ruinous decision by a generation of men, both Catholic and not, to use military means to end this stalemate.

CHAPTER EIGHT

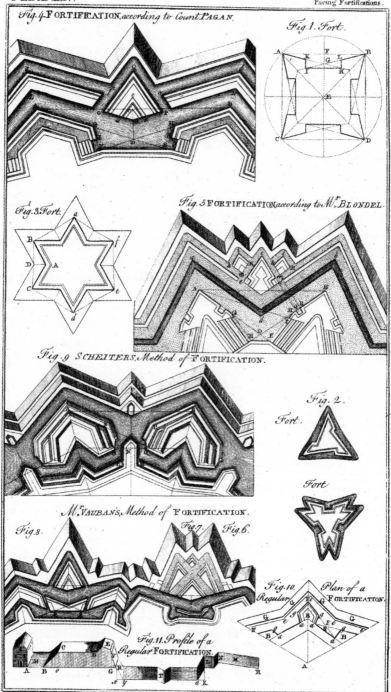

PLATE LXV.

Fig. 4. FORTIFICATION, according to Count PAGAN.

Fig. 1. Fort.

Fig. 3. Fort.

Fig. 5. FORTIFICATION according to M.n BLONDEL.

Fig. 9. SCHEITERS Method of FORTIFICATION.

Fig. 2.

Fort.

Fort.

M.r VAUBAN'S Method of FORTIFICATION.

Fig. 8. Fig. 7. Fig. 6.

Fig. 10. Plan of a
Regular FORTIFICATION.

Fig. 11. Profile of a
Regular FORTIFICATION.

'A harvest of joys'

One way in which all history books fail is that they provide accounts of events which suppose that they are being read by an enlightened outsider. This also creates a shape for events which steers the reader's attitude – so if you are engrossed by a book on the Thirty Years War and are reading about the events of 1645 you know that there are three years to go. But for those who were living the events there were no means of understanding what would happen next – nobody would fight on until 1648 so as to make it a round thirty years. So the shape of historical events is unavailable to those living them, but also unavailable was the status of being that genuinely enlightened outsider. Consequences, good and bad, needless or inevitable, could only be guessed at, and yet seem glaringly obvious to the modern-day history reader. When Charles V agreed to the Peace of Augsburg with the Schmalkaldic League in 1555, only Europe's most lukewarm cynic, or those devoted to a purely private faith, would have seen it as a permanent settlement. The Peace recognized Lutheranism as a legitimate form of Christianity, but not Calvinism. It tried to pin down for good the form of faith in each territory, but such near neutralism was always unacceptable to many. But the stakes were so much higher than this. Belief in this period was, by definition, incompatible with coexistence. Belief was not a form of party dress – gorgeously coloured and elaborate if Catholic; a lot less fun if Calvinist. It was built in that the other faiths had to be both completely wrong and wicked. Luther's ideas were not meant to provide an alternative to existing Christianity, but to replace it – and its failure to do so as well as the creation of other forms of reform left Europe in a state of bad-tempered chaos.

Charles V's abdication led to a drastic change in Europe's structure, with the major sources of power switching to Madrid and to the borders of the Ottoman Empire, leaving the western Empire suddenly as a backwater. Charles was always going off to Tunis or Bologna and while he may have been born a Fleming he soon lost any local affection. The long and incoherent reign of the Emperor Rudolf II in Prague particularly rotted the Empire's structure – because of Rudolf's own prolonged bouts of disengagement, his vicious arguments with his siblings and the dismaying Long Turkish War which ground on through the 1590s and 1600s (and which, of course, was not to start with viewed as Long by its generals). To use a playground metaphor, the extended period of distraction and lack of engagement by Rudolf was rather like in a primary school where all the teachers have disappeared: for a while everyone keeps on playing nicely – but after a few hours they start spontaneously developing slave labour, concubinage and human sacrifice.

Every territory in the Empire viewed the Peace as a mere interlude. Those answering to the Pope recovered their bounce with the soul-searching and creative Council of Trent. The different Reform strands were at odds with one another and people were baffled and fearful at their lack of success. There was also the grand theatre provided by the Dutch–Spanish war, which was understood as a fight between Calvinism and Catholicism, even if this was only partly true. All this meant that any religious changes within the Empire would generate bad ripples. A lot of these changes were personal and effectively just accidental.

One with enormous future implications occurred in the Palatinate. The fervently religious and Catholic Frederick of Simmern had been converted to Lutheranism by his wife Maria. When he became Elector of the Palatinate he sat in Heidelberg in a quagmire of theological earnestness, mulling and disputing with various no doubt grim theologians before deciding that he would move on and become a Calvinist. The early 1560s were then devoted to iconoclasm, mass sackings and friendly overtures to the Dutch. Frederick ignored Imperial threats, but was hamstrung by his own son Ludwig being an equally convinced Lutheran who waited patiently for his father's death (in 1576) to shift everyone back. Ingeniously though, Frederick carved out a small territory for his younger son, Johann Casimir, around the town of Kaiserslautern which could remain Calvinist. Ludwig on coming to the throne duly cleared out the Calvinists but died young, leaving one nine-year-old son (his other sons had died before their first birthdays), Frederick IV, for whom Johann Casimir became regent, and who was therefore raised a Calvinist. As can be imagined, these years saw a certain amount of chaos in Heidelberg, with organs being moved in and out of churches and congregations having to pretend they didn't know various hymns and then suddenly remembering them again. The Palatinate's Elector therefore became, on pretty shambolic grounds, the great beacon for Calvinist hopes in the western Empire, with devastating results for the next generation.

The sheer earnestness of the Palatinate was missing, further down the Rhine, in Bonn, capital of the Catholic Electorate of Cologne. Here theological dispute was reduced to farce, when Elector Gebhard, Archbishop of Cologne, fell in love. There was a precedent for this and the Augsburg agreements permitted priests who wished to marry to resign and change faith. There never seems any suggestion that Gebhard was motivated by anything other than his desire for Agnes von Mansfeld-Eisleben, but he announced to the world that he was not just going to become a Calvinist but stay on as the archbishop of a large, ancient, entirely Catholic territory. The mayhem caused by the marriage in 1583 led to his Electorate being torn to pieces by rival armies. He was hard to defend because he was such an idiot, but the Cologne War was too good an opportunity for others to further the Protestant presence on the Rhine. It also had a profound impact on the other Electors – the Palatinate, Saxony and Brandenburg were all Protestant and if Cologne could also be brought over then the Catholics would become a minority of the seven, with profound implications for the next Emperor's election. Everyone poured in, creating a ghastly sneak preview of the Thirty Years War – including, in a particularly sinister touch, the intervention of thousands of Spanish troops, a key moment in demonstrating that specifically German religious issues could no longer be treated just as Imperial business. Gebhard and Agnes inevitably lost and fled to Strasbourg, leaving Bonn and its hinterland as Catholic then as it is today. The one physical monument to his folly is the distinctive wrecked castle in Bad Godesberg. Blown up during the Cologne War, its garrison massacred and its bleak outline left as a reminder to later generations of the stark cost of disobedience, it is now a luxury hotel.

These were all preliminaries, among others, to the Thirty Years War (1618–48), the catastrophe that is generally reckoned to have killed a third of all German-speakers, many through plague. The conventional view is that it was an almost surreally awful stalemate, with round after round of battles, each triumph petering out and each country humiliated in turn: just a meaningless sequence of actions by out-of-control gangs of horsemen with cheap armour, floppy hats, lank hair and VD. The war would loom large in the nineteenth century as a historical morality tale about German weakness – with the Empire shown as a futile and divided arena trampled over by more powerful outsiders. It became an argument for the creation of the new German Empire in 1871, which would through its unity and strength ensure that such horrors never happened again. But I am struck by the degree to which arguments around the war being uniquely futile can be seen as merely Protestant special pleading: the war was in fact decisive and definitive. It ensured that many areas of Central Europe became Catholic again; it confirmed the Catholic Habsburg stranglehold over the Empire; it ended political Protestantism in France; and it ensured the failure of the Protestant project – corralled into a small group of north-west European countries. Meanwhile Jesuit and other Catholic missionaries spread around the world, from Peru to China, as celebrated by Rubens's vast super-Catholic canvases. The war only took so long because a series of misguided Protestant 'paladins' – the Elector of the Palatinate, the King of Denmark, the King of Sweden – took turns to overplay their hand and be ejected.

Eventual realpolitik French intervention saved some Protestant areas, but only because the French wished to mess up the Habsburgs and ensure they did not become too powerful – France, after all, was itself Catholic and the Protestant states it rescued were simply tools to be briefly picked up and then chucked aside.

To describe the entire course of the Thirty Years War here would be to launch into some fifty to sixty confusing pages. It stemmed from the catastrophic decision, described in the next section, by the young Calvinist Elector Palatine Frederick V (the son of Frederick IV) to accept the throne of Bohemia from a cabal of Protestant nobles – a challenge in all kinds of intolerable ways to the imperial Habsburg dynasty which, unnoticed by Frederick, had unfortunately just revived and refreshed itself after a long period of weakness. Much of the fighting happened in the central and eastern Empire, but one of the war's grim features was the way that wayward, exhausted and unpaid armies were constantly on the hunt for undevastated land – for food, fodder and loot. Almost every area would, perhaps after twenty or more years of security, suddenly find itself the focus of appalling savagery, disasters immortalized in the Lorrainer Jacques Callot's brilliant if horrible engravings *Great Miseries of the War* and Grimmelshausen's remarkable novel *Simplicius Simplicissimus* (1668). Grimmelshausen wrote it in old age, but in some ways it was closely based on his experience in the Imperial army, not least during the fighting around the Black Forest in 1637 and as a garrison soldier in the Rhine fortress of Offenburg. He lived around Strasbourg, becoming very famous and staying alive long enough to witness the French invasion of 1676.

The motives of many involved in the fighting definitely had an end-of-the-world flavour, a sense that an unfortunately rather diverse and mutually hostile spread of Christian Gods were holding various individuals' sword arms. The Emperor Ferdinand II was one of Europe's truly chilling leaders, whose unshakable belief that he had been put on his throne to cleanse Europe of heretics lay at the heart of the disaster. We know a lot about the thoughts of his entourage because Protestant historians have enjoyed themselves over the years picking through sermons and letters for creepy comments.

My favourite is from Ferdinand's ghastly Luxembourger Jesuit confessor Wilhelm Lamormaini, who, in the wake of a particularly unworkably violent anti-Protestant edict, wrote to the Pope that 'no Roman pontiff has received such a harvest of joys from Germany since the time of Charlemagne' – in other words directly comparing Protestants to pagan Saxons and Avars.

As Ferdinand's advisers flapped their arms about with excitement, not knowing whether to pray or self-flagellate first, even the Pope began to worry. Europe's strange self-correcting mechanism now came into play and the clean sweep dreamt of by Ferdinand became impossible, while continuing, pointless ruin rained down. The war in the end outlived almost all its major instigators, grinding to a halt in 1648 after protracted, tortuous negotiations by the next generation. These agreements, known collectively as the Peace of Westphalia, among many other things recognized that the Swiss were no longer part of the Empire – a major breakthrough as the Swiss had spent the war armed to the teeth waiting to be the next item on Ferdinand's agenda. It also formalized an important left-over piece of business: during the disastrous attempt back in 1551 by various Protestant German princes to rebel against Charles V, the bribe offered by them to the French to intervene in return for the Imperial 'Three Bishoprics' had done nothing to help their cause. The French had nonetheless swept in (led by a man called Anne, perhaps oddly) and had held on to the territories ever since in a legal limbo. It was almost a century later then that the Peace of Westphalia acknowledged this transfer. Toul, with its spectacular cathedral, would fall into obscurity: but the confirmed French ownership of Metz and Verdun would have a rich, complex future.

Fencers and soap-boilers

For some years the Musée des Beaux Arts in Antwerp has been shut for repairs, much to the benefit of the whole city as the best of its collection has been found homes in other, less frostily pompous surroundings. So Jean Fouquet's unbelievable painting from around

1450 of a bare-breasted, alabaster-skinned Agnès Sorel, Charles VII of France's mistress, pretending to be the Virgin Mary ('Are you quite sure, Your Majesty? ... Yes but of course: a quite brilliant notion') is in the cosily domestic surroundings of the Mayer van den Bergh Museum and made even more shocking. The great beneficiary though, and with any luck this will be permanent, is that the sequence of guild-sponsored religious paintings, from Quinten Metsijs's *The Lamentation* (1509) to Hendrik van Balen's *Saint John Preaching in the Wilderness* (c. 1622), are back in the cathedral from which they were long absent: chopped up, re-cut, sold, confiscated, burned, but even after so many upsets still one of the greatest sequences of paintings in all of Western art.

The pictures, together with the much patched-up guild halls on the city's main square, have battled into the twenty-first century as fragments of a way of life that dominated Europe's towns and cities from the Middle Ages to the eighteenth century. The guilds, crafts and fraternities that paid for these pictures not only regulated their own trades but organized everything from carnivals to funerals to local defence. The pictures were designed to act as a promotional tool for the virtues of the group that sponsored them. Some are straightforward: so the Guild of Schoolmasters had Frans II Francken paint *Christ among the Scribes*, the scribes in gorgeous clothing and dotted among them several saints and various lucky, immortalized guildsmen. One of the wings of this triptych was paid for by the Craft of the Soap-Boilers, who had to scratch around for an appropriate biblical topic and must have been relieved to find the tangential little story of Elijah rewarding the widow of Zarephath by conjuring up whole jugs of oil from one drop. The Craft of the Wine Taverners have an easy home win with Maerten de Vos's *The Wedding at Cana* (1597) and the Craft of Tailors, in Artus Wolffort's *Adoration of the Magi* (1615), promote their wares simply by giving the kings the most astoundingly lux robes.

There were several 'armed guilds', including the Longbowmen, the Arbalesters (crossbowmen), the Fencers and the Handgunners. These provided security for convoys, training and town defence and were upgraded as new weapons were invented. The Guild of

Fencers had been founded in 1488 in honour of the Emperor Frederick III and his son Maximilian. It was this guild who paid for one of the most famous of these paintings, Frans Floris's *Fall of the Rebel Angels* (1554), the only surviving element from a triptych otherwise destroyed in the great wave of iconoclasm that hit Antwerp in 1566. Floris was probably at the time the most famous Antwerp artist, but principally for his tragically transient, apparently magical contributions to the swaggering Joyous Entry into Antwerp of the Emperor Charles V and his son Philip in 1549. *The Fall of the Rebel Angels* that he created for the Fencers is a virtuoso phantasmagoria, the entire canvas jammed with mutant bodies assembled from atrocious combinations of snake, boar, butterfly, lynx and human. There is no detail not perverted in some way – a nipple becomes a claw, a penis an eagle's head. Up above – to the rescue – come St Michael (the Fencers' patron) and his friends, chopping and stabbing their way through the disgusting heap and, in a smart bit of product placement, using the favoured weapons of the Fencers.

So many places remain haunted by these now long-gone guilds. They were major patrons but their members were also, of course, by definition the creators of almost all the objects that have been preserved in museums. The painters themselves belonged to the Guild of St Luke, named after the apocryphal but charming story that St Luke himself painted from life the real Madonna and Child. All the wonderful things once nurtured by the Craft of Gardeners, Fruiterers and Basket-Makers have long gone, but the Guild of Goldsmiths and the Guild of Ironmongers have left plentiful traces. Guilds sometimes turn up in unexpected places. The Minster of Freiburg-im-Breisgau was built over many years by the townspeople, and guilds paid (among other things) for some of the stained glass, with their symbols as part of the design: immortalizing them with a pair of scissors for the Tailors, a pretzel for the Bakers, a barrel for the Coopers. The Guild of Arbalesters still have the tallest guild hall in Antwerp, topped with a magnificent gold statue of their patron saint St George despatching his dragon. Somehow the Guild of Arquebusiers (who in Antwerp commissioned Rubens's *The Descent from the*

Cross) still have their practice range in Basle, albeit long turned over to other uses. The more workaday guilds tended to thrive without much innovation (the pretzel in a fourteenth-century window is exactly the same shape as now), but others were obliged constantly to mutate. Anyone dealing with the Burgundian or Habsburg courts was producing goods from extremely expensive, scarce materials for a flighty, fashion-conscious clientele with a poor record for payment. Barring a cataclysm bills *were* paid, but sometimes not for a generation.

It has been a commonplace for historians since the eighteenth century to moan about guilds and how they held back progress through their restrictive practices and conservatism, but there is no real evidence for this. The great industrial concerns that sprang up later did make them increasingly pointless, but until then they were responsible for almost every innovation in Europe's history. Indeed, there is a good argument that it was their members' ceaseless mulling and tinkering that allowed Europe to outstrip the rest of the world. Just as over the centuries the needs of long-distance travel and bouts of fighting meant that naval vessels, through hundreds of small and almost unrecorded fixes, became ever more powerful; so, throughout the aggressively self-improving towns of Western Europe, unknown individuals in specific workshops refined locks, hinges, drills, triggers, cheeses, pendulums. Things became miniaturized, alloys more reliable, strawberries bigger, gun ranges longer.

Furniture became more elaborate: Antwerp was again important in this, starting a trend for walnut and exotic woods rather than the unvarying oak. Guilds of carpenters, who used to do the lot, were abandoned in the sixteenth century by more specialized joiners, and then the joiners in the seventeenth century split to form guilds of cabinetmakers. Armour, air pumps, navigation aids, engraving techniques were all being chewed over, in most cases with no record at all of who made this slightly more accurate clock or that handy form of wood-join. Different cities were highly competitive and the guilds tried to keep control over specific inventions, but except in the short term this was impossible. There was always an itinerant element, with so many towns so near to each other, even with quite different jurisdictions – not just with journeymen (in their 'wander years' before joining a specific town guild) on the move, but also such ambulant characters as clockmakers, who would also work as locksmiths, and blacksmiths (who did a lot more than just shoe horses). Gunners and printers were also traditionally footloose, going wherever somebody needed to be shot or better informed.

A sort of summa of both guild and itinerant work has survived in Strasbourg in its Astronomical Clock. This astonishing object has always had a special place in my heart since visiting it with my family in my early teens. Indeed everything about Strasbourg amazed me then (and now) – but the clock most of all. For years I had a sort of super-postcard of it, made from several layers of card and paper, with a wheel on the side that allowed you to make the Four Ages of Man and the Days of the Week rotate through little cut-out windows. I was very sad on a recent visit that this elaborately crafted postcard is no longer made – although I can see that it does not reflect well on me that at an age which is for most boys an eye-rolling frenzy of coughed-over cigarettes and self-abuse I was enjoying making a little cardboard wheel go round.

The clock fills an entire wall in the cathedral's south wing and is an amalgam of several centuries of fixes and upgrades. It was first built in the mid-fourteenth century as towns up and down the Rhine fell into a mania of giant clock-making following the invention of weight-driven mechanics. One feature has somehow survived from this ancient machine, which was strapped to the outside wall – a cockerel automaton that crows thrice and flaps its wings (to remind us of St Peter's betrayal of Christ). This was all drastically upgraded two centuries later by a mathematician and clockmakers and a painter from Schaffhausen. It is hard to convey the sheer lunatic complexity of the resulting confection, powered by an infinity of toothed wheels, and showing the phases of the moon, the saint's day, sunrise and sunset, eclipses, the day of the week, all decorated with a host of allegorical paintings and sculptures: the Four Ages of Man, the Signs of the Zodiac, and Death, who strikes a bell. Theologically it is a bit of a fruit salad, as it features not just Jesus and some characters from the Apocalypse, but also the seven Roman gods in their chariots to show the days of the week. In French these are austerely correct: mardi = Mars, vendredi = Venus, mercredi = Mercury, rather than being largely engulfed by random Nordics as in English.

The whole clock was given a further major overhaul in the 1840s, which fixed the mechanism and added yet more charts, paintings and furbelows. This was a shame in some ways as the new-painted figures, particularly the Roman gods, have an unfortunate fairground flavour, with Apollo looking like a camp game-show host. Saturn, shown in his dragon-pulled chariot, looks particularly banal, munching on the body of one of his children with much the same inattention that someone might eat a burger at a drive-in. The restorer also made the sad mistake of dumping what must have been a wonderful painting called *The Colossus with Feet of Clay* in favour of an uplifting image of Copernicus.

There are so many ways in which the clock is a sensation, but I am currently struck by the way that it represents layer upon layer of invention and refinement. It was always meant as a bravura exercise rather than as something genuinely useful. It required a huge breadth of skills – working in stone, wood, metal; drawing, painting, a fine sense of stage-craft, a near-deranged level of ambition; mathematics, geometry, astrology; theology, gilding, mechanics. It heaps up centuries of knowledge, tinkering and biblical imagery (including a superb Adam's Rib painting) and in its very existence sums up a specific kind of artisanal, guild-based, urban, Imperial pride.

Elizabeth and her children

Britain has always viewed itself as an island of stability and common sense moored offshore from a Continent rife with absurdity and fanaticism. Every neighbour has served as both mortal enemy and figure of fun, whether French, Dutch or Spanish. During the most humiliating of the seventeenth-century naval wars between England and the Netherlands, an enraged John Dryden wrote *Annus Mirabilis*, a poem which is in part a hymn of hate against the Dutch. In one of its wonderfully written yet deeply disturbing climaxes it imagines English ships firing their cannon at Dutch East Indiamen, whose crews are then hideously killed by flying fragments of porcelain and lethal 'Aromatick Splinters' and by an inferno of burning spices: slaughtered by their own high-value commercial products. The poem's gloating nuttiness would seem to indicate that the English and Dutch were eternal, Manichaean enemies, and yet in practice there were bouts of savagery alternating with fond regard, with each country ultimately saving the other from disaster and despair.

As I hope I have already established, the relationship between England, Flanders and Holland had always been a rich, tangled one. Relative English political stability was in many ways made possible by this safety valve of being able to cross the Channel. Many generations of sailors rolled their eyes at yet another incompetently disguised royal pretended to be an Average Joe passenger just happening to need to flee at high speed to the mainland. The process worked both ways, with any number of temporarily or permanently embarrassed foreigners fleeing to Britain and safety, from as far back as we have records to the twenty-first century.

In the seventeenth century the movements across the Channel were particularly rich and entangling. The long, wide shadow of Henry VIII managed to impose its will long after his death, through the reigns of his three children, Edward VI, Mary I and Elizabeth I. As only Mary ever married (childlessly and only four years before her death) there was a weird drought in further royal children, with nobody at all born in the direct line between 1537 and the arrival of the fecund Stuart dynasty of James I from Scotland in 1603. If the modern British tabloid press had then existed, this would have been little less than catastrophic – but it also meant that England was oddly unavailable for the sorts of marriage diplomacy that made Europe's dynastic world function. Elizabeth I's window in which she could have plausibly had children had already closed early in her reign, dooming the Tudors to extinction.

James I took one critical decision which effectively controlled the entire course of his own dynasty and that of the next, and on to the present. In a Europe split by religious hatreds it was genuinely quite awkward to 'place' your children with foreign spouses of the right kind. In the case of his daughter, Elizabeth, he seemed to do well. She had already had an unintentionally adventurous life as the Gunpowder Plot had been based first around the blowing up of her dad and then on her being used as a readily manipulated child monarch. As this did not work out, she was approached by numerous bearded foreigners including, tantalizingly, the great Gustavus Adolphus of Sweden. In the end it was decided that the young Calvinist ruler of the Palatinate, Frederick V, fitted the bill. After a brief period of sybaritic glamour at his Heidelberg court, the young couple unintentionally began the Thirty Years War through the catastrophic decision to accept the throne of the Kingdom of Bohemia, a role previously filled for three generations by a member of the Habsburg family and which was unfortunately already occupied by the latest Habsburg, the tough, zealous and fervent Emperor Ferdinand II. Elizabeth and Frederick spent a year enjoying the facilities of Prague Castle before their Protestant troops were crushed by Imperial forces. In a change of tide invisible until then, Protestantism had now reached its zenith in Europe and was in retreat. The Palatinate was effortlessly invaded by Imperial forces and Heidelberg ravaged, with a pretty classical welcome arch one of the few surviving mementos of Elizabeth and Frederick having lived there. Following some of the worst, most poorly thought-through decisions of the early modern period, Elizabeth and Frederick, still only in their twenties, fled to the Dutch Republic for sanctuary, never to return.

Sheltered in The Hague, the couple passed the time by having as many children as possible. As the interminable war continued, Protestant forces revived under Gustavus Adolphus of Sweden and Frederick left The Hague to discuss with him how he could be made King of Bohemia again. On the way back he became ill and died at Mainz aged thirty-six. Elizabeth now swung into action, devoting the rest of her long life to her children's advancement and the vindication of her and Frederick's political actions. I don't think there is a single painting of Frederick where you do not get a nig-

gling feeling that he was at heart quite a silly person and not a
prince you would put much trust in – it might have just been his
choice of beard shape and clothing, but artists seem to have had an
uncanny ability to reveal the inner prat. Elizabeth was, not necessarily by choice, a sterner figure and even when near destitute in
the 1640s – her 'court' at The Hague in semi-darkness and with
rats and mice scampering around the hem of her frayed dress – she
determinedly pushed her children on.

An entire book could be written just about the escapades of the
nine children who lived to adulthood. The kaleidoscope of opportunities for them depended on the later stages of the Thirty Years
War and on the unfolding disaster of her younger brother Charles
I's reign in England. One child became an important correspondent
of Descartes; another became a painter; a third a duellist and mercenary, killed fighting for the Duke of Lorraine; one married a
Transylvanian prince. Her eldest son, Henry Frederick, as an excited
teenager went to have a look at the sensation of the Protestant
decade: the Spanish treasure fleet, captured by Piet Hein, which
transformed the embattled Dutch war chest. But en route he was
drowned in an accident (in a stretch of water since converted into
dry land). Another son, Maurice, fought as a Royalist in the English
Civil War, became a naval commander and was drowned in a hur-
ricane off the Virgin Islands. Charles Louis, after endless twists and
turns, at the end of the Thirty Years War was allowed to return to
Heidelberg and rule a much smaller and downgraded version of his
father's palatinate. Most famous was Prince Rupert of the Rhine,
Royalist general, whose stylish clothing, corkscrew locks, soft-
leather accessories and damn-your-eyes manner came to define
Cavalier chic before the inevitable fashion change of Cromwell's
no-more-Christmas, black-and-white collection.

In some very old-fashioned history books I was exposed to
when I was a child, Prince Rupert of the Rhine still held sway – his
dashing image designed so that young British man-children would
imprint, in the manner of goslings, on a positive, royal and hierarchical image. He seems to have now disappeared from popular view
completely, which is no great loss. He was in charge of the Royalist

exile fleet (it was during one of its expeditions that his brother was killed) and was part of every one of the incredibly elaborate, painful clashes of honour, treachery and expediency that accompanied the end of the Civil War and the establishment of Cromwell's Republic – a time when the North Sea and Channel were virtually blocked up with clumsily disguised adventurers going back and forth in illegal little ships. As with all Royalists, including his mother, humiliations and strange alliances piled up. The new English king, Charles I's son, Charles II, together with his younger brother the Duke of York (the future James II), were huddled in Bruges, close to despair as Cromwell's regime stabilized and began to make friends. Rupert was fortunately out of the way for the most peculiar of twists when Cromwell's army fought alongside Louis XIV, crushing English exile and Spanish forces, including the troops of the fleeing Duke of York.

This struggle (the Battle of the Dunes, which I deal with later) appeared to be the last straw for Elizabeth and her sons, as well as for her nephew Charles II. But Cromwell's premature death suddenly revealed that the Republic had in practice been held together by the sheer force of his will and that no plausible structure could be agreed on for his replacement. Yet more boats filled with muffled oddballs zoomed back and forth. England remained at war with Spain, so Charles being in exile in the hated Spanish Netherlands sent an extremely awkward message. Once he had agreed to extensive amnesties if he was allowed back, he had to move to Breda in the Netherlands to avoid further Spanish taint, and signed there the United Declaration of Breda which allowed him and his brother to return, together with Elizabeth and Rupert. The most far-reaching bit of Rupert's career then followed, as he created the Hudson's Bay Company and laid claim to one of the world's largest single bits of private land, stretching from the High Arctic to what are now the Dakotas, and gifting the English more musk-oxen than they could ever use. Known for many years as Rupert's Land, it would ultimately allow Canada to spread massively westwards and northwards.

Elizabeth's children then could not have had a more adventurous existence. She was herself born in Scotland, moved to London with her father in 1603 and lived abroad under a boggling range of circumstances from 1613. When she was at last allowed to return to London in 1661 she was sixty-four years old and was seen as a strange creature from a different age, preserving in her manners a world from before the Civil War and the Republic. She died a few months later.

Even after her death however she had one amazing trick up her sleeve. Elizabeth had yet another child, Sophia: tough, clever, impressive and safely married off to the minor German Protestant prince Ernst-August. Following family deaths, military heroism in the war with the Turks and large bribes, Ernst-August clambered up to the exalted rank of becoming a new, ninth Elector (Bavaria had been added as an eighth during the Thirty Years War). In the meantime, an extraordinary series of accidents and tragedies wiped out the Stuart family. Charles II had no children; his brother briefly ruled as James II but was so Catholic and so breathtakingly incompetent that he was thrown out in favour of his Protestant daughter, who became Mary II and her husband who became William III (of whom, more later). The childless Mary died of smallpox shortly thereafter. Her younger sister Anne, the last Stuart, led a truly terrible life, giving birth over and over again to dead or dying children. She had one son, Prince William, who survived: he was therefore the sole remaining thread for Protestant Stuart dynastic survival but he was often ill and died aged eleven in 1700. The crisis was of a slow-motion, but inexorable kind – the childless widower William III, himself always in poor health, would die at some point, to be succeeded in turn by the childless Anne. This would open the way for James II's descendants again, specifically 'James III', his deeply and unacceptably Catholic son. So – blindly ignoring the genealogical sequence which alone was meant to govern kingship – William turned to Elizabeth's daughter Sophia as top Protestant and Parliament established her and her heirs as the true (albeit not true, obviously) line. It then became an unedifying race between the very old but hearty Sophia and the much younger but unwell and distressed Anne as to how things would turn out. Anne duly became queen and managed to stay alive *just* long enough to deny Britain an elderly but admirable Queen Sophia I, who died seven weeks after her. Sophia's grouchy and unpleasant son first became Elector of Hanover and a few weeks later King George I. Elizabeth's descendants have ruled Britain ever since and the years of flight, penury, danger, drownings and rat-infested palaces all worked out.

Uncle Toby's hobby-horse

One of the most relentlessly uninteresting displays of sculpture in Western Europe occupies the ground floor of the Musée des Beaux Arts in Lille. Two huge halls are stuffed with nineteenth-century statues which swamp the visitor in a mix of soft porn and hollow rhetoric. You feel sorry for the sculptors, for the museum guards, for the quarrymen who obtained the white marble; in darkest moods, even for the needlessly gouged-out hillsides themselves. Classical subjects and royalist and republican allegory stretch as far as the eye can see. Even a bust of my favourite catastrophic French royal, Charles X, is so bland that it tells you nothing about him except at the level of his having had hair and a nose.

Perhaps the only poignant feature of the halls is the way that they accidentally preserve the bottoms of various models obliged to shiver for hours pretending to be a goddess or classical heroine or one of the Arts. It is definitely an odd feature of the era that allegorical and mythical women seem obliged at moments of crisis to step out of their clothes – as though it is a contractual precondition if people like Lucretia or Cleopatra want to commit suicide. And how startling it would be to find an elaborate sculpture of a nymph *on her way* to the bath, with a sensible gown on and a little basket for her shampoo, rather than being 'surprised' in the bath in a skittish naked pose. These statues make it a mystery as to how nymphs spend their time when they are *not* bathing or getting abducted. So these cheerless halls instead form an unintentional shrine to ghostly bums-of-yesteryear with the faint, hovering ghosts too of those original gentleman art collectors, almost visible with their elaborate facial hair, distended stomachs, opera cloaks and silver-topped canes.

This mundane experience (topped off by a marble Joan of Arc at the stake, arching her back in fear of the flames and her dress partly unbuttoned to let her breathe more freely) made me worry that the whole of the Lille museum might just be a sort of cultural rag-and-bone shop and, indeed, set me wondering whether modern Europe is simply too weighed down by the rubbish of the past. Should the whole lot be gathered in a huge net, picked up by a helicopter and dumped off the Florida Keys to create the fabulous basis for a new reef, for example? It might be even more pervy to see Joan of Arc with brittle-stars clambering over her breasts, but it would at least be an exciting Green initiative.

As I glumly walked down into the museum's basement, however, everything brightened up. Having failed to do my research I had not realized that here was something magical: beautifully lit and stretching out into the distance was a series of huge tables. Made for the military commanders of Louis XIV and Louis XV, each tabletop is covered in a relief model of a northern border town and its countryside. They are almost eye-wateringly vivid, with every tree, stream and farm building in place but shrunk to 1/600th of its size. No oil painting or surviving ancient street gets you anywhere near as close to a sense of how seventeenth- and eighteenth-century towns used to be. It seems possible (and painfully desirable) to be shrunk to an eighth of an inch in height, step onto the table and walk through these fields of watercolour-soaked paper, and down roads sheltered by shredded-silk trees.

It is almost too obvious a point, but the sculptures of the upper halls were created as cultural objects and now seem for the most part junk, whereas these models made for practical, military use are today among the greatest of all French works of art. At a glance you can see here that in the eighteenth century the now sprawling industrial city of Charleroi was simply a star fortress guarding a river crossing. Calais used to be an isolated walled town on sand dunes – its one-time status as an English enclave suddenly making sense. Namur's never-ending significance as a military objective is simply built into its two-rivers-and-craggy-hilltop combo. There is a bustling, convivial-looking Ypres, its Cloth Hall then only four hundred years old. The maps also make clear how the defences created by the Marquis de Vauban, Louis XIV's military genius, in some cases were as big as the towns themselves – a relatively straggly bunch of houses and churches protected by a monstrous range of sloped walls, water obstacles and strongpoints.

The table-maps are both practical and fantastical. The products of a pre-balloon and pre-aeroplane world, they showed views otherwise unavailable to humans. They also offer a vision of order, rationality and ownership – it is hard not to feel that Louis XIV would ideally have liked the whole of France to be shown on the same scale. He could have then seen everything and known everything. Incidentally, such a table would have had sides that were one-and-a-half miles long, which seems not entirely impossible – perhaps with the Sun King, in tights and wig, hovering above it, moving on crane-borne leather straps from province to province. For soldiers, operating at mere ground level, the table-maps showed up fudges and weak points in the fortifications and perhaps nowhere else are the never resolvable headaches of the period's wars clearer: the more walls to defend, the more troops, the more food, the more ammunition. In the end, the entire military potential of France could be soaked up by these blotting-paper-like towns. In practice nowhere could be secure – with a vast defensive force under siege simply eating every scrap of food within days – or with what should have been a mobile, offensive, marching army made totally impotent by being plonked inside or outside some walls. If all your troops are manning defences you can no longer react to an aggressive opponent. Perhaps more than for any other country, this dilemma defined France's strategic headache well into the twentieth century.

Some of the towns on the table-maps are oddly unchanged – places like Tournai and Maastricht are immediately recognizable. You can see the place where the real d'Artagnan was killed during the Siege of Maastricht in 1673, when he was in fact quite elderly, rather than the bee-stung-lipped young blade in the modern life-size statue that now stands by the city walls. The maps show how for soldiers the surrounding countryside and its valleys and rises were just as important. In an era where everyone lived at ground level, an entire army could be hidden behind a gentle slope; only drifting smoke could give away a regiment behind an orchard. Even the picturesque fields on the tables had crucial military value, down to the smallest wall. It is sadly unknown whether the maps had to be updated and adjusted each time another neglected out-building collapsed on Old Grognard's Farm.

The map-tables had their own adventures. In a symbolically almost banal move many of them were taken away by the Prussians after the defeat of Napoleon. The one for Lille – a rare instance of where Vauban was able to create a pure, regular, colossal star-shape fortress without any frustrating cliffs or rivers in the way – had a rough time in Berlin. It was cut down, lots of the little houses fell off and it was only recovered in 1948 as a very minor part of a much later round of Franco-German post-conflict restitution, with many of the other map-tables destroyed by neglect or bombing.

Looking at the model of Namur, I think of the city's role in *Tristram Shandy* (1767), where the charming if insane Uncle Toby devotes much of his life to his 'Hobby-Horse', building a scale model in his garden to re-enact the Siege of Namur during the War of the League of Augsburg. Helped by loyal, spade-wielding Corporal Trim, Uncle Toby hopes that if he can create a sufficiently accurate version of Namur's defences he will somehow be able to understand the mysterious 'wound in the groin' which he received from a falling chunk of stonework at the real siege. One of many mazes in the book, these endlessly proliferating 'saps, mines, blinds, gabions, palisades, ravelins, half-moons and such trumpery' engulf Uncle Toby's brain.

Uncle Toby was not alone in his perplexity. I have spent much too much time wandering around Vauban's surviving fortresses in places such as Besançon and Arras not to feel that he was one of the greatest confidence tricksters of the early modern period. He created a staggeringly elaborate star ground plan for each citadel, which looks from above like a Christmas ornament, and which absorbed immense resources to build: eradicating farms, diverting rivers, blowing up rock outcrops. He also came up with various ingenious fighting methods – perfecting the bayonet, for example (which meant that by the first decade of the eighteenth century the ghastly pike had at last disappeared), and the use of ricochet-firing for artillery, so that cannonballs would bounce into forts and do horrible, random damage. But what is breathtaking is that he then worked out an infallible way to destroy his own forts, using trenches, mines and mortars. Vauban and his Dutch counterpart Menno van Coehorn encased city after city, with each citadel requiring ever-larger magazines and garrisons, but it was all still contestable as they could, with time and huge resources, then be disposed of anyway. What was attractive about this method of warfare was that it was extremely slow. Casualties – aside from Uncle Toby's groin – could also be slight. Vauban's tactics for taking a city were so irresistible that, given enough time, there would be a point where the garrison was simply obliged by the logic of its situation to 'beat the chamade' – i.e. communicate with the besieger through a massed use of drums that the jig was up. The lines of 'circumvallation' needed as a preliminary to seal off the town and get a siege under way were themselves wonders of the world – at the 1667 Siege of Lille they were fifteen miles long. At the 1691 Siege of Mons twenty thousand diggers were used.* These sieges became an epic struggle between the supplies of the besiegers and those of the besieged. The besiegers themselves in turn were also in effect under siege. At an earlier Siege of Mons, the French had to give up simply because they ran out of forage for their horses. One last fun statistic: a large army with forty thousand horses would need *a thousand tons* of green fodder a day to keep going.

The demands of these sieges were so vast that the French could generally only manage one at a time – which explains the length of Louis XIV's and Louis XV's wars. It also explains how the very small area of the Spanish Netherlands and Dutch Republic was so difficult for Louis to swallow up. I should offer immediate reassurance to readers that I will *not* give an endless account of the

---

* Curiously Racine was present, watching Mons from the French lines through a telescope 'which I struggled to keep hold of, as my heart was beating so, seeing all those good people in peril.'

fighting which convulsed the entire border between France and the Empire, with a few breaks, until Waterloo, several generations later. I apologize here if I miss somebody's favourite encounter, but if this book is to be manageable at all I shall have to choose my battles carefully.

'Too late to be ambitious'

Only three years in the seventeenth century did not involve serious fighting somewhere in Europe: 1610, 1670 and 1682. Troops circulated across huge areas, with many famous commanders equally involved with fighting the Ottomans in the east and the French in the west. The tenuous routes that were taken drew in otherwise harmless territories. The famous Spanish Road, a side effect of the absurdity of Madrid's rule over the Netherlands and lack of control over the seas, obliged troops (for the most part Italian mercenaries) to wend their way from the Italian coast up through Savoy and through (to their relief) some genuine Spanish territory such as the Franche-Comté, occasionally friendly territory such as Lorraine and up into Spanish Luxembourg and Bastogne. At one point a single bridge made the route possible and there were humiliating fees to pay and the need to bring weapons in separate mule-trains. In this way, what was meant to be a struggle purely in the Netherlands entangled others. It also relied on a friendly France, which was also drawn into hostility by anger at Spanish support for specific court factions and in the end simply closed the road entirely.

There was a comparable Protestant road, a highly unsatisfactory one, that led from Scotland (one of the great suppliers of mercenaries) through England, through the rebel Netherlands and down through a mix of the Calvinist (Palatinate, Nassau, Wied, Basle, Zürich) and the Lutheran (Hesse-Darmstadt, Mühlhausen, Baden, Strasbourg). There were fatal gaps (Liège, Trier, Mainz) and the Thirty Years War created endless nightmares for individual parts of this non-self-supporting sequence. Too much is made of the Treaty of Westphalia in 1648 as, while it did end the general fighting across the Empire and modern political scientists have always enjoyed discussing its terms, it marked no real let-up for much of the zone. Most histories note the 'Fronde' rebellion in France (1648–53) as a minor distraction before Louis XIV gets into his stride, but perhaps a million people died. The series of civil wars that wrecked the British Isles from 1639 to 1653 killed a greater percentage of the population than the First World War. By the mid-century the Palatinate had lost half its entire population: whole areas were abandoned, wolves enjoyed their last hurrah and the ecology became so scrambled that great plagues of mice (an old enemy wearily but successfully fought by many centuries' worth of traps and cats) engulfed whole barns. Germany lost the entire population growth of the previous century and a half.

All sides, using different religious measures, viewed the warfare, plague and ferocious weather (this was the time of what we now call the Little Ice Age) through a peccatogenic lens – what was happening had come about through human sin. Random blows of fate went beyond mere human planning. At one point the Dutch river system froze solid and the Spanish could have simply charged across or along this sudden great sequence of magnificent white highways. The Dutch were only saved from catastrophe by the Spanish commander's dithering for a fatal, melty twenty-four hours. On another occasion the Swiss Alps remained so cold that there was almost no snow-melt and Louis XIV was able to get his cavalry across the shallowed Rhine just by wading. Such freaks of nature and the terrible harvests and plagues gave the time its own flavour. There was also a strong intellectual sense that the world was moving into a twilit final era. Archbishop Ussher had carried out his famous calculations and published *The Annals of the Old Testament* in 1650, proving that God had begun Time on the evening of 22 October 4004 BC, with the First Day beginning on the 23rd. It was understood that the Earth would endure for six thousand years, one thousand for each day of the Creation (you can see here a certain number of what might be seen as rather broad, working assumptions), with the Last Days occurring in 2004.

The popularization of such ideas gave a shot in the arm to the gloomier sort of Protestant who could only really relish the idea of things getting even worse. The obsession with the greatness of the ancient world had always given a strong tinge of mournfulness to Europe's intellectual life. The Dukes of Burgundy had surrounded themselves with tapestries of Hector, Alexander and others partly to be boastful, but partly too because they felt themselves to be living in the shadowy afterworld of such figures, not long before God wrapped up the whole rather botched experiment. The great summary of such attitudes came in the Leiden-educated doctor Sir Thomas Browne's *Urne-Buriall*, a long essay written during the 1650s in the wake of Ussher's book, which in astonishing prose roams through the countless, futile ways in which humans have tried to maintain their fame after death.* Browne has the terse, famous line: ''Tis too late to be ambitious. The great mutations of the world are acted, our time may be too short for our designes.' He points out that it does not really matter how famous Charles V may have been as there was now such a little period remaining before everything comes to an end. Hector had been lucky as he had lived so early on that it made sense to be famous. Browne talks about 'the Monument of *Childerick* the first . . . casually discovered three years past at *Tournay*, restoring unto the world much gold richly adorning his Sword, two hundred Rubies, many hundred Imperial Coyns, three hundred golden Bees . . .'. The high summer of being a human was many centuries ago, but now 'Our longest Sunne . . . makes but winter arches'. The endlessness of the next world 'maketh Pyramids pillars of snow, and all that's past a

---

* I was planning to write a whole section on the Dutch cult of the dairy cow: breeding, cheese, prosperity, meadows and then hop on to the lovely world of Dutch horticulture. I regret not writing it, but it had meant perjuring myself by pretending enthusiasm for Aelbert Cuyp's super-boring paintings of cows and the section was really only an elaborate excuse so I could use Browne's otherwise rarely used invented adjective 'retromingent', an adjective applied to animals that urinate backwards, like cows. Browne also invented such words as 'medical', 'coma', 'hallucination', 'incontrovertible', 'prairie', 'precarious' and so on, but retromingent should be the queen of them all.

moment.' I must stop! The only point of this book is to create a ludicrously over-complex advertisement for *Urne-Buriall*.

This sense of gloom was not entirely Protestant. Catholicism was of course just as peccatogenic. Spain's endless setbacks as the century progressed, shifting from predator to prey, are mercilessly portrayed in Velázquez's great sequence of paintings of his master Philip IV, from stylish teenage hopeful to exhausted ruin. In his forty-year reign, Philip was always fighting somebody. The last straw was the Battle of Rocroi in 1643, when a resurgent French army blew to pieces his Army of Flanders. Philip was reduced to falling back on spirit mediums, pleading with the mystic nun Sor Maria de Ágreda to construct a wall of prayer to hold back his enemies. War after war wrecked everyone's hopes, seemingly with the most cynical combinations making old friends into enemies and vice versa. As one war subsided another would flare up. They all seem an absurd tangle to us, but each had its own logic. Societies were organized for war, with armies becoming larger and larger. For the first time a global strategy was followed, with colonies around the world being both great sources of wealth and painfully vulnerable to attack. Much of the planet became an opportunity for an outflanking manoeuvre, and whole expeditions vanished without trace from scurvy, starvation and storms. There are so many examples, but among the grimmest are the frenziedly overstretching efforts by the Dutch Republic to create New Holland in northern Brazil, with its principal cities of Mauritsstad (Recife) and New Amsterdam (Natal), at the same time as New Netherland in northeast North America with its capital also called New Amsterdam (New York). A global Dutch future shimmered briefly into view but was destroyed in the 1650s and 1660s. Resources were poured into protecting the unprotectable as both colonies were devastated, the former's only real trace being Albert Eckhout's wonderful little painting in the Mauritshuis collection, *Two Brazilian Tortoises*.

New Netherland was just one of many theatres in which the rapid and total alienation of the English and Dutch, who had for so long been problematic but considerable allies, was played out. Both were well aware of the other's naval strength and these were strange wars provoked by the jittery conundrum that each passing month allowed one side to build more ships, but each passing month also allowed the other to do likewise. Both sides panicked about their own potential weakness in a very pure example of a destructive arms race. No sooner had relations soured than Andrew Marvell was unhelpfully writing

> Holland, that scarce deserves the name of land,
> As but th' off-scouring of the British sand.

The three wars fought between 1652 and 1674 showed continuing English weakness, most spectacularly in the great Dutch raid of 1667 up the Thames and into the River Medway, where much of the English navy was burnt to the waterline or stolen. I am not aware of his commenting on it, but Sir Thomas Browne must have relished the whole, gloomy, too-late-to-be-ambitious sequence of the Great Plague of 1665, the Great Fire of London of 1666 and the Great Naval Fiasco of 1667. To Louis XIV's delight (he was secretly paying the English) the two sides then tore each other to pieces.

In the Rijksmuseum there is a small piece of stone in a captioned casket which beautifully conveys the point where the whole seventeenth century perhaps changes course. This piece of stone was the first to be touched by the foot of the Stadtholder William III of Orange as he stepped onto English land from his ship in 1688. It is a peculiar object but, more vividly than countless paintings and prints, it encapsulates the hopes and fears of an extraordinary moment. Instead of Elizabeth I becoming ruler of the Netherlands, as had been hoped for a century before, the vexed relationship between the two countries would be resolved by the ruler of the Netherlands becoming ruler of England. With a huge invasion fleet, four times the size of the Armada, and an army of twenty-one thousand men, William achieved what Philip II had not. The same wind that blew his ships south-west through the Strait plugged up James II's warships in the Thames estuary. The fleet was so wide that William had the fun – and I think unique – pleasure of firing salutes off both Dover *and* Calais as he swept past. His timing worked brilliantly as Louis XIV's army was busy destroying the Palatinate and unable to react to the news that the elite of the Dutch army were no longer mounting guard on the Dutch borders but vacationing in Devon. The almost unbelievably incompetent James II, England's worst king in poll after poll, was an elderly, sincere Catholic, a former hero in fighting wars with the Dutch and hopelessly at odds with his Protestant subjects. Betrayed by his Protestant daughter Mary (married to William III), he took the traditional route of flee-ing down the Thames, to the relief of the new authorities in London. In scenes of farce, some honest sailors spotted and arrested him, leading to arguments in a Kentish pub and the potential for either renewed civil war or a royal execution of a kind that had proved so deleterious to James's dad. The authorities arrived at the pub and brought James back to London before 'allowing' him to escape again, this time successfully. Once more, the Channel provided for civilized exile rather than a ruinous bloodbath. And for the first time a large chunk of 'the Protestant Road', from Caithness to Gelder-land, was now under the same management.

CHAPTER NINE

Antonius Leeuwenœchius.

Nancy and Lorraine

I am usually quite meticulous about my notes but I have one small unplaceable sheet of paper. Mixed up with various bits of German vocabulary it simply says: '*The ducal tombs much damaged, lids pushed open by fungus and mould – appalling photos of some white stuff, like billows of detergent!*' I remember the church as eighteenth century with a painted cupola (which does not narrow it down much) and that it was a longer walk away than I had thought, and that there were gloomy trees (again, these eliminate almost nowhere). There were many years when this mausoleum, wherever it was, must have been extremely important – great solemn ceremonies with black horses, stacks of crêpe, grim-faced dowagers, lines of troops, a sense of an old reign ending and a new one begun, silent capless crowds. But at some point the last person stopped caring and all sorts of chemical grotesqueries were allowed to convulse the remains of men and women who had once commanded armies or been middling players on the spinet.

This scribbled note struck me because it is in such strong contrast to the immaculate, beautifully maintained mausoleum in Nancy of the Dukes of Lorraine. This is tucked away in a corner of the Franciscan monastery built by Duke René II in 1487 shortly after he rubbed out Charles the Bold and it forms a striking contrast to the rest of the complex, which has become the last resting place of lots of statues: frightened, badly damaged marble refugees from other parts of Lorraine, forming a sort of royalist Island of Misfit Toys. Survivors of the devastating iconoclasm of the 1790s, they include such masterpieces as Ligier Richier's tomb of the pious and powerful Philippa of Guelders, René II's wife. Once maintained in a sumptuous layer-cake of contrasting marbles, propelled along through the afterlife by the songs and prayers of many generations of priests and choirs, she wound up with her bones and most of her tomb chucked away, reduced to an admittedly still superb recumbent figure, shown in extreme old age wearing her outfit as a Poor Clare – and looking oddly like Darth Sidious.

The circular main chapel of the Dukes of Lorraine is in fine shape however and reflects the dukes' odd ability to keep going despite often mortal threats to their sovereignty. Simply looking at Lorraine on the map shows its problem, with part of its territory of Bar marooned in France and the three enclaves of Toul, Verdun and Metz entangled within its borders. Its political incoherence and status as an Imperial borderland made it a favourite destination for marauding armies to pass through from every point of the compass. Until the seventeenth century, the Dukes had stayed close to the French kings and thrived through being helpful and adventurous. Near the Franciscan church the much restored Porte de la Craffe has wonderful carved silhouettes, wearing elaborate animal-themed helmets, of some of these warriors – Raoul: fought at Tournai, Gibraltar, in Brittany, killed at the Battle of Crécy; Jean I: fought at the Battle of Poitiers, crusader in Lithuania; Charles II: fought in Tunis and Livonia, and at the catastrophic Battle of Nicopolis alongside John the Fearless; René II: killer of Charles the Bold, inheritor of Bar. Their balancing act was always a difficult one though, particularly after Toul, Verdun and Metz were snapped up by France in 1552. Duke Charles IV's luck ran out when he backed the wrong factions at the French court. As an *extremely* minor subset of the Thirty Years War he decided to invade the Metz enclaves of Vic and Moyenvic in 1630, bringing down a French invasion on his head.

Just typing the words 'Vic and Moyenvic' suggests a level of micro-history plunging into madness but, as usual, Vic has its real moment in the sun. It was where the great painter Georges de la Tour was born (in 1593) and married. Almost nothing is known about de la Tour's life except that at some point he moved to the Lorraine town of Lunéville, dying there of plague in 1652. His entire working life must have been entangled with the violence and uncertainty of Lorraine in this period and he worked for Charles IV for a short time. Obviously, there is nothing so babyish as 'the greatest ever painting', but there seems to be a category of a thousand or so, say, which might be claimed as first equal: travelling around Lotharingia, paintings such as Vermeer's *The Little Street* or Brueghel's *The Fall of Icarus* or van Eyck's *Virgin and Child with Canon van der Paele* would qualify. De la Tour joins them with a religious picture (*Joseph the Carpenter*) and a secular one (*The Cheat with the Ace of Clubs* – painted just before Vic and Moyenvic made headlines), which make me happy just thinking about them.

Having started this non-politico-military diversion, I have to mention too de la Tour's contemporary Claude Gellée, born in the Lorraine town of Chamagne, south-west of Lunéville in around 1600. Known as 'Le Lorrain', his long career as a painter mostly happened in Rome, so he falls outside this book's frame. But it is curious that of the three wizard-like great 'French' painters of the seventeenth century (i.e. plus Poussin), two were in fact from Lorraine and none worked much in France. In our long and cheerful marriage, practically the only serious area of dispute between my wife and myself is over the virtues of Claude's work. About once a year this topic will unexpectedly lurch into view at a gallery or somehow just in an unrelated conversation, with her pouring out a shocking stream of derision on how unbelievably dreary and boring his (actually) matchless canvases are. It is years since we have been to the Ashmolean Museum in Oxford together because it happens to own his final masterpiece, that spectral twilit farewell to a lost world, *Landscape with Ascanius shooting the Stag of Sylvia*, a picture that on our final joint trip provoked poorly judged joke snoring noises. Still, even the happiest marriage has to be balanced sometimes by one partner silently soaking a pillow with tears in the darkness and whispering, 'But I will always love you Claude and will never, never let you down.'

To return to the Dukes: Charles IV was forced to flee (with his sister disguised as a soldier) and Lorraine appeared doomed to follow the fate of the Three Bishoprics, engulfed by France. But the

Holy Roman Empire continued to work well and Lorraine's interests were guarded by the Habsburgs. Despite many indignities, the family switched its allegiance completely to the Imperial army and never backed away from being the rightful rulers, even if they were not allowed into their own territory. Duke Charles V of Lorraine was born in exile in Vienna and became commander of the Imperial armies, the ruthless hammer of both Frenchman and Turk, a victor at the epochal Battle of Vienna (1683) and conqueror of Buda. Charles died young at the beginning of the War of the League of Augsburg, pitting Louis XIV against the Dutch Republic, England, the Empire and Spain, but his actions on behalf of Christendom were remembered. In 1697, a battered France agreed to the Treaty of Ryswick (a town in South Holland – Rijswijk), which included a clause to hand back, among other things, Lorraine.

Charles's son Leopold after further setbacks re-established his court at Lunéville, still today a wonderful example of an Imperial 'residence' town despite its now complete Frenchness, its atmosphere of mournful beauty much enhanced by the dense river-fog shrouding the palace when I was there. But this is the reason why the chapel of the Dukes of Lorraine is today still in such good condition. Leopold scooped the pool. The grim, panicked Emperor Charles VI, mouldering in Vienna, had no male children and spent his entire reign persuading his vulpine and inconstant neighbours to honour his eldest daughter Maria Theresa as his heir. A woman could not be emperor but she could, by agreement ('the Pragmatic Sanction'), inherit the Habsburg lands. Leopold's son Leopold Clement was chosen to be her husband – with the plan being that he should be elected Emperor on Charles VI's death. This sparkling future wobbled badly when Leopold Clement, aged sixteen, died suddenly of smallpox. Suddenly his younger brother Francis, previously a total spare, stepped forward. One of the most genial figures of the eighteenth century, the sybaritic, tubby Francis spent many years happily, if unfaithfully, married to Maria Theresa, sitting in their special pavilion in the midst of their new zoo, drinking chocolate for breakfast. He collected gemstones, had innumerable affairs and spent amazing amounts of money on fun stuff while Maria

Theresa actually ran the Empire, fighting successful Prussian and unsuccessful Bavarian predators. From now on the Habsburg dynasty became the Habsburg-Lorraine dynasty.

When this plan for Francis was announced, Louis XV viewed it as intolerable that such a potentially powerful figure should also rule Lorraine, so an elaborate dynastic swap was carried out, transferring Francis to become Grand Duke of Tuscany in return for Lorraine 'reverting' to France. The duchy was then given to the former King of Poland, Stanisław Leszczyński, Louis XV's father-in-law and almost as jolly a character as Francis, who filled the gardens of his Lunéville palace with automata that could sing, milk robot goats, etc. On Stanisław's death Lorraine simply became part of France, but 'Duke of Lorraine' remained as a fossil title of the Habsburg dynasty and the chapel at Nancy a focus of veneration. Francis and Maria Theresa's son, Joseph II, en route to offending his subjects somewhere in his Empire, came to pray here, as did his sister Marie Antoinette, just after her marriage to Louis XVI. As can be imagined, the whole place got a heavy makeover by French Revolutionaries, with the dust and bones of René II and the others orgiastically chucked about. The current chapel was rebuilt in the 1820s as a neo-royalist stronghold. There is a plaque to Marie Antoinette that can hardly contain its rage: 'Thus, adored by the French, this proud daughter of emperors came, adorned with the graces and the virtues, to the throne of Louis XVI'. Many years after her execution, her brother-in-law, the French king Charles X, came to pray here, as did her nephew Francis II, the two tailor's dummies of the Restoration. The morose killjoy Francis shook his head looking at the restored tombs and said, 'All my ancestors wanted was to make Lorraine happy.'

Unlike the sad, chemically forced apart and ignored tombs mentioned at the beginning of this section, the chapel of the Dukes of Lorraine continued to function throughout the oddities of the twentieth century. When the Habsburgs were forced to abdicate at the end of the Great War, the ex-Emperor Charles, after various low-grade semi-adventures, went into exile in Madeira (I mention this because I was recently there and visited his tomb – festooned in legitimist ribbons* – meaning that I have now completed the long-standing dream of collecting *all* the Habsburg imperial tombs). His son, Otto, born in 1912, became the heir to the ex-throne, but was banned from ever entering the former Habsburg lands. A genial, devout and thoughtful character, Otto was doomed to wander the world with a funny batch of passports, promoting pan-European cooperation. As he could not go to Austria or Hungary he adopted the Nancy chapel and was married there in 1951. When he died in 2011 an elaborate requiem mass was held for him. Each year a mass is still held for the Dukes of Lorraine.

I once stayed in a very old-fashioned boarding-house in Vienna where the breakfast room had as one of its decorations a little luridly coloured and yellowing printed card from 1915, showing the ancient Emperor Franz Joseph feeding a baby in a high chair, Otto. This action on his part seems extremely unlikely, but the survival of such a piece of devotional kitsch shows the odd nature of history. In his enormously long lifetime, instead of becoming Emperor Otto I, he was on the run from republicanism, communism, republicanism again, Nazism, communism again, outliving them all and by the end of his life cheerily showered in honorary citizenships by many of the countries he might once have ruled. Somehow, more often than not through no virtue of its own, the House of Lorraine clung on.

Rebuilding the Rhine

Ever since I can remember I have hated Louis XIV. I would not say the same about most other rulers, even those with a consistently anti-British record. It is not as though he came up as an object of scorn in the playground or my parents routinely discussed the Revocation of the Edict of Nantes at dinner. I do remember having history lessons, aged fourteen or fifteen, about seventeenth-century France when the teacher made clear his love of Richelieu and

---

* Just to be clear – it was the tomb festooned in legitimist ribbons, not I.

Mazarin and the civilized and thoughtful world they conjured up under Louis XIII. There was perhaps an implication that it all then became colder and grimmer with Louis XIV.

Off and on for years, when the children were small, we would often find ourselves at Versailles, either en route to a train trip into Paris or visiting a sister who lived nearby. One way or another I have spent a lot of time at Versailles and always disliked it – the sheer chilly dreariness and pomposity; the talentless brown-nosing decorators who did all the Sun King ceiling paintings; the way that nothing about the palace contributes anything warm or stylish. I associate it in any event less with aesthetics and more with the endless hunt for toilets characteristic of holidays with small children. Louis's great building in Paris, Les Invalides, created for his war veterans, has the same family connotations: a whole afternoon was once spent in furious argument there with a stubborn seven-year-old son wanting to buy a 'paper-knife' in the shop which was obviously just a dagger. My – I thought – trial-winning argument that nobody sent him any letters to open anyway, him being only seven, bounced off uselessly. My three-year-old daughter then toddled into the laser alarm of an amazingly ugly giant vase donated by Tsar Alexander I to Louis XVIII which, if she had successfully shoved it over so that it shattered into a thousand golden bits, would have been an action clapped by most present. So perhaps I just associate the Sun King, perhaps unfairly, with that awkward phase in parenting where intentions related to sex, reading, sleep and alcohol are always being trumped by emergency changes of clothing and tantrums about foreign food.

Louis XIV's lifelong, weary pursuit of *gloire* made him into a sort of giant wigged animal restlessly confined within the hexagon of France, battering its edges in a rage just to expand them ever so slightly. He could have spent his time on pleasant trips to the Loire valley with carriages packed with effectively limitless sacks of money, but instead he spent the lot on soldiers, killing many tens of thousands of them so that Lille and Strasbourg should become part of France. Armies of toadying lawyers were paid to come up with various absurd reasons why region *x* should be French or town *y* had ancient historical links with his family, but nobody except Louis believed them and he simply ground his way north and east, conjuring up the active enmity of almost everyone during half a century, a legacy continued under his long-lived successor Louis XV.

Minor but poignant casualties in all this were the ten Alsatian towns of the attractively named Decapolis. These pieces of the Empire had been somewhat ineffectively allied since the fourteenth century, had been ravaged during the Thirty Years War and now all fell definitively into Louis's lap, with the exception (for now) of Mühlhausen (Mulhouse), which continued to have a ring of magic fire around it from being an exclaved member of the Swiss cantons. Schlettstadt, once home of a great early sixteenth-century school of humanists, became Sélestat; Hagenau became Haguenau but nobody pronounced the H any more and Louis had Frederick Barbarossa's palace there eradicated to prevent any further associations with 'Germanness' (the stones were used to build Fort-Louis on the Rhine, bits of which are still there); Kolmar became Colmar, and so on.

There is no space here to deal with the seemingly endless dynastic wars that battered Europe under Louis XIV and Louis XV. The Dutch for a few months in 1672 came close to being destroyed – their incorporation into France being a what-if on a far vaster scale than that of the Decapole. The extra naval heft of a Franco-Dutch state might have devastated Britain, and much of the world might now be speaking French, with all of North America called Louisiana and no French Revolution as Paris would never have had to bankrupt itself fighting the Seven Years War and the American War. The Dutch brushed off all their old anti-Philip II pamphlets and simply dropped in Louis's name instead, portraying him as Nebuchadnezzar, King of Babylon, who (biblically) shouts, 'Kill, kill, for the hunt is good!'

Setting aside pointless conjectures, the grinding nature of European warfare from Louis XIV onwards meant both relatively little change in borders but also a general sense that the real prizes were elsewhere. What headway Louis enjoyed was in part because the

Empire was so fully distracted by fighting the Turks – and indeed Louis had himself somewhat un-Christianly encouraged the Turks to attack Vienna. Briefly it looked as though the Habsburgs would be crushed by the Ottomans and their territories swept away, allowing Louis to absorb the remaining tatters of western Germany and launch his own crusade against the Turks, or simply partition Europe with them. This future is almost too peculiar to comprehend. But with the failure of the Siege of Vienna (not least thanks to Charles of Lorraine), vast swathes of Central Europe in turn opened up to Habsburg power and it was Louis who suddenly appeared to be monarch of a mere cheese-and-wine backwater. The French tugging back and forth with the Dutch the corpse of the Spanish Netherlands was very small beer compared to the apocalyptic Battles of Mohács and Slankamen (1687 and 1691) which had large, mainly German armies racing around ecstatically some five hundred miles into the Ottoman Empire. When not being called Nebuchadnezzar, Louis was sometimes called 'the Great Turk', a potentially mocking rather than admiring name.

While the Habsburgs were enjoying themselves in the east, Louis XIV's general the Count of Mélac was engaging in his since legendary campaign physically to destroy western Germany, with Mannheim, for example, levelled 'like a field'. The intention was to so damage the area between the Rhine and France that it would become a demilitarized zone. Even if it could not be absorbed by France (even Louis admitted he had no claim on places such as the Electorate of Cologne) it could be wrecked. As each town was burned to the ground, each palace and cathedral blown up, a German black legend around France grew up as severe as that of the Dutch with the Spanish.

Perhaps frivolously we at least can appreciate some of the results of the French demolitions as, naturally, these provoked a great wave of rebuilding. Numerous superb new palaces, inspired by Versailles but with a genial frivolity lacking in that chilly pile, sprang up along the Rhine. The Elector-Archbishop of Cologne, Clemens August, built his spectacular Augustusburg Palace near Bruhl, a glamorous confection reflecting the perhaps rather worldly eighteenth-century concerns of the Elector and allowing for colossal parties. He tended to spend the spring and summer here, indulging his enthusiasm for using falcons to catch herons. Perhaps oddly, given its owner's role as a great prince of the Church, the palace had only a tiny little chapel tucked in next to a gigantic hunting-themed room. Clemens August was the son of the Elector of Bavaria and younger brother of the anomalous, luckless non-Habsburg Emperor Charles VII who was militarily humiliated by Maria Theresa and died quickly before his plight got even worse, allowing the Imperial crown to land on Francis's head. There are portraits of Clemens August and his brother at Augustusburg which make them look identical, like those paper dolls whose clothing you can change, one a priest, the other a soldier. In the wake of Allied bombing during the Second World War, this was one of the handful of attractive big buildings left standing on the Middle Rhine and it became the incongruously cur-licue location for many West German state galas.

The Bishop of Speyer built his own magnificent replacement palace at Bruchsal, burnt out in March 1945, but now home to the unmissable German Mechanical Music Museum which, alas, I have no space to write about except to say how much the world owes to the genius of Franz Rudolph Wurlitzer. But the pick of these great structures has to be the palace at Rastatt rebuilt by Ludwig Wilhelm, Margrave of Baden, from 1700 onwards. 'Turkish Ludwig' was, like Charles of Lorraine, a superb example of how effectively the Empire worked in this period. He had fought with Charles at Vienna, com-manded at Slankamen and during the War of the Spanish Succession played a key role in the campaign that resulted in the devastating Battle of Blenheim.* His palace at Rastatt was built over many years, sadly Ludwig Wilhelm himself not living long enough to enjoy it much. Baden was not a big state, but there on the roof is a colossal

---

* This was a classic Lotharingian triumph as the Duke of Marlborough effectively did a 'reverse Spanish road' to race his troops down from the Neth-erlands to Cologne to Koblenz to Mainz to Heidelberg before heading east round the Black Forest and completely wrecking the French and Bavarian armies.

gold statue of Jupiter shaking his thunderbolts in the direction of France at a presumably quailing Louis. The endlessly absorbing military museum in the palace includes a deranged nineteenth-century panorama of the Battle of Slankamen, with some six thousand little tin figures fighting in a desert (presumably because the maker assumed this would make it all Muslim-looking, although it was fought in a quite green and bosky bit of north Serbia). The panorama shows the disciplined Imperial troops marching in ranks against the impulsive uncoordinated childishness of the Turks, who are backed by exotic cannon, prisoner heads on spikes, a camel park, a big janissary cooking-pot, some quixotic old-school archers (perhaps reused from another panorama) and the Grand Vizier's tent, soon to be booty.

The panorama is positively rational compared to the palace's Ancestral Hall, decorated with gigantic statues of nude Turkish captives in chains, sighing, groaning, pulling at their top-knots and threatened on every side by gilt plaster decorative swirls. The ceiling shows the Apotheosis of Hercules (i.e. Ludwig Wilhelm) flanked, inevitably, by his chums Magnanimitas, Nobilitas, Auctoritas and so on. The palace also has some amazingly retro tapestries celebrating Ludwig Wilhelm's friendship with William III, Marlborough, etc., the tapestries mainly showing French houses being set fire to. After Ludwig Wilhelm's death, the Treaty of Rastatt between the French and the Empire was negotiated here, ending their parts in the War of the Spanish Succession. The elegant little wood-panelled room has been preserved where Marshal Villars, signing for the aged and bitter Louis XIV, and Prince Eugene of Savoy initialled the agreement.

'Turkish Ludwig' rode the crest of a particular moment of glamour – colossal wigs, unironic allegory, pretty furniture – and through many setbacks his palace has somehow survived, albeit with its surrounding area rather hedged in with much-later-built shops, such as *Top Hair*, *Hair Impuls* and *S + B: Body Wear (and more!)*, providing a cheerful frame. Ludwig's greatest monument though is in the Stiftskirche in the town of Baden-Baden where he is buried. Taking up an entire wall, it might be said that his tomb decorations effectively corrupt and end an entire fun genre. But if so, this is in a good cause. The tomb is almost impossible to look at there is such a confusion: cascades of armorial decoration, skulls, flags, cannon, attractive allegorical girls representing something or other, a hapless Turk being clawed at by an eagle (i.e. the Empire), while another has the claws of a lion (i.e. Baden) sunk into his face. Death (a cloaked skeleton) acts as a sort of gloating circus master, while a litter of grenades, cannonballs and abandoned kettle drums are scattered at the monument's foot. A stretched Hercules-style Nemean lion skin has Ludwig Wilhelm's many virtues carved onto it: 'Protector of the Empire, Atlas of the Germans', etc. I love this stuff, obviously – it takes Louis XIV's architecture and allegory and, on behalf of little Baden, reduces them to camp absurdity. All these great battles, grand alliances and the rest may be long forgotten, but from grand wigs to Hair Impuls life goes on.

Sperm by candlelight

The Old Church in Delft is externally a bit of a disaster, with its clumsy tower slumped to one side at an alarming angle (but remaining steady like that for some six hundred years). Internally though it is a magical advertisement for Protestant whitewash – pristine, severe and elegant. Its tombs are many and enjoyable, particularly Admiral Tromp's, with its life-size marble armoured figure, lying with its head propped up by a cannon covered in a flag, capturing the moment of his death at the Battle of Scheveningen – but even the biggest tomb is swamped by the sheer height and whiteness of the interior, which frowns down in Calvinist rectitude on human folly.

Delft's churches, like many others across the Netherlands, are an extraordinary mishmash. From the seventeenth century onwards other Europeans marvelled at the religious tolerance of the Republic. The British Isles, for example, had been made almost ungovernable by frenzied religious hatreds, with civil wars, massacres, exiles, rebellion and four regime changes in less than fifty years, before

William III's invasion and coup yoked British resources to Dutch needs. Throughout these British ructions, Zeeland, Rotterdam and the Hague found themselves dealing with often bedraggled yet snooty English exiles turning up in small boats – these provinces' coasts providing the vital safety valve that prevented more English regime opponents from suffering the fate of Charles I. His sons, the future Charles II and James II, were at different points grateful for Dutch hospitality, even if the marriage of James's daughter Mary to William III ended with the destruction of James's own serio-comic attempts to re-impose Catholicism on his surly and derisive country. It was while twiddling his thumbs in Breda that Charles bought one of the greatest paintings now in the Royal Collection, Brueghel's *The Massacre of the Innocents*, painted almost a century before, a horrifying portrayal of the New Testament story, but updated for the 1560s with armoured Spanish troops killing Dutch children. An earlier owner, the Emperor Rudolf II, found it so upsetting that he had all the children painted over, so a mother is weeping in despair over a parcel on her lap and another mother is fighting with a soldier over a swan, while horsemen thrust their lances into a group of farmyard fowls.

The Brueghel was only one striking example of a whole world of paintings, plays, poems and songs execrating the invaders of the Low Countries. These foreigners were, whether Spanish or French, Catholic. The Republic defined itself by being Calvinist and, as in England or Ireland, faith became both a cultural and religious marker, often hard to tell apart. In miniature, the Republic became a lesson in the limits of reform. As all other variants on Catholicism found, having broken Rome's monopoly it was impossible to persuade everybody, even if they agreed with the break, what the substitute should be. This was also not helped by the different religious experience of each Dutch province and the degree to which each would go to almost any length to defend its local interests. Calvinists themselves, with their focus on discipline and biblical exegesis, found it impossible to maintain a united front, with a terrible splitting sound never far off. Like a cake recipe, once you start mixing ingredients, you can never pick them apart again, and each reform movement had to blunder ahead throwing into the mixer ever more bizarre things, cheered on by one group and mocked by others. Every attempt to go back to basics was thwarted by the real basics being that the cake had been already baked by one and half thousand years of the Catholic Church. Ideas around reform spun off in every direction. There were extreme 'Cocceians' within the Reform church whose close study of the Bible led them to believe, for example, that God did not really part the Red Sea, a revolution- ary suggestion that went down poorly with mainstream opinion more concerned with God's anger being brought down on the Netherlands by (as usual) dancing schools, tobacco, coloured hank- ies, etc. Outside the official Church, the Mennonites' severe attitude towards the unacceptability of violence led them through many convolutions to agree that they could pray for the success of the Dutch state, but not to pray specifically for the success of its armies.

One English traveller marvelled at how the Republic was like a great fair where all the different peddlers of religion tried to drum up business with their 'Phanatick Rattles'. The final victories in the war with Spain had in any event brought in a block of straight- forwardly Catholic territories in the south such as Breda and Maastricht which could not realistically be converted – there was simply no longer that sort of zealous sense, particularly as, to the horror of the Elect, there seemed to be a declining interest in Cal- vinism even among Calvinists. In this splintered, riven environment there was even space for Spanish Jews (but not in Maastricht, where a ban stayed in place until the 1790s), who settled into non-guild industries and trades such as tobacco-spinning and diamonds.

The opposite approach was taken by Louis XIV, who in the 1680s disposed of all remaining protections for Protestants, result- ing in some 250,000 leaving France and settling wherever they could find a welcome – including the area of south-west London I live in, where there is still a grand, if battered Huguenot cemetery. The influx of thousands of French-speaking Calvinists added to the mayhem in the Netherlands as 'Walloon' churches were set up to accommodate the refugees (there is still a very beautiful one in Delft, just by the Old Church). A new, if semi-detached, group of

exiled French academics further enriched an intellectual life already
crazily contradictory and fecund. Among these was Pierre Bayle,
who had taught at the Academy of Sedan, set up by a fervent
member of the Principality of Sedan's ruling family, to teach French
Calvinist clergy.* When Louis shut down the Academy, Bayle
moved to Rotterdam and spent much of his adult life teaching there
while never learning a word of Dutch. Bayle has many virtues, but
above all he cut through all the parrot-house of fervent, loopy,
pious voices bickering across the Republic with the resounding,
magical and new statement that drags humankind forward into a
fresh era: everyone has 'the right to be mistaken and to hold ill-
founded views.'

It is hard to know who to point to in this ferment of interest –
in the 1650s Delft is home to Fabritius, Vermeer, Steen and de
Hooch, for example. But the Old Church there contains the mod-
estly elegant tomb of perhaps the most important of them all
(obviously we don't need to choose really), a narrow pyramid of
grey marble to commemorate Antonie van Leeuwenhoek. While
Bayle made the comment which allowed humans to cross a new
intellectual frontier, Leeuwenhoek was using his strangely powerful
and steady eyes to cross another. Over a tremendously long life (he
died in 1723) he sat for the most part in Delft, fiddling for year
after year with tiny glass lenses, tubes and candles, their light inten-
sified by concave mirrors. A young Leeuwenhoek can be seen in the
background of Cornelis de Man's nauseating painting *The Anatomy
Lesson of Cornelis 's-Gravesande* (a dissection carried out in the Bap-
tistry of the Old Church!), upstaged by the moustachioed corpse,

---

* The Principality of Sedan, like the related micro-state of the Duchy of
Bouillon, was absorbed by France in the seventeenth century. During the Allied discussions in 1815 it was decided that France should keep Sedan, which
was then the headquarters town of the Prussian occupation forces, a decision
which had a huge impact on subsequent French history. Bouillon was attached to the Grand Duchy of Luxembourg, and therefore, through twists and
turns, became part of Belgium, allowing Godefroy of Bouillon to become a
national Catholic hero.

its chest opened, its ribs making me promise never to eat rack of lamb again, and its flensed skin spread over its arms like a napkin.

Leeuwenhoek was himself a great chopper and slicer and did terrible things to dogs. He was supplied by a local butcher, who must have scratched his head at the gentleman's funny needs more than a few times. He was fascinated by eyes, from bee to cow, and at one point tinkered with a whale eye the size of a baseball thoughtfully brought to him by the captain of a Greenland whaler pickled in brandy.* His the-world-before/the-world-after break-throughs were to discover sperm and micro-organisms.

It is impossible to exaggerate the importance of what Leeuwen-hoek did: one day he identified red blood corpuscles, the next flagellates and rotifers. His discovery of sperm was in itself a bit of a semi-breakthrough as nobody knew, having established their existence, what these little characters did or why. Supplying himself with a steady stream of his own subjects for study, Leeuwenhoek could not work out what they meant. The Great Spermist Contro-versy that now developed – which he did not agree with himself – lay in the belief that each sperm had a tiny homunculus inside it from which the human grew. Operating at the far outer reaches of what a contemporary lens could do, many claimed to see such a thing, crouched at the base of the head – a tiny, tiny elem-ent in an already tiny object. The fascinating argument emerged that logically the homunculus must in turn have, like a series of Chinese boxes, but not actually box-shaped obviously, myriad further tiny men in his testicles, who in turn ... Perhaps with powerful enough lenses it could be discovered how many more generations of humans God planned there to be?

It had long been a party piece in scientific European circles to use a lens to see fleas and mites, but the discovery of micro-organisms was equivalent in importance, on the tiniest canvas, to the discovery of America, launching vast enterprises without which our world would be unimaginable. Leeuwenhoek's strongest surviv-ing lens is x266, enough to enlarge a bluebottle to the size of a

---

* The eye, not the captain.

spaniel, fortunately not all at one go, but also powerful enough to allow extraordinarily small animalcules ('diertgens'!) to swim into view: 'I make the proportion of one of these small Water-creatures to a Cheese-mite, to be like that of a Bee to a Horse'.

Leeuwenhoek became a great celebrity. He was a favourite of exiled English gentlemen with time on their hands – John Locke came to have a peep at some dog sperm in 1678 and the future James II the year after. Peter the Great passed through on his special barge and, in a curious instance of the Republic's trading reach, could talk to Leeuwenhoek in Dutch, having picked it up on various Russian Baltic docksides. Leeuwenhoek does not seem to have been a particularly winning individual and, despite his fame, I'm not sure I would particularly have wanted to shake his hand, but as the Dutch battled wave after wave of invaders, he and Bayle and many others were transforming the world in ways which had far greater repercussions than the Siege of Namur.

Gilt and beshit

A strange constant in a long stretch of Western European history was the blocking of the Scheldt by the Dutch to asphyxiate the trade of Spanish-controlled Antwerp. A small piece of territory still ruled by the Netherlands (Zeelandic Flanders) is left over from this period of enforced quarantine from 1585 to 1792. One of the greatest ports in the world became a stagnant backwater. The Spanish turned instead to the small settlement of Dunkirk. Taken from the Dutch in 1583, it was built up in the following decades into Europe's premier pirate port. It bristled with ever more ingenious stone castles, walls and strongpoints which, in a world of scarily vulnerable wooden ships, made it invincible. A spectacular approach to the harbour was built between two, almost mile-long, massively armed protective moles carved through the enjoyably named Splinter Sands (Dunkirk wallowed in sand and has always been the toast of dredger captains and crews). Once permitted past the entrance to the moles (armed with devices which would blow to smithereens anyone trying it on), ships could be hauled down the channel and into the fortified harbour. The moles meant that no unfriendly ship could even think of coming within range of the happily carousing pirates, barmaids, loblolly boys and so on who roared and smoked in the tavern-packed town. The Spanish could also rely on wildernesses of shifting sandbars and reliably awful squalls and storms to make any attempted blockade into a nightmare. Dunkirk became the great home of the frigate, a new type of shallow-water attack-ship which swarmed down the Channel or into the North Sea.

The first half of the seventeenth century was an English nadir. With songs and folklore of the Armada's defeat still humiliatingly fresh, southern England was now navyless. Dunkirkers could massacre and sink entire fishing fleets and the Channel emptied of merchants. At the western end of the Channel, corsairs from Morocco could with impunity raid Cornish coastal villages and abduct their inhabitants as slaves (perhaps provoking a short-lived craze for pasties in Fez). The roots of the Royal Navy lay in this crisis, as huge ship-building programmes gradually allowed for more anti-Dunkirker patrols. After the English Civil War, Cromwell's new Republic had tentative discussions with the Dutch about joint sovereignty for mutual protection, as the two Godly states fought the Catholic Hydra. When these came to nothing, Cromwell allied with France, both against Spain and against the various members of the exiled English royal family sheltered by Spain, some lurking in the Spanish Netherlands. Aside from taking Jamaica, the key result of this war was the Battle of the Dunes in 1658. Unable to approach Dunkirk from the sea, there was no choice but to march along the beach, creating a battle on a strangely restricted site between the French army, braced by six thousand psalm-singing New Model Army troops, and the defending Spanish. After a very short, very violent fight, Dunkirk fell and, as a treaty condition, became an English possession. This was 25 June 1658, 'the mad day', when Dunkirk was Spanish in the morning, French at noon, English by the evening. Ownership of Dunkirk at last fixed all of London's security worries, allowing control of the Channel and a fabulous base into which troops could be loaded for use against any future threat. But after the Restoration – in a typically heavy-lidded and brocaded moment – Charles II decided, to the incredulity of his ministers, to sell it to Louis XIV, and so Dunkirk became for ever French – one more silty element in the ancient County of Flanders at last brought to obedience.

This meant that when war broke out again – inevitably – between France and England the town turned into an even worse nest of buccaneers: cussing and belching in the footsteps of the Spaniards, again grabbing or sinking English ships, effectively with impunity, lurking behind the further upgraded and, if possible, even more bristling Splinter moles. The damage was amazing: during the War of the Spanish Succession, the French captured or sank close to a thousand English ships, thanks to such characters as the swaggering, much eulogized but obviously very annoying French hero Jean Bart. As this monstrous conflict staggered to its end, the exhausted French as part of the Treaty of Utrecht agreed to demilitarize Dunkirk, and it became a more routine port. English visitors noticed however that the dismantled fortifications were carefully piled up as thousands of numbered and categorized stone blocks which could, in time of emergency, be quickly popped back into place, like the world's heaviest Lego kit.

The whole of the eighteenth century was spent by the British trying to keep the southern Netherlands in friendly hands (and, indeed, this has been true ever since). Every combination of allies was tried in order to achieve this, including even a further period of allying with the French themselves. In another of the treaties that ended the Spanish succession war, the Austrians in 1714 took over the old Spanish Netherlands. This allowed a member of the French royal family to become King of Spain, but shorn of some of the lands which would have given him a Philip II-like heft. The new Austrian Netherlands were reinforced against future French predation by a series of 'barrier fortresses' manned by Dutch Republic troops, in places such as Tournai, Ypres, Namur and Ghent. These proved hopelessly flimsy as the Austrians soon lost interest in their remote and hard-to-defend territory, and the Dutch went into an economic death spiral. Both the British and the Dutch agreed about the barrier's importance, but the sheer weight of France leant on it heavily. In a series of epic wars (the War of the Austrian Succession, the Seven Years War, the American Revolutionary War and the French Revolutionary Wars) the British battled to fend off the French before eventually the whole lot was swept away in 1794 and incorporated into France, the outcome that the British had dreaded for generations.

The British argued endlessly about their Continental commitment, which became more closely integrated with their sharing a ruler – generally called George – with the Electorate of Hanover: a worthwhile but awkward-to-reach territory well to the east of the Dutch Republic. An extreme though plausible argument could be made for the British Empire itself being largely a displacement activity for the frustrations of fighting in Flanders. Generally the French were held back during these wars by different combinations of allies in the Austrian Netherlands, but there was never any question of mortal damage being done to France itself, which remained impregnable behind its Vauban fortresses. It became a clever British strategy to use its huge navy to deflect the French through forcing them to defend absurdly remote colonies, which once grabbed could then either be kept or used as bargaining chips in Europe later. As one British official attractively put it in 1813: 'Antwerp and Flushing out of the hands of France are worth twenty Martiniques in our own hands'.

There is something shark-like and unappealing about the British in the eighteenth century – they created a great and fun literary and domestic culture at home, but abroad there seems to be no end to the bad faith and violence. The American Revolutionary War was such a disaster not least because at last all Britain's potential European allies had been so frequently betrayed, nagged, lied to, let down or bullied that they finally lined up with France, shutting Britain out and taking turns to be awkward. By 1780 Britain was managing to fight Spain, France and the Dutch – with others gloatingly neutral – as well as the Americans. At last everyone had seen through Britain as an ally, making it impossible for the British to concentrate on the Thirteen Colonies in what should have been just a minor policing operation, he says controversially.

The triumphs and disasters of these endlessly extended eighteenth-century wars now have little resonance, but for many tens of thousands of British troops, the journey across the Channel was a rite of passage, heading off yet again to Flanders and points east, cursing their seasickness but at least relieved not to be dying of fever on the Spanish Main. Sometimes their transports could be trapped against the coast for days by adverse winds or flung about by appalling storms. There were also all kinds of safe-conducts for clumps of diplomats – each time the gunsmoke at last cleared, other, more voluntary British travellers at last were allowed to cross the Channel – and many of the wars' major treaties were signed in towns dotted up and down Flanders and the Rhine: Nijmegen, Aix-la-Chapelle (Aachen), Rastatt, Amiens; even the Anglo-American negotiations to end the unsatisfactory War of 1812 were carried out at Ghent.

This subject, of course, is a book in its own right, but the ink would hardly be dry on one of these treaties before any number of British ne'er-do-wells would come across from Dover to see what had been closed off by years of fighting. The most famous flood of British travellers was after the Treaty of Amiens in 1802, during the wars with Napoleon, when after ten years it was at last possible to go to France without carrying a musket. But it was equally true after earlier wars, as happy French inn-keepers and barmen casually wiped down a few surfaces, chucked a fowl in a pot and waited to fleece the new tourists. The Treaty of Aix-la-Chapelle in 1748, for example, had roistering characters such as William Hogarth and Tobias Smollett making the trip, the latter reporting that in Ghent he had talked with a Frenchman who explained carefully that France had *let* the Duke of Marlborough win his battles in order to thwart the machinations of the king's mistress.

Hogarth is the real hero though. He went over to Calais with a few mates just, it seems, to get drunk and provoke a punch-up. He was a near-miraculous artist, but also a near-unhinged sort of patriot. When asked to admire any specific piece of French furniture or ornaments he said: 'What then? But it is *French*! Their houses are all gilt and beshit.' He expressed his amazement at the impact of the 'little distance as from Dover', suddenly finding himself face to face with 'a farcical pomp of war, parade of riligion, and Bustle with very bussiness in short poverty slavery and Insolence'. He was arrested patriotically sketching the old English fortified gate. Hogarth's revenge was one of his greatest paintings: *The Gate of Calais*. Making Calais into a stage set, viewed through an archway, every inch of the picture is crammed with derisive anti-French detail. A fat monk slobbers over a huge piece of beef for British visitors, while starveling, rickety French soldiers eat tiny bowls of grey soup. A wretched Jacobite lies on the ground with a raw onion to eat ('brozing on scanty french fair'). A group of fishwives gawp reverently at a ray which they have arranged with a small fish to look like the Virgin Mary and Baby Jesus. In the far background some absurdly handled Catholic service is going on. But the whole painting is dominated by the Gate, sunlight catching the carved English coat of arms. Hogarth paints himself sketching it, with a hand reaching out to arrest him.

A generation later, after the Seven Years War, Smollett was able to return and create a marvellous prose equivalent to *The Gate of Calais*: his hymn to dyspepsia, *Travels through France and Italy*. Like all British visitors, he first engaged with the old Burgundian stamping grounds. Boulogne was his first focus of contempt and dismay and *Travels* initiates the tradition of the incredulous, comic British travel book, where readers can both marvel at foreign idiocy and warm themselves on their own national greatness. I feel sad not to have space to quote entire pages, as Smollett rages against his Continental surroundings. He cannot quite believe the awfulness of French food or French manners or their spindly, dirty furniture. He uses wonderful, now extinct words: just on a couple of pages: chalybeate, zonic, corinths, endemial, mundic. He piles on contempt for everyone in Boulogne – the nobility, living in 'dark holes' in the Upper Town, have 'no education, no taste for reading, no housewifery, nor indeed any earthly occupation but that of dressing their hair and adorning their bodies'. Their only pastimes are playing cards and going to church. He is very funny both about the French ('volatile, giddy, unthinking', 'a frivolous taste for frippery and shew', 'utter strangers to what we call common decency', etc.) and Catholic 'mummery'. He reserves a special hatred for a revered Virgin Mary, a statue carried off by Henry VIII but later found, miraculously, drifting back into Boulogne harbour in her own little boat: 'At present she is very black and very ugly, besides being cruelly mutilated in different parts of her body, which I suppose have been amputated, and converted into tobacco-stoppers'.*

The sheer hysteria of Smollett's scorn ('They are hardy and raw-boned, exercise the trade of fishermen and boatmen, and propagate like rabbits') gets wearying after a bit, but as he shouts and grinds his teeth, he invents a new genre. Laurence Sterne, who also took advantage of the war's end to get across the Channel, was appalled by his predecessor and nicknamed Smollett the dreadful 'Smelfungus' in his novel *A Sentimental Journey*, which describes a Sterne-like figure's Continental adventures and ends with the wonderful line

> So that when I stretch'd out my hand, I caught hold of the Fille de Chambre's
>
> END OF VOLUME II

Sadly, while *A Sentimental Journey* was once a cult book, it now seems (to me, anyway) boring and incomprehensible (unlike his endlessly curious and funny *Tristram Shandy*). This may just be because Smollett got there first in my affections when in my teens. Sterne set up *A Sentimental Journey* to be a rebuttal of Smelfungus's egregious book, but I soon get impatient with its tinkly tweeness and side instead with Smelfungus (or indeed Hogarth), shouting at innkeepers and gagging on foreign food. Continuing to keep this sort of British visitor (known to the French as *les goddams* or *les rosbifs*, among other things) out of the Channel ports must in itself

---

* French Revolutionaries would both burn the famous statue (only a partial hand survived) and eradicate the great church in the Upper Town in which she had lived, originally founded by Godefroy of Bouillon's mother.

have been a profound argument in favour of Louis XV prolonging the Seven Years War to Eight Years or even Nine.

Adventures in tiny states

One of the guiding spirits behind the French Revolution was a sense of exasperation at the total irrationality of Europe's political landscape. Great swathes of territory looked on the map like a spilt packet of muesli, with scattered bits of land arising from some five-century-old family dispute or an emperor's reward for some long-forgotten piece of battlefield courage. In many ways, it was these scraps of territory which were the most eloquent exhibits in any critique of aristocratic rule. This was even recognized by some of the rulers themselves. The hyper-rationalizing Habsburg Emperor Joseph II, sitting in Vienna in the 1780s, exhausted himself trying to swap his ownership of the remote and awkward Austrian Netherlands for adjacent Bavaria: a demeaning situation that must have done its part to fuel incipient Belgian nationalism. In the end any rationalizing of scattered land fragments was a threat to almost everybody in the Holy Roman Empire. All the little states huddled together in a squeaking panic, warmly encouraged by Frederick the Great. Frederick behaved rather like Lewis Carroll's Walrus, sobbing with sympathy for the poor little oysters even as he eats them up, and had a wonderful time generally irritating Joseph II by feigning a pro-oyster stance. It would take the cataclysm of the French Revolution to both sweep up the territorial debris and end semi-feudal rule – but even that proved only partial, with many aristocrats *still* escaping through the Net of Rationalism.

There are so many pre-1789 oddities scattered across the map that it is hard to have any discipline writing about them. I could spend my whole life drifting from anomaly to anomaly, almost all, on closer inspection, having curious places in European history. With inward sobs and special pleadings, I can only realistically restrict myself to talk about two: Montbéliard and Neuchâtel.

Montbéliard is a dozy little town in the south of the Franche-

Comté. With its dusty squares, shuttered houses, Café du Commerce and smell of hot baguette, it seems to be an identikit summation of everything that makes France so attractive. But then, you walk around a corner and, perched on a monstrous crag, is a chaotic, toothy, part-ruined German Schloss glowering down – as though you have ambled in a few moments from *Jour de Fête* into *Escape from Colditz*. For some four hundred years Montbéliard was an isolated territory, attended by some smaller little splotches around it (including the Fiefdom of Saint-Hippolyte, which need not detain us), owned by the Dukes of Württemberg, whose main territories were unfortunately a hundred miles or more away, with their capital at Stuttgart. Inserted between the Burgundian and then Spanish-ruled Franche-Comté, the lands of the Bishop of Basle and Habsburg-ruled Further Austria, Montbéliard was as spatchcocked and nutty a piece of territory as anyone could hope for. The Dukes were a classic example of rulers whose territory was not big enough to make them serious European figures but also not small enough to be left alone. Their own incompetence and brutality meant that they also had a notably antagonistic relationship with their leading subjects – who could reduce the dukes to raging impotence, gnashing their teeth in their Stuttgart palace – with their endless talk about privileges and exceptions and refusal to be taxed. The Dukes loved Montbéliard, or more properly in their time Mömpelgard, as, even if the place was tiny, they could swank about and be more feudal there. At one moment of particular humiliation, it was the only territory they had left.

The Dukes had the additional problem of having converted to Protestantism. Mömpelgard was converted by a Swiss-French preacher, Guillaume Farel, and this isolated it from its mainly Catholic neighbours. Within the Holy Roman Empire, Protestant rulers never resolved the problem of how to find jobs for their sons. The Empire's framework remained organized around Catholicism, and Catholic rulers could find any number of lucrative posts for family members within the Church hierarchy, including such idle, nicely dressed ones as being the canon of a cathedral. The only Protestant route for large families was to bundle everyone into the army. The

Dukes of Württemberg went even further – selling their own subjects as soldiers to other countries – but it was a genuine headache
for a cash-strapped and sprawling place like Württemberg: how do
you keep a respectably parasitic aristocratic lifestyle for family
members who – in an odd form of discrimination – were absolutely
forbidden from earning any money by, say, settling down to run a
pub or shop? Sometimes reigns produced a lot of children and what
to do with them all produced ducal despair. For this reason
Mömpelgard tended to be handed over to a junior family branch
to rule just to spread the limited Württemberger cash around. The
absolute low point was Leopold-Eberhard, who ruled at the beginning of the eighteenth century and lived in a frenzy of silliness,
betrayal and sexual incontinence (enjoying at one point several
daughters of the same guard captain). His legacy was the epic,
long-running lawsuit of the 'Mömpelgard Bastards', who dogged
his cash-free successors in the hope of affording fringe-aristocratic
lifestyles.

On the face of it Mömpelgard was just a comic anomaly. Whenever there was a war some bright commander would remember
Mömpelgard and invade it. It was a regular pit stop in the Thirty
Years War and during the War of the Spanish Succession the garrison was under orders simply to give up at once if anyone in a
French uniform appeared. It is a shame that we have no record of
what ordinary Mömpelgarders thought of all this. Once Louis XIV
had taken Alsace off the Vienna Habsburgs and the Franche-Comté
off the Madrid Habsburgs, Mömpelgard found itself in the front
line but somehow held on until it featured in the general clearance
sale of 1793, becoming together with a chunk of north-western
Switzerland part of the wonderfully named new French department
of Mont-Tonnerre. After the Napoleonic Wars were over it remained
part of France. But Mömpelgard has, like so many such places, curious byways. It was always an enclave of Protestantism and, falling
outside Louis XIV's jurisdiction, it was not affected by the Revocation of the Edict of Nantes in 1685 that ruined Protestant life in
the rest of France. The town therefore has the oldest Protestant
church in France – a beautifully severe classical box from around

1600. It was also the town where the great Protestant scientist Georges Cuvier grew up. A superb statue of him in the main square pushes the sculptor as far as he can go, by successfully rendering flesh, cloth, hair, fur, paper, leather, silk and a chunk of fossilized bone in bronze. Cuvier's virtues are almost endless and I felt elated to so unexpectedly bump into him. Minor yet excellent achievements include inventing the words mastodon and pterodactyl, which tap directly into my very earliest and most fervent enthusiasms, as well as being the man who first studied the mosasaur. To mark this dinosaur link the local museum has (alongside superb plaster and resin models of the Pears of the Franche-Comté) a spectacular cast of the skull of *Sarcosuchus imperator*, an appalling crocodile twice the size of any living one – the fossil *'une découverte 100% française!'*.

Mömpelgard's other strange claim on everyone's time is that, after centuries of make-do-and-mend, sexual abasement and middling-dukedom humiliation, the rulers hit pay dirt. Friedrich Eugen, the Duke of Württemberg's younger brother, lived there and, through the machinations of Catherine the Great and Frederick the Great, his daughter was chosen as the wife of her son and heir, Paul. Catherine had been herself a minor German aristocrat before marrying the Russian tsar, conniving in his murder and becoming one of Russia's greatest rulers – so little Sophie Dorothea was following in distinguished footsteps when the heir Paul came to Mömpelgard to whisk her away from the dozy pear orchards of the Jura to the grandeurs and cruelties of the Romanov court. Converting to Orthodoxy and changing her name to Maria Feodorovna, she spent many years under Catherine's thumb, turning out children. Sophie then found herself eerily echoing Catherine as Paul I (a deeply weird and unpleasant man) was also murdered after a short reign. She tried to do a Catherine and take over the state, but nobody paid any attention and her eldest son became Alexander I. An extraordinarily regal and appealing character, she spent many years working on the fabulous Pavlovsk Palace outside St Petersburg (or rather, watching other people work). She invented the fun idea that she would remain the most senior woman at her son's court, meaning that she was the central focus rather than the elbowed aside tsar's wife, marching about resplendent in all kinds of surreal costumes. She lived long enough to see her second son, the cheerless martinet Nicholas I, take over.

A similar story of important unimportance can be told about the nearby micro-state of Neuchâtel (Neuenburg). A compact, tangled and beautiful place, in the sunlight its sandstone buildings give the impression of being made from huge slabs of golden pastry. It shares with Mömpelgard the same sense of ancient self-sufficiency. The town was converted to Protestantism by the same preacher as Montbéliard, Guillaume Farel, in 1530 and the entire contents of its great and ancient church, the Collégiale, were dumped in the River Seyon. The local ruling family died out in 1707 and, admittedly on a somewhat restricted electorate, the inhabitants had an ancient right, otherwise only enshrined still with the Pope and the Emperor, to choose their new ruler. Among the jostle of candidates (including that perennial hopeful Louis XIV), the burghers had the brilliant idea of choosing the Prussian king, Frederick I, on the grounds that he was so far away he would be unlikely to interfere much. Frederick agreed, briefly excited about its possibilities as a launch pad for attacking France, but then stymied by the farcical tangle of neutral and unfriendly territory in the way. Despite attempts to give it to someone else, Neuchâtel remained in Prussian hands (with the traditional Revolutionary and Napoleonic interlude) until 1848, latterly as Switzerland's only monarchically-ruled canton.

Neuchâtel has many claims on European history, even if it was a dud from the Prussian point of view. It was the home of Philippe Suchard, the great Chocolate Supremo, whose Neuchâtel factory spread so much happiness around the world (the cantonal museum features pre-1914 shop window displays of Suchard products from the wonderfully randomly selected towns of Algiers, New York, Gotha and Ploesti). It was the original home of absinthe. When under the rule of the old Scottish Jacobite renegade George Keith, tenth Earl Marischal, on behalf of Frederick the Great, Neuchâtel provided crucial sanctuary for Rousseau in 1762. Viewed as a moral and religious leper, Rousseau had been hounded from place to place and was eventually kicked out of Neuchâtel too (it became a standard local sport to throw a stone through one of his windows), settling on the pretty if tiny Bernese island of St Pierre to the north-east, before being expelled again, this time moving on to Strasbourg and then to London. To match Cuvier in Mömpelgard, Neuchâtel had Louis Agassiz, professor of natural history at its university and theorist, among many other things, of the Ice Age, the first man to realize that Switzerland was simply the tiny modern remnant of an appalling Greenland-style ice-sheet that once crushed down on the northern hemisphere. One of the Prussian government's last acts in Neuchâtel was to pay for his research trip to the United States, where he stayed and went on to revolutionize American science.

There is no end to what can be said about Neuchâtel in fact – its calico, its fountains, its freakish automata, its wristwatches, its wonderful Cenotaph of the Counts. Much of its territory was thinly populated Catholic farmland, with families who lived through the terrible expedient of exporting unwanted family members, leaving never to return. Neuchâtel sold its men as soldiers and as tutors and its women as governesses. Like much less grand versions of Mömpelgard's Maria Feodorovna, Neuchâtel girls were highly valued in Russian aristocratic circles for what was seen as the unique purity of their French. In the nineteenth century this became an even more vigorous asset as the French girls from France were marked as regicidal bacilli. In an upper-class world in which normal conversation was held in French, Neuchâtelaise became essential teachers, scattered on aristocratic estates from the Baltic to the Urals. For these girls it must have been like going to the Moon. To grow up making daisy-chains in some lakeside meadow and chatting with your favourite cow, then a few months later being bundled up in bear fur in a frantic sleigh, its bearded driver invoking the names of all the saints as he races his wild-eyed horses across a frozen lake pursued by howling wolves, must have been quite something.

In the time of the periwigs

There can be few happier hymns to Dutch urbanism than Zaad-straat (Seed Street), one of the principal thoroughfares of Zutphen. From every angle it heaves with charitable and educational founda-tions, towers, old glass and grand private homes. Of course, on closer inspection there are many more recent architectural fixes and fiddles, but its dominant flavour is at latest early eighteenth century. Delft's town centre is famously stranded in the later seventeenth century, with much of it still looking like Vermeer's *The Little Street*, painted shortly after the accidental explosion that had destroyed much of old Delft in 1654. Everyone must love this flavour of ancient brick, much repainted window-frames and worn steps and I have several times made a hysterical pitch to my ever more fright-ened and irritated family that we should move to a Delft canal-house and throw ourselves into the language and employment issues later; make it a bit of an adventure. For the Dutch themselves though it was far from an adventure. These great market squares, town halls, churches and homes survive in such profusion because they were frozen or pickled in the nightmarish collapse of the Dutch way of life in the eighteenth century, a collapse only really fixed in the twentieth. What we enjoy now is a spin-off from the wretched experience of living *after* the Golden Age.

The eighteenth century mocked the Dutch. What was for Brit-ain and France a time of boom and drama was for the Dutch Republic a disaster. If you were, say, Russian, historically your hopes could never have been high, but for the Dutch to have known *such* fortune – a fortune intimately linked with Calvinist predestination – and to then participate in such failure was truly horrible. Even maps of the world taunted their owners, preserving high-water-mark reminders in far south-east Asia (Arnhem Land, Van Diemen's Land, the Tasman Sea, New Zeeland) of a long-lost supremacy, just as much smaller-scale maps of New York remained littered with fossil remnants of Dutch North America (Staten Island, Brooklyn, Harlem, Bronx, the Tappen Zee, Yonkers, Spuyten Duyvil). Mauritius had been snatched by the French, its very name replaced by Île de France, losing for now the connection with Prince Maurits, once Governor of Dutch Brazil, another distant memory. The second half of the eighteenth century was further mocked by the Stadtholder William V, aged three at his accession in 1751 and whose terrible inability to rule became clearer with each passing year (in a self-critical moment he himself looked back on his own military training and said that he qualified perhaps to be a corporal).

Disasters came from every direction. The revered cows once glowingly painted by Cuyp were devastated by wave after wave of rinderpest. The fishing fleet collapsed, the navy shrank, entire industries seized up in just a generation. Leiden's huge textile industry fell to pieces and the town's population nearly halved, with farm animals grazing on its once grand squares. Salt refining (a Dordrecht speciality) nearly stopped. In a horror specially reserved for the Dutch, creatures called 'pile worms' appeared in the 1730s and began munching their way through all the wooden bits of dikes. After about 1720, the Dutch East India Company (abbreviated in Dutch to VOC) was no longer dominant in Asia, and after about 1740 the Dutch lead in technology disappeared. Everyone in Leiden was proud of how Peter the Great had come there to see its great scientific triumphs and tour the Hortus Botanicus; that Linnaeus had published his *Systema Naturæ* and *Fundamenta Botanica* there – but by the second half of the century it was clear that it had become a backwater. Even worse, the Austrian Netherlands were thriving, with Brussels a boomtown and, during the long and vigorous viceroyalty there of Charles Alexander of Lorraine, canals, roads and industry sprang up and the population went up in a sneak preview of the Belgium to come. What had made the Dutch Republic so successful in the seventeenth century somehow conspired to wreck it in the eighteenth, with the particularly unfair feeling that Britain and France had copied Dutch techniques and then used their larger scale to crush Dutch competition. Meanwhile in The Hague, William V (his very name a derisive parody of his great predecessors William the Silent and William III) presided over his pettish, corrupt and self-indulgent court, an era that would be remembered as 'the age of periwigs'.

It was in this atmosphere that the extraordinary excitement around the American Revolution surged across Europe. The eighteenth century saw rising European globalism, rapid economic growth (for some countries), adventure and enterprise – but it was incremental and had few of the astonishments that had made the previous two centuries so mind-boggling. Now everyone was used to drinking coffee, tea and chocolate and the last dodo was long since eaten. In this world of relative dynastic steadiness (Britain: people called George; France: people called Louis), the American revolutionary years of 1775–83 were a feast of fun: intellectually challenging, with widely sought engravings of new heroes and, above all, the happy spectacle of British disaster. After Britain had pigged out on its winnings from the Seven Years War, dumped its friends and become Europe's first super-power, it was too good to be true that after so short a period of lording it, it might lose its biggest colony. The French poured everything they could into messing the British about, and around 1780 it looked as though their empire might crack up completely. For the Dutch, the great temptation emerged: should they, as the French proposed, join forces in the Indian Ocean and carve up the British Empire there, just as the French and the Americans were doing in the western Atlantic? William V remained neutral and pro-British, but as the American War unfolded and the British became both ferocious and despairing in its prosecution, the Dutch were awkwardly placed. Not least, the almost unbelievably tiny but enterprising Dutch West Indian island of St Eustatius became the key entrepôt supplying weapons to the American rebels. American naval vessels attacking shipping around the British Isles used Dutch harbours. 'Neutrality' became increasingly intolerable to the British, who boarded and confiscated at will ships thought to be providing goods for the Americans.

And so, the terrible fiasco of the Fourth Anglo-Dutch War unfolded. For those brought up on the magic deeds of earlier struggles, the innumerable engravings and popular tales of Admirals Tromp and de Ruyter, it was too much to bear. The British swiftly

swept up Dutch ships and colonies, and destroyed the boom
entrepôt of St Eustatius, which has not troubled history further. The
antiquated Dutch navy was simply unable to risk its total destruction
and stayed in harbour, allowing the British to blockade the coast
and wreck the Dutch economy. The only plus was that the disappearance of Virginian tobacco gave a brief and highly delusive boost
to Dutch tobacco. In 1782 the Dutch Republic became the second
country, after France, to recognize the United States.

The Austrian Netherlands took advantage of this struggle to end
the ancient Barrier Treaty with the Dutch, kicking out their garrisons and demolishing the forts. The forts were useless in any
event – a victim of the same malaise that meant the Dutch could
not pay for anything else. Normally the British would have
objected vociferously, as the Barrier was central to their Continental policy against France, but this obviously was unlikely to happen
given that the British were fighting the Dutch too. The Austrian
Netherlands therefore gained what proved to be a very short period
of full if local sovereignty at last.

The independence of the United States, finally agreed to in
1783, was an odd result for the French. Versailles could not have
been more buckled-shoes/gateaux-in-the-shape-of-palaces/tinkly
music, a queasy blend of self-indulgence and frosty protocol. There
must have been more than one beautifully manicured hand drum-
ming on a cherry-wood desk in some impatience, mulling over the
fact that France had lost thousands of troops and bankrupted itself
to help bring into being a huge new republic, already much larger
in area than it and standing between France and its rickety, thinly
held colony on the Mississippi. In even the short term the British
seemed oddly undamaged by this – certainly humiliated, but with
the rest of their empire intact and with continuing cultural, linguistic and financial links to the United States which France could not
break. It was though the *republican* bit that was most striking.
Republics had been small historical oddities – the Swiss, stagnant
Venice, some bits of religious obscurantism inside the Holy Roman
Empire such as the Abbey of Essen – and now they suddenly
seemed chic, big scale and workable. As the Dutch wound up their

war with the British, they looked askance too at the hapless William V, who while not a monarch was, as hereditary Stadtholder, close enough. He was so widely despised that he managed to be both personally against the war and yet blamed for its disasters. Before the end of the decade, the overwhelming implications of these events would sweep up first the Dutch and then the French and a new era would begin.

CHAPTER TEN

Heroic and ominous

In 1781, through sheer bad luck, one of the great unintentionally comic figures of the eighteenth century decided to visit Ghent. The Emperor Joseph II was absolutely in earnest about everything he did but, like a Habsburg Monsieur Hulot, left a trail of chaos behind him. The vagaries of death dates and Salic law meant that he inherited from his father Francis I the role of Emperor in 1765 but continued under the watchful eye of his mother, the wise and experienced Maria Theresa, for a further fifteen years as she ruled the Habsburg lands, sometimes allowing him to help for an afternoon just to be kind. Joseph emerged from this unlooked-for tutelage in a rage of thwarted energy. It was probably fair to say that his mother's court had become rather old-fashioned by the end (a sort of wilderness of hassocks, incense, spindly, flower-motif chairs and singing children) and Joseph, once off the leash, set out to drag this inheritance into the fresh air. A devout Catholic, Joseph wished to axe what he viewed as all the uselessness and mummery of the rococo Church. He ejected monks from their monasteries and turned the buildings into schools; he kept up a quixotic battle with Tyrolean Christmas-crib-makers; he yearned for his subjects to be 'useful' and to shock them into becoming devoted servants of his state.

It had never crossed his mother's mind as a good use of her time to visit the Austrian Netherlands, but Joseph was different. Characteristically he had two contradictory projects in mind. One was to drag the province from its priest-ridden, obscurantist mire and make it into a wealthy, humming part of the Empire. The other was to get rid of it completely, swapping it for Bavaria, which was experiencing inheritance problems of a kind that made it vulnerable to its incorporation in the Habsburg lands. In 1781 he arrived in Ghent, having already left a long trail of outraged feelings and bafflement behind him. As was traditional he went to St Bavo's to see the *Adoration of the Sacred Lamb* – and was appalled. Van Eyck's extraordinary figures of Adam and Eve (naked as per Genesis) struck him as obscene. Tangled in his own sexual misery, Joseph seems to have had a sort of breakdown in the face of these admittedly harshly, near medically nude figures. He commanded that they should be repainted but in animal furs (i.e. as per a bit later in Genesis). Luckily he wanted fresh panels done rather than getting a modern painter to treat them like paper dollies and stick clothes on the originals. The result was magnificently silly, with Eve in a proto-mini-skirt and the two of them transformed from being the burdened, austere parents of humankind into Flintstones swingers.*

This sort of plunging, chaotic intervention wrecked all Joseph's initiatives. Nobody thought the Bavaria swap was a good idea and ultimately a coalition of smaller states plus Prussia prevented it. By then Joseph had long lost patience with the Austrian Netherlands. He had banned gambling, closed down over a hundred and fifty monasteries, dumped a whole range of attractively old-fashioned religious practices and drawn universal hatred on himself. He railed against 'provincial dullards governed by women and monks' and attacked Flemish speakers as 'narrow-minded . . . obstinate . . . lunatics . . . idiots'. He seems to have entirely failed to notice that places such as Namur and Brussels were growing and industrializing in a British way (as was Liège, in the neighbouring diocese). The British were mischievously involved, encouraging Joseph to force the opening of the still-closed Scheldt just to wind up the Dutch (the farcical 'Kettle War'). Indeed, the British became strongly in favour of Joseph's rule and against the Bavarian swap for the unacknowledged reason that continuing Habsburg incompetence in Flanders was just right for them. Being treated in this

---

* Adam and Eve accessorized both ways can now be seen in the cathedral – but with the originals back in their rightful place.

way – patronized, bullied, derided and viewed as something to be swapped – the inhabitants in the end revolted, inspired by the French Revolution. Within weeks all the provinces except Luxembourg had expelled Habsburg power and Liège had chased out its prince-bishop and become a republic. On 11 January 1790 the United States of Belgium was declared, news of which reached Joseph in Vienna as he was dying of TB contracted while fighting the Turks at the other end of his now collapsing empire.

The Belgian recoil from Joseph's poorly thought through ideas of modernity was increasingly national but also wholeheartedly Catholic and viewed with bafflement and distaste by more radical neighbours. The situation in the Dutch Republic in the same decade had, in the wake of the tremendous strain and humiliation of the war with Britain, resulted in a left-wing revolution in 1787 as the Patriot party ejected the weakened and periwigged Orangists, with William V fleeing across the Channel, using I think the very same beach outside The Hague that Charles II had used in a more positive and exciting context in 1660. Tragically both Patriots and Orangists viewed the values and decisions of the other as the reason for Dutch shame and each could create narratives where they alone were the true inheritors of the heroes who fought the wars with Spain (Wedgwood's factory made a lot of money from selling the appropriate commemorative china figurines of William III, de Witt etc. to both sides).

As the area weakened and become more unstable and incoherent it oddly became absorbed again by the Holy Roman Empire. The Austrian Netherlands had never left it, but to the horror of the new Dutch Republic a fresh page in its abasement was turned by the invasion in 1787 of a Prussian army led by the Duke of Brunswick, a German who had been for many years William V's adviser. Having successfully fended off the Spanish for eighty years, the Dutch now found that the Orangist-backing Prussians were able to cross the country and reach the sea in about four weeks. In 1789 a Prussian army under Brunswick crushed the newly declared Republic of Liège and in 1790 an Austrian army ended the United States of Belgium, the Habsburg Empire having immediately regained its sense of purpose and ruthlessness under Joseph's younger brother, Leopold II. These were all traditional *Reichsexekutionen*: Imperial interventions to re-impose 'order', loosely defined. The Liège and USB actions post-dated the most important event of all – the French Revolution. But the Revolution was itself created in part by the sense of total shame and failure in Paris at seeing France's ally, the Dutch Republic, overrun by the Prussians without even consulting what was meant to be Europe's premier state.

The pace of change was now simply extraordinary. The opening phase of the French Revolution was generally met with pleasure – for good reasons (a New Dawn) and bad (British glee at what appeared to be the total collapse of their generations-long enemy). In many ways the fizzing hysteria of the next few years bursts the bounds of this book. Everywhere had its weeks of excitement/ terror/betrayal/recrimination. Decisions and loyalties which seemed rational one day became fatal the next. Society after society became shaken apart, each town suffering its own mini-drama. Just in the Austrian Netherlands, the process which caused revolution in 1790 resulted in an Austrian army restoring order, followed by a French invasion in November 1792 that expelled the Allies (the Battle of Jemappes), a counterattack in March 1793 that expelled the French (the Battle of Neerwinden) and a further and (as it turned out) decisive French invasion in June 1794 that resulted in the province becoming part of France (the Battle of Fleurus).* These repeatedly shook to pieces every social assumption. All the little town halls, guilds and civic militias lay in ruins and the habits of obedience, heredity and order were lost. By the time of Napoleon's defeat in 1814 an entire generation had grown up who simply could not understand what the 'periwig' obedience and hierarchy of the eighteenth century had meant.

---

* Jemappes is a village outside Mons. It was such a key victory that in 1795 the French memorialized it by creating the department of Jemappe out of the old County of Hainaut, the former enclave of Tournai plus bits of Liège and Namur. The humiliation of living somewhere named after your own defeat lasted until 1814.

With the French royal family trapped in the Tuileries palace in 1792, the allies and aristocratic émigrés clustered along the Rhine decided that the invasion of France could not be delayed and were buoyed up by the ease with which invasions had been so readily achieved in the Dutch Republic, Liège and the Austrian Netherlands. The Duke of Brunswick was once more in charge and put his name to an unhelpfully apocalyptic manifesto that stated that if a hair on the head of the royal family was harmed Paris would cease to exist.

We have the great good luck that Goethe was in the Allied invasion army (as was a young Kleist) and wrote an account, *The Campaign in France*, which captures the chaos and horror of the proceedings brilliantly. It is also unintentionally funny about him – with his leather-doored coach and carefully cut out little paper maps of each campaign. He knows very well that he is Germany's Mr Famous and between the lines there is some amazing special pleading and scrounging. One can imagine that he left a bitter trail behind him of soldiers, servants and inn-keepers swearing never to read *The Sorrows of Young Werther* again. But their rage is our gain as Goethe records the creeping unease of the Allies marching west into an unrecognizably strange France. Very early on this is shown in the devastating Siege of Verdun, held by a revolutionary garrison and with the Allies effectively destroying the town to force its surrender. In an unprecedented gesture, the French commandant commits suicide; a captured soldier kills himself by throwing himself off a bridge ('heroic and ominous' as Goethe called it). This was not the sort of choreographed, 'reasonable' fighting which had in some measure prevailed in the eighteenth century. It was also impossible not to be appalled by the news from Paris, where the Tuileries palace had been stormed, the royal family imprisoned and hundreds of their Swiss bodyguards slaughtered.*

As Goethe negotiated with various military couriers to take back to Germany for him boxes of looted Verdun sugar-plums, extraordinary scenes were unfolding in Paris, with thousands of volunteers

---

* Commemorated by Thorvaldsen's extraordinarily eloquent and sad *Lion Monument* in Lucerne, carved in the very different world of the 1820s.

(whipped up by Danton's 'Audacity! Always audacity') pouring in from the provinces to take on the lumbering Allied army. Even worse, back in April Claude Joseph Rouget de Lisle, sitting in Strasbourg, had written what would become the 'Marseillaise', that sinister precursor to the frenzies of nineteenth-century opera. Nobody had really sung in public before about the desirability of soaking France's fields with the enemy's blood. Although it should really be called the 'Strasbourgeoise', it was carried to Paris by Marseilles volunteers answering the call and ever since they have had the credit.

Goethe picked up a recent copy of the Paris newspaper *Le Moniteur* which gloatingly stated: 'The Prussians may reach Paris, but they will not leave'. In scenes reminiscent of Charles the Bold heading towards the Swiss cantons, the Duke of Brunswick marched into disaster. At the Battle of Valmy it proved completely impossible to break the French lines. Even if the Allies had done so, they were now massively outnumbered, under-supplied and marooned in hostile territory – had they somehow reached Paris they were not remotely equipped to besiege it, let alone, as Brunswick had once suggested, erase it. In pouring rain (which Brunswick blamed for the fiasco – and which certainly did not help), the Allies turned back. It turned out to be a little under twenty-two years before they would return.

'The old times have gone'

The ecclesiastical Electors along the Rhine had a fantastic time in the wake of the French Revolution, a frenzy of enjoyment before their world disappeared for ever. Long used to being somewhat disregarded backwaters, Trier, Mainz and Cologne filled up in 1789 with frightened, vengeful and confused French émigrés. There was also the double-dip fun of two Imperial elections in quick succession, with Leopold II crowned in October 1790, dying fifteen months later, and his son, Francis II, crowned in July 1792. This was a disaster for the Empire as Leopold was exactly the sort of experienced, pragmatic and clever leader the Allies needed and his death left behind a pretty sorry bunch. The hysterical, free-wheeling dynamism of the Revolutionaries and then of Napoleon was genuine, but it was also made possible by the accident of duff, charisma-free opponents. For the ecclesiastical Electors however, it was all too good to be true – vast, elaborate ceremonies, crates of incense, the best china, top-drawer house guests. This mêlée of Imperial dignitaries and angry French émigrés was unique. Francis's coronation proved to be a last hurrah, but at the time it seemed to show the robust nature of Imperial life and be a model of decorum, protocol and tradition to set against the Paris funny-farm.

Klemens Wenzeslaus of Trier was Louis XVI's uncle and his territories, particularly the city of Koblenz, were overrun with French aristocrats. Friedrich Karl of Mainz was frenziedly opposed to the Revolution and his extensive palaces were soon also turned into a bedlam of aristocrat spongers and weirdos who were not used to earning a living but who, cut off from their estates, soon ran out of money. In a move that destabilized the entire region's credit, they increasingly issued 'assignats', which promised future payment by Louis XVI. The initial warm welcome became increasingly strained as mobs of aristos and their increasingly desperate dependants day after day cleared the ham from Friedrich Karl's to-start-with generous buffets. He became ever more upset as his very small tax base failed and unemployed Frenchmen trampled all over his pretty riverside gardens and stole his silverware.

Nonetheless Mainz and Trier had never been more glamorous, with the Emperor, the King of Prussia and any number of Imperial figures major and minor. The émigrés included the future Louis XVIII and Charles X, who stayed for a while in the monastery attached to the wonderfully zany Trier church of St Maximin. One of the great oddities of this period was that Louis XVI himself, as head of the French state, was obliged at the end of 1791 to decry Friedrich Karl and Klemens Wenzeslaus for treacherously harbouring the enemies of France, such as his own brothers. The archbishop-electors were, against the backdrop of the unfolding disaster at Valmy, living on borrowed time and after the chaotic

retreat, the Count of Custine's French Revolutionary army swept
through Speyer, Worms, Mainz and Frankfurt in the autumn.

Goethe gives a startling description of the post-Valmy shambles,
dwelling on the awful details that attend defeat: desperate horsemen riding their coaches over the bodies of dying horses;
blacksmiths frantically trying to fix broken axletrees; Goethe himself trapped in a great wallow of red mud (where he felt like
Pharaoh in the Red Sea); wounded, looters and the infected ill
staggering about in the endless rain; starving troops leaving heaps
of dead horses by the roadside with strips of flesh torn from them
with bayonets; dead troops stripped naked for their uniforms. The
Allies marched back into the devastated remains of Verdun less than
six weeks after they had so gleefully headed out of it. Goethe talks
about the conflicts of loyalty that would now be the defining
horror of European life for a generation: the fates of those who
cheer the wrong side: the families ruined by a single incautious
gesture; the families thrown out of their homes by the failure to
make that same gesture. He also describes the hatred now felt for
the French émigrés (their 'mischief, insolence and waste') as their
credit collapsed, ruining stables, inns and dressmakers and wiping
out pro-royal goodwill across the Palatinate and Rhineland.

More or less by accident Mainz became in the following year
the focus of Europe's hopes and fears. Easily captured by the
French during the post-Valmy chaos, it became the Republic of
Mainz, filled with French troops but also with excited pro-
Revolution German 'Clubbists'. These included the very wonderful
Georg Forster, who had accompanied his father as the botanist on
Captain Cook's second voyage, written a magical account of his
experiences, been the inspiration for the young Alexander von
Humboldt and was almost certainly the only Mainz insurrectionary
to have personally seen the sea-ice fields of the Southern Ocean.
The siege was one of the first major shows of strength in the wake
of the killing of the French royal family in January and Goethe's
account has an unmistakable sense of Europe's now wading into
something like Brueghel's *Triumph of Death* – a vast and seemingly
endless contest between two sides who to win must be willing to

destroy everything. In three ruinous months Mainz was essentially burned flat, with the huge cathedral's bulk making it an easy target for banks of Allied cannon. To conserve food, the Clubbists expelled all women and children across the Rhine and the city as an Imperial, ecclesiastical, artistic centre effectively came to an end ('Ashes and ruins were all that was left of what it had cost centuries to build up').

Eventually the French surrendered, their troops marching out west under condition of not fighting the Allies for a year (they were used to crush the counter-revolution in western France instead), singing the now already rather gratingly over-familiar 'Marseillaise'. A stream of carriages followed, carefully picked over by the Allies hunting for Clubbists (Forster had gone to Paris, where he died of rheumatic fever in January during the Terror). The French deputy Merlin de Thionville, as he was leaving, stopped and addressed the furious anti-Revolutionary crowd, pointing out that it would best for everyone just to stay quiet and not look for vengeance, as they would all be held responsible when the French returned, very shortly.

The subsequent course of the war bursts this book's banks. The Austrian Netherlands became definitively French after the Battle of Fleurus in June 1794. Antwerp became Anvers, Brussels Bruxelles, Ghent Gant, Mechelen Malines, Leuven Louvain. Just as terrible rain had played into Revolutionary hands at Valmy, so at the end of 1794 disaster struck Dutch royalists as their traditional defences, the great river systems, all froze solid and a French army simply marched unimpeded from south to north with somewhat cold feet and hooves. Stadtholder William V fled by fishing-boat to England, dying there unmourned eleven years later. The old Dutch Republic, that had reshaped Europe and much of the world, that had once provoked more expiatory pilgrimages and angry scenes in confessionals in Spanish ruling circles than any other country, now came to an end.

The west bank of the Rhine was occupied definitively by the French in the autumn of that year. Mainz became Mayence; Speyer Spire; Koblenz Coblence; Aachen Aix-la-Chapelle. In 1797 the great magic circle of fire the Swiss had successfully put around themselves, based on military heroics from many generations before, sputtered and went out. Their independence was swept aside under conditions of absolute humiliation. Among the many wonders being carted to Paris were the poor bears from the Bern bear-pits. There remains in Bern today a wistful little monument: a bear cub, left behind by the French, stuffed and equipped with a tiny sword and laurel-wreath and holding a little shield inscribed: *The old times have gone 1798.*

The great French gingerbread-baker

It is tempting to start talking about Napoleon, but the dilemmas of the era are just as readily dramatized through the figure of the Abbé Grégoire. Born in the Duchy of Lorraine under the reign of Stanisław Leszczyński, he was elected on behalf of the clerical estates of Nancy to go to the Estates-General meeting in Paris which initiated the Revolution. His achievements were many and extraordinary, perhaps the least of which was the invention of the word 'vandalism' to describe what the Revolution was doing to Europe's art. He was a republican, a hater of privilege, in favour of the abolition of the monarchy and of Louis XVI's trial. He helped found the Institut de France, he was in favour of universal suffrage and crucial in developing new arguments against slavery and against anti-Jewish and anti-black discrimination.

What could the anti-Revolutionary Allies do against such a man? He manages to be both a highly attractive and thoroughly sinister figure, but his beliefs meant ruin for the powdered types who had once so confidently gathered at Mainz. As the French rolled out their new ideas and practices across Europe, the world of Stanisław Leszczyński quickly came to seem palsied and remote and the Allied heads of state mere panicked sheep. Napoleon systematized and fixed in place the French Empire (which Grégoire voted against) but intellectually most of the heavy lifting had already been done. It found, as in Mainz, many supporters across Europe, some creepy and opportunistic but many simply excited to wave goodbye to the old patchwork of privileges, exemptions and oddities.

The French task was also much helped by the creepy and opportunistic nature of its opponents. The Prussians, Russians and Habsburgs may have been proclaiming legitimacy, decency and old-school standards but they were in practice just as wolfish as anyone else. Others watched in disgusted amazement as they carried out the final partition of Poland in October 1795, the end of a generation-long process of destroying one of Europe's great states. They all greedily increased their holdings and Prussia gave itself for the first time a long land border with Russia, an almost unnoticed decision which would have world-changing implications. Everything seemed up for grabs, from a legitimist just as much as a revolutionary point of view. The Habsburgs agreed in 1797 to acknowledge French rule over the Austrian Netherlands and in return were tossed Venice – another of Europe's most ancient, grand states (but with Napoleon having already picked it over for artworks, including – a gratuitous piece of information but it *is* my favourite painting – Veronese's *Wedding at Cana*, conveniently accessible in the Louvre as a result). The disappearance of Venice filled the Dutch with horror. The two states had always matched each other – one maritime republic in the Mediterranean, the other in the North Sea. The Dutch suddenly felt very vulnerable – and would indeed, after a short period as a kingdom under the rule of Napoleon's younger brother Louis (or, temporarily, Lodewijk), end up as a mere northern part of France (with 's-Hertogenbosch Bois-le-Duc; Nijmegen Nimegue, etc.).

One of the great commentators on these years was the splenetic and very funny British cartoonist James Gillray. He had always portrayed the world as a sort of chimps' tea-party, and professionally could not believe his luck with the arrival of the French Revolution and then Napoleon. You can sense his almost gagging with happy disgust as each further degradation and brutality kicked in. It was all a tremendous upgrade from having to hate the French just because they were Catholic and ate frogs. In the palace museum at Rastatt someone has recently had the superb idea of taking one of Gillray's greatest cartoons and blowing it up to fill an entire wall, printing it on cloth. It was in this palace in 1797 that the serious business of 'compensation' began to be discussed by the princes of the Empire now that so many of them were losing their properties to the west of the Rhine. Gillray's cartoon of 1806 shows the culmination of the horse-trading and bad faith which destroyed the Holy Roman Empire. A little Napoleon (Gillray always showed Napoleon as little, but he was in fact a perfectly normal height) in outsize hat and boots is shown as 'the Great French Gingerbread-Baker', taking from the oven little gilded gingerbread new monarchs: the King of Württemberg, the King of Bavaria and the Grand Duke of Baden, decked out in trashy cake decorations from a bag Napoleon has on the floor: tiny crowns, sceptres, etc. In the background Talleyrand is kneading the dough, helped by a Prussian eagle. Fuelling the oven is a pile of easily flammable garbage that has been swept there: a fat-bottomed Dutch doll, a skull with the crown of the Holy Roman Empire, a dirty piece of flag from the French Republic. Behind him is a wicker basket filled with 'True Corsican Kinglings for Home Consumption and Export'. There are endless funny details, made more visible when blown up to wall-size: on a side table there are some 'Little Dough Viceroys' waiting to be baked, including Gillray's lifelong bugbear Charles James Fox, whose early enthusiasm for the French Revolution had previously led Gillray to draw him on numerous fun occasions as a regicidal poltroon and traitor.

Napoleon's genius lay in nudging everybody who had any power into helping themselves to weaker elements in the Empire. Nobody could hold back, but by grabbing that monastery or those pretty vineyards, they were not only agreeing to France's eternal ownership of the Left Bank, but making Napoleon the sole real guarantor of their own new holdings. If the Austrians conceded the southern Netherlands to France in return for getting a cheerful place like Venice for themselves, they effectively admitted that Napoleon was the arbiter of anything that attracted his gaze anywhere in Europe. This was much more poisonous and deep-rooted than simply losing a battle and giving territory to the victor. Prussia waved goodbye to Jülich and gained Essen, but at what cost?

Everywhere ancient families in their tiny castles and ecclesiastical oddities dating back to the Carolingians found themselves dispossessed. Nothing about this process was progressive let alone revolutionary as these bits of Toyland were simply being gorged on by other, luckier, equally feudal characters. One of the great beneficiaries was Baden, which went from being a classic sad patchwork to a compact, plausible state, absorbing Konstanz, Freiburg and the Black Forest as well as the territories on the Right Bank that had belonged to the Bishops of Speyer, Strasbourg and Basle. Its Grand Duke, Charles Frederick, who had started off as plain little Margrave of Baden-Durlach, died in 1811 at just the right point, having quadrupled his territory and created a magnificent inheritance for his successor, who then had to deal with such unhappy bills-falling-due issues as the death of thousands of his subjects fighting in Russia and Germany for Napoleon.

The genius of Gillray's cartoon is to show these new monarchs not just as gilded bits of cake, but as passively plopped down on Napoleon's baking paddle. It shows how it would be the easiest gesture in the world for him to tip them into the 'Ash-Hole' with other regimes that had failed him. The fast-forward atmosphere of life in Napoleon's Europe was exemplified in 1804 by his crowning himself Emperor of the French. In a blind panic (there can only be one emperor) the Habsburg family scrambled to get all their Holy Roman regalia out of Regensburg and safely stowed in Vienna where the Emperor Francis II rustled up the new title of Emperor of Austria as, confusingly, Francis I. Both Napoleon and Franz could draw on the Treaty of Verdun as the French and German inheritors of Charlemagne, although Napoleon had pole position in now owning Aachen and the Rhineland imperial sites. The Holy Roman Empire, with its ancient, confused roots, was at an end and the Habsburgs reduced to being a regional power, albeit a very large one. Their centuries-long role in Western Europe now stopped. If German-speakers were no longer living in a patchwork quilt of small-to-medium polities, then what should be the replacement? Who now owned the quilt? Effectively people have been writing in with answers on a postcard ever since, with sometimes dire results.

The immediate solution was the Confederation of the Rhine of 1806, by which Napoleon began to call in favours from his brittle little gingerbread friends. It was through the Confederation that over a hundred thousand of its most luckless inhabitants found themselves marching into Russia, together with some twenty-five thousand from the Low Countries. The jaw-dropping sequence of events that began with the Grande Armée crossing into the Russian Empire on 24 June 1812 and ended with the Battle of the Nations outside Leipzig less than sixteen months later destroyed Napoleon's Empire. It also pitted 'his' Germans against the Germans fighting with the Sixth Coalition forces, both sides thinking of themselves as standing for truth and justice. For the first time Prussia and Austria were entirely *eastern* forces, facing a Confederation of the Rhine allied to France. The Confederation marked yet another, as it turned out, transient phase in shaking the Rhineland to bits and nobody, from the Swiss cantons to the North Sea, could have any idea what the right political order really ought to be.

Nationalism was the obvious answer, but this presupposed clear, crisply defined blocks of homogeneity, with no mixing of language or religion or custom and a smooth relationship between town and country, none of which existed anywhere. The Abbé Grégoire had once thought about this a lot. Looking at Revolutionary France's now complete ownership of Alsace, Saint-Just had said that Alsatian women should be forced to remove their traditional bonnets as these were 'not French'. Grégoire had gone further: the German 'patois' spoken by so many Alsatians was itself unacceptable. Indeed all non-French speakers – Basque, Breton, Flemish – were, simply through speaking or writing, disloyal. French citizenship could only be expressed in the French language. The stage was being set for the nineteenth and twentieth centuries.

Armies of the Ocean Coast

The fate of Calais has not lost its power to shock. It was one of the string of coastal towns – with Boulogne, Dunkirk, Middelburg and

Rotterdam – where, during a few weeks in the summer of 1940, the full impact of new aerial technology showed itself in the West. Calais was then also repeatedly bombed in 1944 by the Allies, leaving a town which has almost nothing to indicate that it was once ancient and complex. Outside the old centre there are a couple of striking things, most immediately the colossal late-nineteenth-century town hall, its architecture of neo-Assyrian-Venetian-Byzantine-Burgundian inspiration, with a bit of LSD thrown in, making any sane viewer question the whole idea of civic government. There is also Rodin's *Burghers of Calais* (1895), now positioned in front of it, seemingly to create a dialogue about the merits and demerits of nineteenth-century aesthetics. Of course, the Rodin wins – not only as a monument to Calais's epic siege by the English during the Hundred Years War but, inevitably, as an accidental preview of Europe's terrible future, the six anguished figures having more in common with the 1940s than the 1340s, and looking almost unrelated to the bourgeois stolidity of the 1890s, when the sculpture was loathed by all those who had commissioned it.

While central Calais cannot escape being a place that has been pounded into the ground and then hastily rebuilt, it remains also unavoidably exciting, because it is a port, with beaches, moles, cranes, seawalls and the frequent, magic spectacle of ferries manoeuvring into terrifyingly restricted harbours. Seeing the colossal *Côte des Flandres* churning and hooting away, crazily out of scale with its surrounding buildings, en route to Dover, made me wonder if I should simply get a flat in Calais and spend my days sitting on its balcony, flanked by machines that delivered cans of beer to one hand and bowls of nuts to the other, just staring at ferries.

This is by way of preamble to mention an elegant column, topped with a bobble, on the harbour front. The column only survived the Second World War because of the transformation of Calais in the autumn of 1939 – huge modernizing works were carried out to allow a constant flow of British troops and matériel into France. The column was taken away for safe-keeping and re-emerged after 1945 as almost the sole decorative survivor. It commemorates what could be seen as one of the most politically freighted moments of the nineteenth century, when on 24 April 1814, King Louis XVIII stepped back onto French soil. Days before, Napoleon had signed the Treaty of Fontainebleau, resigning as Emperor and going into exile on Elba. The monument has an engagingly kitschy bronze royal footprint decorated with fleurs-de-lis and announces that it was here that Louis 'finally returned to the love of the French'. It was more than twenty-one years since his elder brother had been executed in Paris. His own age, bulk, habits and realism accidentally made him an ideal returning king, even if he had to flee again indecorously less than a year later, this time to Ghent, returning once more after Waterloo had been won.

That Louis should have landed at Calais was symbolically perfect. The story in the west of the previous two decades had in many ways been that of how two opponents – Britain and France – tried but could not get to grips with each other. Other enemies the French could deal with, but Britain remained out of reach. Equally Britain – while it handed out huge sums of money to Continental allies so that they could be beaten again by Napoleon a bit later on – could never work out the means to land anything more than glancing blows itself. From Calais, the two great adversaries could on a clear day see each other across the Strait, but neither could come up with a winning plan. Both sides massively fortified their most vulnerable point – the hulk of the Fort de l'Heurt can still be seen on a shoal off the beach at Boulogne, a monstrous eroded block built by Napoleon, used as an anti-aircraft platform by the Germans and eaten away by countless storms into its current, surreal shape. Control of the Strait remained for years the central issue. The British had the advantage that their security always lay in their navy and could therefore focus purely on turning out heaps of ships, crewed by sailors from the kingdoms' innumerable harbours. The French, as was traditional, had to split their resources, in the end always plumping for their land army – but therefore ensuring British supremacy at sea.

In 1797 the French forced the Dutch to send out what proved to be their final fleet, devastated by the British at the Battle of Camperdown and bringing down the curtain on a once heroic naval power. In the summer of 1799 Holland became the scene of an extraordinary Anglo-Russian invasion led by the Duke of York. Some forty thousand troops marched down the blameless North Holland peninsula hoping that the supporters of the exiled Stadt-holder would rise up and that the French army would somehow not notice. It suffered the traditional fate of amphibious forces: a few days of success just from surprise, followed by the entire power of a Continent-wide empire rallying itself very slightly to shake the intruders off. The invasion's only success was to destroy a last, desperate attempt to rebuild the Dutch navy – but it also raised unresolvably horrible issues for the Dutch, for whom no plausible independence seemed possible ever again.

The conundrum of London and Paris continued to play out for years, both on a global scale (with the British passing the time by gradually taking all the Dutch and French colonies) and on a local one, with telescopes trained across the Strait for a generation. In 1803 Napoleon began a serious and sustained attempt to invade. The ideally named Army of the Ocean Coasts sprawled along nine miles of encampments, backed by huge supply dumps at Amiens, Arras and elsewhere. With all the coast under French control and the Scheldt open for shipping, the now ancient and emaciated port of Antwerp became a major potential asset – 'a pistol pointed at the heart of England' as Napoleon gleefully pointed out – and work began on the Bonaparte Dock, which is still there. To whip up enthusiasm for the invasion, Napoleon put the Bayeux Tapestry on display in Paris, showing how it was done. The region was stripped of trees to make hundreds of invasion barges – a wonderful draw-ing survives showing them crowded into their special harbours, looking a bit like gaming chips. By March 1804 some hundred and twenty thousand men were encamped. A spectacular British raid on Boulogne in October, using fire-ships and 'torpedo-catamarans', must have looked fantastic for lucky spectators on the ramparts of the Old Town but, once the amazing bangs and sheets of flame had subsided, little damage was done.

Napoleon had the usual problem that the eight hours or more needed to get his barges across were in military terms an age. It had to be done at night to have any chance of surprise and the night was too short in the summer, meaning the stormy horrors of a winter crossing. The risks of committing to what could readily prove just a chaotic massacre were too great. Troops rowing twenty-two miles would have in any event been totally exhausted and it was unthinkable to waste space needed for soldiers and equipment on separate teams of rowers. Tests on the barges showed they wobbled and floundered even just outside the harbour. Napoleon passed the time enjoyably, however – instituting the Légion d'Honneur in a grand ceremony at the camp outside Boulogne, and a couple of weeks later popping over to Aachen with Josephine to ponder destiny by Charlemagne's throne. As usual he said fantastic things, perhaps best of all: 'Eight hours of night in our favour would decide the fate of the universe.'

As Napoleon piled up men and equipment, the British piled up fortifications, canals and weapons dumps, and Dover Castle was made invulnerable to anything except just the sort of massed heavy siege-artillery which was almost impossible to transport by sea. In a way, it was a big shame Napoleon did not try it out, as his reign might have ended in 1804. There is a similar counterfactual about Operation Sealion in 1940. The last straw was in July 1805, when the Battle of Cape Finisterre, while a draw, showed that the British navy was so powerful it was insane for thousands of seasick elite troops, exhausted from rowing, to bob about in jollyboats off Dover in the vague hope that the Royal Navy would not notice. Napoleon lost interest and marched the army off to destroy Britain's Continental allies again. The Battle of Trafalgar then ended any future possibility of a French invasion. None of this resolved the problem of how one side was to defeat the other. It was, for both sides, like a nightmare I once had where I was somehow being forced to take a bite from a colossal apple, but it was so big that however wide I opened my jaws I could not get my teeth into its horrible flat green surface. I feel suffocated again just writing these words. The British settled on a policy of indirection, tying down French troops in Spain, a move that undoubtedly spread French troops out, but not fatally. An ambitious attempt was made to re-run the absurdities of the 1799 expedition. This time it was decided to attack Zeeland. In 1809 some forty thousand troops were landed on Walcheren. Walcheren is now simply part of the Dutch mainland, but then the Zee features of the area were much more marked, with Walcheren and its ports still an island, at the heart of the VOC network and with Middelburg a significant European town. Like the Anglo-Russian expedition, the Walcheren expedition is not part of British folk memory as it was an almost incredible shambles. The point had been to draw French troops away from Central European allies, block up the Scheldt, damage French warship construction, prevent Antwerp becoming a threat and destroy Flushing as a French base. The invasion took so long to organize that the Austrians had already been defeated by Napoleon by the time it was launched and the island proved to be merely a humiliating holding-pen in which several thousand troops could die of sickness without the French having to lift a musket.

Some months later the force was withdrawn and the British effectively just waited for a strategy to turn up. This came in the shape of Napoleon's pan-European invasion of Russia in 1812, its catastrophic failure, his consequent retreat and a series of annihilatory battles in Germany that broke his power. Britain was important in providing leadership, money and arms but was a bystander during these events and the Strait a military backwater, the Royal Navy patrolling the world against enemy ships that had ceased to exist. It was also plunged into a separate war with the United States. At the end of 1813 Wellington's British-Spanish-Portuguese army emerged in south-west France, and Prussian, Russian and Austrian troops at last broke through into eastern France. Beset on every side, Napoleon gave in. Flanked by implausible young noblewomen in white dresses and holding flowers, plus a bunch of vengeful, decrepit old aristocratic roués who had frittered away their best years around Piccadilly Circus, Louis XVIII stepped ashore.

Europe reordered

It is unlikely that Napoleon himself particularly appreciated this, but the Battle of Waterloo was in symbolic terms the most beautifully appropriate way to end his reign. Napoleon did not stay long on his strange little principality of Elba, where he designed the Elban flag to include Childeric's bee symbols (they remain on the flag today, ensuring that at least one little island in the Tuscan Archipelago is for ever Merovingian). His surprise return to France was dramatic but effectively pointless. Almost unlimited numbers of Austrian and Russian troops were pouring over the Rhine and would have totally engulfed him even if he had somehow won Waterloo. The symbolism of Waterloo lay in its at last providing the British with the opportunity to confront their great hate figure. As banker of the coalitions and as the most relentless of Napoleon's enemies, Britain had of course been crucial. But, as with several of his royal French predecessors, Napoleon only had a passing interest in colonial empires and naval derring-do – in 1803 he had been perfectly happy to sell the eight hundred thousand square miles of French Louisiana to the United States. His loss of nerve with the Army of the Ocean Coasts (paid for by the Louisiana sale) showed that he could not defeat the British any more than they could him. Waterloo therefore ended everything perfectly. The Russians, Prussians and Austrians had already given him major defeats and now, outside this small Brabantine village, the British, with substantial support from the re-formed Dutch, anti-Napoleon German exiles (the King's German Legion) and the ideally arranged arrival of the Prussians, could also feel they had a major and decisive military role, ten years after Trafalgar.

It was therefore yet another part of Napoleon's stylishness that, even in the manner of his defeat, as he was being packed off to the most remote spot anyone could find on a map, he was able to bring all his enemies together in such a warm and communitarian way. For the Dutch too, their conspicuous role in the battle, marked by the heir to the throne being wounded, wiped away a generation of exile, horror and humiliation. The vast Lion's Mound monument on the battlefield – very un-Dutch in its arrogance – has to be seen as a great sigh of relief, rather oddly expressed in thousands of tons of soil. The conclusion of the war was therefore fortunate for the Coalition and meant there was a surprising level of trust and respect between the various leaders. Just to make sure the French tried no further tricks, Wellington was put in charge of an Allied army of occupation, with the British headquarters at Cambrai, the Russians at Maubeuge, the Prussians at Sedan and the Austrians at Colmar.

With the human and geographical wreckage of twenty-three years of war strewn across Western Europe, the Allies now had to take an absurd range of political decisions in a short space of time, almost none of which stuck. I may well be forgetting something but, aside from the unimaginative decision not to revive the ancient Republic of Gersau (a small ledge of flat land on Lake Lucerne), nothing agreed by the Allies was not drastically questioned over the following century. As with every attempt at a rational, universally agreeable final settlement, it simply created a new range of upsets and debacles.

The reason the fighting had gone on so long remained the insurmountable one that France was gigantic and very rich and enjoyed the same geographical advantages (i.e. most of its frontiers being secured by mountains or lots of water) that it had always had. The Habsburgs took the opportunity in 1815 to express no further interest in their isolated and indefensible western territories, confirming the disappearance of Austrian rule in the southern Netherlands, Freiburg and the Forest Towns – a final farewell to the legacy of Mary the Rich. Switzerland reconstituted itself after being tugged to pieces by Napoleon's experiments. It gained territory in the south (the Valais) and the Prussian enclave of Neuchâtel joined the federation, but with the Prussian king still in charge. The city state of Mulhouse, for many years an associated Swiss exclave, had voted to join France in 1798 and did not revise that decision – although its inhabitants' hopes for a quiet life would be dashed from 1870 onwards.

The litter of bits and pieces around the Black Forest which Austria had owned were split between the Grand Duchy of Baden and the Kingdom of Württemberg, making this neck of the woods look rational for the first time in its patchworky history. Of all the successor states, Baden, with its capital at Karlsruhe, has always struck me as the most plausible – geographically coherent, commanding a long stretch of the Rhine, with a good education system and a range of interesting smaller cities: Konstanz, Heidelberg, Baden-Baden, Mannheim. But as with every attempt to make things clean and tidy, it had problems – oddities such as the Hessian exclave of Bad Wimpfen, or an amazingly unhelpful block of territory which was essential to Baden's integrity, but which meant that the Rhenish Palatinate, given to Bavaria to rule, was unfortunately separated from Bavaria. This could only have been resolved by in turn splitting Baden's territory in two – so the cock-ups of yesteryear were just updated and bad blood between Baden and Bavaria was kept on the boil.

Baden was, however, like all the western territories, simply too small. It was about half the size of what would become Belgium and faced directly onto French Alsace in a ridiculously vulnerable way. All along the Rhine lucky or unlucky princes who had once ruled a variety of micro-states ruefully looked back on their game efforts to join Imperial forces in the attack on France back in 1792, which had promptly resulted in the annihilation of their territories. Baden was fairly well run, had a convincing army and a grand tradition, but its independence next to such a potentially sulky behemoth was a negative one – it was fine only as long as France was in a good mood. This meant that Baden, far from being a reliable beacon of what became 'Third Germany' strength (i.e. not part of either Prussia or Austria), was always frantic to be an ally of someone bigger and stronger.

The rest of the border with France was arranged in a sequence of botches which even on paper seemed very unlikely to hold her in – and yet the arrangements were made entirely with that aim in mind. The enormous Allied occupation army, it was briefly argued, could become permanent and be paid for by the French – but the British were anxious to go home and start inventing railways, and the Austrians were equally keen that the Russians (whose many thousands of troops were engaged in mystical religious ceremonies in Champagne under the increasingly deranged eye of Tsar Alexander I) should be safely transferred out of Western Europe and back into their snowy fastnesses. The Allies were in the fortunate position of all being aware that in different ways they had each contributed a lot to the final victory and therefore were at relative ease with each other and willing to cooperate, but some basics (like – could the Russians please leave before things went terribly wrong) united in many cases only three of the four.

Each bit of the arrangements north of Baden came a cropper. Bavaria was given the Rhenish Palatinate as a major bolster for maintaining a tough front with France, but it was made absurd by the aforementioned Baden territory separating it from Bavaria proper. A series of crude swaps were done between Bavaria and Austria, extricating Austria completely from the Palatinate in return for Bavaria handing over chunks of the Tyrol. Incidentally, one of the very minor sadnesses of all these shifts was the disappearance of a number of beautifully named French administrative units – with the Département du Mont-Tonnerre being transferred into the history books and split between the Bavarian Palatinate and Hesse-Darmstadt. Almost as much to be regretted was the matchlessly named Département des Forêts, which just briefly put the Ardennes under a rational structure, before being divvied up again between three countries. Obviously pretty names count for less than the horrors of Napoleonic colonial oppression, etc. but still.

Two enormous decisions were taken to deal with the rest of the rickety fence designed to stop French resurgence. Suggestions that a British force be stationed on the northern French border, perhaps garrisoned in some permanent new block of British fortified territory such as Dunkirk, were ignored by London, which was already demobilizing most of its army. Instead British strategy was based on two pillars, both of which proved in quite different ways fantastically awkward. The first was to create a large new, northern country: a rebuilt Kingdom of the Netherlands which would take over the whole of the former Austrian Netherlands and the phantom old territories of the Bishop of Liège. This brought into existence an entirely unfamiliar medium-sized unit, which would have been unrecognizable even to the Dukes of Burgundy. It made sense, both as a reward for the Dutch role at Waterloo and because a new Netherlands would have the resources to be, in conjunction with Britain and Prussia, a serious threat to France. It was a good idea for everyone except, as it turned out, the region's inhabitants.

The most far-reaching British brainwave, however, was the insistence on Prussia taking on border-guard responsibilities. The authorities in Berlin had been badly shaken by the previous decade's events as their kingdom had almost ceased to exist under Napoleon. With the happy outcome of 1815 and Prussia's central place in it, they wished to consolidate a larger Prussia in the east – for example, by swallowing the whole of Saxony, which had engaged in some very poor decision-making re staying loyal to French alliances. In the west the small but valuable Prussian territories based around Kleve had been regained, but they no more made Prussia a major western power than did its flaky little role in Neuchâtel. The British were aware that it could be awkward having a militarily vigorous new power in the west, but this seemed a lot less important than caging France. At the first sign of its getting Revolutionary or Napoleonic again, the idea was for the Allies to rush in and stop it – and this required Prussian troops with a big enough block of land to give Berlin a serious stake, although it was a long way from the rest of its territory.

The resulting Rhine Province brought together the ancient religious electorates of Cologne and Trier, the lands of the Bishops of Westphalia and innumerable bits and pieces, from Xanten to Aachen to Prüm. Koblenz became its capital. The Prussians also created the Province of Westphalia, a mass of disparate fragments, seemingly of little value, spread across the north-west of the German-speaking lands with its capital at Münster. Curiously, the fact that the Prussians had secured many of the key ancient Imperial sites did not really have any future cultic relevance for them, as Berlin remained much more significant – although Cologne and the completion of Cologne's cathedral became an important goal in the 1840s. This new inheritance was a mixed bag and at least two things fell into Prussia's lap which would have huge significance. The first was Karl Marx being born in the Rhine Province in 1818. The second was the acquisition, barely noticed at the time, of the entire Ruhr Valley. The County of Mark was an old Prussian property but the absorption of the rest of the Ruhr – most crucially the independent Abbey of Essen, ruled for centuries as a women's religious republic and home to the quietly industrious Krupp family – quite accidentally scooped up Germany's industrial future. As with similar areas of Britain, the Ruhr was a region that united coal, iron ore and water and which by 1815 already had a serious industrial function. But this was nothing at all compared to its mad growth in following decades – a growth which made even previously quite buoyant German states like Bavaria or Hannover into mere orbiting fragments.

Of several congratulatory congresses held by the Allies, the meeting at Aachen in 1818 was the most genial. The Emperor Francis I of Austria, Tsar Alexander I, Frederick William III of Prussia and the non-royals Prince Metternich, Lord Castlereagh and the Duke of Wellington were in attendance, with other figures such as Goethe and some senior Rothschilds. There was a fun visit to see the sacred relics of Charlemagne, effectively, in the wake of Napoleon's visit there, decontaminating the place with a strong spray of hysterical reactionary mysticism. There were discussions about having a permanent Allied army in Brussels which could swoop on the French – but this came to nothing as the most enthusiastic supporters were the Russians, who everyone else really wanted to go home. They had a cheery visit to Spa and one to Waterloo, where the Duke of Wellington gave one of his – what must have already been somewhat dreaded – battlefield tours. In a measure of how shaky everyone's confidence was, Tsar Alexander insisted that for his journey from Aachen to Waterloo all Dutch troops (who were viewed as a security risk, having in some cases fought for Napoleon) had to leave the region and be replaced by a bodyguard of Swiss mercenaries. This followed one of the many hundreds of rumours about Napoleonic secret agents planning to kidnap him.

Perhaps the strangest discussions were for a gigantic European-wide army to be ferried by the British navy to South America to crush the colonial rebellion there against Spanish rule. This is one of the most daft what-ifs of all – but consistent with the new atmosphere of anti-republican hatred and the cult of obedience which swept European ruling circles. Fortunately the British had recent experience of this being a poor idea, having been humiliated some years earlier in an attack on Buenos Aires and having had a thankless time in their own recent war with the United States. We know that events would unfold in ways that ruined the visions of the men at Aachen, but it would have been an even more curiously different direction for history to have taken if this Latin American expedition had been launched – with unfortunate peasant lads from the Urals or Worcestershire battling electric eels, piranha and boa constrictors in the name of monarchical solidarity.

'What is there to fear if you are a slave?'

With their business wrapped up, the monarchs and aristocrats at Aachen prepared to leave but were held there much against their will by a peculiar technological problem. To commemorate the end of the war and Britain's central place in the Battle of Waterloo, the Prince Regent (ruling in place of his incapacitated father George III) commissioned Sir Thomas Lawrence to paint portraits of all the key figures gathered at Aachen. Like an amazingly slower version of some railway station photo-booth – to which the subject had to return once a month to see if the picture had fallen yet into the little tray – this process just took too long. The vast, sumptuous Waterloo Chamber at Windsor Castle is still there, preserved and unmessed-about-with by the odd accident of none of the Prince Regent's successors having any aesthetic interests. The Chamber enshrines perhaps the last moments of glamorous male fashion as 'The Great Renunciation' began to bite and wealthy men shifted to simple black, grey and white clothing. All kinds of gorgeousness are here – unbelievable waistcoats, military dress uniforms of astounding chic.

I remember once seeing an early nineteenth-century Parisian advertisement for imported English fashion: *chapeau de Robinson?: Incroyable!** Even the most zany reactionaries like the Emperor Francis I would not have dreamed of wearing a wig any more and the spirit of 'new Roman' austerity would soon make everyone look as boring as the British Prime Minister Lord Liverpool in his Lawrence portrait (white shirt, white cravat, black coat, hardly even any side-whiskers). Also preserved, perhaps, is the irritation and boredom of the world's most powerful men forced to hang around while Sir Thomas worked up his scumbling.

The portraits are more revealing than the subjects would wish. The principals – Alexander I, Francis I, Frederick William III, William I of the Netherlands – are, despite the best efforts of Lawrence and others, visibly not up to their jobs. Despite declarations of monarchical solidarity, the handing out of tons of medals and reviews of immaculately turned-out troops, none of these figures inspire confidence – it is as though despite their protestations Napoleon had sucked the life from them. Their triumph in 1815 does not in the end feel like a triumph – in different ways each of their societies had been severely smashed up and the basis for their families' rule over their countries had become shaky. Their ministers in their portraits look much tougher, and Metternich is even more sensationally dressed than his master Francis I. It is hard not to imagine that in private conversations the ministers might all have rolled their eyes at the mystical, querulous royal oddballs they had to put up with. In a sure sign of failure, many at Aachen were prey to mad fantasies about Freemasons, cosmic plots and the idea that lurking in a room, somewhere in Paris, there was some Arch Fiend sitting like a spider at the centre of a vast web of global revolution. For some years, anywhere in Europe, all it would take would be for a gang of desperate peasants to torch some feudal symbol or other and the Congress partners would go into paroxysms. They wished

* The French returned to British male fashion at the time of the early twentieth-century Entente Cordiale, with one fashion journalist cooing about a devastating ensemble in loud checks: '*un peu Edouard VII, un peu «cad»*'.

to collaborate in a pan-European police force, stamping out even the tiniest flame of dissent, but they did this in such a jittery way and with almost no positive vision (beyond obedience, and the building of endless canals) that further revolutions were inevitable.

The French were now hemmed in by a tangled array of very unconvincing military arrangements. Dutch troops sat in flimsy border fortifications such as the clumsily repurposed castle at Bouillon and slow work began on various German fortresses. The different political German political entities created the 'Confederation', a loose cooperative organization, with an assembly in Frankfurt, which replaced the Holy Roman Empire. Some of its members were picturesquely tiny, as in the old Empire, but it was strikingly different from its predecessor in clearly being *German*. It may have had some minorities (particularly Czech and Polish) but unwittingly it set out the framework (including with the minorities) for arguments about Germany that were only resolved after 1945. The Confederation's main practical aim was to provide an arena for Prussia and Austria to keep engaged in penning up the French Revolutionary monster. Confederal fortresses were created in a number of locations, including Mainz, Ehrenbreitstein (an ancient heap of rock opposite Koblenz), Luxembourg, Landau, Rastatt and Ulm. Engagingly, these were to be paid for by France. Chunks of these forts still litter the landscape – but they suffered from the increasingly hard-not-to-notice problem that France was no longer a threat. Decades went by with generations of Austrian, Prussian and Bavarian troops rotating through these extremely expensive and ever more pointless buildings. In the end their main contribution to European history was an accident at a confederal gunpowder store in Mainz which killed or injured hundreds of people and required yet more rebuilding work on the haggard cathedral.

The jittery and weird atmosphere of this period came to a head in 1830. My favourite French monarch, the self-immolatarily reactionary and dim Charles X, mocked the memory of Revolutionary and Napoleonic France with his demands for legislation which would punish those stealing sacred vessels from a church by having the offending hand cut off. These sorts of shenanigans resulted in

a relatively minor burst of protest in Paris, at which Charles panicked and fled to England. A new regime was formed by a cousin
whose family had some Revolutionary credentials, Louis Philippe.
It was an indication of how little the Congress of Europe could do
that no action was taken. The vast effort that had originated in the
wish to ensure the safety of the Bourbon family had come to nothing. Indeed, France seemed to have little difficulty in continuing to
act as a great power – it had successfully invaded Spain in 1823 to
re-impose reactionary rule and, earlier in 1830, had begun its long
military involvement in what became Algeria. Now its example in
disposing of Charles X would have a huge impact on its northern
neighbour.

The new United Kingdom of the Netherlands was a deeply
unhappy place. It is hard to exaggerate just how much the Dutch
had been traumatized by the treatment of their country. Waves of
barely resisted foreign intervention, humiliating switches of regime
and eventual incorporation into France as merely a further small
group of departments mocked a great past. It must have been
unbearable to see the great tombs to the Republic's naval, military,
intellectual and artistic giants in the churches of Delft, now merely
a minor town in Bouches-de-la-Meuse. They had been obliged to
become helpless bystanders as their troops died in Russia and the
British helped themselves to their overseas colonies. The new
Dutch state had recovered sufficiently to have seventeen thousand
troops at Waterloo and ended the war undoubtedly in the winning
camp. It was in this context that the old Austrian Netherlands was
handed over – to enlarge the kingdom from two million inhabitants
to five million and to make it a plausible (or somewhat plausible)
counterweight to France, and resolve the problem of what to do
with these bedraggled southern territories.

The attempt to amalgamate two societies which had for well
over two centuries defined each other by mutual hatred and contempt was not a success. The religious, social and linguistic
problems were overwhelming. William I of the United Netherlands
wanted everyone to read and speak 'proper Dutch' – a necessary
action in creating a viable state, but awkwardly at odds with the

different history of Flemish in the south and of the southern elite
speaking French. Technocratic building of canals and redevelop-
ment of Antwerp was not remotely enough. It was also awkward
that the south not only had a larger population, but was also
becoming, in much the same way as the Ruhr, curiously proto-
industrial. Liège, even before the Prince-Bishop had been kicked
out, was famous for manufacturing vigour and great seams of coal.
In a curious piece of continuity though, the Cathedral of St Lambert, which Revolutionaries had begun to tear down in 1794, was
still being taken down and its stone sold despite the notionally
neo-Catholic environment – the last major bits finally going in
1827. Brussels too was formidable – it was already one of Europe's
largest cities, with a population over a hundred thousand, and not
at all readily swallowable by the regime in The Hague. But, given
that the south had in itself never had an independent identity, it
was hard to imagine what it would look like without some form of
external master – whether Burgundian, Habsburg, Spanish, Austrian or French.

The overthrow of Charles X's reign had shown that the post-
Waterloo structure was in as bad a shape as St Lambert's Cathedral.
The trigger in Brussels was a performance of Auber's opera *The
Dumb Girl of Portici*, with its rousing (or, to be honest, very mildly
engaging) duet 'Amour sacré de la patrie' ('Better to die than stay
miserable! What is there to fear if you are a slave?'). After the performance at the Théatre de la Monnaie, crowds poured out and
revolution began. With southern units refusing to fight, William I
turned to the Congress powers for help. But, for their own reasons,
none was enthusiastic. The most helpful were the French, who suggested that a large central block of the southern Netherlands could
be incorporated into, say, France – with the western areas of Flanders as a British protectorate and Prussia taking Luxembourg and
Maastricht. Once this had been studiedly ignored, the Congress
system worked well for what was now described as 'Belgium'.
Continuing fear of France, but also the deep-seated and peculiar
tensile strength of the south kept it intact. Horse-trading in the east
built on earlier horse-trading when in 1815 William I had swapped

with Prussia his family's ancient ownership of the German Nassau territories for what now became the Grand Duchy of Luxembourg. This made sense as part of the United Kingdom of the Netherlands, but was now isolated by the Belgian Revolution. Meeting in London, the Congress powers decided that Belgium should become independent but neutral within the borders of 1790. The Dutch refused to accept this and invaded. This led to the grim Siege of Antwerp, where French troops marched in to support Belgium and to winkle the Dutch out of the Antwerp citadel. This short and horrible campaign (immortalized in some shocking paintings in Les Invalides) devastated Antwerp and ended with over a thousand combat deaths. In 1839 the Dutch finally acknowledged Belgian independence and at a further London conference the borders were fixed: the Dutch kept Maastricht, but Luxembourg was split in two, with the majority becoming part of Belgium (including such places as Bouillon and Bastogne) and the east remaining in the possession of William I as Grand Duke of Luxembourg – the state that still exists today. This bizarre survival was one of the last surviving pieces of debris from East Francia, a still privately owned ducal enclave.

The future implications of a neutral Belgium were, of course, enormous. It became a powerful industrial and colonial state, and a blatant example (along with Baden) of why Max Weber's ideas about Protestantism and Capitalism were completely wrong. Its neutrality matched Switzerland's but on the basis of external guarantors – Britain, France, Prussia, Russia and the Netherlands – rather than its own strength. It used its neutral status to finagle its way into the Congo. The process that guaranteed its borders suggested a great future for reasonableness and novel forms of international law. The Dutch only recognized the boundaries with great reluctance, and some surreal little anomalies still remain today – most notably the Baarle-Hartog and Baarle-Nassau territories, a series of fragments of Belgium inside the Netherlands, sometimes just individual fields, that reflect (for reasons which I have puzzled over but ultimately given up in despair over) ancient land agreements between the Duchy of Brabant and the Lords of Breda. As readers may have noticed, I love territorial anomalies – but these seemed too silly to visit, even with the tantalizing knowledge that there is a pub partly on Dutch and partly on Belgian territory which, reflecting different licensing laws, allows you to keep drinking just by jumping over a line on the floor.

CHAPTER ELEVEN

Strange happenings underground » The New Rhine »
The Translation Bureau of Barbarian Books »
Baden in turmoil » A Newfoundland dog in Luzern »
Grand Duchies, Empires and Kingdoms

Strange happenings underground

I grew up, through sheer good luck, in the end house of a new development, a late 1960s mini-town built on the site of what had been vast Victorian gardens, which meant that while everything was new red brick and concrete, some garden features had survived, such as a charismatic monkey-puzzle tree. The luck came from being in the end house as, at the hyper-impressionable age of five, I was able to spend months, round-mouthed with wonder, staring out of the window at the monster earth-moving vehicles manoeuvring in the sticky red mud as they began work on the next section of houses. I would draw these hydraulic diggers obsessively, filling endless little notebooks. There was a superb caterpillar-tracked yellow Poclain which I fear became to me something like a modern God. This obsession with excavation equipment elided easily into an enthusiasm for dinosaurs and I went through a phase of sketching both diggers and dinosaurs together indiscriminately before, leaving behind childish things, I switched entirely to lovingly worked if wonky drawings of triceratops, stegosaurus and their friends. Visits to the Natural History Museum in London (where emotions were so high I practically had to be sedated to get me out) and ownership of a sensational book of colour illustrations of dinosaurs roaring at the sky or trying to eat each other completed my religious training.

I mention this because in my teens I used to feel a twinge of sadness that I might one day unthinkingly cast aside the Cretaceous and Jurassic playmates of my childhood. One of the pleasures of being in my fifties is realizing that I still love dinosaurs just as much and have seriously overshot growing out of them. This is the key background to my walking through the streets of Maastricht for what I thought would be a routine but fun visit to the town's natural history museum. Such places *always* include something surprising – particularly if they have a 'brown room', where glazed, desiccated and insect-riddled old stuffed creatures sit wistfully in glass cases. But when I entered the museum the whole world spun round: this visit was more than just a quick glance at a dust-coated pufferfish. Over all these years I had never put two and two together. In the unlikely-to-happen event (albeit one I have prepared for most of my life) of someone challenging me to name my favourite dinosaur I would without hesitation have said: the mosasaur. This horrifying marine reptile had provoked in my prized big dinosaur book a masterpiece of speculative illustration – a deep-green big-flippered torpedo of toothed malice. But I had never thought about the meaning of its name, which turned out to be 'lizard from the Meuse', and it was first discovered just outside the town called 'crossing of the Meuse': Maastricht.

The discovery of a jumbled block of fossilized teeth, bones and jaws by some nearby miners in 1770 was the starting pistol for a new understanding of the Earth. A superb engraving from the time shows five brawny miners pushing the dreadful object on rollers watched by two *Sturm-und-Drang* savants in cloaks who gesture their astonishment. The celebrated object, 'The Great Animal of Maastricht', was trundled off as booty to Paris by the French Revolutionary army in 1795. There were countless arguments: was it a whale or crocodile? Why was it crushed and compacted? How old was it? The great Cuvier studied it and confirmed the creature was a lizard, albeit one of staggering size. In 1822 the heroic early palaeontologist William Conybeare named it 'mosasaur'.

The Maastricht museum turns out not just to have a very good 'brown room', but to also be a mosasaur shrine. It has one in a specially built 'mosaleum' and another, christened Lars, in a laboratory being gradually extracted from its rock. They even have an admittedly somewhat speculative painting of a dead mosasaur being eaten by proto-sharks. The impact of the mosasaur's discovery was enormous. It was followed up by my hero Mary Anning's discovery of plesiosaur fossils in Dorset, but also by two further bombshells: the unearthing in 1856 of Neanderthal ('Neander Valley') man about fifteen miles east of Düsseldorf and in 1861 of archaeopteryx in Franconia. To a curious extent it can be argued that the very idea of this newly revealed ancient past is intimately linked with industrialization. Each of these finds were made by miners in quarries where they were simply digging deeper than before. The impact they had on ideas about the nature of the world (allied with books such as Lyell's *Principles of Geology*) raised catastrophic problems for Christianity, discarding the last vestiges of belief in Bishop Ussher's timeframe. The mosasaur shook to pieces man-oriented timescales. If the Creation happened in six days then what *was* this object? There were some ingenious attempts to square the circle, such as that God placed the bones there to test our faith by giving the Earth the false disguise of great age, but these fooled few. The ultimate conclusion, that it was part of a creature that splashed about happily eating everything else in a shallow Dutch tropical sea bordered by gigantic ferns some hundred million years ago, certainly required something of an intellectual wash-and-brush-up.

The mental and religious stresses of the period were added to and entangled with what amounted to entirely new human populations. There are so many examples: a little French Flanders town like Roubaix, with 8,000 people in 1800, balloons to 125,000 a century later; Duisburg, 4,500 to 92,000; Lille, 70,000 to 200,000. Some of these were immigrants (Poles and Silesians poured west into the Ruhr), but a combination of the availability of work and improved life expectancy meant that Belgium at independence had some four million inhabitants and on the eve of the First World War had almost four million more, new people acting in different ways. There were many horrible new jobs for these new people and it is impossible to read *Germinal* without recoiling in total dismay as Zola revives Bosch's and Brueghel's visions of damnation in modern mining. There was a direct line from the mosasaur's discovery to the agonies of firedamp, flooding and collapsed shafts.

One very strange mine was set up around Kelmis, a small town in Limburg, near Maastricht and just across the hills south-west of Aachen, to dig up zinc ore. There had been works there since the fourteenth century at least and there had been peevish disputes between the Dukes of Brabant and the Imperial City of Aachen about who really owned them before the region had settled into the Burgundian/Spanish/Austrian Netherlands. Napoleon ('Au palais des Tuileries, le 30 ventôse an 13') made the mine over to one Jean-Jacques-Daniel Dony on a fifty-year lease and as almost everything was ruled by France at that point nobody really noticed. Dony thanked Napoleon by giving him an elaborate portable campaigning bath made of zinc, which is now in the marvellous Kelmis museum. With Napoleon's defeat however there was an explosion of fusty nitpicking, with lots of experts waving old bits of paper around to show where exactly the new border should run between the new United Netherlands and the new Prussian Rhine Province. Under the unique circumstances of two potential owners, entirely new to the area, arguing a border which itself had mutated wildly over the previous twenty years, and which had before then been sunk in the jigsaw of the Empire and owned by now defunct priests, it was impossible to come up with a good compromise. Several districts (Eupen, Malmédy, St Vith and others) were given to Prussia and these would in due course become the entirely bogus 'unredeemed cantons' of Belgium and get dragged back and forth during the two world wars. The value of the zinc ore concession so goaded both sides that it was decided to make it into perhaps Europe's least-known state, Neutral Moresnet. It proved much more enduring than its initial Dutch and Prussian sponsors, lasting until 1914, while its flanking states mutated into Belgium and Germany.

I would not say that Neutral Moresnet deserves an entire book to itself, but it gets close. A near triangle, with a population of about three thousand, Neutral Moresnet was so small that if there was a fire it had to call in the Prussian fire brigade. It was of course helpless to administer itself except through joint Dutch–Prussian adjudicators. Technically the Dutch still have a stake in the territory today as the mood was so filthy after the Belgian revolution that they never acknowledged the end of their role as a guarantor of Neutral Moresnet – but the chances of this becoming a live issue in the twenty-first century are quite small. The smart little Neutral Moresnet administrative building has a very prominent Belgian shield put there in 1952 after the area became finally and definitively part of Belgium, but some local artisan at irregular intervals must have chiselled off quite an array of earlier shields. The zinc ore was one of the building blocks of nineteenth-century industrialization – not just for baths, but for everything made of brass, for paint, for wire. The Kelmis museum is filled with beautiful technical drawings of ornaments, pumps, winches, shafts – indeed, so beautiful are these drawings that it seems inadequate that industrial art is not treated as a serious field in its own right.

Slightly unfortunately the relentless demands of the region's factories meant that the mine was totally scraped out by the 1880s but there was no means by which either side could agree to end Neutral Moresnet. There had been a fun period when young Belgian men went to live there to avoid military service, but the Belgian government eventually noticed this and fixed it. There is a wonderful postcard of the spot where Neutral Moresnet and the countries of the Netherlands, Belgium and Germany met and which was an undemanding minor tourist attraction. Next to the stone markers in the picture is a little lemonade stand run by the elderly Widow Lausberg – a stand which by that point probably generated the territory's entire GDP. The disaster that overwhelmed Neutral Moresnet was impossible to predict: the attentions of the World Congress of Esperanto. The completely terrible plan was hatched to make Neutral Moresnet the first Esperanto state – its three thousand people the helpless playthings of madness. It was renamed Amikejo (place of friendship) in 1908 and Kelmis became the world Esperanto capital. Esperantists fanned out (seemingly all in straw hats and with large moustaches), organizing picnics, holding language-teaching classes and generally terrorizing the locals. The man who let them in, GP and stamp-collector Dr Molly, seems never have had to pay for his enthusiasms. I have been simply unable to find out if they attempted to convert the Widow Lausberg

or get her to rewrite her little lemonade stand's sign in Esperanto –
a research failure for which I apologize.

This peculiar idyll came to an end in the summer of 1914 when
German troops swept through. It became part of Belgium in 1920.
Aside from its exemplary museum, the most important trace of
Neutral Moresnet lies in the church of Notre Dame. In the porch
is one of the most remarkable of all war memorials. As a parting,
final expression of a century of neutrality, the monument lists the
seventy-nine dead and missing from Neutral Moresnet but refuses
to say whether they fought for Belgium or Germany – they are
simply 'sons of Kelmis' who are 'in death united'.

The New Rhine

While in theory old-regime German towns must have been fun,
with their unfailing patterns of tolling bells, nightwatchmen, guild
parades, public punishments and city gates clanging shut at dusk,
there is a tiny counter-argument that they were in practice unbelievably boring. The image of old Heidelberg in the operetta *The Student
Prince* with everyone laughing, carousing, high-stepping, waving
from windows and singing, 'Drink! Drink! Drink!' was, of course, far
worse than the reality – but nonetheless daily life must have been, save
for the occasional approach of a French army, monotonous.

Basle is a good example. Two very beautiful maps were made,
one in 1615 and one in 1847, and they show practically the same
place the same size, minus some walls and gates and plus a new
railway and factories. The idea of growth, which defines our own
lives, was simply not a historical factor for many places and at most
times, with the economy instead simply consisting of a steady
churn: its rewards handed out in predictable patterns, and with
occasional natural or military disaster from which towns might take
a generation or more to recover. The beautiful area of Basel around
the Lohnhof shows this make-do-and-mend atmosphere well, filled
with houses some five hundred years old and which have had any
number of functions over the centuries. The Lohnhof itself is a

complex of religious buildings on top of a surviving stretch of city wall. The Augustinian canons who once ruled it were kicked out in the Reformation but the buildings themselves have since been through all kinds of implausible fixes. From the nineteenth century it was taken over by Basel's police and the hotel I stay at in the Lohnhof was for many years the city's women's prison, giving the rooms, with their great thick walls and deeply indented doors, an extraordinary mournfulness.

One of Basel's greatest sons, Johann Peter Hebel, author of the wonderfully entertaining heap of Rhineland tall stories *The Treasure Chest*, recalled how as a child in the 1760s there was still a pre-scribed distance from any gentleman at which he had to doff his cap. The Pietist stranglehold on the town meant that no plays could be shown on Sundays and as that was the only day off for most people, it meant there were no plays. Even as late as the 1840s the famous university with its four ancient faculties only had a grand total of sixty-two students. By the 1860s, when Nietzsche arrived to perk things up as Professor of Greek, it had risen to a hundred.

This sense of small-town doziness drove many Germans mad, but there were respectable arguments in its favour. Jakob Burkhardt, the towering figure in nineteenth-century Basel, articulated the idea that the genius of the Germans lay in being 'Greek' rather than 'Roman': a world of self-sufficient, proud, cultured and essentially pacific city states devoted to their own needs. The new German nationalism in the Prussian sense – wallowing in power and con-quest, crushing the diverse, buffet-table atmosphere of the old – was a Neronian perversion of what had made Germans typically rather nicer than, say, the French. Burkhardt's became a highly influential argument – indeed the continuing basis of the Swiss German cri-tique of their more northerly relatives and an argument used both by the Weimar Republic and post-1945 West Germany. But from the point of view of the broad and unhappy main stream of modern history, it was seen as backward, quaint and snobbish. Burckhardt's writing desk has survived him and in its wonderful Spartan simpli-city remains a reproach to the late nineteenth century, both in ideas and aesthetics.

Basel itself was now buffeted by change. In the eighteenth century it had been ruled by the enjoyably named 'Ribbon Lords'.
Basel had a central role in that quintessentially pre-Bastille object
the ribbon, for which there was an unassuageable thirst, tied or
draped around every part of the human body. As in the rest of
Europe, the piecework was done in thousands of households scattered across the countryside ruled by Basel, whereas the profits
accumulated behind the lovely doors of the Basel townhouses.
Some of this old world was swept away by Napoleon, but despite
huge pressures, Switzerland, including Basel, re-emerged in 1815
with much of its stuffiness intact. It was a curious measure of how
rattled and neurotic post-Congress-of-Vienna forces were that the
Prussian king viewed Basel as such a relatively liberal hothouse that
he banned his subjects from going to the university there, despite
none of them having applied.

What did for old Basel was steam, and the actions of the Badenese genius Johann Tulla. The harnessing of steam swept through
work and transport in a generation. The Basel map of 1847 shows
just a handful of factories, but Basle soon became one of the quintessential industrial European cities, its population quadrupling in
the following fifty years. Oddly the ribbons provided the leap, as
experiments with new forms of artificial colour created the synthetic
dye industry. In 1842–3 there was a final, failed attempt by Basle
conservatives to stop the building of the railway from Strasbourg, on
the sensible grounds that 'French ideas' would trundle down those
tracks – which they did. Guild restrictions crumbled in 1854 and by
1869 the old city walls had gone, apart from those holding up
structures like the Lohnhof. These were amazing changes, but nothing compared to what was happening to the Rhine.

Johann Tulla was a military engineer from Karlsruhe obsessed
by the Rhine's inefficiency and uselessness. Under the Holy Roman
Empire there were so many petty sovereignties along its banks
(people like the *three* Counts of Leiningen!) that no action could be
taken. Indeed, enjoyably, rival digging and ditching works in the
eighteenth century went on in the Bavarian Palatinate on the west
bank and Baden on the east, both reshaping their riverfronts to try

to make the current swamp the rival opposite shore. It was daft stuff like this that made the most eloquent case for German unity – during the 1848 revolutions, anti-insurgent Badenese forces, who were meant to be using their artillery against a rebel army holed up in the Palatinate town of Ludwigshafen, instead mucked about flattening the smart new Palatinate port facilities next to it. In any event, the Rhine was a tangled mess, with over fifteen hundred islands in the seventy miles or so below Strasbourg and territories washed away or emerging quite randomly, depending on great convulsions of water discharged by Swiss snow-melt or distant storms. Tulla spent his life turning the Rhine into the gigantic, straight drain that it is now. Ultimately the 220 miles from Basle to Worms was reduced by fifty miles. Most of the islands disappeared, almost all the flood-plains became fields for crops.

The casualties created by these changes were tragic. It had been one of the world's great fish rivers (Strasbourg was famous for its salmon) and the disappearance of thousands of ponds, pools and bits of murk also meant most of the fish disappeared, further discouraged by places such as Basle and Ludwigshafen pouring newly invented industrial effluent into the river. Beavers packed up. It also ended the strange world of the itinerant 'gold-washer'. The River Aare wiggled down from Bern, discharging gold into the Rhine which had been sifted since Roman times. As the engineering works peaked there was a final bonanza for the Bavarian and Badenese governments with huge hauls, but the new, fast, even flow which, as Tulla had predicted, dug a deeper river-bed, meant that there was no way to pan any more. In German museums you can see particularly cherished old medals or presentation coins made from 'Rhine Gold' but by the 1870s they were no longer made. Oddly, Richard Wagner's great hymn to the metal was premiered in 1869 with the Rhinemaidens singing 'Rhine gold! Rhine gold!' as a sort of promotional jingle – but, almost to the year, for a product that was no longer in the shops.*

---

* For those readers who say: 'Oh, he just stole that joke from David Blackbourn's great book *The Conquest of Nature* – shameful I calls it,' I can only urge

What *was* in the shops were countless tourists – as much made from steam as the new factories – impelled up the Rhine by steam-trains and steamboats and guided by Baedeckers printed on steam-presses. The Rhine's flow had meant that many categories of boat could only travel once, from south to north, where they were broken up and sold for timber. The most spectacular of these were the huge log rafts with crews of up to five hundred men and made up of several thousand logs, converting the Black Forest into the wood pilings on which cities such as Amsterdam rested. But now steam removed all obstacles and anyone could travel across Europe in any direction. Basle became the gateway for that quintessential form of Victorian tourism, the visit to the Rhine Falls, followed by the Swiss excursion, either to admire the sublime or to help failing lungs. For English tourists the route along the Rhine and into Switzerland was healthful also in a moral sense, as it allowed travellers to avoid France, which for much of the nineteenth century was viewed both as a military enemy and as a pants-down moral sump. When in *Dombey and Son* Mr Carker and proud Edith flee England and end up in a hotel in Dijon, Dickens hardly has to sketch in any further detail to convey that they *can fall no lower.* 'Clean' Switzerland and 'Dirty' France were no contest, with matching general British enthusiasm for 'picturesque' Germany defined by Prince Albert and by his and Victoria's children ruling or marrying so many chunks of it.

The acme of Victorian hotels, Basle's The Three Kings, is still there and it is still possible to have a stilted tea on its balcony looking over both the Rhine and the great bridge that marks where the river shifts from west to north. Just sitting there I felt myself channelling a nineteenth-century self, reading a pocket book of sermons, keenly aware of the need for a top-up splash of eau-de-Cologne and worrying about my enthusiasm for stays and corsets.

---

them to borrow my copy, where it clearly has at the bottom of page 105 my scribbled 'exactly in line with Wagner!' but *when you turn over the page,* only then does Blackbourn make the same point, where I have written Oh rats! and drawn a sad-face.

It was on this balcony that the great (well, very mildly engaging) drama of Trollope's *Can You Forgive Her?* opens.* It was also here that the famous photo of Theodor Herzl was taken during the First Zionist Congress in 1897. This was an event widely viewed at the time as cranky, but which would come to define the following century and was in many ways only made possible by the strange neutral space and extensive hotel facilities of Basle, in a Europe which was otherwise beginning, as Herzl rightly perceived, to act in an ever more frightening way.

The Translation Bureau of Barbarian Books

During the (as it proved) calamitous conference held by the Japanese navy in May 1942, after it was proposed that the carrier fleet should be sent to attack the small American base on Midway Island, Admiral Yamamoto asked whether there was anxiety about how the fleet would respond should the American carriers intercept them. Magnificently, one of his commanders exclaimed with a contemptuous gesture: '*Gaishu Isshoku!*' – 'One touch of the armoured gauntlet!' I hope this was said in the sort of croaking semi-shout favoured by bull-necked samurai in Kurosawa movies, but his exact voice pitch is sadly beyond my research abilities. I also hope that he said the same thing before every staggeringly successful decision taken by the Japanese in the previous few months, when he would have been right – perhaps, indeed, his naval colleagues had only raised objections to the invasion of Malaya or to the attack on Pearl Harbor for the fun of hearing him struggle to his feet – a mass of braid and jingling medals – to bark, 'One touch of the armoured gauntlet!'

At many points when writing this book the *Gaishu Isshoku*

---

* Britons and Americans abroad are one of the giant subjects I have no room for. Henry James treats the Channel as something like the River Styx, with the plots of many stories and novels stemming from that transition. The closing pages of *What Maisie Knew* become ever more crazily over-reliant on the timetable of the Boulogne ferry.

attitude has occurred to me as essential to world history. If nobody believed this unthinkingly, there would be few wars. Both sides must have military men with such values – but with one side's swaggering shouters proved, in the event, thoroughly wrong. The scale of Japan's land grab in 1941–2 was astounding and had very few precedents, but it had an interesting one that proved comparably disastrous, if slightly longer lasting: the explosion across the world of Dutch power in the seventeenth century. I mentioned this earlier, but it is worth returning to. As with the Japanese in the twentieth century, the Dutch had specific forms of technology and belief which were allied to the (as it proved) only temporary weakness of their opponents: in the Dutch case the French, English, Spanish and Portuguese. For a couple of generations blameless individuals from Zeeland and Holland found themselves masters of the world. Voices who questioned this strategy were shouted down – and were, for quite some time, wrong. Great empires were carved out in the Hudson Valley (New Netherland), northern Brazil, southern Africa (Cape Town), the Indian Ocean (Ceylon and Malacca), the West Indies and Java (Batavia/Jakarta, founded in 1619). Many of these were then lost as an assortment of vengeful rivals took turns to destroy the grossly overstretched Dutch.

It was impossible for anyone to manage such a sprawling mess and it is curious to imagine what might have happened if the Dutch had concentrated just, say, on colonizing and defending North America. The Portuguese ejected them from Brazil and – in perhaps the most globalized war yet fought by humans – Luso-Brazilian and Tupinambá troops defeated Kongo-Dutch forces in Angola. The English ejected them from New Netherland. Entire colonies appeared and then vanished. Evanescent Pomeroon, with its tiny, diseased capital of New Middelburg, was founded in South America in 1650 but burned to the ground by French pirates in 1689. Political fossils still scatter the world today. The Caribbean island of St-Martin/Sint Maarten is still crazily split in half according to a French–Dutch treaty of 1648. The Dutch island of St Eustatius, as mentioned earlier, briefly became the focus of global attention in 1780 as the main hub for sales of weapons to the American rebels, prompting Britain to declare war on the Dutch and raze St Eustatius to the ground, which did not take long. On the other side of the world the sign saying 'New Holland' was painted over by the British and replaced by 'Australia' and the island of Timor remains today split into the three fragments that had been argued over between the Dutch and the Portuguese for centuries, with the unplanned side effect of Timor-Leste's long modern agony.

Time and again, the Dutch completely misunderstood their wider strategic situation and sapped their strength in a mass of futile conflicts which by the late eighteenth century had ruined their country. Forced to side with Napoleon, they had to stand by and watch as the British used this as an excuse to take over Cape Town, Guyana, Ceylon, Malacca and Java, much of which they kept. The absolute dark point came in 1810 with Napoleon's decision to absorb the Netherlands completely into France. With events now vastly beyond their control, the Dutch simply had to wait on events. After Waterloo, years were spent wrangling with the British over who should rule what bit of south-east Asia, with the newly founded Johore port-town of Singapore a particular source of Dutch rage.

At the Napoleonic nadir, with the Dutch having to reconcile themselves to living in departments called things like Zuyderzée, there was only one place left in the world where their flag continued to fly: the tiny artificial island of Deshima in Nagasaki Bay. For 214 years the Dutch had had the exclusive European right to trade with Japan, a peculiar and as it proved thoroughly marginal privilege in an island country essentially self-sufficient and bristling with anti-foreigner feeling. The Japanese had been disgusted by the inroads of Jesuit-fuelled Christianity and turned to the Dutch in return for their not indulging in the smells-and-bells hysteria they associated with the Portuguese. The settlement, founded in 1641, was monitored intensely, with spies checking that work carried on uninterrupted every Sunday and that Christians who died in Deshima were packed off prayerless, simply put in bags and dropped into the bay. Bibles had to be nailed inside special barrels. There must have been a near comic tension in the compound, with someone just absent-mindedly humming a snatch from 'The Lord is my shepherd . . .' risking everyone being put to the sword.

As part of the same Dutch sugar-rush frenzy of invading everywhere, Deshima started off as the focus of grand plans for joint Dutch–Japanese attacks on Macao and Manila, but through sheer luck the moment passed and no scarred, hoarse and lacquered old Japanese general struggled to his feet with some gauntlety metaphor on his lips. Very little actual trade was done at Deshima but it had some value to the Japanese as a link to the world, with Dutch ship captains questioned on arrival about political news. They were selective and perhaps mischievous with this news: for example, it was only when a British frigate came into Nagasaki Bay during the Napoleonic Wars that the Japanese found out the United States had been independent for a generation. Deshima was a boring and disappointing spot – Japan had ample supplies of almost everything it wanted and, like China, was a culture of a complex density that made it uninterested in European antics. The sheer longevity of Deshima gradually, over many generations, let it drift marginally into Japanese culture. Eventually, as some Japanese officials became interested in European scientific ideas, a tradition of *Rangaku*, 'Dutch studies', emerged, followed by the creation of the Translation Bureau of Barbarian Books. Bulk trade proved much less important to Japan than the impact of the occasional small book slipped into a jacket pocket.

For Europeans, Deshima might have remained just a minor cul-de-sac, a peculiarity swept away when Commodore Perry's American fleet entered Tokyo Bay in 1853 and Japan was forcibly 'opened'. It had one extraordinary claim to fame though – the presence there, from 1823 to 1829, of Philipp Franz von Siebold. A young German doctor, worryingly lacking in medical experience, Siebold was recruited as part of the rebuilding of the Dutch East Indies after Napoleon's defeat. He was one of those amazing nineteenth-century characters who through their actions intellectually and imaginatively tied together the planet – Humboldt and Bates in tropical America, Gandhi in Natal, Napoleon in Alexandria, Wallace in Borneo, Kingsley in Gabon, al-Afghani in Cairo, Darwin in the Galápagos. It is impossible not to feel irritable about the mass of low-hanging fruit available to these people. They saw things with new eyes and were able to convey that newness to others, creating an excited ferment of which we are the mere inheritors.

Siebold, for example, was a miraculous handler of seeds and seedlings. He broke the Chinese monopoly on tea. All previous attempts had failed, but he studied Japanese techniques for conserving seeds and successfully got a batch to Java which, by 1833, had some 500,000 tea-plants. One small loam-packed box thus began a revolution (continued only later by the British in Assam and Sri Lanka) as well as landing a devastating if accidental blow on China's import–export balances. He became the great conduit for bringing Japanese plants to the rest of the world, working with the Hortus Botanicus in Leiden. Oddly his future became an unwitting side effect of the Belgian revolution, as the plants he had sent to the National Herbarium in Brussels and the botanical garden in Ghent fell on the wrong side of the new border from his masters in The Hague. Years were spent negotiating their return. What plants these were! I am not sure how this calculation was done, but in Dutch gardens at least it is estimated that three-quarters of the plantings are Siebold descendants. It is thanks to him that my grandparents in West London had the front of their house choking with dusty hydrangeas. The house I grew up in was, at the time, believed to be the place where the five members of the family ran in and out, ate, slept, lived out our lives – but no: we and it were merely a support mechanism for a wisteria of terrifying size. One of Siebold's original wisterias, the ancestor of countless subsequent colonizers, is still in Leiden, still sporting its sinister, all-conquering little mauve flowers after more than a century and a half. Between the Hortus and Siebold's own hothouse, chrysanthemums, lilies, azaleas, hostas, peonies, magnolias and ginkgos proliferated and Japan's great garden culture filled the West. Less happily, Japanese knotweed has also taken over much of the planet thanks to a single plant from Siebold's collection.

Siebold's former house in Leiden is now one of Europe's most absurdly enjoyable museums, packed with some of the heaped piles of *stuff* that he brought back and demonstrating his restless interests as, with various assistants, he catalogued, nurtured and engraved his holdings and spread one of the great human aesthetics around the world. It is impossible to know where to begin – there is everything from sumo-wrestler prints to lacquered picnic sets to the skull of a giant salamander and an unfortunate Japanese otter so overstuffed it looks like a bolster with residual head and feet. Siebold's curiosity fills the house, from his interest in Japanese obstetrics to his writings on acupuncture. An artist attached to Deshima, Kawahara Keiga, produced beautiful images for Siebold, of stingrays, crabs, pomegranates, of a giant-salamander hunt in a wooden landscape. He also did a little painting of Siebold, his Japanese courtesan Kusumoto Tagi and their little daughter on a Deshima observation balcony looking out over the bay with a telescope.

Siebold's collections were the result of disaster in Deshima. A blind eye was turned by the Nagasaki authorities to some of the tiny island's oddities. For example, there were only a handful of Dutch there but there could be up to fifty Japanese 'translators' looking after them, who would in fact be medical students visiting Siebold. Siebold introduced the cataract operation to Japan and would swap doing these operations for artworks and information. Siebold had to use intermediaries to get much of his information on Japan and the authorities in far-off Edo were in an increasing panic about the activities of various circling, nosy foreigners. Sketching the coastline or defences or creating maps was punishable by death (it was a crime in Europe too – hence Hogarth's arrest in Calais). Through sheer bad luck some sketches created thanks to Siebold's friend, the Court Astronomer, Takahashi Sakuzaemon, were found. Takahashi was imprisoned, with all his teeth torn out to prevent him from biting off his tongue to avoid testifying – he later died in prison. Siebold himself was lucky simply to be expelled.

Siebold later became famous in Japan, seen as a great medical benefactor as well as perhaps the single most important figure in exporting Japan's culture to the world, both through his plants and through his publications (including the massive *Flora Japonica* and

Fauna Japonica). The success of Siebold's work was blamed, by the final Dutch ruler of Deshima, for drawing unwanted attention to Japan and hence to the disaster of Commodore Perry's 'Black Ships'. It is a shame that Siebold was himself such an unpleasant character, perhaps the reason he is not more widely known, but legacies act in strange ways. When Siebold left Japan he saw a small boat in the harbour from which Kusumoto Tagi and their daughter waved goodbye. That daughter, Kusumoto Ine, became Japan's first female doctor of Western medicine and in her own right a startling result of Nagasaki's tiny entrepôt.

Baden in turmoil

The events of 1789 to 1815 laid out effectively the gamut of human behaviour, in dramatic and tragic terms. For those coming of age in its aftermath it seemed they had missed an epoch of giants. When Jenny Marx wrote from Trier in 1845 that 'life here is a pocket edition' she was speaking both on behalf of those living in a decayed cathedral town on the Mosel, and on behalf of all Europeans. The Revolutionary and Napoleonic years were like a huge Sears catalogue, found reliably on the doorstep each year, and with something for everyone. Different people turned to different pages and with different forms of nostalgia, curiosity or dread – everything from a special deal on poles on which aristocrats' heads could be publicly paraded to bulk rates on reliable, poorly educated peasant militia who could be let loose on bourgeois liberals. Kits for burning chateaux or for printing up inflammatory posters, romantic refits for wrecked Catholic churches to stun the faithful into fresh obedience, everything you need to smash down barricades. There were pages giving printed forms with wording for timely concessions to mobs, and others announcing distracting military adventures abroad.

With the news in early 1848 that Paris was convulsed by a fresh revolution, everyone ran to their catalogues, frenziedly trying to find the right page. The revolutions that broke out across Europe were real and sometimes very violent, but both sides were almost

incapacitated by self-consciousness: they could already see the massacred nobles, just as much as they could see the mob fleeing like
frightened animals from a well-aimed volley. The thousands of
prints and paintings of 1848 all have this rather worn quality and
yet Europe was a very different place when it came through the
other side. All classes shared a terror of repeating the sort of frenzy
associated with the 1790s,* and no new Napoleon emerged to
sweep the Continent – but the excitement and strangeness of 1848
were real.

The whole point of the sort of religiose, side-whiskered regimes
that ran Europe was to hold off the mob, but many of the most
ardent conservatives (a term invented in this period) saw this as
merely an ultimately doomed rear-guard action. Only so much
could be done by finishing Cologne Cathedral or handing out colour lithographs of young, slightly more open-minded members of
royal families. The years between Waterloo and 1848 were in many
ways very attractive. Although hardly lacking in violence, it was an
era when politicians remained aware of the horrors that had defined
their youths and were tensely non-escalatory. The Paganini–
Schubert–Liszt soundtrack was agreeable and recognizably middle-
class cultures spread, but it always felt like an interlude. Everything
was played out in an atmosphere of regretful aftermath, following
the death of various giants whose legacy was endlessly chewed
over: not just Napoleon, but Hegel, Byron, Beethoven, Goethe.
Darwin had spent his five years going round the world, but nobody
yet knew what that meant; steamships and trains proliferated but
were not yet ubiquitous.

A good example of how 1848 developed is the Grand Duchy
of Baden. Of all the new states that consolidated during and after
Napoleon, Baden should have been one of the most likely to suc-
ceed. Its compact and cheerful lamb-chop shape, its busy Rhine
towns, some revered and ancient, others new and industrial, its

---

* A frenzy which would in fact be achieved outside the framework of this
book by the horrors further east involved in suppressing the Hungarian Revolution.

dense agriculture and timber forests all pointed at its being a possible extra Belgium or Luxembourg. It was at the technological cutting edge, boldly building its first railway (from Mannheim to Heidelberg) in 1840, but unfortunately choosing a different, big gauge to all its neighbours (a gauge which would end up being used only by the Russians) and which required expensive, recriminatory and sheepish unpicking a bit later. Tucked away on the borders with France and Switzerland and with innumerable ancient links to Strasbourg and Basle, Baden had every reason to be a cooperative, mild and independent place. Somehow, though, it never settled down and it became a case history as to why Germany ended up united.

Baden's capital of Karlsruhe was a first indicator of unease – founded in the eighteenth century as a gigantic expression of absolutism, its street plan in the shape of a fan, with the ducal palace at its base. This really poor idea gives it something of a flavour of an American grid city,* but one in which you are caught in an Escher-like nightmare in which to get any place you have to travel in a peculiar zigzag. It reminds me of a pot experience I once had where I was under the impression that my legs had gone all bandy and were marching off in different directions. In this unfortunate city lurked the dukes, elevated by Napoleon to grand dukes. Napoleon's vision for Baden was an unflattering one. He handed it places which had belonged to others (such as Heidelberg, the right-bank lands of Strasbourg and Speyer and the Black Forest Towns) to ensure permanent enmity with its neighbours. The thin northern strip of Baden along the Rhine was designed to be useless, a prophylactic between France and the rest of Germany which would be incapable of defending itself and could be burst through by the French army. Napoleon's needs came to nothing as, in one of the great moments in the wars, memorialized in endless prints scattered through Badenese museums, Tsar Alexander I and his Russian army crossed the Rhine into France at Mannheim. As the tide of

---

* It inspired Washington, DC (through sheer bad luck Jefferson visited Karlsruhe), giving it the same mind-bending, baffled quality.

fighting swept west of 'liberated' Baden there were a host of sticky questions to be asked, not least around the Grand Duke's being married to an adopted member of Napoleon's family.

As the new, post-Napoleon age of monarchical legitimism began, the Grand Dukes were therefore poorly positioned to make big claims for themselves. There was also no reason at all why an inhabitant of Konstanz, Freiburg or Mannheim, say, which were new to the duchy, should particularly feel like crooking the knee to such a gang. The Grand Dukes were a dynastic fiasco. The enormously long-lived Grand Duke Karl Friedrich had a son, Karl Ludwig, who spent many years with his wife having five daughters in a row. At last they had a son, Karl, but Karl Ludwig, having waited forty-six years for his father to die, packed it in and died himself. Karl at last became Grand Duke in 1811, but then died childless shortly thereafter. This meant a dynastic dead end and Karl's surprised uncle Ludwig took over, who was twenty-three years older than his predecessor and then died too. Luckily old Karl Friedrich had had two families (this thicket of Karls will soon clear) – he remarried later in his vast life morganatically, i.e. his wife was insufficiently posh so her children were debarred from inheriting. As they were the only ones now left, legal twists and turns gave the job to one of these children, Leopold, who was about the same age as the Grand Duke two back.

This shambles is only worth recounting because it is from its implausibilities that the potent myth of Kaspar Hauser emerged. He was a simpleton who claimed to have been locked up for much of his life in a stable and whose condition baffled the era's savants. He became rumoured to be the true child of Karl, snatched and imprisoned by the morganatic mum so that her own genes could kick in. The story made no sense – but it did at least lead to Werner Herzog's wonderful film *The Enigma of Kaspar Hauser*, which manages to be a sort of essence of both the 1820s and the 1970s at the same time. That the story became so widely believed was ruinous for the Grand Dukes, reflecting a sense across Baden of their rulers, not as legitimate, ancient, fathers of the nation, etc. but as frauds.

Each European country had its own 1848. Baden was particularly quick off the mark. In Baden there were immediate concessions as huge, threatening crowds gathered in the main towns, filled with excitement about the revolution in France. Democratic problems emerged within weeks: Jews were given full civic rights at Karlsruhe in April, but just as noticeable were anti-Jewish riots in Heidelberg and a great crowd of peasants outside Ettelheim swearing to stand together for 'Freedom, equality and the murder of the Jews'. Freedom of speech too often seemed to mean the freedom to be anti-Semitic. Later the reliably disgusting nationalist Prussian historian Heinrich Treitschke saw the whole of 1848 as being egged on by its 'Oriental cheerleaders'.

The Baden revolution swiftly spun out of control, despite Grand Duke Leopold's attempts to manage it pragmatically. An immediate gap appeared between liberals and radicals, as elsewhere – with the former often being pushy bourgeois civil servants who could generally be bought off by someone in the royal family commenting favourably on their wives' dresses. Radicals – including Karl Marx – were appalled by the way that the revolutions were made by great crowds building barricades or refusing to work, but that the gains were going to a small slice of the middle class, who now generally turned on their lower-class former allies. In the wake of the end of censorship of newspapers, radicals pointed out that for most people what really mattered was the 'freedom to feed' rather than the 'freedom to read'. Radical lawyers such as Friedrich Hecker and Gustav von Struve tried to drive Baden on to genuine insurrectionary revolution, with Struve deriding those in the new Chamber of Deputies as 'the sixty-three rabbits'.

The rigid monarchical solidarity across Europe seemed to many Germans only beatable through German nationalism. The German Confederation was essentially an instrument to fight the French (expressed in Baden by the ever-proliferating Confederal fortress at Rastatt) and to maintain a reactionary 'Habsburg' order by smothering the slightest peep of liberalism. In Baden insurgents marched from Konstanz only to be dispersed by Confederal troops, with the leaders fleeing into Switzerland. In a second attempt a new, united, federal Germany was proclaimed by Struve at the little Badenese town of Lörrach, which by highly technical definitions became for a few hours Germany's first capital, before Struve was arrested.

The slightly comic opera aspect of Baden's revolution ended though with one final, brutal convulsion, the May Uprising in 1849, which, fuelled by thousands of mutinous troops, at last heaved Leopold out. A large Prussian army marched in on Confederal orders, led by the future Wilhelm I of Prussia, and the revolutionaries were crushed in scenes of extraordinary savagery after a three-week Siege of Rastatt. Special courts there and in Mannheim and Freiburg executed twenty-seven of the revolution's leaders. Struve himself escaped (as did the young Friedrich Engels) into Switzerland and lived a long, curious life, like many exiled '48ers, on a circuit of conspiracy, crankiness, poverty and an attractive, continuing idealism. A surprising number became involved in the American Civil War. All together, for a variety of motives, some eighty thousand Badenese left. Throughout the three waves of the Baden revolution there had been a fatal inability to manoeuvre through the splits between liberals and radicals and too vivid a fantasy that the often isolated and hungry small towns of Baden were, on no evidence, filled with baying, Paris-style sans-culottes. Large enough crowds were generated to make a cheering and exciting mob, but this always proved much smaller than the forces arrayed against it.

Grand Duke Leopold returned to Karlsruhe and his descendants continued to rule Baden until the final and total dynastic fail of 1918. Baden became entangled in Napoleon III's plans for a 'southern tier' of German states which would resist a Prussian-controlled united Germany, but Baden was in practice riddled with pro-Germany enthusiasts and thousands of Badenese troops under Prussian leadership took part in the 1870 Siege of Strasbourg during the Franco-Prussian War. Gustav Struve lived long enough to see the beginning of the siege – he had been resident in Vienna under a general amnesty for '48ers, now viewed as harmless and irrelevant. One of the problems Struve had faced many years before, as he tried to announce a German Republic, had been trying to define who was in and who was out of such an entity. Standing in Lörrach, symbolically at the point where Baden joined onto Alsace and Switzerland, Struve concluded that these places too were themselves by language necessarily part of his Republic. If he had lived to see the aftermath of the Siege of Strasbourg, with Alsace incorporated into what he would have seen as a grotesque parody of his vision for Germany, he would have been appalled – but he would also have seen it as in some ways correct. He died just in time. Hecker had also escaped Baden and had fought in the Union armies in the American Civil War. When he visited Imperial Germany in 1873 he shook his head sadly: 'Republicans eke out a meagre existence in dark caves like the last of the dinosaurs'.

A Newfoundland dog in Luzern

My interest in Switzerland is an entirely summer one. Many years ago my family took the eccentric decision to have a winter sports holiday in a context where my parents had previously restricted us to sitting agreeably in various French squares slurping chocolate milk or beautifully coloured aperitifs, depending on the drinker's age. I think the decision to take up skiing was a semi-serious gesture by my father, but sadly I never got round to asking him for a post-match assessment of what he had really had in mind for Europe's most contentedly immobile family.

I must have been thirteen or fourteen. My only clear memory – aside from being cold, wet and baffled – is of our spry old instructor's face. We were all being pulled up the mountainside on a button-seat surface-lift, leaning back on the seats, our skis pointing straight ahead. Somehow I had got to the top, but each of the succeeding button-seats came up empty and Jean-Claude and I, peering over the edge, could see various Winders sprawled at different points down the slope, with discarded poles and skis dotted here and there – a couple of them making pantomime beetle-on-back gestures. I will never forget, turning to Jean-Claude, seeing his eyes, brimming wells of sadness in his seamed, granitic face: a lifetime devoted to the rigours of *alpinisme* mocked. Once we all got to the top and found our poles and skis we were too exhausted to do much more than make jokey slaloming gestures and hum the theme tune to *On Her Majesty's Secret Service*. I did not dare to glance across again at Jean-Claude. The following year we went on a barge holiday in Alsace, which was equally ill-judged but at least returned most of us most of the time to sitting down.

Taking on board this major seasonal reservation, Switzerland is so compelling that one of my many regrets about completing this book is the lack of further excuses to wander from town to town. Who can ever forget the remarkable sound made by the Fribourg funicular railway ballasted by human waste? Or the severe shock of being in Montreux and seeing how functional and dull the hotel was where Nabokov spent so many years of his life? Or the beautiful austerity of the cenotaph to the Counts of Neuchâtel in the Collégiale? As the sun pours down Switzerland becomes a sort of paradise. Bern's city centre is built on its defensive cliff-top, the federal buildings glittering and looking oddly like Queen Amadala's palace on the planet Naboo. The site is carved by a tight loop of the Aare and in midsummer cheery individuals put their clothes in plastic bags and then jump into the aquamarine river, the current taking them round the town and dropping them reasonably close to where they began.

Switzerland practically invented the idea of tourism and there is a camp pleasure in following in the footsteps of every royal, writer and ne'er-do-well of nineteenth-century Europe in gasping at the prison cellars of Château Chillon, shedding a tear at the poignant monument in Lausanne Cathedral to Lord Stratford de Redcliffe's young wife or thinking last thoughts when admiring the statue to the gloomy, peripatetic Empress Elizabeth of Austria in Montreux, her endless wanderings brought to an end in Geneva by a sharpened-file-wielding anarchist. The trains and steamboats and grand hotels that made it all possible are so untouched by passing time that these themselves attract last thoughts – the many, now ploughed-under generations of trippers and tax exiles who have admired the same views, enjoyed the same faultless waiters. The acme is Luzern or Lucerne – a grand lake-port still stuffed with hotels, cafes, vistas and excursion boats, thronged with the ghosts of earlier card-sharps, sexual adventurers and remittance men. Things which would once have appeared merely tacky – such as the Mirror Labyrinth and Edouard Castre's colossal panorama painting of the internment of a French army during the Franco-Prussian War – are now priceless survivors of Victorian travel. The short summer season gives Luzern a hectic quality, with excursion boats zooming out into the complex of lakes loaded to bursting with visitors. A brass band plays Meat Loaf's 'I'd Do Anything for Love (But I Won't Do That)'.

If I were old, rich and unreasonable I would settle here in a trice, thumping my walking stick on the hotel's parquet to summon a waiter to fix me up with another wilfully obscure aniseed or fermented-walnut liqueur. I would attend church at the magnificent St Leodegar's – built in a particularly full-tilt style during the Thirty Years War after its venerable predecessor had been burned to its foundations following a poorly managed attempt to shoot a jack-daw on the roof.* Above all, I would go for repeated walks along Lake Luzern's western shore, a tangle of boatyards, offices and little parks leading down to one of the nineteenth century's principal musical shrines: Wagner's house at Tribschen.

I have never been an obsessive Wagner fan – I love *The Ring of the Nibelung*, particularly *Siegfried*, but attempts to move out beyond this have all failed. Every shot at listening with an inward smile of concentration and reverence to *Lohengrin* or even *Tristan and Isolde* has always ended up after an hour or two with trips to the biscuit cupboard, resultant crunching noises that mess up the lavish orchestration and then a sudden, overwhelming urge to check emails. Wagner's sheer nastiness also gets in the way of veneration:

---

* In the strangely confrontational style of this period there is a carving on the church of St Leodegar himself, a Burgundian priest, holding the drill with which his eyes were removed during one career low point. He is traditionally prayed to by people with eye problems, whereas, it might be argued, he should be the very last person you would want to contact on this issue.

the anti-Semitism, the wheedling, the lies and betrayals. His role as supplier of Nazi theme tunes is obviously not his fault, but it does not help. Many years ago I was listening to *Ring* highlights at my parents' house in an ecstasy of teenage pretension when my grandfather tottered into the room in a genuine fury, shouting at me to turn off 'Hitler's music'.

Despite this or because of this I have found myself repeatedly visiting Tribschen. Wagner was there because, even many years after his own participation in the 1848 revolutions, he was still a wanted man. That he could live in total safety in this big bourgeois house, just outside a town which so many of his enemies would have visited in private capacities, is a perfect example of how critical Switzerland has been to Europe's politics and culture. If Wagner had been captured he would probably have been first condemned to death and then reprieved – but only to a similar extent to his friend August Röckel, who wound up spending thirteen years in solitary confinement in some horrible Saxon fortress. Such a fate would have knocked Wagner's career on the head just after he had completed *Lohengrin*. Whether or not this was a good thing for the future of Europe it is, of course, hard to say. It would have prevented the Kaiser from having a special horn made for his new car that played Donner's motif from *Das Rheingold*. It would have denied key bits of theme music to the 1930s – but perhaps life in Europe would have been even worse? There is nothing to say that, say, French light opera might not have filled the void left by Wagner's prison confinement, so that instead of *Götterdämmerung* being the backdrop to dictatorship, documentaries about the same period would have instead the blood-chilling, nihilistic melodies of Bizet's *La jolie fille de Perth* or Offenbach's *Le roi Carotte*. But I have become distracted. In many ways, Wagner's prolonged exile (in Switzerland and in France) made him more desirable – a king-across-the-water figure. Liszt could conduct *Lohengrin* in Weimar, its 'Bridal March' could conquer Europe, but Wagner could not be present himself.

Amazing things happened at Tribschen. The lovely *Siegfried Idyll* was first performed here on the stairs outside Cosima Wagner's window on Christmas Day 1870. The young Nietzsche visited

Wagner here constantly and they would have had wide-ranging, borderline demented discussions looking over the lake at grand Mount Pilatus (oddly believed to be the burial place of Pontius Pilate). It was at Tribschen that Wagner played on piano the entire score of *The Mastersingers of Nuremberg* for Liszt — an event that strikes me as so frighteningly boring that (perhaps unfairly) it triggers involuntary memories of sitting in church as a child almost crying with dismay at the yawning acres of time during Veneration of the Cross services. Nietzsche himself became besotted with Wagner's music entirely on the basis of a piano reduction of *Tristan*, a curious example (like the *Meistersinger* run-through) of how almost impossibly remote we are now from the technological, temporal and sonic context in which all this great work was actually created.

The house is a fan-boy shrine and filled with old programmes, scores, the actual piano on which Wagner played for Liszt. My favourite is a glass case which contains the tiny whip Wagner used to chastise his Newfoundland dog, Russ. This absurd object brings everything back to a happier level. It is impossible not to think of Tribschen's gaslit interior, with the tiny maestro in his velour cap, capering with rage as he ineffectively whacks his pony-sized pet, with the shadowy, weird Cosima Wagner and Franz Liszt towering over him like carnival-parade giants. In a triumph of pointless internet research I have worked out that the dog and the composer must have weighed about the same.

Wagner wrote the almost unbelievably brilliant Act III of *Siegfried*, Nietzsche wrote *The Birth of Tragedy*. Liszt was rather in transition, shifting from Europe's top long-haired seducer to his latter-years, warty Abbé persona, but he can be forgiven anything for his much earlier *Years of Pilgrimage* piano pieces which crystallize a particularly effervescent Swiss romanticism. I can never quite be sure when I am just making retrospective pretentious claims, but I'm fairly certain that my enthusiasm for Switzerland is based on many years of preliminary listening to Liszt's 'Obermann's Valley', 'By a Spring' and 'William Tell's Chapel'.

It was in every respect a most peculiar household, with Cosima being Liszt's illegitimate daughter, and Cosima and Nietzsche miles younger than the others. In a way Nietzsche and Wagner were both knitting together different cultures in much the same way Philipp Franz von Siebold had linked things Dutch and Japanese. Charlemagne's regular invasions of the Ruhr to kill Saxons had unfortunately deprived Germany of paganism and had indeed been so thorough that no trace of a record of it remained. Wagner, to create an ancient panorama of mythological Germanism, had therefore simply to steal outright completely unrelated Icelandic sagas and, using the crudest surgery, staple their gods to the *Nibelungenlied*. Nietzsche, as Professor of Philology at Basle, continued Burckhardt's ideas about the German genius being inspired by city-state Greek rather than imperial Roman civilization, but also already hinted at the Indian philosophy that would so preoccupy him. Both were obsessed with Schopenhauer. Wagner was at the height of his greatness, and could magic up music which makes even something as silly as Siegfried's rescue of Brünnhilde from the flames thrilling and deranging. Nietzsche was writing a chaotic and often quite boring book, but one which contains flickers of what he will become so adored for: 'A storm seizes everything decrepit, rotten, broken, stunted, shrouds it in a whirling red cloud of dust and carries it into the air like a vulture.' Only the 'fire-magic of music' (i.e. Wagner's) can renew and purify the German spirit.

It is striking that the two men who would be most blamed for providing the backdrop to the Third Reich – and who were, undoubtedly, in some ways fairly nasty individuals – were sitting by Lake Luzern and only tangentially linked to the vast dramas of German unification happening around them while the *Siegfried Idyll* was being debuted. Nietzsche served briefly as a medical orderly in the war, but had given up his Prussian citizenship when he moved to Basle and remained stateless for the rest of his life, having no patience at all for the Second Reich. Wagner was plunged into composing about a world of gods and heroes, but also ultimately of treachery and the death of ambition which ends with the Rhine flooding its banks and Valhalla in flames, a long way from the rational, economically-driven world of Bismarck's new Reich.

Grand Duchies, Empires and Kingdoms

Luxembourg remains one of Europe's strangest entities. Somehow, through innumerable evolutionary twists and turns, it has survived. After all the Prüms, Touls and Salm-Salms have long been tidied up and given to reasonably careful national owners, Luxembourg – so often menaced, truncated and kicked about – has reached the twenty-first century. Luxembourg City is one of the great, weird European landscapes. Many major towns start, of course, on a defendable, flood-resistant hill, even if it is merely a small rise now invisible under a traffic crossing. But Luxembourg battles with Edinburgh or Budapest in any Most Craggy City contest. Even today, the geological cataclysm that sits at its heart is off-putting, with only one road from the south jumping the huge gap into the Old Town. There are few more defendable spots and over the centuries this has made it extraordinarily attractive to conquerors or would-be conquerors.

Luxembourg's contribution to European history was the run of Holy Roman Emperors who preceded the Habsburgs, most importantly the great Charles IV, who in the fourteenth century ruled the Empire from Prague (he was also King of Bohemia) and imposed the document known as the Golden Bull of 1356, which regulated the Seven Electors and the Empire's overall structure until the French Revolution. Luxembourg was passed around by various owners but, like a bathtub duck, however often it was pushed underwater it bobbed up again. Only twice was it threatened with total disaster – under Napoleon it became merely part of the department of Forêts and under Hitler it was subsumed in the Gau Moselland. Otherwise, it has always suited someone somewhere for it to exist. It was in the 1860s, though, that it briefly became the focus of all eyes.

We tend to think of the post-Waterloo nineteenth century as remarkably rational and peaceful in relation to later Armageddons. But this is all relative, and in its middle decades the century was flaky, violent and chaotic with dynasties and ancient polities crashing to pieces all over the place. Largely for technological and accidental reasons, wars tended to be short, but they were murderous nonetheless and led to huge changes. I am writing this in 2017. If you were to take the twenty-five-year-period 1846–1871 and track back the same number of years from the present it would take you to 1992. In that time within Europe the only serious fighting occurred in Bosnia and Kosovo and, more recently, in eastern Ukraine – each of these being essentially civil conflicts with external stirrers. 1846–1871 – the period not coincidentally of Napoleon III's regime in France – saw civil wars, revolutions and major inter-state conflicts in and between almost everyone. It would take most of a page just to list the conflicts. Even Switzerland cracked – with the brief Sonderbund War of 1847 creating the modern, federal state and ending the archaic loose alliances between cantons. And this is to exclude such global convulsions as the American Civil War, the Indian Mutiny, the Second Opium War, French involvement in Mexico and the 'Black Ships' action in Japan, to name but a few. Almost the only major European state that did not see its integrity directly threatened was Britain – but even the British spent the whole period in anxious defensiveness, pouring money into gigantic new ironclad battleships, and the charming, charismatic sea-forts that still dot the coast off Portsmouth, and worrying about the defence of Canada. The French never attacked Britain and the Americans never attacked Canada – but this was only because they both wound up having other things to do.

The Lord of Misrule at the heart of so much of this was Napoleon III. Most of my adult life I have worshipped Émile Zola's novels excoriating his regime. Indeed I am proud to have spent my early years in the south London suburb of Norwood, where Zola spent his post-*J'Accuse* exile. It may be because of spending too much time reading such wonder-works as *Nana*, *Pot Luck* and *The Kill* but whenever the words 'Napoleon III' come up, my free-association mental response is always 'poor sexual hygiene'. This was obviously Zola's intention, but it is not helped by the spread of photography in the period, which particularly puts prominent Parisian men in a very poor light: with their bellies, their trousers that look as though they were changed only seasonally, their dirty-looking whiskers and such gruesome characters as Napoleon's venal cousin 'Plon-Plon'. It must have been a horrific period for women.

But moving back to a more politico-military level, the curiosity of the period was that five European kingdoms or empires – Britain, France, Russia, Austria and Prussia – were comparably strong, assertive and wedded to violence. Indeed, the principal non-court expenditure of the state was on fortifications, troops, ships and weapons. Britain and Russia had substantially avoided the 1848 revolutions (although the latter helped Austria crush the Hungarians), while Austria and Prussia had retained their regimes through their military men and still owed their legitimacy and romance to their roles in the destruction of the Napoleonic Empire. Usually European history's instability seems to stem from one out-of-control monster being brought down by a coalition of smaller states – but it turns out that even in the mid-nineteenth century, with a fair balance of power between five major states, there was still no peace.

Napoleon III was a quintessentially Lotharingian figure. He was the nephew of the real Napoleon and the son of Napoleon's brother King Louis of the Netherlands – although recent DNA tests on their blood show that in fact Louis was *not* his biological father, explaining why Napoleon III always suffered from the awkward problem of not looking even faintly Napoleonic. Fuelled by the – as it proved – mistaken belief that he was born carrying the Flag of Greatness, Napoleon flitted around the edge of France, lurking in Switzerland or England and engaging in two comic coups – one fiasco in Strasbourg and one even worse in Boulogne, featuring a paddle-steamer, a tame vulture pretending to be an Imperial eagle and the effortless arrest of everyone involved as they struggled ashore in heavy surf. In the wake of the 1848 revolutions he was able to use the Napoleonic aura to become voted president of the new French republic and then through a 'self-coup' organize an upgrade to emperor in 1852.

The adventures of the Second Empire are too numerous for this book, but Napoleon's odd form of activist liberal imperialism sent

French troops all over the world, with results both incoherent and lasting. He was crucial in destroying Austrian rule over northern Italy and therefore in creating the Kingdom of Italy from what had always been before a jumble of smaller states. In return for his military role, the Kingdom of Piedmont, the initiator of Italian unity, handed over to France the ancient territories of Savoy south of Lake Geneva as well as the County of Nice (Nizza). As the King of Piedmont now became king of the whole of Italy this was a relatively minor swap for him, but a major addition for France. In the later twentieth century Savoy made France into a major winter-sports destination and gave it control over Evian mineral water – two unanticipated pluses. The name-that-fails-to-rise-to-the-occasion peak of Monte Bianco became the no-less-flat Mont Blanc. Some local cafe chat about how it might have made more sense for Savoy to join the Swiss Federation was rapidly quashed by French troops. Evian aside, it had the unfortunate effect of making Britain again absolutely hostile to France – the British seeing Napoleon now not as the quixotic liberal supporter of Italian unification over Austria's fossil obscurantism, but as an acquisitive adventurer in the same mould as his uncle.

The 1848 revolutions and the Italian wars, combined with extensive colonial activity, made all borders seem up for grabs and Napoleon III was central to this sense of the tree being shaken to see what fell out. While blithely interfering in Mexico and sending soldiers to Asia, Napoleon had unfortunately failed fully to take on board the significance of Otto von Bismarck, who became Minister President of Prussia in 1862. With a strange, devastating confidence, Bismarck spent nine years wrecking all opposition and creating the German Empire. There were many secrets to his success, but at the core was his willingness to wait – he would have been just as happy creating a new Germany under Prussian rule, say, ten years later than he did. He could feel the crazily expanding strength of industry, the growth of nationalism and the pliability of his opponents and I am compelled to admire his sheer ability, even if the result was ruinous. But then, given the generalized nationalist hysteria of the period, as much in evidence in the United States as in the United Kingdom, it is very hard to imagine a future in which Germany was *not* united.

Luxembourg exists today because it was felt in 1867 that it was not important enough to fight over. It had the strange status of being a grand duchy ruled in a personal capacity by William III, King of the Netherlands, but also being part of the German Confederation – indeed Luxembourg City's vast, gnarled defences had been further upgraded to make it a key Confederal fortress for penning in France.

It is hard not to see the rulers of the various European states at this moment as a group of only feebly reformed alcoholics being presented with a tinkling, wheeled trolley of rainbow-hued liqueur miniatures. They knew how their grandfathers were bamboozled by Napoleon I into various forms of fake cooperation which allowed them to grab this, that and the other and then in the end be humiliated and destroyed: and yet, with shaking hand, they nonetheless reach for that glowing little bottle of Chartreuse. Much of this temptation was played out in colonial contexts: it was routine in the 1850s and 1860s to come up with all kinds of swaps, nods and winks. Some of these did indeed work out – for example, the creation of Italy. But hardly a month went by without Vienna being offered Romania or Silesia, or Prussia nodding at France to get Luxembourg.

The great catastrophe for Napoleon III was the very violent but extremely short war between Prussia and Austria in 1866, which in a few weeks made clear what had been beforehand genuinely up in the air: that Prussia was more powerful and would now indeed be the dominant European state. Napoleon (like all the other European leaders) had enjoyed the tension between Berlin and Vienna as it allowed everyone to be played off against everyone else. The overnight reduction of the great Habsburg monarchy to a zombie underling of the Hohenzollerns – incapable (as it proved) of further independent action until it destroyed them both through declaring war on Serbia in 1914 – made post-1866 Europe a fundamentally new place. It was not helped by Napoleon III's regime being so personal that, with his only son a child ('Lou-Lou'), the regime leant too heavily on the energy of the increasingly puffy, soiled-looking and exhausted figure at its helm.

In the aftermath of the 1866 war Prussia scooped up all the remaining independent German states north of the River Main, marching into the Free City of Frankfurt (the mayor shot himself), the Kingdom of Hanover and the Electorate of Hesse. This left France with only a handful of very cowed southern German allies – most importantly Baden and Bavaria. In a pathetic attempt to regain the initiative Napoleon bribed the gigantic and very unpleasant William III of the Netherlands via his mistress to see if he would be willing to cough up Luxembourg. Bismarck secretly winked at this, although there are arguments both ways: that he wanted to let Napoleon have a minor fillip to cheer him up, or he wanted to trap him and then destroy him by riding to Luxembourg's rescue. William decided that a necessary preliminary was, wearing his Confederal Luxembourg hat, to ask Prussia. The news of this discussion caused a huge surge of German fervour, beyond Bismarck's ability to control. It showed very clearly the passions which would now have to be dealt with. The fury at the idea of Luxembourg becoming part of France was felt even in notionally pro-French places such as Baden. At a conference held in London in 1867 Luxembourg had its personal link with the King of the Netherlands confirmed and was made neutral (confirmed by all the powers except Belgium, which could not sign because it was itself neutral and a sort of 'ward of court'). The Prussian garrison had to leave and the city's fortifications be dismantled so it could not be seized and used in any future conflict. This decision meant that over the following years Luxembourg was probably the world's largest building site as some fifteen miles of underground defences and ten acres of fortresses were taken down. The upside of this for Luxembourg was that many of these defence works, once cleared, made superb terraces for growing roses, a surprise new area of specialization, which meant that by 1914 Luxembourg was exporting some six million rose bushes a year.

Things would prove a lot less rosy for Napoleon. At the end of Zola's *Nana*, in one of the greatest scenes in nineteenth-century

French fiction, Nana, the dazzling prostitute who had stood at the pinnacle of Napoleon III's Paris, is dying in horrible agony, diseased and impoverished. None of her notional friends and protectors notice, as they all look out agog at the frenzied crowds marching through the streets of Paris, yelling: 'To Berlin! To Berlin!'

CHAPTER TWELVE

Kilometre pigs » French exiles »

Metz and the nationalist frontline » Expanses of baize »

Bullets, tusks and rubber » Rays and masks

Kilometre pigs

Vauban's great citadel for defending the newly acquired French city of Arras never had a starring role, managing to survive as a major military facility from 1672 to 2010 with only a few moments of direct threat. At the beginning of the First World War a small group of Germans reached it, defaced some of the prettier fittings, had their photos taken in the officers' lounge and then retreated. Part of the vast complex was used as a German prison in the Second World War and there is a monument to 218 individuals from across Europe who were executed there.

Given that it was only evacuated by the French military in 2010 you would like to feel that the sounds of marching boots and sergeants' shouts could still be heard on the wind, but this would be untrue. The parade ground looks like a car park *manqué*, too remote from the town centre to fill even this role. Almost the only notable building is an extremely battered chapel. It was decommissioned during the Revolution and patched back together by Napoleon III. The crumbling façade is meant to feature facing carved profiles of Louis XIV and Napoleon III, but the former is badly worn and the latter carefully chipped off. Inside there is an unbearable monument to the many thousands of engineering troops stationed at Arras who were killed during the Great War. There are grander and more lurid monuments but nowhere else I think gives more of a sense both of the out-of-control nightmare of France's war and of how long ago this was – a building that must have been for many years a serious focus for countless regimental and family pilgrimages now just seems chilly and abandoned.

At the back of the chapel there is a set of slate tablets put up in

1875 listing troops from the Arras garrison killed during the Franco-Prussian War. There are a number scattered across the epochal battles of Spicheren, Le Mans, Sedan; the sieges of Metz, Bitche and Belfort; a surprisingly large number in putting down the resultant 'Paris insurrection'. What struck me was that, like all such French monuments put up after the fighting had ended (fighting which in total killed or wounded some 280,000 Frenchmen) it does not use our term (the 'Franco-Prussian War') but calls it instead simply 'the war against Germany'.

Many of the wars of the mid-nineteenth century still have a somewhat decorative quality, however horrible in practice, as they either settled an issue (Italian unification; Austrian subservience to Prussia) or settled nothing (the Crimea). They are remembered in brightly coloured, dramatic paintings, made with advice from retired officers over precise details of sashes, shakos, swords and regimental buttons. The 'war against Germany', however, moved all this along, and was the founding disaster of the modern era. Over the years I think I must have read every account that has been published in English and indeed read one three times – perhaps in the weird hope that it might come out different, but of course it never does.

Napoleon III's army was widely viewed as the best in Europe, but while it had fought around the world, the regime had never used it in a context where France itself might be endangered. Even during the wars in Italy, it seemed inconceivable that a serious defeat might result in an Austrian army marching vengefully on Antibes – a peace treaty of a traditional kind would be arranged and life would continue as normal. Prussia's brief and devastating war with Austria in 1866 horrified Napoleon, whose whole reign was based on the pleasures of patronizing Berlin and playing Vienna and the non-aligned German states off against one another. Suddenly most of Germany was united with Prussia, and Austria went into a state of catatonia. Until that moment Prussia was widely derided, not having fought anyone serious since 1815.

It is hard to imagine this now, but there was widespread contempt for Prussia across the Rhineland, where the substantially Catholic population saw little value in their Prussian masters –

which was not to say that this meant they would welcome French rule. France was far larger than Prussia; Paris was twice the size of Berlin and Napoleon III ruled over a global empire, from Martinique to Saigon. The war of 1866 forced all Europeans to think very quickly about how to react to Bismarck's new, very big Prussia. The still independent southern German states (Baden, Württemberg, Bavaria) which had once been comfortably supported by Austria suddenly found themselves feeling too small. But they also felt swept up, despite themselves, in the excitement of German unity and agreed to various Prussian military proposals that defanged them as opponents, in a context where their fangs were in any event not much to write home about.

The pace of change swamped Napoleon's regime. It went from being Europe's premier state to friendless and crumbling overnight. As recently as the early 1860s one of the triumphs of France's Rhineland policy had come to fruition with the completion of the great bridge across the Rhine linking Alsace and Baden – a wonderful Gothic confection, like a chunk of cathedral, first snapped in half to make the two bridge-towers and then pulled apart like taffy to create its central span. Baden became a genuine neighbour of France and numerous Badenese worked in Strasbourg, a trend which naturally continued once Strasbourg became Straßburg in 1871. The bridge was blown up by French troops in 1940.

Bismarck realized that Napoleon needed to be tricked into war and defeated if Prussia was to complete German unification. He enjoyed this very much, investing in a Swiss railway because he knew it would annoy Napoleon and having scurrilous, vague conversations with nothing written down urging him to grab Belgium. Napoleon had thought that just as he supported Italian unification and got Savoy and Nice in return, he could be benign about German unification and gain perhaps the Saar and Bavarian Palatinate. But Prussia defeated Austria too quickly – and in any event had no intention of giving France anything. There was a particularly pathetic scene in September 1868 when Napoleon was having dinner with his officers and deliberately served Rhine wines, just so that he could say: 'Gentlemen, I hope that you yourselves will shortly be harvesting this wine.' As skittish and aggressive proposals leaked from Paris around the futures of Luxembourg, Belgium and the Rhine, potentially helpful countries such as Britain came to see France as out of control and Prussia as thoughtful and statesmanlike, even though Bismarck was effectively goading and making fun of Napoleon, sure that sooner or later he would do something stupid.

Eventually a row over who should become the King of Spain (in itself a sort of Looney Tunes version of the big-screen epic *The War of the Spanish Succession*) resulted in a conflict which had become viewed by both sides as inevitable. The result was shameful. Napoleon's regime was much more successful than his uncle's (it lasted seven years longer) and defined itself by its constrained but real liberalism, its modernity and its devotion to its army. Incredibly, there were, after years of huffing and puffing, no actual plans to invade the North German Confederation, admittedly quite tricky because its border was mostly masked by Belgium and by independent Baden. There was a tentative nudge over the border into Saarbrücken (a very similar, equally pitiful move was made in 1939) during which 'Lou-Lou' fired a cannon for the first time (there is still a commemorative marker stone), presumably much to the delight of his cousin 'Plon-Plon'. But otherwise Napoleon III's generals all seemed paralysed – as though the weight of historical expectation was too much and the shadow of the real Napoleon too vast. The actual fighting was 'boring' in as much as the French generals allowed themselves to be herded like sheep. Britain had made it clear that Belgian and Luxembourgeois neutrality was serious and would be defended and this, combined with Swiss neutrality, should have provided France – once it had decided not to invade anyone – with an attractively clear and straightforwardly framed theatre to defend. The French rifle was much better than the Prussian and this was the opportunity to unveil the ultimate secret weapon, the machine gun, or 'hell machine' as the Prussians called it. Unfortunately the latter, while horrible, could not be moved from side to side as it would in 1914 so it tended to pointlessly hit one unfortunate Prussian thirty times rather sweep the front.

Foreign observers all looked on in incredulity as the French generalissimo, Achille Bazaine, dithered and havered, seemingly unable to function under the sheer weight of Napoleon's ghost on his back, ludicrously missed the open goal of the Battle of Mars-la-Tour and then, with his 180,000 troops, retreating into the Metz fortress complexes and starving. The besieging Prussians refused to let out deserters, pushing them back in so that they could do the useful work of helping to chew through the last foodstocks. What had been a major army which could have retreated to the French interior, grossly overstretching Prussian forces and perhaps doing a Valmy, therefore stayed stuck on the border, rotting to pieces and eventually surrendering in the most humiliating moment in nineteenth-century French history. Throughout the major fighting, the Prussians would only ever pause because they assumed they were being led into a cunning trap, which in each case turned out to be simply a piece of rank incompetence. The Prussians won partly by default and partly because of their amazing ability to keep marching over huge distances, hypnotizing and baffling French troops who could not believe where the enemy had already reached – the wonderful term *Kilometerschweine* (kilometre pigs) sums up this achievement. This great marching legend would, however, effectively ruin the German army in 1914.

The main surviving French army was trapped against the neutral Belgian border at Sedan and unable to manoeuvre. It was surrounded and destroyed, with 120,000 troops killed, wounded or made prisoner. After this the fighting became bitter but minor. One crucial French hot-air balloon from Paris with instructions for a fresh military gathering in Tours was unfortunately blown to Norway. One last reasonable size force, led by General Charles-Denis Bourbaki, found itself in winter, running out of supplies. Bourbaki tried and failed to shoot himself and then led some 87,000 troops across the Swiss border where, as per neutral convention, the Swiss disarmed and accommodated them in what was itself an extraordinary humanitarian epic – commemorated in Edouard Castries's colossal and endlessly enjoyable panoramic painting in Lucerne. This was a major event in Swiss history as it showed the value of staunch neutralism. Some ten thousand troops wound up in

Neuchâtel – an extraordinary number when the town itself at the time only had around twelve thousand inhabitants. Auguste Bachelin did a number of sketches and paintings, including a superb one which wallows in the sheer oddness of the military life, with scarlet baggy-trousered Zouaves, breastplated cuirassiers and spike-helmeted Prussians (prisoners of the French swept up in the mêlée), bearded and phlegmatic, reduced to weaponless impotence, marshalled along by a handful of armed Swiss troops. For many years a French exclamation for a total shambles was '*Quelle armée de Bourbaki!*', which it would be fun to revive.

One of the smaller but nonetheless despairing tragedies was the Siege of Strasbourg. The speed of events was overwhelming. The disastrous Battle of Froeschwiller on 6 August suddenly put Strasbourg in the front line with a state of siege declared the next day and buildings blown up to clear fields of fire. At the time Strasbourg Cathedral was the tallest structure ever built and from its spire it was possible to see twenty-five thousand Badenese troops on the march, the grand duchy's German nationalism easily trumping any sense of Rhineland solidarity. Incoming French troops thought that the German-dialect-speaking locals must be traitors and, even before the siege had begun, nationalist tensions had been hydrated that would poison the region for many years. The siege lasted forty-four days, during which time 194,722 projectiles landed in the city. The cathedral roof was burned off (the gargoyles vomiting molten lead) and the spire only held together because of its lightning rod. At one point the bombardment coincided with a severe thunderstorm which caused the town dogs to howl – apparently a uniquely eerie combination. The most lasting disaster, aside from 861 military and 300 civilians dead and 10,000 homeless, was the destruction of the New Church, France's second library and the great depository for French Protestant texts: some 400,000 books were destroyed and thousands of ancient manuscripts. A vast number of items by Gutenberg were burnt (he had lived and worked in Strasbourg), but the greatest loss was Herrad of Landsberg's *The Garden of Delights*, a masterpiece with some 330 brilliant illustrations, created by a nun a generation younger than

Hildegard of Bingen. Scholars from Berlin had specifically written to the military pleading with them to watch out for *The Garden of Delights*, but to no avail.

One curious element in the siege was intervention by the Swiss. In 1576 during discussions between different Imperial cities about how they could work together to defend their Protestantism, the city of Zürich proved it could bring effective aid by successfully getting a boatload of still-hot porridge all the way to Strasbourg down the Rhine in less than twenty-four hours. This rather odd precedent (still celebrated today – and part of the original pot survived the New Church fire) led a group of Swiss citizens to approach the Prussian military and propose escorting non-belligerents from the city. This showed Swiss neutrality in action (the French, Prussians and Badenese had been unsure about whether to trust the Swiss) as almost two thousand residents left before what it was assumed would be a truly horrible final assault. In a strangely Swiss touch each individual had to prove they had enough money to pay for their own keep.

The issue of Strasbourg's survival became urgent. The garrison town of Belfort, far to the south, held out until the final French surrender and remained French. It became clear that if Strasbourg gave in then, like Metz, it would be on the Prussian shopping list for annexation. Despite attempts to create a revolutionary atmosphere in the walls, the position eventually became hopeless and the town indeed surrendered. The only positive beneficiary of this awful sequence of events was the Alsatian sculptor Frédéric Bartholdi, who was involved in the defence of Colmar, traumatized by the fate of his homeland and now created the two great monuments to the war: the statue that greets you as you walk down the avenue from Basle railway station commemorating Swiss help for Strasbourg (and featuring a jaunty relief of the boatload of porridge) and the colossal, brilliantly strange and disturbing seventy-foot-long Lion of Belfort, which glowers on the side of the fortress of Belfort and must make just going to the shops in the streets below seem both heroic and somewhat bathetic. He went on to become the world's most famous sculptor with the Statue of Liberty – twice as high as the lion was long. The idea came to him just after the war as the new German Empire was proclaimed (as insultingly as possible) in Louis XIV's palace at Versailles, and Alsace and a chunk of Lorraine, including French-speaking Metz, were absorbed into that empire as the Reichsland Elsaß-Lothringen. Bartholdi's home town became Kolmar, Séléstat Schlettstadt, Strasbourg Straßburg and some fifty thousand people left their homes for ever. The Statue of Liberty has undoubtedly become the great symbol of New York, but the torch she is carrying is at least as Alsatian as it is American.

French exiles

If you turn left out of the car park in front of the railway station of the southern English town of Farnborough, cross a particularly hostile and depressing giant roundabout and stand at a specific time on a Saturday afternoon by a locked metal gate at the bottom of a wooded hill, there will be a click and the gate will open, allowing you to walk up a driveway to one of Europe's oddest sites: the last resting place of Napoleon III, his Empress and his son.

If you were the ruler of the United Kingdom or Prussia, say, much of the nineteenth century had the potential to be almost uniformly enjoyable – lots of money, respect, stability (with one Prussian wobble in 1848), terrific outfits to wear, coins with your face on, relatives to visit, parties. France was very different and Europe is dotted with memorial sites to the chronic instability that was only resolved in the wake of Napoleon III's crushing defeat by Prussia in 1870 at Sedan. I have a shaky-handed inability to stay away from sad scenes of French royal failure. I know I shouldn't be in Farnborough but, nonetheless, here I am once more breathing in the cold, mouldering air of another *nécropole dynastique*.

There are four of these spots. The first and grandest is of course the Church of St Denis to the north of Paris. In two spasms of frenzied Revolutionary violence in 1793 the tombs of some hundred and fifty of these royals were jemmied open and their contents, from Clovis onwards, tipped into a trench and smothered in quick-lime. After Napoleon's departure, Louis XVIII (who had spent a number of unhappy years in Essex and Buckinghamshire) had the grim job of reconsecrating the legitimacy of his line. This was done through the can-this-get-any-worse expedient of shovelling all the surviving bits and bobs behind a marble wall in St Denis and then engraving on several big tablets a solemn contents list of names and ages. Presumably what is behind the wall is something like the inside of a terrible Hoover, with scraps of Louis XIV entangled with Philip Augustus's desiccated hair. The wall is really one of the worst places in France and easy to imagine bursting outwards, deluging bystanders in horrors.

As usual with burial grounds the main purpose is to offer consolation to those who survive the individual's death – as they or their grandchildren die, the grief/relief/pleasure associated with that death drifts off, and we are left with what is emotionally a mere stone husk. For dynasties though, the stakes are much higher. For centuries St Denis was the site that validated the monarchy, with every new king crushingly aware of being only the latest link in a chain going back to Clovis, Peppin and friends. Each ceremony carried out also implied an unending future sequence, matching and then outrunning the mere present – like the scene in *Macbeth* where the witches show Banquo his myriad royal descendants.

Louis XVIII completed his work at St Denis by having himself buried under a smart black slab. His younger but elderly brother Charles X then managed to alienate everybody by his insane devotion to camp, 'brocade' Catholicism and his pretence that nothing had happened since 1788. Kicked out in 1830 and exiled in Habsburg-ruled Gorizia, Charles died there and was buried at the Franciscan monastery of Konstanjevica (now in Slovenia). Once this accidental burial place was established it became, like St Denis, the unavoidable destination for his pretender descendants on their deaths: the notional Louis XIX and Henry V, their wives and a stray sister. In both life and death they underwent all kinds of indignities: the memories of greatness blown and deference ended; selling jewels and scrounging for cash. But in death at least they managed to continue an eternal future claim to the throne – one which has been disregarded by everyone except a tiny handful of legitimists who still leave long-life plastic wreaths on the chilly tombs.

Louis XVIII and Charles X spent many years on their various 'travels', cadging abroad to dodge the guillotine. England became the invaluable safety valve for French royal instability, with the Channel ports intermittently crowded with blowsy courtiers and carts full of battered paintings and dinner sets. Everyone knew the drill – if things get rough, head to Boulogne. After Charles X's removal, the throne was handed to Louis-Philippe, a member of a cadet branch of the family. He precariously clung on for eighteen years before also getting the message and hot-footing it to England in the wake of the 1848 Revolution. He ended up living in Surrey and being buried in a Catholic chapel in Weybridge (now a Korean church). Before it had all gone wrong though, Louis-Philippe's family poured money into the absolutely staggering necropolis at Dreux, west of Paris, a crazed mass of white-marble, full-length statues of leading family members and, again, designed to be merely the starting point of a great sequence of French rulers.

Louis-Philippe's brief tenure mocks the necropolis. All in all, it is a shame that such places should wind up being just unintended commentaries on human vanity. It is fun for the rest of us, but unfortunate for the families, and for the priests who have to keep offering prayers there, without themselves tactlessly alluding to the all-flesh-is-grass folly around them. In the end, in the firmly republican French world of the 1870s Louis-Philippe's corpse was allowed to leave Weybridge and settle down in Dreux.

After Napoleon III seized power, Louis-Philippe's family held their nerve and continued to treat Dreux both as a dignified reproach to an upstart and as the ante-chamber in which to wait to regain power. As the rest of nineteenth-century France's history played out, they were completely ignored, with dead family members piling up and each getting a pricey and elaborate tomb paid for. Some of these are superb – Louis-Philippe's great-grandson was an explorer who discovered the source of the Irrawaddy and died of malaria in Saigon in 1901. For perhaps the only time white marble is used as a medium for showing someone in a tropical suit holding a white marble map and, his head convulsed to one side, in the throes of a malarial spasm. It is one of the last great uses of a traditional funerary framework to do something quite new and strange. But while he may have lucked out after his premature death by getting a superb sculptor, Henri of Orléans was never really going to become king. His tomb was a last gasp – three generations on from royal power and the family now began to cut costs, with mere plaques and standard-issue near-bourgeois memorials.

Which brings us back to Farnborough and to Napoleon III, nemesis of the Orléans family, but a man who had always been more familiar with the south of England than he would have liked, having spent chunks of time there in earlier exiles. When his own final moment of disaster came with his capture after the cataclysmic Battle of Sedan, Napoleon and his Empress Eugenie followed in the now well-worn footsteps of Bourbon and Orléans to southern England, sulking in a house which is today the headquarters of the Chislehurst Golf Club.

He died in 1873. Again, every effort was made to maintain the dynasty for future use, but his and Eugenie's only son, 'Lou-Lou', was killed in the Zulu War and the line came to an end. Eugenie, who lived on for many years, created the Farnborough necropolis and endowed a small monastery to pray for the family's souls. A handful of monks remain but the abbey is the near helpless victim of surrounding, spreading Farnborough, with many objects stolen and with the lead repeatedly stripped from the roof, making the Imperial resting place a gloomy spot. All the elaborate trappings on the tombs, including fun Zulu material for the Prince Imperial, have either been pinched or locked away. One great oddity is that back in 1873 the French government objected to Napoleon being buried on British soil – but for obvious reasons did not want the body returned to become yet another revanchist focus. The ingenious – albeit insane – decision was taken to import neutral Swiss soil to form a layer under Napoleon's coffin. And so the last Emperor of France appears to have finished up his restless life in Hampshire but is actually in Switzerland.

Metz and the nationalist frontline

Nationalism seems to be a universal side effect of specific levels of literacy and communication. There is little point in grumbling about it. Even the most seemingly low-self-esteem nation will come out fighting the moment anyone suggests problems with its honesty, womenfolk, national stew, etc. Every country at some level assumes that other countries are worse – the dial can always be moved favourably to turn others' success into mere brashness and materialism or cultural confidence into mere narrowness and jingoism. Nationalists prop themselves up by imagining they are living in a circle of virtue outside which shamble those not so blessed, despite their having near-identical beliefs and stews. Perhaps a distinction can be made between patriotism, which is a legitimate, sometimes vexed affection for and pride in the world one grows up in and knows well, and nationalism, where that central space tends to be hollow but given shape by the imagined foibles, vices and plots of those *others* about which, in practice, one knows little or nothing.

The highly contested decision by Bismarck to grab Alsace and much of Lorraine after the Franco-Prussian War was spurred by nationalism and was the founding disaster of the twentieth century. Strategically it made sense – Bismarck rightly pointed out that the French had trundled through Alsace many times before and it would prove true that the Germans easily defended it in 1914. Only five years previously the Habsburg Empire, threatening Prussia's ever more dynamic role in the German-speaking world, had been rapidly defeated, but with no annexations, and then became as meek as a lamb until destroyed in the First World War fighting shoulder-to-shoulder with the Germans. Many argued against the Alsace-Lorraine annexation, but there was such a wave of nationalism – from newspapers, politicians, academics – that the Germans took the fatal decision.

Alsatians largely spoke German dialects and the decision to absorb them was meant to be for ever. In a spirit of stern Nibelung justice the Germans let the fortress town of Belfort, which had successfully held out for a hundred and three days, remain French, creating both a strange little department that exists to this day and, indirectly, the euphonious Métro station Denfert-Rochereau, named after the fortress's vigorous commandant. Lorraine was split, with the Germans taking much of its industrial land in the north-east and the city of Metz.

It seems unlikely, but France might *just* have accepted Alsace's loss if it had not been for Metz – Metz was an unquestionably French-speaking city and Germany's acquisition was an overtly voracious one. The Germans were not particularly upping the levels of greediness: earlier French conquerors heading east or north were always claiming that city *x* and then city *y* were critical to France's future security and would have kept going all the way to Moscow making the same claim (oh – hold on – they did!). Anyone could point to Metz and say how incredibly strategic and essential it was, and then move on to the next place and make the same point. It was always an uneasy German possession, transgressing the whole point of language nationalism. By pandering to these bull-necked and scarlet-faced German sentiments, Bismarck catastrophically failed to think about France's matching fury, which never really moved on, bubbling up periodically under a welter of impotent loathing for Teuton greed. The Germans tried to be reasonable by allowing anyone who wished to leave the new Reichsland a two-year grace period, and many thousands did. It is interesting that so many of the most influential figures in twentieth-century French history had roots along this new frontier: Poincaré from Bar-le-Duc led France through the Great War; Lyautey from Nancy allowed France to revel in the distraction of spreading its national destiny across North Africa; Maginot, who lived in a Lorraine village destroyed during the Great War and was instrumental in creating his Line; and Dreyfus, from Mulhouse (then Mühlhausen), who emigrated, joined the French army and through no fault of his own tore apart the French state in the 1890s.

These figures all grew up in a deluge of printed, painted or sculpted kitsch about the horrors of German actions against Alsace and Lorraine, entities invariably pictured as outraged women. One famous image shows Marianne, the personification of France, with a limb sawn off. In a statue which still sits in a square (now named after Maginot) in Nancy, the provinces are two helpless little girls trying to comfort each other. Many cartoons showed either Marianne or these other girls being hauled away and raped. No politician could ever propose a friendly attitude towards Germany without provoking nationalist curses and another round of cartoons featuring semi-pornographic images of lost honour. Sometimes the issue simmered down, but the idea remained that these two geographical areas were in fact ravished and humiliated daughters of France. Germans could point out until they were purple in the face that this was land snatched by various French monarchs from the sixteenth century onwards and that somewhere like Mulhouse had been Swiss less than a century before, but nobody in France was listening.

The Germans could have tried to placate France, perhaps by at least handing Metz back, but this immediately came in turn to look both shamefully weak and beside the point. In the longer term the Germans understood that Metz would, with patience and social engineering, be duly absorbed. Many French-speakers left and German settlers arrived. Implacable generational churn put children through schools who assumed Strasbourg was Straßburg and were proud to live in the western lands of Europe's greatest state. With control of education, government offices and the army, the Germans could reasonably expect the Frenchness of Metz to dilute to a barely tastable flavour over a century or so.

Today Metz is an almost ridiculously interesting city, its different layers enshrining the battles for its soul and the confused motives of all concerned. It is still split architecturally between the cathedral hill, which is completely French (shutters, puzzling little bits of wrought iron, perverse, tangled street patterns, Catholic, artisanal, funny smells), and the new Imperial city at the bottom of the hill (bombastic, four-square, humourless, an emphasis on drains, totally bananas architecture), which might as well be Wiesbaden on steroids. Of course these stereotypes are all wrong – except that this is what both sides themselves felt. Kaiser Wilhelm was deeply involved in the rebuilding of Metz, treating the whole city as a sort of toy box. However unpleasant a figure he was, he did brilliantly engage with the importance of symbolism's ability to reshape attitudes. When the city walls were demolished he intervened to keep the magnificent Germans' Gate – a mishmash of pepper-pot towers, firing platforms and machicolations sprawling across a pretty tributary of the Moselle. Named after the Teutonic Knights, whose hospital stood by it, this was always the point where travellers left the city to head to the Rhineland, so there were Imperial reasons for Wilhelm's enthusiasm – but this does not stop his instincts being sound. His drastic vision for the cathedral also worked. At the nadir of Gothic's fortunes in the eighteenth century, the French concealed what now seemed the irredeemably barbarian shambles of the cathedral's architecture with a skirt of classical arcading and a pillared gateway. Sensibly Wilhelm had this all demolished and replaced by standard-issue rather leaden German Imperial Gothic, drawing on the vast ateliers of sub-sub-William-Morris figures who could carve any quantity of tendril and any weight of saint. Attractively, the French, when they took Metz back in 1918 (and again at the end of 1944), kept the elaborate Latin inscription marking Wilhelm's role. A lot of things were got rid of (the German Garrison Church was not very accidentally burnt down, for example) but keeping the inscription was a brilliantly judged piece of historical courtesy. Inside the cathedral a little plaque marking the deaths of two officers in German Kamerun (Cameroon) and South-West Africa (Namibia) has also been kept – again, something which could so easily have been chipped off, but which adds a strange resonance that can only become greater over time.

But Metz above all else is known for its extraordinary railway station. This building, again closely supervised by Wilhelm, brings together a vast range of Imperial neuroses and was meant to be the western terminus of Germandom. Built as a Nibelung hall plus railway tracks, it is both a monstrosity and a wonder, forming part of an ensemble which also includes a post office which looks as though you need to have chainmail and a horned helmet just to buy a stamp from it, and one of the world's very few medieval-style water-towers. With its Charlemagne Hall, mythological, faux-runic carvings and hunkered down Romanesque clock-tower, the station is almost lovable, even if originally designed just as a backdrop for Wilhelm's visits in ever-stranger uniforms. Many of the carvings are designed to enchant bored children in waiting rooms. Its main purpose might have been to get as many troops de-trained and re-trained as quickly as possible in a future war, but it achieves this with great style.

There is a famous statue on the outside of the booking hall. It shows a Roland figure with sword and Imperial shield looking frowningly towards France. His face was modelled on that of Graf von Haeseler, the head of the XVI Army Corps stationed at Metz, an ancient Prussian officer who had served in the wars with Denmark, Austria and France many years previously. At the end of 1918 an occupying French soldier scrambled up there and put a sign on the shield saying, 'Hey! So what is he still doing here?' ('*Eh! Bien celui ci que fait-il encore là?*') In 1919 his shield was re-carved as the Cross of Lorraine; this was then again redone as the shield of the city of Metz in 1940 and in 1945 his German head was at last lopped off and replaced by a French one with an Asterix moustache.

Expanses of baize

Like much of the Western world, our local shopping mall a couple of years ago was seized by the bizarre fashion for putting your bare feet in a tank and having the dead skin bitten off by little Middle Eastern fish. It would be easy to rant about how this sums up everything that is most hopeless about the twenty-first century, etc., but I was mainly saddened both for the fish (who cannot actively *want* to be in south-west London) and for the activity being described as a 'fish spa pedicure'. As helpless as the tiny fish themselves, the word 'spa' itself continues its relentless journey both laterally (around the globe) and downwards (into ever more humiliating contexts). The name of the original town of Spa springs from other, similarly odd words in the linguistic rubble formed by the Romance-Germanic frontier in the Ardennes: places like Theux, Trooz, Ovifat, Ster and

St Vith. We are so inured to the word Spa that we are no longer struck by its oddness. The practices first worked out here for turning illnesses into a happy racket have changed the world.

The sheer grandeur of these original spas remains astonishing. I grew up in a small spa town in south-east England and while the water is no longer a draw, it is still strikingly elegant. But it is a mere village compared to such monsters as Spa itself, Wiesbaden and Baden-Baden. By the nineteenth century their town centres were jammed with gargantuan palaces for water, in an arms race to inveigle and then keep the wealthiest, biggest-spending clientele. The spas' social function was invaluable – transferring as much money as possible from the aristocracy and new bourgeois elites into the pockets of others. Strange skills with fingertips, playing cards or nasty-flavoured water brought staggering riches to an arbitrary cross-section of outsiders. The few hours taken up with bogus treatments had to be supplemented, just to pass the time, by drinking, gambling and infidelity. Small groups of money-with-menaces spivs could engage in all kinds of blackmail, flitting from spa to spa in their elegant clothes, pencil moustaches and oiled hair and having a field day. Random maid-servants, walking into a hotel room to find themselves face-to-face with the whipped bum of the Finance Minister, could set themselves up for life. Medalled statesmen and their wives could savour the gap between their public, palm-court gentility and their private perversions. Activities once confined to a very narrow group in the privacy of palaces became a major economic proposition. Wandering through the magical suburbs of Wiesbaden today, with its seemingly endless rows of Imperial German villas, it remains something to marvel at that such happy homes could be found for so many blackmailers, quacks and sharp-minded prostitutes.

The carnival played out in the great spas was always highly unstable, and a change in the international situation, or spasms of fashion (a great opera star coming to Baden-Baden, royalty deciding to try out the Bohemian spas this year) could lead to boom or bust. As each spa was in essence just a large assembly of bedrooms and administrative offices there was always a danger of being

reconditioned as a military headquarters in wartime – whether the
Germans in Spa in 1918 or the Americans in Spa in 1944 or Wiesbaden in 1945. They could also be converted into sprawling
military hospitals. At the very worst (as in the case of luckless
Vichy) they could be turned into the capital of a collaborationist
government. Today the battle between the spas continues, with ever
bigger water-slides, dafter treatments, more luxurious shops, all
frantically trying to distract the visitor from the whispered possibility that they might be quite boring places.

My own spa research has always been a bit muted and shy. Years
ago I spent days summing up courage to go to one of the great
Budapest baths, anxious to see their surviving Ottoman architecture.
In most of the really echt baths there is no English spoken or written, and once I had plunged nerve-racked through the doors, it was
unclear what the metal tags meant, what the lockers were for, which
corridor led to the men's pool. I was also anxious about being
propositioned and not being able to politely say no. I had therefore
practised a Hungarian phrase which would have come out as something like 'My sorrys but me am differently othered'. Having at last
got into the pool, admired the dome for a bit and with the hot
spring water roaring in, I then switched to become ever more furi-
ously sulky that my fellow-bathers must have had a quick glance at
me and felt Eros dwelt elsewhere. There was another occasion when
I was basted in mud and salt crystals and put in a machine that made
me feel like a hog-roast, but these events are too silly to dwell on
further.

The key nineteenth-century spa breakthrough technologically
was made by an Irish doctor, Richard Barter, who invented what
became known as the Hiberno-Roman spa. Unlike the Turkish use
of steam, this allowed people to sweat in a room with dry heat. The
greatest of the Hiberno-Roman spas is in Wiesbaden, named after
Kaiser Friedrich III, Wilhelm II's short-lived war-hero father, who
remains the town's presiding genius, his hirsute form once subjected to any number of water and heat treatments. I thought for
research I should really try the Hiberno-Roman baths as their
Babylonian-style interiors are apparently wonderful. But they

require total nudity, which I felt I could only carry off if I could walk around leaning backwards about forty-five degrees so that my stomach would be stretched flat rather than acting as a gruesome sort of pelmet above my genitals.

One aspect of Wiesbaden that I could not avoid however was the famous casino. Gambling, legal or illegal, has always been almost as important as blackmail in the success of spa economies but the idea of walking in on such a heavily coded and expert space filled me with dread. My only experience of gambling was some desultory blackjack on a cruise ship and I worried that, just as I cannot start a packet of biscuits without finishing it, I would be flushed out at once as an until now latent reckless, wild-eyed high-roller who would have to be collected the next day by my wife from a padded cell, my shirt stiff with spilt Cointreau, screaming about the queen of spades.

I dolled myself up, although only to the pathetic extent of a jacket and tie, abandoning my ideal gambling alter-ego wish-list (bottle-green smoking jacket, splash of toilet water, discreet rouge, teeth a little loosened by syphilis). I left my credit card behind and stuffed a pocket with cash but I was in the end far too timorous to get involved, perching on a bar stool sipping a martini, munching the unlimited free nuts and staring at the fantastically beautiful room, with its ideal combination of cut glass, polished cherry-wood, gleaming metal and expanses of baize. I was quickly hypnotized by the postures and actions of the croupiers – another fascinating group who have traditionally done so much to transfer money from the pockets of the wealthy to other socio-economic groups. The vast room was like a fully-functioning temple with a wholehearted con-gregation, regulated by the complex sets of exaggerated actions and muted sounds made by the staff. Even roulette, surely the stupidest game of all, became utterly compelling. A fevered-looking man had created at a separate table huge paper charts, colour-coded with marker-pens, from which he was plotting his roulette strategy. I kept waiting for the discreet nod which would commit him rather than me to a padded cell (itself perhaps a room with charming polished cherry-wood elements), but suddenly he won some colossal sum,

with lots of gasps and chuckles from other players but not a flicker
of feeling from the hieratic croupiers as they heaped his winnings.
By this time I had already had way too many nuts and was not even
sure I could remember the rules of blackjack, certainly not well
enough to dare to take on the groups of wizened pros hunched over
the tables. The evening ended absurdly as I tried to saunter out with
the blank arrogance of a many-times-married shipping magnate but,
not having realized that a casino's outer doors are locked, was
reduced to battling with a recalcitrant knob until rescued by an icy
and meticulous functionary. I could have sworn I heard titters from
the bar staff.

Wiesbaden is immortalized in Dostoevsky's *The Gambler*, a rats-
in-a-sack phantasmagoria of bankrupts, imposters and snobs. His
picture of 'Roulettenberg' as a sort of open sewer, a carnival of
disgust, is with rather odd pride marked by the Wiesbaden fathers
with a grand banqueting and business-meeting room in the spa/
casino named after him. I cannot really convey how much time I
have wasted trying to work out whether this decision was a brilliant joke or just flat-footed localism. Nobody seems to know. A
sad side effect of my research though was to discover that the gorgeous casino rooms I wandered through with such aplomb were in
fact a fake. If only Dostoevsky had arrived a little later he would
not have lost all his money. The little Grand Duchy of Nassau, of
which Wiesbaden was the capital, chose the wrong side in the
Austro-Prussian War of 1866 and was crushed by Prussia with the
ease of an elephant shifting slightly in its sleep. Shortly afterwards
all casinos were banned throughout Prussia (one of the legal moves
which made Monaco, an even more mini version of Nassau, famous
as the home of Monte Carlo). I knew that the casino itself post-
dated Dostoevsky and had been opened in 1907, but had wrongly
assumed that people like the Kaiser were all whooping and frothing
at the tables as the little ball went round: medals leaping, spurs
gouging the thick carpet littered with dropped monocles. Sadly the
cherry-wood rooms were then a 'wine salon' and the casino opened
only by enterprising characters during the post-1945 American
occupation.

One of the pleasures of *The Gambler* is that it preserves the important role of Russians in the nineteenth-century spa economy. Wiesbaden became a favoured haunt because of Grand Duke Adolf's brief marriage to a niece of the ferocious Tsar Nicolas I (who sent Dostoyevsky to Siberia). Grand Duchess Elizabeth Mikhailovna died aged eighteen, while giving birth to a stillborn daughter less than a year after her marriage. This was both a tragic event and a novel one as her burial at Wiesbaden was problematic from an Orthodox point of view. The traumatized Adolf solved this by building the Russian Orthodox church of St Elizabeth on the Neroberg, a beautiful wooded area above the town, haunted by the ghosts of thousands of slowly walking posh hypochondriacs. The church is a sensational shrine both to the Grand Duchess and to 1840s official taste, the sort of panicked classicism which was about to be blown away by the 1848 revolutions. With their own Orthodox church to pray at and the tomb of a famous, melancholy Romanov heroine on site, Russians poured into Wiesbaden, with Dostoyevsky merely part of the general churn. These transients became permanent after the First World War when a mixed bag of White refugees settled, subsequently buried in the adjoining graveyard.

The Russian link was a peculiar one. After their marriage, Tsar Nicolas II and Alexandra Feodorovna – previously just plain Alix, a German princess from the nearby Grand Duchy of Hesse-Darmstadt – worshipped here. Following the Revolutionary historical twists and turns that first killed them and then, generations later, made them – after the collapse of communism – into Orthodox saints, there are now icons in the church to St Nicolas and St Alexandra the Passion Bearers, a striking leg-up for the former spa guests. In 1990 Mikhail Gorbachev visited Wiesbaden and at his request a Russian sculptor created a statue of Dostoyevsky, which now decorates the gardens by the casino. As with the business executives chewing over how to achieve year-on-year growth in the Dostojewski-Saal, this statue revels in the sheer rhino-hided gall of spa towns – one of the nineteenth century's greatest writers went to all the trouble of writing a novel to warn the world that Wiesbaden is a pullulating, verminous trough and this is blandly converted into yet another tribute to the town's star-power.

Bullets, tusks and rubber

One of my more recent moral collapses has been to start picking up old copies of *Le Petit Journal* at French flea-markets. This addictive paper produced lavish colour supplements from the 1890s onwards, wallowing in a particularly lurid, feverish chauvinism mixed up with wonderfully unregulated advertisements: for example urging women to increase the allure of their breasts by dosing up on rather vaguely named 'Oriental Pills' (results within two months), or extolling the virtues of hammerless revolvers, exotic pomades, beautiful, sturdy accordions and *Royal Windsor*, 'the celebrated hair regenerator' which returns grey hair 'to the natural beauty of youth'. I hesitate even to mention *Le Petit Journal* it is so addictive. A remarkably cheap pile of them in the superb market inside Lille's Old Stock Exchange made all my other plans for the day seem flimsy and missable – how could some second-division cathedral compete with flipping through grotesque murders, royal visits and colonial derring-do, all told in a wonderfully lip-smacking, pudeur-laden prose? The distance it provides from, say, the British experience in the same period is like holding up a dirty mirror to one's own country – it seems so much more chauvinist, vicious and weird, but only because the topics and language are unfamiliar. The issue of *Le Petit Journal* I have to hand deals with the capture of the African leader Samory Touré with a terrific front-cover picture: two snorting horses galloping side by side, on one the cloaked Samory, on the other plucky Lieutenant Jacquin, waving his sabre and clutching the rebel by the throat. Or there is a painting of a French submarine in harbour, with a cheering crowd looking on, from straw-hatted young men gawping at this miracle of modern technology to older gaffers in bowler hats, baffled by these new-fangled techno-marvels, yet proud to be French ('*The British, it should be noted, despite their habitual phlegm, did not have the strength to hide their disquiet . . .*').

These illustrated newspapers are a curse – like the internet, they are stronger than the reader and can draw you into any number of disgraceful and bizarre stories (my eye wavered over one issue with the headline 'Nuns burn alive in their own convent'). As you can pick them up individually and more or less at random (I have ones in front of me now, for example, from July 1901 and October 1898) you are only dipped briefly into a story and with no possible follow-up. But this makes their vivid oddness and hysteria all the more striking: a very brief insight, say, into the still-unfolding Fashoda Incident or 'an abominable crime' with no solution. Anarchist outrages, flag-strewn opening ceremonies, caravans of Roma ('savages') mingle freely with moustache wax and anti-hernia gadgets. It's all-polluting yet gripping. The most famous of all *Petit Journal* covers was from the Dreyfus scandal. Captioned 'The Traitor', it showed the Alsatian colonel surrounded by rows of French troops, a magnificently breast-plated and plumed officer snapping Dreyfus's sword over his knee. Despite the caption, it is fair to say that our eyes have moved on since that issue was published: we all look at the almost blank figure of Dreyfus and think of the nightmare of treachery that has engulfed this blameless man – but at the time, almost every reader would have gloated over the traitor's humiliation, and a striking number would have equated Dreyfus's treason with his being Jewish.

Colonial adventures are central to the lurid press. The capture of Samory Touré and the destruction of his West African army are discussed in *Le Petit Journal*, while decrying how 'certain powers' had supplied him with modern weaponry. Two years later the Brussels Convention, which was set up to take further action against slaving, slipped in an extra clause in which its European signatories agreed to stop selling Africans guns – a key moment in inter-colonial control and the point when the system became a completed cage for the Continent. The ghoulish pre-1914 European enthusiasm for colonial violence was essentially fictional – an endless series of fights, shocks and lurid excesses with no risk to the actual reader or his country. A temporary setback during the conquest of Indochina may have made honest French patriots excoriate their government, but no Vietnamese army was ever going to bombard Calais.

This was a golden era for two massive colonial ports: Rotterdam and Antwerp. Rotterdam drew on centuries of Dutch control over the East Indies and parts of the West Indies, now operating on a phenomenal extractive scale. Antwerp, though, was something new. It at last recovered its great place in European commerce, having been blocked up and pickled for much of two centuries. In 1900 its population had grown by six times in a hundred years. Beginning in the 1870s, King Leopold II was able to use Belgium's neutrality to pose as the benevolent guiding force behind his International African Association, penetrating the Congo basin for scientific and philanthropic reasons. Leopold would have grabbed anything – he tried at various times to buy the Philippines, Taiwan and Borneo – but the Congo actually worked out, not least through his employing the loathsome Welsh-American Henry Morton Stanley. Under the cover of Leopold's amazing, all-encompassing lie, Belgians who would have lived blameless lives in the factories of Liège found themselves standing in tropical forests trying to persuade the local people to work for them. Most famously, a bureaucratic method to account for each bullet issued to Congolese enforcers was invented: a severed hand of the person killed by the bullet had to be brought back to base. Photos of this innovation gradually reached a wider and ever more appalled public.

Antwerp's huge new cargo sheds were heaped with tusks and rubber and a smallish number of Belgian and other investors made a lot of money. But in the process – through disease, dislocation, overwork and massacre – the Congo Basin probably lost half its population. Even the shape of the modern state of Congo on a map makes clear that it was created as a huge reservoir, with a little tap in its south-west corner by the old port and capital city of Boma to drain off everything of value and transfer it to Antwerp.

Leopold's position was confirmed in 1885 and he ran the 'Congo Free State' in seeming total indifference to the moral cost. His most famous employee proved to be Joseph Conrad, the temporary captain of a Congo steamer. The hallucinatory, nauseated visions of Africa in Conrad's short story 'An Outpost of Progress' and novella *Heart of Darkness* have fixed for ever a specific place and time. Just as sinister is his vision of Brussels as a 'whited sepulchre', with the surreal company offices filled with barely animated ghosts and its director with 'his grip on the handle-end of ever so many millions'.

The weakness of Leopold's monstrous personal estate turned out to be that Belgian neutrality set it aside from the tougher power blocs of the other European empires, whose owners could more closely control who visited their colonies and why. The French expeditions against Samory Touré, relished by the *Petit Journal*, were, just as in the Congo, the most incredible, careless bloodbaths, and if Conrad had been employed to help out Cecil Rhodes during the Matabele Wars, we would perhaps have as vivid a sense of Britain's ability to create a charnel-house as we do Belgium's. In any event, a number of foreign experts could not be prevented from investigating, most importantly Roger Casement. Oddly the two men who would define the Congo, Conrad and Casement, met there years before when one was just a sailor and the other a railway engineer. Casement's later reports turned Leopold's Congo Free State into a moral monster in the clutches of what Conrad called Leopold's 'masquerading philanthropy'. It was taken over from Leopold by the Belgian state in 1908 – becoming the Belgian Congo – and was from then on ruled with merely the same sort of impatient violence as its neighbours.

Some 5,800 tons of elephant ivory landed in Antwerp in 1901. Incredibly, a key use for the ivory was in billiard balls. The superb, if sometimes harrowing, Museum by the River (MAS) in Antwerp has a photo of the English billiards mogul James Burroughes sitting nonchalantly on a net-bagged heap of twenty thousand balls and even wearing a Leopold II-like beard, as though this was the sign for a poorly concealed freemasonry of scoundrels. It was estimated that this many balls would have required some 2,100 elephants to be shot. In return for such cargoes Antwerp exported Belgian railway and building materials, canned goods and weapons. There is a

1909 photo of a festive carnival float in central Antwerp heaped
with tusks and rubber and everyone seems entirely cheerful.

The continuities for Antwerp are definitely very odd. Back in
1508 a Zeelandic ship arrived with the first sugar cargo from the
Canary Islands, and in the late nineteenth century the craze for
bananas was fed by cargoes into Antwerp from the Canaries, later
replaced by new plantations developed around Boma. It is so difficult to write about colonialism as a separate topic because it is so
intimately entangled in Europe's own history – cheap bananas may
seem trivial (as indeed do billiard balls) but they were a part of a
global system which shaped Europeans' behaviour, development
and history. When in 1891 another upriver expedition by Leopold's goons marched into the Yeke Kingdom they simply shot
dead Msiri, its long-time ruler, and annexed the entire region to the
'Free State', just in time to thwart Cecil Rhodes. This led to the
creation by Leopold of the Union Minière du Haut Katanga, which
soon left in the dust the little bits of money got from poor elephants, pouring out vast amounts of copper, manganese, tin, cobalt
and (somewhat later) the uranium used in the Manhattan Project.

The Union Minière changed the shape of Belgium's economy
and defined many thousands of lives. Somehow the horrors of what
went on and their more banal impacts have to be intertwined. Leopold and his associates (and Rhodes and his) genuinely thought
they were bringing light into the darkness. This feeling was much
added to by the importance of Belgian missionaries, whose activities provided an intimate link to countless Catholic congregations
back home – a spiritual shock-force in parallel to the mercenaries
and oddballs clearing the ground militarily for them, and immortalized in Hergé's thoroughly awkward *Tintin in the Congo*.

One of the great non-human dramas of the Congo was the discovery of that wonderfully elegant giraffid the okapi. As an okapi
enthusiast I felt it was almost too much to take in that Antwerp Zoo
(in perhaps the only entirely positive legacy of the Congo) was the
home of the international okapi stud-book, with okapi bloodlines
treated much like horses'. Europe's first okapi arrived here just after

the First World War – a traditional Antwerp exotic import with roots in the far, far earlier arrival of dodos, sloths and cassowaries.

The First World War ended this long period of low-risk, high-entertainment sunshiny European fighting. Colonial wars were cheap and created an endlessly unrolling narrative of excitements, generally with almost no sense at all that colonies themselves might be problematic. They happened off-stage – it never crossed Leopold II's mind to visit the Congo himself. There is a self-congratulatory but beautiful monument to French colonial military prowess put up in Boulogne's Upper Town in 1898. Its opening ceremony would surely have been celebrated in *Le Petit Journal* if I could dig up the right issue. It very precisely lists the names of the Boulonnais killed in France's post-Napoleonic wars and 'repacification' campaigns, in date order. This precision is itself interesting, as in early periods nobody had any records of this kind. So it is a bureaucratic monument among other things and gives a fair sense of the relative levels of risk and violence to which European troops were exposed. Twenty years after its first unveiling, the structure of the monument had to be drastically changed and individual soldiers' names dropped for the last addition.

Deaths	Campaign
4	Madagascar
3	Senegal
1	'Other colonies'
2	Mexico
2	China
26	Crimea
29	1870–1 [Franco-Prussian War]
17	Tonkin [Vietnam]
5	Algeria
4	Tunisia
1,642	1914–1918

Rays and masks

I had got off the train in Ostend and was walking towards the sea-front when I found myself, quite unconsciously, developing a slightly rolling gait. To my horror I felt a desire to stick my thumbs into my belt and tip a non-existent hat further back on my head. When I glanced up at the sky to tell whether or not a storm was brewing, then instinctively glanced across at the Van Eyck pub with a view to wetting my whistle, it became clear that I had fallen victim to another bout of camp suggestibility and that at some unconscious level just seeing a few flags, seagulls and boats had made me start channelling various idiotic dredged ideas about being some sort of Jack Tar on the spree. Hitching my non-existent bell-bottoms and shifting my non-existent chaw of tobacco from one cheek to the other, I tried to take control of myself, disciplining and restraightening my *H.M.S. Pinafore* legs.

Being in Ostend, it did strike me as unsurprising I should start channelling my inner hornpipe. For quite accidental reasons I had spent some eight years writing only about places which were inland aside from Hamburg and a couple of spots in the Baltic, a sea that I find hard to feel is fully legitimate. In the superb *Asterix in Switzerland* one of the running jokes is that Asterix's enormous and not very bright companion Obelix is throughout the story always asleep, underground, indoors or drunk, or it is night-time. He therefore never actually sees the country he and Asterix are visiting, and is able to report back to his Gaulish village on the last page that Switzerland is flat. I feel rather the same about Europe. Endless trips around the Carpathians or the Swabian back country had blinded me to the way that Europe, far more than any other continent, is defined by its sea-coasts. Indeed it is the strange, gnarled sea geography that runs from St Petersburg round to Istanbul that makes Europe quite different from any of its gigantic neighbours. Its superfluity of navigable rivers rushing down from random heaps of mountain terrain both break Europe up and connect it together, generating a mass of attractive sub-units for human use.

This new enthusiasm for a bit of salt spray made me a bit uncritical of Ostend, with its joyless, heaped-up apartment blocks, the result not least of relentless Second World War bombing. To celebrate my new, nautical mental reorientation I plunged into the North Sea Aquarium. It proved to be a classic of the genre, featuring a poorly gurnard, a lumpsucker which appeared to be having a nervous breakdown and some chipper blennies. There was also the wonderful issue of fish names in different languages – with the lumpfish also being a *Seehase, Lompe* or *Snotolf.* A huge stuffed sunfish (always my favourite) once again raised the old issue of its being called a moonfish by all our neighbours (*poisson lune, Mondfisch* or *maanvis*). We will never know what ancient piece of somewhat unimaginative naming associated its bizarre circular shape with either the one of the other heavenly body. The pleasures of the aquarium were endless, with bits of fishing equipment, bones, old maps, helpful advice about eating prawns and a tank full of turbot, the latter with that curious camouflage stippling of black and yellow dots which makes them look pre-breaded for frying – as though you would expect them to also have a helpful slice of lemon tied to their tails. There was a sad lobster with such low energy and so little room to move around in that various red growths had sprung up from his armour. One particularly happy surprise was an energetic thornback ray, flapping against the glass. I suddenly realized that this must be the same species of ray that features in Hogarth's painting *The Gate of Calais.*

Ostend on balance did turn out, once you had got used to the salt smell and the gulls (and setting the aquarium aside), to be slightly disappointing. When Belgium became independent its short coastline had to have a resort somewhere and so, by default, Ostend got the job. I had assumed, given the region's enthusiasm for allegorical railway stations, that on arrival there I would be greeted by some huge fresco, or a statue of a semi-nude figure of Belgica being embraced by a bearded, trident-wielding Poseidon. Presumably there had once been such characters but, again, bombing wrecked them all. This sense of exhaustion is shared with Calais and Dunkirk, both also so devastated in 1940 and 1944 that they have never really recovered their grace. They all cry out for

some huge plan to start again from scratch and there are few traces
of what made them, at different points in their history, so historically dense and powerful.

Ostend was very much the vision of Leopold II; who poured
some of the money he made from the Congo into its development.
This genuinely evil figure is still commemorated on the seafront by
a statue, his immense beard prominent, surrounded on one side by
cheering, heavily clothed Belgians and on the other – incredibly –
by cheering, clothing-free Congolese. There is also a tablet recording
locals who had died in the good cause of civilizing the Congo. In
the light of the system used at one point to check that Congolese
trackers chasing runaways were not secretly hoarding bullets, someone recently had the brilliant idea of cutting off the hands of the
Congolese, turning what had been stuffy and offensive into a genuine artwork for the first time. With any luck the hands will never be
repaired.

Ostend's great claim to fame (aside from Marvin Gaye's living
there in the early 1980s and recording 'Sexual Healing' in an
Ostend studio) is the lifelong presence of James Ensor. He has
always been one of my heroes, with postcards of his paintings of
grinning carnival masks, skulls, dolls and elaborate hats dotting the
area around my desk ever since I can remember. He lived much of
his life above his uncle and aunt's shop, which sold the sort of seaside gewgaws that were incorporated into his paintings. I generally
do not see much point in visiting artists' houses as they do not seem
to have all that much to do with the work itself – even Rubens'
house in Antwerp, while fantastic in itself (why did we ever abandon
leather wallpaper – or wallleather I suppose?), seemed interesting as
a great seventeenth-century house more than as saying much about
Rubens. Ensor is an exception because the shop and the seafront
were his personality and somehow the shop has survived the bomb-
ings and become a museum, still done up with hanging pufferfish,
disgusting fake 'mermaids' in glass cases and heaped seashells. The
overstuffed sitting room has a good reproduction of his *Christ's Entry
into Brussels in 1889*, the vast painting (now in Los Angeles) that for
decades filled the wall and can be seen in photos of Ensor and his

friends, lurking behind them in all its terror and brilliance obscured by pot-plants and a piano.

I have loved Ensor for so long that it did feel like a real pilgrimage. The ossified, weird flavour of the museum, even though it was only put together long after his death in 1946, seems plausibly accurate. Here at last I was in the house of the man who, back in the 1880s, had created such marvels as *Death Looking at Chinese Objects* and *The Astonishment of the Mask Wouse*. In 1936, two remarkable writers, Joseph Roth and Stefan Zweig, were in Ostend, both exiled by the horrors of Central Europe and twisting and turning to create futures for themselves under terrible circumstances (Roth died of alcoholism in Paris in 1939; Zweig and his wife committed suicide in Brazil in 1942). At one point Zweig decided to visit the elderly Ensor. He was allowed into the shop and walked quietly up the stairs to the main room. Here he saw Ensor in a flat cap, his back to him as he played quietly on his piano in total solitude, surrounded by the macabre trinkets of a lifetime and with *Christ's Entry into Brussels* filling the entire wall behind him, the picture heaving with masked, leering figures, for the most part ignoring the tiny spiritless Christ in their midst. Overcome with unease, Zweig turned round and went quietly back down the stairs.

CHAPTER THIRTEEN

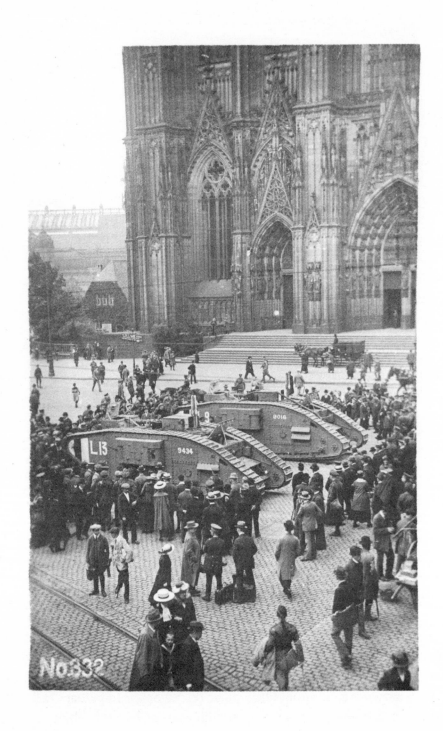

'Barracks, barracks, barracks'

In the decades before 1914, Europe became a vast, chaotic building site. Architecture lurched about crazily, devouring then regurgitating a buffet trolley of unrelated styles: Byzantine, Aztec, Greek, Javanese, Carolingian – an incontinent thrashing about which caused such indigestion that it forced modernism to come to the rescue, kicking in the stained-glass and copper-tendril front door and arresting the lot. At the time it must have seemed both stimulating and deeply confusing. We are ourselves now so far out of modernism's shadow that we can pick our way around these buildings in the same spirit as we enjoy a gigantic box of soft-centre chocolates: in other words – before abandoning the food/aesthetics metaphors – no longer for sustenance but for fun. The gleeful panache of such buildings as Victor Horta's Hôtel Tassel in Brussels or the extraordinary Winter Garden of the Ursuline Nuns just outside Mechelen now seems a summit of cheerfulness and it is hard to recapture how from the 1920s onwards most intelligent opinion would have seen them as walnut-whirls with a turd filling.

One striking oddity was that so many places became just much more medieval. Ghent was a battered, grimy factory town which, largely in the run-up to its hosting the 1913 World's Fair, turned its historic centre into a wonderful fantasy of Burgundian style. Standing on the entirely made-up St Michael's Bridge, looking at a superb array of similarly made-up pinnacles, curlicues and doodads, I suddenly felt urban, proudly mercantile, prayerful; I seemed to be wearing pointed shoes, a felt hat, brightly coloured tights, with a dagger and leather florin purse on my belt, and perhaps feeling a first hint of plague. The real buildings, such as the fabulously blackened, carcass-like front of St Michael's Church, blend seamlessly with the fake – such as the superb new medieval building stuck to that church's north-east corner. This is true throughout Ghent, as historicist obsessives triumphed. The Gravensteen, the battered, much abused old castle of the counts and dukes, had been raided as a stone quarry for years and had the indignity of being used just as a back wall for various shops. Plans to demolish it were quashed and it was so crazily over-restored that it looks as though human-size Playmobil figures should be guarding the battlements. One of the Gravensteen's many pleasures is seeing how the real urban environment was reshaped, inspired substantially by historicist Grand Opera sets, in ways that would then in turn have a huge influence on history-themed movies.

This is an endless subject and some slight sense of discipline has to be kept. In the Netherlands, for example, it seemed in 1869 fairly uncontentious to sell off the huge, magnificent rood loft from the Cathedral of St John in 's-Hertogenbosch, a classical work in coloured marble from the early seventeenth century, which could not have been more unfashionable in an era of Gothic fancy. It ended up in the collection of the Victoria & Albert Museum, where it remains today on spectacular display (and could perhaps, in a nice gesture, just be handed back to the cathedral for free at some point?). Unexpectedly, this patrimonial sell-off caused a spasm of horror across the Netherlands and launched a vigorous new Dutch conservation movement. The vagaries of taste and fate almost led to the fabulous Knights Hall in The Hague being demolished, before it was rescued, rebuilt, given its two charming, medievaline towers and restored to its central place in Dutch political life. This was in large part thanks to the energy and wisdom of the great Pierre Cuypers, architect extraordinary (Amsterdam Central Station, the Rijksmuseum), who not only renovated the hall but also, to the delight of so many generations, added the magical flourish of the Binnenhof fountain, a fantasia of flowers and monsters and heraldic shields topped by a gold statue of Count William II. The fountain started off life (as with bits of Ghent) as part of a World's Fair and this sense of international and local rivalry made such *grands projets* (fuelled by steam, petrol and electrical breakthroughs, plus unparalleled sums of money sloshing around) into a near-universal aspiration. There is a fine example in the French Flanders town of Douai where someone (sadly I have been unable to find out who or why) decided in 1900 that it made sense to commission for the Town Hall an absolutely colossal painting by Auguste François-Marie Gorguet as part of the newly medievalled 'Salon Gothique'. This delirious picture shows a cavalcade through the streets of Douai in 1355 by the French king John the Good. The picture (which is in four chunks, interrupted by vaguely olden-times carved doors) is a summa of the genre: bursting with flower-carrying maidens, little page-boys, austere prelates, stern elders and a seemingly unending parade of brilliantly caparisoned horses (one head-to-hoof in gold fleurs-de-lis), armoured men and weapons. With part of my mind whirring with scenarios for getting myself elected as a *douaisien* local councillor so I could legitimately report back on parking issues in this very room, I simply stood there flabbergasted. As with the wilder reaches of art-nouveau architecture, Gorguet's painting seems designed as a frenzied goad or a Technicolor emetic that will force into existence Malevitch's *Black Square*. But it is in itself extremely fun. Two startling bits of modernity, however, are also marked by Douai Town Hall. Just outside there is a plaque marking the first ever helicopter flight, a one-minute hover in 1907 by the Gyroplane Breguet-Richet No. 1. As the centre of early French aeroplane construction, Douai also hosted the world's first fatal mid-air collision in 1912. Relatedly, on wooden Gothic panels, the town hall has a scarcely comprehensible list of the hundreds of citizens who were killed in the First World War – the list is so long that it almost seems like a list of the town's entire population.

Other forms of more aggressive building were going on further to the east. There is an enormous crappy Germania monument looking out across the Rhine and towards France from a hill opposite Bingen. This monster was built to celebrate the Franco-Prussian War and German unification. It features the usual banal allegories of War and Peace and a matronly Germania statue holding the victor's laurels, all on a vast scale but – entertainingly – nonetheless made vanishingly small by the surrounding countryside. Up close it couldn't be worse (although getting there on a little gondola lift swinging over vineyards is fun), but over in Bingen the gap between its known size and its actual tininess accidentally makes it a welcome symbol of human transience and weakness. The statue's great claim to fame was that during its construction anarchists managed to pack a huge bomb into the new road up the hill, planning to detonate it under Bismarck and Wilhelm I at the opening ceremony. In one of history's stranger twists, it simply did not go off. The French anarchist Émile Henry said the explosives might have been better used just to blow up the dreadful statue itself.

More mad, and a joy for ever, was Germany's great gift to Alsace: Schloß Hochkönigsburg, later renamed, under new management, Château Haut-Koenigsbourg. Kaiser Wilhelm II wanted his eastern and western borders to be marked by major castles to show (or assert) the German Empire's ancient continuity. This was readily done in the east with the renovation of old Teutonic Knight buildings, but in the west Louis XIV and other invaders had done an effective job in erasing Germandom. Hochkönigsburg was a battered stump high in the Vosges, an old Imperial fortress destroyed by Swedish troops in the Thirty Years War. From 1900, using the latest technology, it was rebuilt as a delirious fantasy by Bodo Ebhardt. Bodo, like Wilhelm, can by some lights be seen as not strictly sane. With blithe indifference to the original ground plan he threw into the mix absolutely everything he could think of – towers, a windmill, a portcullis, a drawbridge and a chapel of the purest camp: even down to a separate little high balcony so that Wilhelm can *like the emperors of old* observe the service separately from the vulgar below. Even the guttering is done in a rough-hewn way to make it seem all ancient.

On the bus up the mountainside there is a stop for the leading – and apparently not as cruel as one might idly think – Alsatian tourist attraction of Monkey Island, but in practice this cannot hope to compete with the real Monkey Island of the Schloß. Wilhelm would hang out here with his friends, surrounded by pictures of his great predecessors Charlemagne, Godefroy of Bouillon, King Arthur and King David, with stuffed capercaillies and hundreds of old weapons. Guests would come in through the carved gateway twinning Wilhelm's coat of arms with those of Charles V, making explicit the new German Empire's claim to be the successor to the Holy Roman Empire, with all the problematic border issues for its neighbours that this could imply. The actual Kaisersaal, where Wilhelm would entertain his guests, is, with its antler chandeliers, wall paintings of shields and funny smell, disappointingly like a provincial Ratskeller dragged from a basement to the top of a mountain, but this is a minor quibble.

Setting aside fun buildings, the technology that could recreate entire medieval castles was also being used to pile up real fortifications along the borders. The French response to the Franco-Prussian War was to build an extraordinary tangle of strongpoints behind the new French–German border known as the Séré de Rivières system, its main strength running from Verdun through Toul to Belfort. Resources were poured into three generations of tunnels, supply dumps and fortresses. Like a nightmare inside the synapses of the French military mind the network proliferated over the decades – endlessly expensive, soaking up huge numbers of troops, technologically harassed by weapons innovations that made each generation of updates a bust even before the concrete was dry. Decades of war games came to nothing and whole, extraordinarily lucky year-groups of French troops passed through the system unscathed except by boredom. Eventually the luck ended and the gigantic and now antiquated fortresses at Verdun became one of the most terrible places in human history.

Belgium's fort-building was designed not to fight a war but to make an unspecified aggressor (which, in practice, could only be Germany) think twice about breaking its neutrality. Liège was defended by a series of enormous structures which, like the French ones, lurched from being state of the art to being painfully vulnerable in a very short time. A National Redoubt of forts was created circling Antwerp, not just one of the world's biggest ports but the place that could most easily be reinforced by troops from some of the powers that guaranteed Belgian neutrality. Given Belgium's many peaceful years it was difficult to maintain readiness and a sense of realism. The Liège fortresses were genuinely very powerful though, albeit catastrophically undermined by the handful of 'Gamma guns' and giant howitzers developed by the Germans and Austrians just in time, in 1913–14, the latter (a 'Big Bertha') demonstrated to Wilhelm only in the spring of 1914.

The Germans themselves built up and reinforced their own fortress complexes. Above all Metz, the key city acquired in 1871, became the hub for everything – both a colossal defensive position and the place from which men and supplies from the Empire could be channelled to the Front. Even after years of post-war demolition of many of its forts, Metz is still defined by its defences. There are strange walks in its outskirts where bafflingly oversized buildings, like moss-covered Aztec temples, loom up above you or old German barracks or cold stores suddenly turn up round a corner.

In a way all this was a harmless activity for people who liked to work outside or make things from concrete, but there was always the chance, in many years very hard to imagine, that the fortresses might actually swing into action. The endlessly peripatetic D. H. Lawrence visited Metz in 1912. He was kicked out as an implausible suspected spy. In a letter he wrote that Metz was 'a ghastly medley . . . new town, old town, barracks, barracks, barracks . . .'

War plans

In the decades after the Franco-Prussian War both sides relived in excruciating or exalted detail every moment of their great conflict. The French looked back on a war marked by incredulous prostration – in six weeks Napoleon III's armies had been effectively destroyed. If they boldly marched forward (as at Mars-le-Tour) they were defeated and if they stayed put (as at Metz) they were defeated. The long-drawn-out final months of the war were a shameful agony with no heroes and the horrors of the Commune. The Prussians calculated the colossal indemnity payable by France exactly in proportion to the one extorted by Napoleon I from them back in 1807. As Napoleon III went into his English exile and then died, much of the execration could be heaped on his shoulders. The new Third Republic went through periods of revanchism, particularly during the picturesque episode of 'Générale Revanche', the absurd Georges Boulanger, who in the late 1880s huffed and puffed about fighting the Germans, dithered and then suffered electoral fiasco before fleeing to Brussels and shooting himself. But the Republic more often just focused on growth and finding allies. In Lille Cathedral there is a side altar which features a painting of the Count of Chambord, the legitimist pretender to the throne ('Henri V'). The very existence of this picture is a residual trace of treason and shows the poisonous gulf within France between the Republic and much of the Catholic Church, influential parts of which had seen the defeat in the Franco-Prussian War as the result of secularism: 'Catholic Christians, Protestant Christians, Christians of all name and all party, on your knees!' The unhelpful Bishop of the newly truncated diocese of Nancy and Toul roared vengeance, claiming there was an 'essential difference in the afterlife' between a soldier who died dutifully and one who retreated. Nancy itself became a revanchist boom-town, fuelled by thousands of emigrants from the new German territories. French Lorraine became one of the most militarized places in the world, but also a huge centre for metal industries – its steel built the Eiffel Tower,* a structure that has always defined the period's many enjoyments, alongside reading Zola's novels about how awful Napoleon III's empire had been,

---

* The Eiffel Tower was the final, winning riposte in one of the sillier elements of Franco-German rivalry. With Strasbourg Cathedral now in the Empire, the Germans owned the world's tallest building. This was then trumped by the Church of St Nikolai in Hamburg. The French counter-attacked with the frankly ridiculous new giant metal spire to Rouen Cathedral. This only bought them four years of supremacy before Cologne Cathedral was completed. For a shocked interval, the endlessly delayed Washington Monument took over, but then five years later the Eiffel Tower nearly *doubled* the size of the world's tallest building, but only in the almost incredibly babyish context of a building which only existed to be tall.

with its gripping account of the war, *The Debacle*, showing a heroic, genuine France betrayed by the squalid speculators' fairground of the old regime.

France remained split but ever more elaborate use was made of the sacrificial image of Joan of Arc, and the battlefield of Mars-le-Tour became a great national shrine, with ceremonies held just inside the French border that were partly bitter but also held the chance of reconciliation, with many Germans attending. 1891 saw a new era with the creation of the Russo-French alliance: the isolation that had produced the disaster of 1870 would not be repeated – Germany was now hemmed in. In the run-up to the Great War, a banquet was held in St Petersburg to celebrate eternal Russo-French friendship and which featured as part of the decoration plants grown in the soil of German-occupied Lorraine, so soon to be redeemed. How and when the soil was transported I have never been able to find out, but it has to be said that, whatever the circumstances, this was a thoroughly loopy idea for a table setting.

For the Germans, an era of self-congratulation opened, but it was a nervous one. They felt certain that France would try to reverse what had happened. They looked back at the many campaigns of earlier centuries that showed how extremely hard France was to invade, how, for example, even the grand alliance of much of Europe ground to a halt at the Battle of Malplaquet in 1709, never getting more than a few miles across the border; how Napoleon I was defeated almost entirely outside France; how in 1870 the French armies had been just astonishingly obliging, clinging to the frontiers and eventually being chased into Metz and squashed against the Belgian border at Sedan. It remained one of the great what-ifs as to how differently the war might have gone if a major French force had managed to manoeuvre west or south-west, extend Prussian communications and defeat each spread-out invading army in turn. As it was, France's generals seemed to treat the war as though they were visiting the barber, simply waiting in a row for their turn.

From 1871 to 1914 both sides tried to work out a solution which, given how long this period proved to be, was both urgent and yet oddly deferred. General Bazaine, who spent the rest of his life in exile, became the great hate figure for the French – his fatalism and passivity had resulted in the death or captivity of 180,000 French troops at Metz. A policy of relentless aggression was the obvious response to Bazaine's shameful example – a vast French offensive to liberate Alsace and Lorraine and then threaten Baden. As with the Prussians in 1870, the hope was for a cataclysmic, decisive battle quite near the French border as, if the Germans did not prove cooperative, the idea of a drifting and dispersed offensive, marching through dozy swathes of Swabia, many miles from any serious population centres, seemed unlikely to be war-winning.

The Germans became a victim of one of Wilhelm II's idiocies. It has to be remembered that while he was a charming initiator of building projects such as Schloß Hochkönigsberg and the Roman camp at Saalburg, he was a despairingly useless ruler. Bismarck had a secret 'reinsurance' treaty with Russia guaranteeing mutual neutrality. With Wilhelm's accession to the throne and dismissal of Bismarck, Wilhelm decided not to be encumbered by the treaty but rely instead on his frank man-to-man relationship with the tsar. What was viewed as a shrewd chess move by Wilhelm was viewed as sinister and frightening by the Russians, who promptly signed their treaty with the French. This transformed German neuroses and began the long, fretful process of creating a war strategy that would so completely eviscerate France, on the same timetable as in 1870, that the bulk of the German army could then safely redeploy to the east and defeat Russia.

It is commonplace to say that Belgium is a small country, but this is in some contexts just not true. The nature of its position made it loom large – indeed between the Channel and the Swiss border half of the entire French frontier was with Belgium. Belgian neutrality was of a strange kind. The Netherlands was a sovereign state which chose not to engage with any European alliance and its out-of-the-way geography made this possible. Switzerland was also sovereign but guaranteed its neutrality by having a massive army, in the early twentieth century some 250,000 strong and purely defensive. Belgium was sovereign but in a way heavily compromised by its neutrality being imposed from outside by the Great Powers through what would in 1914 become known as the 'scrap of paper'. As with earlier versions of Belgium, its neutrality suited a number of countries as it meant at least one area of the map was not subject to endless fantasies by moustachioed and booted officers: for France it meant security in the north, for Britain a guaranteed friendly coast and for the Dutch it helped ensure their own neutrality.

The Prussia that signed the 'scrap' back in 1839 had been a purely defensive country in the west – one of the policemen designed to box in France. In 1870 the Battle of Sedan happened because Belgium was neutral and the French troops had nowhere to go – the Prussians crushed them against a legal abstraction. As the decades went by the phantom of Sedan hag-rid the Germans and the cult of von Moltke, Roon and others made these generals into the gods of an earlier and better time. Rapid technological change also made the tactics of 1870 ever less feasible, and their replacement foggy. Officers grew old, retired and died enacting secret war games for the defeat of France. The map of France and Germany's border areas became what must be the most intensely studied piece of land in European history, with every wood, defile, plain, bridge and height scribbled over, with both sides going on absurd mufti-clad walking holidays on enemy territory – bits of the Vosges and Ardennes must have been simply clogged with rival gangs of trekkers with hair en brosse, a clipped, ramrod-spined manner and poorly fitting civilian clothes. To say 'enemy' though would be wrong as it was a hostility which remained theoretical. Alfred von Schlieffen went from young commander in 1870 to Chief of the Imperial Staff, a post he held for fifteen years, before expiring in 1913 shortly before his eightieth birthday without fighting anybody for most of his life. It was Schlieffen and those around him who came to the fatal conclusion that a war with France could only be achieved through taking a route through Belgium.

This all matters so much because it was these plans for the broad strip of land from the Belgian coast to the Swiss border that would

destroy Europe and initiate a period which could only be compared
to the horrors of the Thirty Years War. The French commitment to
Plan XVII to invade Alsace-Lorraine from bases stretching from
Verdun to Belfort and the German commitment to what became
known as the Schlieffen Plan (although it was much fiddled with,
creating a further area of unresolvable controversy) would between
them result in some 330,000 French casualties in the war's opening
weeks and about the same German. This was already uncontrollably
more than in the entire Franco-Prussian War and with the other key
difference that not only did both plans fail, but they were only one
element in a war which, partly triggered by the invasion of Belgium,
rapidly encompassed much of the world. Plan XVII never got anywhere beyond a brief occupation of Mulhouse and a glimpse of the
Rhine, and the Schlieffen Plan turned into a hubristic disaster as
Joseph Joffre, the French commander-in-chief, abandoned the Plan
just in time and actually manoeuvred in the way his predecessors in
1870 had so painfully failed to. Neither side won and both now
stared at catastrophe as, once the German retreat from the Marne
had ended, a line of trenches formed from the Belgian coast to Switzerland, much of it through the core of Lotharingia.

The Battle of the Frontiers

For centuries Britain's one obsessive concern was with the security
of the far side of the Channel. A long way behind this came the
security of Ireland, and after that everything was optional as vast
expanses of empty sea and a handful of countries with tiny, shivering populations to the north made the foreign-policy issues easy.
At some point in each century expeditionary forces were sent to
fight the Spanish or the French or the Dutch. In the later nineteenth century, Dutch and Belgian neutrality were invaluable,
allowing Britain to focus on its continuing, entangled enmity with
France. Once, when walking round the Isle of Portland on the English south coast (pushed into doing so by the descriptions of its
stone quarries in Hardy's *The Well-Beloved*), I came across a huge

hole in the ground that turned out to have been the site of a Victorian super-gun, which had used a mathematical grid to aim at any quadrant on the approaches to the Portland anchorage and blow up whatever was there. The area around Portland is dotted with sea-forts and strange lumps left from old military buildings, each put up at huge expense following yet another war scare with France. These non-wars have always fascinated me, with their strange hybrid sail-and-steam warships and colonial standoffs. In a way it is only through a strong historical sense of non-war that war makes sense. Franco-British rivalry in the Sudan (or indeed Russo-British rivalry in Central Asia) could have created famous, history-changing cataclysms – but did not.

The Entente Cordiale between Britain and France in 1904 ended this long and expensive antagonism and meant that the Channel was no longer an active front. Portland's guns were promptly dismantled for use elsewhere. The Entente was a miracle cure for France, which now ended the western isolation that had dogged it since 1871. Oddly much of the agreement was about often extraordinarily petty colonial disputes – a swap of the tiny British-owned Los Islands off the coast of Guinea in return for the removal of residual French rights in barely inhabited parts of Newfoundland. Perhaps most significant was the agreement to leave Siam alone, allowing it to remain independent. These issues were symbols: from now on France and Britain would stand together. As with all such understandings, they were defensive, in as much as Germany would be unlikely to attack such a behemoth; and offensive, in as much as France now felt that with British support (and also Russian support – a longer-standing agreement) the possibility of a war of revenge with Germany came into realistic view.

The entente worked well for ten years but came under ever greater pressure from the gung-ho military attitudes of both the French and German armies and the British and German navies. The alliance system was attractive as it made the stakes extremely high and therefore, it was assumed, no area of disagreement could be sufficiently important in itself to unleash what everyone understood would be a cataclysm. Various crises, in North Africa and the Balkans, were managed reasonably well, but each time tempers were shorter and there was more of a sense of mutual humiliation. The assassination of the Habsburg heir, Franz Ferdinand, in Sarajevo initially seemed just another of these bad-news items but, scattered across Europe, a mixed bag of politicians and generals drifted into a reckless fatalism which now led to truly terrible decisions.

The war need only have involved Serbia and Austria-Hungary. When Russia made it clear it would protect Serbia other states were dragged in that were otherwise completely indifferent to Serbia. In each case treaty obligations seemed at the time unbreakable, and yet the cost of breaking them would have, in retrospect, been tiny. So Germany supported Austria-Hungary, France supported Russia and Britain supported France. The only intelligent actor was Italy, where it was correctly seen that no gain could be involved and the Triple Alliance with Germany and Austria-Hungary was cheerfully betrayed.

It is striking how, compared to now, technology then really was revolutionary and very hard to get a grip on. When the basset-hound-faced von Schlieffen stood down as Chief of the Imperial General Staff in 1906 the first powered flight had happened only two years before and was of no practical interest. The execution of his endlessly fiddled with final version of his plan would be brought low by many things, but at a key moment a single small French spotter-plane buzzed overhead, its pilot noticing the derangement between the relentlessly marching German 1st and 2nd Armies – the famous 'gap' – and the last shred of Schlieffen's vision collapsed. Louis XIV's wish to be able to see his country from above had at last come true. As a gigantic re-run of the Franco-Prussian War, the opening moves in 1914 seemed oblivious to the implications of the many chilling upgrades the world had received since 1870. If it had been possible to build the Panama Canal and London Underground, or manufacture the rails for the Trans-Siberian Railway, what would it mean if those same technologies were turned to military use? Or if enjoyable new telephone technology could also be used to move troops around, would the very idea of the large 'surprise' attack become impossible?

Of all the countries involved in 1914, Britain was most reluctant as it had nothing to gain. As in 1939, this meant disastrously bad signalling, with the Germans confident in both cases that Britain would stay neutral. The Germans added to this belief because they had no means by which they could defeat Britain, so they were eager to read British dithering as genuine backing out. It will always be unclear what might have happened if the Germans had not invaded Belgium, but this is by most definitions irrelevant as the Germans never seriously considered any other scheme. But for Britain the idea of the Belgian and French coast under German rule, with the naval bases that could be developed there over, say, the following twenty-year period, was an intolerable problem. I have always assumed that it was the 'Berlin genes' of those Germans involved that fatally blinded them to the historical trap they were marching into: the Prussian emphasis on battlefields further east, with no military knowledge (except for a few weeks around Waterloo) or care for the Low Countries and their intricacies, but this is unprovable. In any event, Britain had gone to great trouble to help create Belgium and it was crucial to defend it. So completely by accident two alliance groups fought each other in alignments that made it almost impossible for either side to win. Germany never had any rational plan for invading Britain, and the Allies, as it would prove after four years of fighting, had no plan for invading Germany either. Unrealized by almost everyone (except such eccentrics as Lenin, safely tucked away in his Zürich coffee house) each passing week would not only kill unimaginable numbers of people but it would also grind to pieces Europe's entire culture.

I must have read dozens of accounts of the opening weeks of the war, some repeatedly, and they have the force of religious texts: each reading makes even the greatest fiction vapid. The entire hubristic idea behind the German plan was effectively mad – a technical concept which *required* France to be beaten in six weeks *so that* the army could then move east to defeat Russia, and without enjoying any serious margin over French manpower. In any event that margin dissolved just marching through Belgium. Much of the German outrage at continuing Belgian resistance came from its being at odds with the plan, which went wrong immediately with the failure to destroy on time the Liège forts. The anger at 'betrayal' by Britain also stemmed from its not being a country featured in their crazily over-elaborate, endlessly footnoted and crossed-out invasion plan.

As the war's opening stages were played out across the entire landscape of Belgium and France, in countless towns, roads, fields and woods, there are few places where it is possible now to get a sense of what happened. One that keeps its terrible sense of drama is the Belgian town of Dinant. Backed by its great cliff and controlling a key bridge on the Meuse, a number of generals found themselves pointing to its dot on the map. As the Germans marched towards France, Dinant was one of the few places where a coherent defence could be mounted – with the stakes very high if the Germans could pour over its bridge. In confused, brutal fighting, French troops raced to reinforce the Belgians on the heights above the town, not knowing that most of the entire German army was heading their way. Dinant fell to the Germans but the fighting was confused and – braced by stories of civilian snipers from the Franco-Prussian War – the Germans came to believe that the inhabitants had been firing on them: 674 people were rounded up and shot. The town, already devastated, was then systematically wrecked, with 1,100 buildings destroyed. These horrors – allied to other events such as shootings in Louvain and the burning of the great library there – indelibly marked Germany, within days, as being an amoral, militaristic, marauding power. Allied propaganda enraged Germany – in posters and speeches the Germans pointed out that in the previous two centuries Prussia had fought thirteen wars, France thirty-five and Britain forty-nine; that since 1871 Germany had barely used its army whereas Britain had been killing twenty-six thousand Boer women and children in concentration camps. But it was too late. The German army in the west imposed draconian discipline on its troops and the anti-civilian violence almost disappeared, but for both Allied and much neutral opinion Germany now became a different kind of enemy, outside the pale of civilization.

Dinant is so shocking to visit because it is easy to see its geographical importance, the vulnerability of those living there and how strangely new the buildings all look for such an ancient place. The bridge is a most chilling place. On different parts of the front, particularly the Ardennes, the French started digging trenches a couple of days after the fighting stopped in Dinant – and this became the only rational way to reduce casualties. In Dinant the fighting was in the open and the absolute vulnerability of the human body to the complicated mixes of metal and chemical filling the air meant that for both sides the sort of courage needed to run forward over the bridge was near super-human. The French troops who at one point rushed the bridge were massacred. One who was only wounded while all those around him died was the young Charles de Gaulle. During the war's opening months, the future of the twentieth century was in fact scattered everywhere: de Gaulle in Dinant, Churchill in Antwerp, Röhm in Lorraine, Göring in Alsace and Hitler outside Ypres.

As the Germans headed south their campaign fell to pieces. On 23 August 24.5 German divisions were bearing down on 17.5 Allied ones. By 6 September, as the French initiated the Battle of the Marne, the Allies had 41 divisions. Italy's declaration of neutrality freed up 6 new French divisions, 2 more arrived from North Africa and a further British division was shipped into Zeebrugge and Ostend – while the German army (its horses needing two million pounds of fodder a day, its boots falling to pieces) began to experience a nervous breakdown. Oddly none of this was visible to the generals of the Imperial High Command who, as Joffre began to move, were under the impression they had already won. How many of them were already beginning to think about which artists to commission for super 'warlord' oil-paintings in the manner of those done for the heroes of 1870? By 6 September a huge part of the front had already 'frozen', from Switzerland to Verdun and beyond. The French had already sustained 320,000 casualties; the Germans only a few less; much of the small British force was dead – these were levels which already simply had no meaning or precedent. They made the rulers of each country absolutely committed to using every industrial and human means to prevail and therefore justify through further catastrophes the catastrophe that had just happened.

In all the near-meaningless big statistics there are specific moments which make things a lot harsher and more graspable. In the exemplary new war museum in Ypres there are a number of tall, grey, closed-off areas which look deliberately boring so that children do not enter them. Inside one is an account of events in Vottem, a village north of Liège. A brief flurry of fighting before the front moved south left the villagers with wounded Belgian and German troops to care for, who they put in separate rooms. There were also a number of dead (eleven German and twenty-two Belgian). The villagers were terrified of reprisals and decided that before burying the dead they would photograph each one so that there was an undisputable record of who had been killed fighting. Some of these pictures are on display. Each corpse, wearing his uniform, is put on the same chair with its head held upright by someone seizing its hair. I feel that a fair split can be made: how I saw the world before going into the display and how I saw it after coming out. I am not sure anybody should be allowed to see these pictures and I cannot bring myself to describe them. The villagers were right – the pictures convinced the Germans when they came back that Vottem's civilians had reacted properly and had remained neutral. But what has been left behind in these photos is something that lives in a different world from the official, carefully controlled media of 1914, and the little space they inhabit in the museum is itself a sort of uniquely powerful commemorative chapel to a Europe that had now gone completely wrong.

Kilomètre 0

Most maps of the Western Front in books, to show the trench line in sufficient detail, tend to leave off the most southern part of the battlefield. Very little happened here, but I have always been curious: if the trenches in the north ended in a quagmire of opened sluices and the sea, how did they end in the south? A brilliantly detailed and thoughtful new French map, created for the 1914 centenary, which should be compulsory for all Great War obsessives, showed the precise spot and I thought it was an appropriate way to end research on this book to drive from Basle to southern Alsace and visit 'Kilomètre 0', hiking around whatever survived.

Europe is dotted with strange geographical anomalies. My favourite is a German-owned oblong of forest and farm, some 50 metres wide and 350 metres deep south-west of Aachen, which sticks into Belgian territory. Perhaps understandably, nowhere have I found an explanation. It makes no sense whatsoever and I can only hope there is a reader out there who has the answer. A similar, if very slightly larger, oddity sits at Kilomètre 0 – a block of Swiss land known as 'the Duck's Beak', some 400 metres wide which sticks out east for a kilometre or so into French territory (then, in 1914, German). The tip of the beak was where the trenches ended, some 700 kilometres from the English Channel. As I had hoped, it could not have been more atmospheric, with a local group of enthusiasts having rebuilt some small pieces of trench and put up interesting information boards.

The Germans planted trees to camouflage their concrete bunkers and these trees, now massive, have torn the bunkers apart with their roots, in one case crushing a chunk of concrete into a ball. It was midsummer and everything was clogged with moss and ivy. There was an almost Amazonian level of birdsong, with charismatic woodpeckers scooting overhead plus an eldritch beech martin putting in a fleeting appearance. At one point the war's changing technology is perfectly preserved. Two machine-gun bunkers remain, trained on the small bridge over a stream. One night in 1917 a group of Germans ran forward and blew up the current bridge's ancestor: as tanks had just been invented, for the first time in human history someone could cross the bridge and rush the bunkers without being mown down.

The very furthest point of the German trench system (setting aside the great bales of barbed wire which have long been cleared away) is a large, reinforced dome, now in pieces, which had once held a *Revolvierkanone* – a formidable sort of Gatling gun, a 'stopper' to end things with a flourish. On Swiss territory the army has rebuilt to mark the centenary a wooden bunker of the type used to defend the Duck's Beak during the War. Swiss neutrality was guaranteed by an army in 1914 of some 250,000 men, more than enough to dissuade either side from trying to slip round the bottom of the trench line. The bunkers were wooden so that they could protect Swiss troops from the shrapnel and stray bullets happening a few yards off, but also to express their neutrality – it would not have been difficult to destroy such a bunker but it could not be ignored. The area is so interesting it deserves its own book. The 1743 border markers remain; one side shows an attractively carved Bear of Bern (the then overlords of the Beak), but on the other the sovereignty has changed so often that pretty crests are long gone, gouged and battered from repeated updates. Presumably after 1945, someone has decisively chiselled in a large, crude F.

Very early in the war Kilomètre 0 became a backwater, with fighting moving ever further north. Once the Germans had begun to retreat in the face of French counter-attacks on the Marne they found it very hard to stop. They kept trying to 'fix' French forces in front of trenches so that German troops further west could hook behind them. These tiny versions of the Schlieffen plan failed too and as each side tried the same manoeuvre the only response was more trenches, first just scratches in the ground or pre-existing railway embankments, but soon thickening up. Eventually both sides reached the Channel and ran out of room. The Belgians secured a tiny block of national territory on the coast by flooding in front of it and hunkering down, never surrendering. It is hard to exaggerate the damage the Belgians did to German war plans. This was Germany's fault in that it had been a mere idle assumption that Belgium would surrender, just as it was idly assumed Britain would remain neutral. The complications of this campaign, it could be argued, saved the Entente. Some sixty thousand German troops were diverted to besiege Antwerp. This created a range of moral problems around Dutch neutrality because of the famous Dutch ownership of the mouth of the Scheldt. Both Berlin and London dithered about whether or not military logic forced them now to attack Dutch territory. For Berlin it meant further diversion of resources and for London it was a bit awkward, given that the war had begun for the defence of a plucky neutral.

The decision to let the Dutch remain untouched had huge repercussions. The Germans intended to win a brief war by destroying the French army, having herded it into a pocket against the borders of Lorraine in a variant on what they had achieved at Sedan. Once this failed, a series of reckless improvisations made Antwerp for a few days the focus of Europe. Churchill, as First Lord of the Admiralty, in an amazingly impetuous move, left his office and rushed to Antwerp, diverting naval troops to its defence. It was all futile as the Germans simply swamped the area with men. In the Army Museum in Vienna, one of the most alarming exhibits is a reinforced cupola from the Antwerp forts with an appalling dent from one of the Škoda siege guns that destroyed it. Control of the great port could lead to nothing without a declaration of war on the Netherlands to break through the Scheldt and neither side had the extra troops or political capital to do this. Historically-minded Antwerpers must have rolled their eyes to find themselves once again blockaded in. This diversion of German troops northwards meant that the British and French were able to secure Dunkirk and Calais, and communications between the two countries, through the Royal Navy and ever more elaborate minefields and patrols, were never broken by the Germans – another completely unresolvable and fatal problem unanticipated by Berlin. A fair case could be made for saying that this little sequence of events meant the Germans had already lost the war.

Throughout the rest of the conflict, through this series of accidents, the Germans therefore only controlled the short Belgian coast. Bruges emerged with some surprise from its medieval torpor to become a U-boat base, with its canals able to feed submarines through Ostend and Zeebrugge. This made it comparable to seventeenth-century Dunkirk, with no Allied technology which could properly neutralize it. Towards the end of the war the British tried to block its exits by sinking ships, but this was initially thwarted by the German commander, using a dodge made famous by the Dutch back in the sixteenth century. He simply and cheaply moved the navigation buoys so that the British expedition was led directly onto a huge sandbank. Bruges was never important though, as the Germans were so closely hedged in by British countermeasures. If the long, many-harboured and powerfully resourced ports and rivers of the Dutch coast had been available to the Germans it would have been a different story – and in 1940 the Germans did not make the same mistake, although they made a different one instead.

The rest of the war in the west consisted of a series of attempts to end the strange accident of the trench line. On the whole whoever attacked lost somewhat more men than whoever defended, but the enormous numbers of casualties could be replaced when the next year's worth of men became the right age to put on uniform. The balance of forces mocked all strategic novelties. The Germans were helped by being on the defensive. They could rationalize a future win by simply keeping hold of Belgium, Luxembourg and industrial northern France. The Allies had actively to expel them in order to win. Most of the land fought over had in itself no value. In early 1917 the Germans carried out 'Operation Alberich', a retreat across a large section of the line to massively reinforced, shorter, more rational new positions some five to ten miles east: the Siegfried or Hindenburg Line. As they retreated they took 125,000 French civilians with them to work in the Reich, blew up every house, cut down most of the trees, poisoned all the wells and strewed mines and booby-traps throughout the ruins. The following March, Ludendorff's vast surprise attack on the British spent much of its energy simply retaking the same ground. Every attack was either annihilated by entrenched opposition (the First Battle of the Somme) or became a mutually flaying horror (Verdun) or, during rare actual breakthroughs (the March 1918 offensive), simply presenting flanks which could be crushed by the enemy's reinforcements pinching in the mouth of the developing 'sack' of advancing troops.

For the British, Ypres ('Wipers' – a further anglicizing readjustment in a process going back many centuries) and Arras became the key towns anchoring their line, with both places eradicated during

the fighting.* Arras is still the home today of one of the many
ingenious attempts to break the deadlock: the old limestone quarries south of the town, the 'Carrières Wellington'. I had idly
assumed these were named for the Duke of Wellington, but this was
true only indirectly as it was some 500 New Zealand miners who
named them for their capital city. In a good example of the war's
slowness, it took six months to prepare these quarries which then
allowed thousands of men to be funnelled forward to initiate the
April/May 1917 Battle of Arras. After the initial shock of the British blowing up huge mines and men leaping from the tunnels, the
same horrific logic set in, with the British suffering some 158,000
casualties to the Germans' 125,000.

Everywhere commanders struggled with the impossibility of
their situation. In 1918 Ludendorff's decision to attack resulted in
his taking casualties on such a monstrous scale (some 700,000 by
the time the offensives had petered out) that the German army at
last began to malfunction. Immense numbers of American troops
had been landing all year and this combination made the German
position impossible. Much of the American Expeditionary Force
was spread between Verdun and Nancy, and the Meuse–Argonne
offensives involved well over a million US troops. Again, dotted
around were the men of the future: Truman, Patton, Marshall, with
Eisenhower still waiting to be shipped when the war ended and
Bogart one of the sailors taking them back from Europe. The combined series of French, British and American offensives crushed the
Germans who, facing revolution at home, sued for an armistice. At
that point Lille, Tournai, Courtrai, Bruges and Ostend had been
liberated and the British were at Ghent. The Americans broke the
Kriemhilde Line and the French, in a perfect bit of timing, liberated
Sedan a week before the Armistice was signed.

---

* Very briefly the Germans got into Arras at the beginning of the war, but in
the frantic manoeuvres of the 'Race to the Sea' they were forced to retreat. It
was this complex, terrifying, mobile campaign that Foch directed from Cassel
(chapter 7).

Red, yellow and blue

Through my own language failures and panic in the face of schematic transport maps, much of the research for this and my other books has been carried out through long, involuntary walks through various suburbs. At a specific level of tiredness I convince myself that I know how to get back to the bed-and-breakfast which, as it proves, was so cheap online because so remote from the town centre. This has provoked in me much interesting inward mulling over the nature of human consciousness and the tragedy of our having no external referee to adjudicate on our internal stupidity. Completely exhausted, with the rain coming down ever harder, I would repeatedly delude myself that I was practically born and raised in Zutphen or Namur or Konstanz and head off at a confident loping pace, like a native tracker, towards my distant goal, as it got dark. On almost every research trip I would find myself stumbling into bus stations, sports fields and industrial estates or puzzling over a canal seemingly moved from somewhere else. Cursing my lack of a smartphone, I would fail to notice the slight but fatal curve in a road that meant I was now travelling south rather than west, itself a compass point only established by a vague smudge of light attributed – wrongly – to the setting sun. I was good at the geography in my head but terrible at interpreting it, but I always ended up in the right place, never actually having to slump despairingly into an uneasy sleep in the yard of a wire-and-cable factory, for example: a distinct possibility on one occasion.

Altogether entire days' worth of time must have been frittered in this way, but unless it was raining really hard, or I found myself walking next to the crash-barrier on a dual carriageway, I never felt downhearted. To escape from all the churches, marketplaces, guildhalls and museums was to re-emerge in the world of actual private life: of battered housing projects, wittily named hairdressers, garages, coffee shops and graveyards that made everywhere into a variant on my own home in south-west London. These walks and their mismanagement have been in some ways as important to writing these books as all the reading, conversations and gallery visits.

It is hard to convey exactly why, but perhaps these walks formed a sort of prayer-wheel whose turning reminded me over and over again of one key fact: that the first half of the twentieth century reached into all these houses and through war, occupation, economic growth or economic collapse, shaped the lives of everyone in them. Having a house that was small or tucked away down a cul-de-sac or in some remote bit of the countryside exempted none of its inhabitants from a series of regimes which, armed only with card indexes, rubber stamps and signatures, had near-total reach.

More often than not I would find myself wandering through three periods of housing – new estates from the 1920s, post-bombing quick rebuilds from the 1950s or new estates from the 1960s. The first of these soon became a wonderland for me. Hopelessly lost once in the outskirts of Breda, I found myself taking a crash course in the infinite charm, perverseness and variety of post-1918 Dutch domestic architecture: a seemingly inexhaustible use of dark bricks to conjure up strange chimneys, elaborate and characterful doorways and walls, zany windows. This style had many sources but in part at least it springs from De Stijl.

A side effect of the Great War was to trap various people in places they did not intend to be. My favourite has always been Joseph Conrad and his wife, accidentally stuck in Habsburg Galicia as all hell broke loose. One of the slight annoyances in writing this current book has been the habit of talented figures born and raised within Lotharingia's geographical scope to up and leave for a capital city at the first chance, particularly Paris, taking them out of the narrative. A promising North Brabantine figure like Vincent van Gogh escapes there at the first chance. Post-1918 heroes of mine like Max Ernst and Paul Klee also zoom off, infuriatingly, albeit providing excuses for wonderful later museums where they grew up, in Brühl and near Bern respectively. This was also true of Gelderland-raised Piet Mondrian. But happily for me, Mondrian found himself back from Paris in the Netherlands when war broke out in 1914 and was trapped north of the electric fence that kept the neutral Dutch away from the German-ruled Belgians. The Dutch experience of the war was miserable, spared from the Western Front, but caged in, exhausted and half-starved, their traditional role as Europe's great entrepôt suspended by the British blockade and by Germany's stranglehold on their supply of coal. But it was in this unpromising world that De Stijl was born.

The roots of De Stijl are endlessly contested and tangled. Its key figures seem not to have liked each other very much and frequently were only in touch by letter, but by the time the movement finally collapsed in the early 1930s it had conjured up an almost ridiculously enjoyable aesthetic, fragments of which shine from every suburban street. Of course, De Stijl is hardly without competition for the modernist crown (Bauhaus, most obviously) but the group of painters, architects and designers thrown together outside Utrecht by the world war seemed to be working in a frenzy to come up with fresh reasons for admiring European culture in a context in which it had otherwise completely failed. As far as I am aware, there is sadly no film of the deeply odd Mondrian dancing 'geometrically', but otherwise De Stijl chairs and houses and posters and food-pack designs still make the world a better place. Mondrian developed the idea that only the colours red, yellow and blue were legitimate, placed in a black and white grid. Theo van Doesburg's *Stained-Glass Composition IV* from 1917 has inspired countless painfully neither-here-nor-there church decorations ever since, but in itself has a cheerful bounce infinitely adrift from the military horrors happening a few miles to the south. Just to take van Doesburg's perky 1919 design for a box of Gouda cheese: this alone should act like a fall-of-Jericho aesthetic trumpet-blast. Such prewar junk as the blowsy neo-Olmec Kaiser Wilhelm equestrian monument at Koblenz (1897) should spontaneously collapse into the Mosel if the cheesebox was simply waved beneath the bronze horse's nose.

This restless, fiddly Dutch modernity still springs up everywhere today – curvilinear houses, curious murals, school buildings, shop signs, all preserving an inter-war optimism and inventiveness. Too enjoyable to ignore is the great documentary *Philips-Radio-Film* (1931), directed by Joris Ivens with music by the Surinamese composer Lou Lichtveld. It shows a factory in Eindhoven as a sort of industrial symphony of metal, glass, flames, innumerable little moving parts and strangely artisanal elements, such as men hand-blowing light bulbs. In half an hour it encapsulates everything that was new, fun and surreal about the period, now a world away from 1914 – of thousands of light-industrial jobs and their associated suburbs and green-field sites, of mass consumerism and comforts, the spread of radios, cars, pylons. This was happening everywhere: long-time dozy Rhine towns in France, Germany and Switzerland which had begun to perk up in the 1890s now drastically reshaped themselves: medicines, chemicals, chocolate bars, pills, dyes, fabrics, biscuits.

If De Stijl began behind the north of the wartime trench line, then beyond the southern end of the Front there was a matching outfit in Zürich, the Cabaret Voltaire. It had a related function to De Stijl, incubating much of the post-1918 world. In itself Dadaism is almost unrecoverable. Much of it seems to have consisted of people in funny hats making machine-like movements while babbling random words. I don't think I have ever seen a photo of an event at Cabaret Voltaire and not felt an instinctive sense of relief that I was not there. *But* Arp, Ernst, Kandinsky, Klee, de Chirico pass through its unfunny doors, and personal heroes like Kurt Schwitters and his collages and Oskar Schlemmer and his fabulous Triadic Ballet could not have existed without it. De Stijl and Dada even joined forces through the endlessly various Theo von Doesburg.

Unfortunately for us all, the greatest of all early twentieth-century performance artists was also lurking just round the corner from the Cabaret. Lenin had, like the Conrads, been stuck in Galicia in 1914 and had with difficulty got to neutral Zürich. Here he wrote *Imperialism: The Highest State of Capitalism* and lived a life of harmless absurdity, glowering through the windows of his favourite cafe* and dreaming of world revolution, harmlessly trapped and irrelevant

---

* When I last was in Zürich I had an in-the-footsteps-of-Lenin espresso there – enjoyably it was festooned with posters for Baz Luhrmann's bloated and corny film of *The Great Gatsby*, its Flapper Capitalism almost designed to make Lenin's ghost eat its own beard with rage.

while the Great War ground on. But help was at hand from the Foreign Office in Berlin. This is a scene which needs ideally to be shown like a silent film, with lots of uneasy, jerkily walking characters with big moustaches, black coats and derby hats, to a soundtrack scored for an out-of-tune pub piano and swannee whistle. As millions died, Arthur Zimmerman, head of the German Foreign Office, did more perhaps than anyone to accidentally destroy his own country. In a short space he and his associates came up with two brilliant plans. The first was to send a telegram to the Mexicans suggesting a treaty with Germany whereby, in the event of the USA declaring war, Mexico would get back Texas, Arizona and New Mexico. As the British had control of all transatlantic cables, this insane proposal was immediately decrypted and gleefully passed to the US, releasing a wave of fury which contributed to the American declaration of war. Only a few weeks after this coup, Zimmerman agreed to the equally brilliant plan that the Germans should spring Lenin from Zürich, transport him on a sealed train across Germany and through Sweden to St Petersburg to help foment revolutionary unrest and thereby undermine the Allies. So even as the most terrible war in human history ground on, strange Lotharingian exceptionalism first protected Lenin and then unleashed him on the world.

Lenin's train trip was itself a sort of Dadaist exercise, with a chalk mark on the carriage floor to show which bit was Russian territory, very limited toilet facilities and Lenin banning smoking – which of course meant a huge toilet queue as everyone smoked in there. As the train pulled into a southern German station locals stared speechlessly into the carriage as Lenin and his friends wolfed down fresh white bread rolls from Switzerland, a fairy vision for Germans whose bread for years had mostly been made of wood-pulp and potato peelings. As usual, historical what-ifs are a bit futile, but in retrospect neutral Switzerland's great service had been to provide Lenin with bread rolls, coffee and a nice warm library where he could have dozed harmlessly for the duration. Instead Zimmerman, having helped doom his own country in one world war, had laid the groundwork for its destruction in a second at the hands of the Soviet state Lenin made. Rather like Schlieffen, he would have the luck to die himself (in 1940) just before the full impact of his long-term miscalculations became evident.

Kaiser Wilhelm, still under the impression that he could win, spent an enjoyable 1918 doing some very retro mulling of a kind that Henry the Fowler or Otto the Great would have found congenial: putting together fresh monarchies. He thought the Saxon monarchy should take over a revived Lithuania and tried to persuade the King of Württemberg to take on Poland – a part of the world Württemberg had no links with whatsoever and which the king viewed as a distraction compared to his eager plan to take over Alsace on the tipping-over-into-insane basis of this including the Württemberger 'lost lands' that had many years before scattered the area (and including old Mömpelgard). All these fun discussions about precedence, medals, honour guards, uniforms, possible wedding bells came to a sudden stop as armistice and revolution swept over Germany, disposing of the whole world of emperors, kings, dukes and others. In November 1918 at the German military headquarters in Spa, as Kaiser Wilhelm resigned in a fury and fled into exile, he memorably snarled that 'The Foreign Office has completely filled its pants.' Little did he know that there would be plenty more where that came from.

Shame on the Rhine

For anyone who gets a funny feeling when they hear the words 'epaulette', 'shako' or 'regimental silverware' the Badenese military museum in Rastatt is the equivalent of the Folies Bergère. Room after room is crammed with the pommels, spurs and cross-beltings of yesteryear. The entire history of the rise and fall of Imperial Germany could be told from objects here: how a small state such as Baden became swept up in it, was provided with just over forty years of enjoyment, but was then led to total ruin. There is a heavy silver banqueting centrepiece commemorating German troops who died in South-West Africa in 1904–5: a source of pride then, but which we would now entirely associate with the genocide carried out by those troops on the colony's inhabitants.* One room dedicated to the First World War is so striking that it should be compulsory for anyone wanting to understand Europe's twentieth century. I can only quickly mention three things, but these are enough: a fawning painting of Ludendorff as military visionary; a series of deft life sketches of Germans in the trenches shooting down their British attackers; and, most startling, an elaborate painting of Goltz Pasha's coffin lying in state in Baghdad in 1916. Goltz was a Prussian who as a young man fought the Austrians and was at the Siege of Metz. In his seventies he became in 1914 the notably brutal governor of occupied Belgium and then went to the Middle East where he died, having humiliated British forces at the Iraqi town of Kut. The painting shows a coffin draped in a huge Imperial flag with a spiked helmet and fez placed on top, flanked by monstrous candles, heaped flowers and a matching Ottoman and German honour guard.

These pictures are all so unnerving because they were prepared for a world which did not happen: one in which Germany emerged from the Great War victorious. Goltz Pasha's painting, in the palace built by 'Turkish Louis', was meant to show the continuity of German glamour and power in the Islamic world. Under other circumstances children today would have been reverently shown the portrait of a visionary Ludendorff and admired the drawings of an earlier generation defending their trenches bravely with their old-fashioned machine guns. Standing, freaked out, by these images, I could see how the wreckage of the hopes in these pictures might have become an indelible problem for some Germans – indeed how even the continuing existence of the absurd South-West Africa table decoration, once the Allies had taken all of Germany's colonies, might have contributed to the survivors of the Great War's disastrous sense of bitterness and wish for revenge.

The focus on 1918 as the end of the First World War is incorrect.

---

* Extraordinarily, because of Namibia's tortuous and strange subsequent political history, the full-scale version of the monument is still standing in Swakopmund – but surely for not much longer.

Some American war memorials (like the huge one in St Louis) give
it as 1919 to include the Siberian intervention. But in many ways,
given such era-defining events as the Battle of Warsaw (1920) and
the capture of Smyrna (1922), the war really only ends with the
post-Smyrna Chanak Crisis, when the British decided they could
not defend the neutral zone around Istanbul and the Straits against
a resurgent Turkish army. On the Western Front, the calling of an
'Armistice' in November 1918 proved an absolutely terrible decision. The Germans had effectively surrendered in the face of total
military defeat, but the term 'Armistice', with its implication of a
soldierly and honourable ceasefire, allowed German opinion to see
it as more of a peace between equals. The enraged Kaiser went into
Dutch exile and the revolution that ended Imperial Germany
seemed to most Germans to have fulfilled Allied wishes. They no
longer lived in Bismarck's country. In a huge ceremony at the
Brandenburg Gate in Berlin, the new socialist President of the
German Republic, Friedrich Ebert, uncontroversially said to returning troops: 'I salute you, who return unvanquished from the field
of battle.'

Of course, there were many Germans who understood the
defeat – indeed some who welcomed it as the end of a terrible and
delusive era of imperial braggadocio and who looked to the renewal
of a more modest 'small German' state. The Allies understood it
quite differently though. The Armistice was just the beginning, and
a mere change of regime would not let the Germans off the hook.
The implacable blockade continued, allowing the British to control
all the neutrals, permitting them just sufficient imports to keep their
own economies going, but nothing left over to sell on to the Germans. Gradually the blockade had brought the Central Powers to an
abject state, with everyone by 1918 underweight and exhausted and
all the once great cities shabby and decaying. The unprecedented
movement of millions of troops around the world generated the
devastating 'Spanish' flu pandemic of 1918.

Germany's armed forces were dismantled and its colonies gifted
to various of the Allies. The least noticed and most uncontroversial
of these hand-outs were the hundreds of small Pacific islands from

the old Spanish East Indies which the Germans had bought in 1899 and which were now (as it turned out ruinously) Japan's. The Belgians took over two small pieces of land from Prussia (partly through an antiquarian claim based on the old Principality of Stavelot-Malmédy) as well as Neutral Moresnet, giving them a small, completely pointless and aggrieved German-speaking minority. Belgian troops occupied Germany from Kleve down to Aachen. They also took the small, densely populated part of German Africa adjacent to the Congo known then as Ruanda-Urundi.

The French of course took back Alsace-Lorraine (some 300,000 Germans would leave). Straßburg became Strasbourg again, lots of streets were renamed again. The giant statue of Kaiser Wilhelm I was wrenched down and a crashed German fighter-plane fixed mockingly on its plinth. Some odd things were allowed to stay: the Kaiser-Wilhelm University while (fair play) renamed, still to this day on the front of its university library has carvings of characters like Lessing and Goethe to inspire its students. The Germans in Schlettstadt (now renamed again Séléstat) had built the wonderful Humanist Library (celebrating the town's great period in the sixteenth century) with an external cladding of polychrome tiles incorporating the words *STADTBIBLIOTHEK-MUSEUM*. Short of chiselling out a large part of the facade the French could do nothing much about this. Various ingenious attempts to at least partly cover it up failed, so as it was being rebuilt in 2017 the German text prevailed in a highly attractive if accidental comment on the confused nature of Alsace's cultural patrimony.

The Rhineland was taken over by the Allies. The French botched together a bit of Prussia and a bit of the Bavarian Palatinate to invent the Saarland, a coal-producing area which they occupied and which, through a number of twists and turns, has continued stubbornly to exist as a separate if very small German province to the present day. The French army also occupied a great swath of land from Wiesbaden southwards and three key bridge-heads. The British controlled Cologne and the Americans an area between Verdun and Koblenz.

Huge gangs of workmen around the former Allied frontlines

began to build the cemetery sites that would enshrine the Allied
dead (the Isle of Portland supplied 600,000 British gravestones),
while other gangs were, further to the east, demolishing any sort
of fortification that could possibly help the Germans in a further
war, even though these structures had on the whole not been
involved in any way in the actual course of 1914–18. Some of
these forts were of great antiquity and the Rhineland was denuded
of many striking objects. The only exception was made for Ehrenbreitstein, where a huge stars-and-stripes flew, and whose American
commander (the extraordinary General Henry T. Allen) refused to
be involved in such historical vandalism. Thanks to his stubborn-
ness this gnarled, sprawling and startling object still frowns down
on Koblenz.

The only other major military survival was Metz, because it was
now again part of France. Its endlessly proliferating fortifications,
the work of thousands of men over decades, had also played no
role at all in 1914–18. This strange displacement activity showed
a basic Allied problem: because the Armistice had happened before
their troops had entered Germany, they had never needed to engage
with the issue of how you would in fact invade such a big, densely
populated and complex country without taking the most terrible
casualties. After all, the Germans – famously – had just spent four
years finding it impossible to invade France. This nightmarish
quandary would emerge even more bleakly in 1939–40.

As the Allies had never invaded Germany, many Germans themselves felt the entire occupation to be illegitimate, and even before
the terms of the Treaty of Versailles were known (with its German
signatories obliged to march past a long row of hideously mutilated
French veterans) the inhabitants of the Rhineland felt as much
tricked and lied to as defeated. Almost every family had its own
disaster – dead or wounded soldiers, victims of the flu, malnour-
ished children. Inflation, dislocation and the collapse of any real
economy criminalized the entire population. A country once
known for its meticulous, fair bureaucrats and public services
collapsed into a welter of fur-coat, sex and jewellery bribes. For
traditional middle-class families with savings and pensions every-

thing melted away in a few weeks, the choice being between starving to death and plunging into the black market. Protection rackets sprang up everywhere. From 1921 hyperinflation finished the last traces of pre-war Germany. It was estimated that the money needed to buy an egg in 1923 would have bought 500,000,000,000 eggs back in 1914. Starving crowds roamed the countryside outside Cologne attacking farms and pulling up half-grown crops. This moral collapse, even when Germany briefly stabilized between 1924 and the Wall Street Crash of 1929, meant that there was no serious trace left of the stuffy, proud Wilhelmine empire – except within parts of the army and the memories of those who had fought in it. The more I think about it, the more it feels that the Second World War happened just as soon as it was possible.

The Allies were never able to create a united front. The Americans wanted to go home as soon as possible; the British, once the German fleet was in their hands, had again become strategically without real enemies. Blame has been heaped on the French for their enshrining hatred and revenge in the Treaty, but it was their territory which had been wrecked. There are so many figures, but among the more striking ones would be the 448 million square yards of barbed wire that needed to be dismantled; the 33,000 miles of roads and 700,000 houses rebuilt; the thousands of poisoned wells; the blown-up coal mines and wrecked industrial equipment. And who would pay the pensions of 700,000 French widows? Entire cities, formerly prosperous and successful, such as Cambrai and Arras, were going to have to be rebuilt from scratch, while the equivalent German cities along the Rhine had not received so much as a dent.

The formerly German-occupied north was in ruins: during the war some of its inhabitants had been resettled outside the zone through Swiss intermediaries, and Herbert Hoover's famous campaign had kept alive millions of starving Belgians, but in 1919 it was quite clear to the Allies which country should now pay for all these ruins. There were several clumsy attempts by the French and Belgians to create satellite states on the Rhine with bribes, short-sightedly poured into local communist parties on the grounds that they could be relied on to make things even worse. But the impulse to collaborate in return for becoming an Allied satellite was almost always trumped by German solidarity, although the young Konrad Adenauer was briefly tempted. The violent 1923 occupation of the Ruhr by the French and Belgians left the Allies isolated and morally in an ever worse state. Many pessimists felt that their only protection from a second war was to keep Germany economically wretched and militarily feeble, but the colossal reparations demanded by the Allies (which would guarantee German weakness) could only be paid by an industrial and financial powerhouse (which would not be weak).

One curious aspect of the Rhine occupation was how German anger came to focus on the French use of African troops. By 1918 the Allies were drawing in forces from all over the world (with, for example, tens of thousands of Chinese working as stevedores in the Channel ports). But even in 1914 the Tirailleurs Sénégalais, drawn from all over French West Africa, from Mauretania to Togo, were already on the Western Front and some 135,000 fought there throughout the war. The Germans were unable to use their own colonial forces as their colonies were so quickly over-run or bottled up by the Allies. A pathological racism gripped the German army, with countless cartoons and posters deriding such things as 'the 5th Gorilla Regiment', 'the latest addition to the *Grande Armée*'. The Germans were outraged that a 'white' war for the future of Europe was being undermined in this way. Captured African troops were fitted into the fake scientific obsessions of the period. A remarkable if horrifying exhibition in Frankfurt in 2014 focused on this issue. German scientists had analysed and photographed the black prisoners of war producing a powerful series of photos of faces so detailed that every cicatrice and pore has an unnerving clarity and in some the photographer and his equipment can be seen reflected in the subject's eyes. One truly terrible photo shows a POW with his entire head covered in plaster, his hands stiff with distress, for some futile collection of 'African facial types'.

The French attitude towards their own African troops was confused, but a mixture of standard-issue racism and admiration: after all, some thirty thousand African troops were killed. A great monument to the Tirailleurs was put up in Rheims (and quickly taken down by the Occupation authorities in 1940) but it would be too much to suggest it was a colour-blind relationship. Black troops were extensively used in the occupation of the Rhineland, partly because troops from metropolitan France were desperate to be demobilized, but partly indeed to humiliate the Germans. Except under very limited circumstances (circuses; world fairs; a Cameroonian kettle-drummer in a Badenese regiment) this was something new for Germany. There were many cases of rape by Allied soldiers, but the handful that involved Africans caused 'the Horrors on the Rhine' – a welter of salacious and appalled reporting across Germany about 'black bastards', part of the same pathology that saw 'Jewish profiteers' in every agony of the hyperinflation. An ever more elaborate theory of defilement and treachery came to dominate much of the German explanation for 1918: an army betrayed, the war dead mocked, an undefeated nation brought low by the bullying and lies of the mongrel Allied coalition.

CHAPTER FOURTEEN

Dreams of Corfu

A few miles outside Utrecht is a grand house which must have a fair claim to be one of the most resonant sites in Europe. If part of the point of sitting in a church is to dwell on human transience and folly, then this house would qualify as a religious building. Wandering through its mournful rooms the visitor is caught in a labyrinth of horror, and at its heart, popped on a chair in its former owner's bedroom, is a pretty cushion stitched with the words *Deutschland, Deutschland, über Alles, über in der Welt.*

Kaiser Wilhelm lived for over twenty years in Huis Doorn, becoming older and older, plotting and fantasizing, ranting and cheese-paring. As he died after the German occupation of the Netherlands in 1940, his house was briefly inherited by his family. Hitler's defeat then allowed the Dutch government to confiscate it. This sequence of events meant that the entire house was kept intact, exactly as Wilhelm had arranged it, and not sold off or looted. To wander around Huis Doorn then is to sink into the Kaiser's vision of home-furnishings – this bust, this pot, this collection of cigarette lighters, this painting of the estate in Corfu which he still owned but would never again be allowed to visit.

The Kaiser's flight to asylum in the Netherlands was one of the minor yet epochal events of 10 November 1918. Seemingly safe in the German-occupied Belgian town of Spa, surrounded by his generals, and shielded by Europe's largest employer of the 1910s, the German army, Wilhelm was suddenly brought to realize that far from being Supreme Warlord, he was now just an embarrassment. As the German revolution unfolded across a country exhausted, enraged and despairing, what had only a few weeks earlier been unthinkable suddenly became obvious – Germany had lost, and the tangle of monarchical and imperial regimes that ruled it were at an end. Generation after generation of the Hohenzollern family, traceable to eleventh-century Swabia, were now irrelevant. From being at the apex of the Central Powers, Wilhelm was now a peculiar sort of private individual. One day the government in Berlin had pronounced his abdication; the following day the Armistice ending the war was signed, the German army stood down and the monstrous trench system dissolved.

There is an extraordinary photo of the Kaiser and a few men of his entourage pacing the station platform of the Dutch border town of Eijsden, on the Meuse below Maastricht, on the afternoon of the 10th. Its blurriness makes it all the more spectral, as though the uniforms, deference and Prussian hierarchies stretching back centuries are visibly dissolving. Wilhelm was alert to the unhappy precedent of the slaughter of the Tsar and his family that summer, and realized he might have only hours in which to act. Dumping the classy white-and-gold imperial train on the grounds that just a handful of disgruntled German artillerymen could make short work of it, he fled to the border, pleading with Queen Wilhelmina of the Netherlands to give him asylum. Aware that any roving band could have grabbed him, Wilhelm stood in Eijsden waiting for permission to proceed, with a catcalling crowd (not shown in the photo) gradually building up around the station.

At midnight Wilhelmina agreed – both the logical result of monarchical solidarity and a practical application of Dutch neutrality – and Wilhelm was whisked to Amerongen Castle, where he had the exquisite humiliation of sleeping in a bed once used by the all-conquering Louis XIV. And so began the Kaiser's *via dolorosa*. He bought Huis Doorn the following summer and moved in together with fifty-nine railway cars of goodies from various Berlin and Potsdam locations and millions of marks handed over by an ambivalent, over-legalistic German government. The hope throughout the coming years was that the organic and irresistible nature of Hohenzollern rule would prevail over the mere blip of losing the Great War. The logic of Wilhelm, or at worst of his son, returning to Germany seemed obvious. For many Germans, however, he was the bombastic warmonger who had betrayed them. Even Hitler, who could in some moods see the logic of Wilhelm coming back, realized that he was simply too discredited and unpopular. Indeed the whole world of waxed moustaches, shining cuirasses, ceremonial swords and ostrich feathers had been utterly drained of its magic during the annihilatory course of the war and, perhaps within mere moments of the Armistice, suddenly seemed embarrassing, silly and out-of-date. The Nazis stayed in close contact with Wilhelm, but in the end he was utterly incompatible with their New Germany.

Huis Doorn preserves in aspic this weird leftover. In what can only be seen as either a mania of self-loathing or (I fear this is more likely) dumb lack of imagination, Wilhelm packed Doorn with mementos of his great ancestors, paintings of successful wars and photos of his old palaces. It is hard to know what is worst. Did he spend much time looking at the model Viking ship made out of silver and presented by his fellow twenty-one German sovereigns and the German city states on his Silver Jubilee in 1913? Did he enjoy having all his Scottish stuff – kilt, claymore and *sgian-dubh* – as a reminder of carefree times at Balmoral as Queen Victoria's pampered grandson, before he became the Most Hated Man in the World? Did he cry at the frankly insane white marble bust of himself as Frederick the Great, with the familiar Wilhelm features topped by a wig and tricorn hat? His smoking room was filled with things actually owned by Frederick the Great (paintings, snuffboxes, weapons), the mere presence of which would have hag-ridden a more imaginative man. Why didn't he surround himself with pictures of his most useless predecessors? I would have given myself a more flattering framework by decorating my study with things owned by the hapless and despairing George William or that bulky mystic Frederick William II.

The Allies enjoyed themselves at Versailles, coming up with ever more outlandishly nasty places of exile for Wilhelm and applying pressure on the Dutch to spit him out. There were plans to have a gigantic show-trial in London, but it was pointed out that such an event could undermine the whole principle of monarchy, and get really out of control if the British ruling house's countless royal German chums popped up. The world drifted on to other things. The security detail at Doorn were terrified of snatch squads, assassins or bounty-hunters sneaking in, and during the winter the moat ice had to be smashed each night – one of the last times in European history when a moat had a real value. But it was a measure of Wilhelm's draining prestige that nobody even had a go. The horrible indignity of his position made his aides inwardly pray for his death. They assumed that if the Allies successfully extradited him, as their representatives came up the drive he would shoot himself or, failing that, one of his officers would intervene with a quick sword-thrust to prevent the final fiasco of a shuffling, fettered ex-Nibelung Lord in the Tower of London. He grew a beard, initially to make him unrecognizable for if he should do a sudden flit.

The years went by, with everyone sitting around crystal-laden dinner tables in full uniform while the Kaiser prosed away about Jews and Freemasons and ever more baroque conspiracy theories involving the long-term malice of the puppet-master-from-beyond-the-grave Edward VII. There would be champagne toasts when one of his countless German democrat enemies was assassinated or died; rage at the betrayals from Berlin, incredulity about the Ludendorff–Hitler putsch attempt ('You can't set up a new Reich from a beer hall!'); euphoria at the Third Reich; delight at British defeat in 1940 ('The ordeal of Juda-England has begun'): but all as a minor bystander. His notional liberation with the invasion of the Netherlands in May 1940 meant nothing – he could never be allowed back to Berlin and was now in his eighties. He died on 4 June 1941, a few days before Operation Barbarossa sealed the Third Reich's fate. The complex historical gusts that blew around the graveside can hardly be summarized – the thoroughly evil Reich Commissioner for the Netherlands Arthur Seyss-Inquart, the thoroughly ancient Prussian commander August von Mackensen, who had started his career getting an Iron Cross during the Franco-Prussian War, Wilhelm's son, the highly notional 'Wilhelm III', and a huge wreath from an absent Hitler.

At an unrelievedly grim meeting of the French cabinet on 12 June 1940, the Prime Minister Paul Reynaud – as Paris was about to fall and the Germans began to dispose of the Maginot Line – battling a mixture of defeatist and treacherous colleagues, exclaimed to those wanting to cut a deal with Hitler, 'We're not dealing with Kaiser Wilhelm but with Genghis Khan.' It was a measure of the sickening pace of change that the man once seen as the enemy of the world was now the soft option.

Walls and bridges

The young Richard Cobb, who went on to become one of the great historians of France, was in the British army in 1944 when it liberated French Flanders and Belgium. On the basis of awe-inspiring numbers of drinks in uncountable numbers of pubs he built up an unrivalled picture of what life had been like under German occupation in both world wars. In cities like Lille in 1914–18 there had been very few male adults as they were all in the French army. Those remaining were taken off to work in labour battalions. In the first winter most supplies of wood were used up (including things like staircases) to stay warm. For the German army, the French and Belgian civilians were the lowest priority and the blockade hit them before anyone else. Just as the British moved all the inhabitants of Arras and Ypres out, so the Germans did the same for towns like Mons, with Brussels becoming a vast refugee camp. Cobb spoke to one Lillois who remembered the awfulness of Lille station, with its vacant ticket offices and its ever tattier posters boasting of easy, glamorous trips to Paris or Nice, now seemingly for ever on the wrong side of the trench lines. With its huge main square, Lille was ideal for German military parades and many photos survive of row upon row of spike-helmeted troops parading beneath cheery prewar advertisements for now mockingly unavailable brands such as Persil and Bovril.

Humanitarian organizations were able to make a cynical case to the occupiers for letting trapped civilians out so that feeding these 'useless mouths' would become a French headache rather than a German one. Occupied Douai, ingeniously, expelled all its vagrants, prisoners and prostitutes into unoccupied France. The Swiss gradually transferred civilians from places like Lille and Tourcoing down the Rhine, through Basle and across the Jura back into France. Cobb talked to one man who had eventually followed this evacuation route as a child. His memory of Basle was one of astonishment: he had never seen young men not in uniform before.

The issue of young men haunted the inter-war period. Just to restrict the numbers to the four countries that physically faced each other on the Western Front, the war ended with three million dead and ten million 'wounded'. The latter was a term that encompassed everything from a bullet in the arm to lifelong confined care in one of the huge buildings that now sprang up across Europe. Every country battled to work out its response. The British spent the 1920s and early 1930s creating what are always referred to, correctly but strangely, as the biggest human funerary sites since Ancient Egypt. The Ypres Salient and the Somme became the main focuses for graveyards and carved memorial stones designed to last for ever. Countless friends and relatives would take the ferries each summer to visit the graves in a dreadful form of tourism that created its own new ecosystem of hotels, coaches, taxis and restaurants.

It had originally been planned that Ypres itself would have a central role, with its ruins a permanent focus, but the inhabitants not unreasonably wanted their homes back. It was then decided to make it into a new, modern town to put the past behind a place which had had just too much history. But the inhabitants, again not unreasonably, asked that it should be rebuilt exactly as it had been. Sir Reginald Blomfield, when building the Menin Gate (inspired by the Porte de la Citadelle in Nancy) to commemorate the nearly fifty-five thousand British and Commonwealth troops with no known graves, was driven mad by Belgian obstinacy.* The sightline running from the rebuilt Ypres Cloth Hall to the Menin Gate

---

* He fretted too about designing the Gate to make it as hard as possible for Belgians to turn it into a *pissoir*.

was ruined by a small group of solid citizens who insisted that they would not move their shops a centimetre. These shops are still there, selling a dazing array of offensive kitsch, from chocolate poppies and helmets to Passchendaele beer.

Many of the fifty or so different nationalities fighting in Flanders by 1918 put up monuments – the extraordinary Canadian one at Vimy Ridge for example, the site continuing the region's irredeemable enthusiasm for exclaves and political anomalies through the French making it permanent Canadian territory. The British signed off with Sir Edward Lutyens' monument at Thiepval to the Missing of the Somme (some seventy-two thousand men), at a huge ceremony in 1932. I have spent so much time wandering around battlefield cemeteries, but have always found excuses *not* to go to this. Just in photos it looks unbearable. In any event everything is encapsulated privately and simply in Blomfield's little St George's Memorial Church in Ypres, almost anonymous on its corner. Everything inside it was put there to commemorate specific deaths, either within regiments or families or schools, and it still seems to contain a sort of essence of 1920s shock and grief.

The French commemorations focused on Verdun, which became a great national shrine during the inter-war period, with its ossuary containing the bones of some 130,000 unidentified French and German troops, and with a drastically different aesthetic to the British cemeteries. Its formal inauguration happened in the same week as Thiepval, in August 1932. For the British, Thiepval was meant to draw a line under any further British involvement in the Continent. Almost a century had gone by between Waterloo and Mons without any British troops in Europe and it should be at least as long before it happened again. A host of novels, memoirs and poems published throughout the 1920s had, while all the cemeteries were being constructed, gradually turned the British experience from a heroic one to a woefully mismanaged waste. For the French and Belgians the hope that they could actively cow and shape Germany as they had tried to in the Ruhr gave way to increasing fatalism. Both, alongside the funerary monuments, embarked on vast projects which would no longer aspire to dominate the Germans but would simply keep them out. The Belgians, having been invaded once, correctly guessed that if the Germans did it again they would not bother with Dutch neutrality and would instead march straight through the Maastricht appendix and into Belgium. Their response to this possibility was to build the largest fortress in the world, Eben-Emael, which incorporated every technical and military innovation available to the early 1930s. The French went even further, building the Maginot Line, which would seal in Alsace and make any renewed German invasion suicidal. These were not in themselves confident gestures.

In the early thirties a form of what appeared to be gloomy, cynical conservatism ruled Europe, of a kind which only in retrospect would seem attractive. No politician proved able to manoeuvre his country out of the Great Depression. Everybody tried to ignore the critiques from the far right and far left. The characteristically named Centre Party in Germany, with its roots in post-1848 Rhineland Catholicism, tried to hold the line but was so ideologically broad that it was necessarily timid, with disastrous results. Its traditional core was in places such as Koblenz and Cologne which had been most humiliated by the Occupation. Its breadth from left to right meant that it had housed both Matthias Erzberger, who had signed the Versailles Treaty for Germany and been duly shot dead by a right-wing hit squad in 1921, and the oleaginous Franz von Papen, whose catastrophic, silly manoeuvrings let in Hitler. The Centre Party confusingly therefore included both figures who had administered the 'stab in the back' which had betrayed the German nation and war dead, *and* figures who believed in such a theory. This meant that the Rhineland was in some ways both a sufficient bulwark against Nazism that Hitler viewed it (in an echo of Bismarck) with great suspicion, *and* nonetheless hopelessly suggestible to Nazi revisionism.

The process by which Hitler came to power in 1933 was focused on Berlin, but was at every point really about the Western Front. While the Nazis only ever received a third of votes they could, once they had seized power, rely on a vastly greater constituency created by those who believed that 1918 had been a trick. The many conservative army officers who despised Hitler and were hated by him in turn almost all agreed about the need to break the shackles of Versailles. Germany had been so shaken about, starved, criminalized and filled, from the Republic's founding, with untruths about why and how the Great War had ended that it was always doomed to undo its humiliations. The French and Belgians had tried to control Germany and keep it down with the occupation of the Ruhr, but by 1924 had been persuaded of its futility by the British and Americans. After that they concluded that they had little choice but to wall themselves in and hope for the best – the work on their vast fortress systems began with Germany still a democracy and Hitler far from power.

The glamorous, militaristic Third Reich found support not only from those wishing to overturn Versailles but also from those fearing and hating Communism, conservatives who might have otherwise still stayed distanced from Hitler. The extra disaster lay in Hitler's chaotic ideology happening to include rabid anti-Semitism – this had the worst implications, but it was possible to imagine a just as violent, dictatorial and warlike German regime without this emphasis (under, say, Hitler's predecessor as chancellor, General von Schleicher, who in his short reign had used many of the same military trappings – and who Hitler murdered during the Night of the Long Knives in 1934).

The weary sequence of events is well known: each aspect of the Versailles Treaty would now be undone as rapidly as possible. Some key elements lay in the east (particularly the 'Polish Corridor' and Danzig) but the critical moment lay in the remilitarization of the Rhineland in March 1936. This was preceded a year before by a plebiscite administered by the League of Nations in the Saarland. This was France's only serious spoil from 1918, but in line with the Treaty the inhabitants had to decide their own future. The plebiscite was fair, with the territory flooded with British and Italian troops under League of Nations command, but disastrous, with an overwhelming vote to re-join Germany. Years of handing out Marianne dolls to schoolchildren, bribes, threats and encouragements to learn French had made no difference whatsoever in the face of a German nationalism just as mad and self-sufficient as France's own. The French left and the Nazis moved in.

The Rhine's left bank remained the great guarantee and tripwire for Belgium and France. The German army was still small and undertrained, the German air force only re-founded a year before. As they marched in German troops were under orders to retreat in the face of resistance, but there was none. Only four years after the Thiepval and Verdun commemorations, but also in societies that had been themselves shaken badly by the Depression, by the threat of communism and by a great intellectual wave of belief in the futility of the Great War, it was impossible to imagine a counter-invasion of the Rhineland. The French needed British assistance, but neither country in the end could conceive of re-opening the spigot of 1914.

The Western Allies in all their military planning still faced the crucial problem of how to go about invading Germany, which had been unresolved in 1918 and, as it turned out, would remain so in 1939. The Great War had been entirely occupied by the straight-forwardly heroic task of taking back national territory seized by an invader. How many years and deaths would have been required to reach Berlin? The Germans had secretly been building lines of fortification east of the Rhine since 1934 – but these were now left in favour of the great West Wall, or Siegfried Line (a British term reconditioned from the Great War). This, oddly, became known as the 'Limesprogramm' – reviving the Roman Empire idea, much beloved of Wilhelm II, of a sequence of anti-barbarian forts. Again, without irony, the original 'Limes' being built to keep *Germans* out seems to have escaped everybody – but Nazism was such a hopeless mess of Caesarian, Wagnerian, Nordic and Fordist impulses that it is too easy to pick holes. Work began on what were planned to be some twelve thousand forts and bunkers from Kleve to the Swiss border, to be finished in 1952. Unlike the Maginot Line and Eben-Emael, however, these forts (which by November 1938 had already used over a million tonnes of cement, almost seven million tonnes of gravel and sand and employed well over half of all German concrete mixers) were there not for defence, but simply to hold off Allied troops while any German opponent in the east (such as Poland or

Czechoslovakia) was first destroyed. If there ever had been an opportunity for the Allies to stop Germany, it was now passed.

The Kingdom of Mattresses

One of the more gloomy/peculiar things to do in the Rhineland is spend a night at the Hotel Dreesen in Bad Godesberg, south of Bonn. With its old-fashioned, mournful gilt and riverside location, for more than a century it has been providing a very mild inland holiday experience. It lies at the heart of Nibelung country, with the Rhine down which Siegfried travelled from Xanten to Worms, and with the Siebengebirge (Seven Mountains) in which Brünnhilde once slept on the opposite bank. A quick ferry journey across the river takes you to the guilty pleasure of the Nibelung Hall, built in 1913 to commemorate the centenary of Wagner's birth. Enjoyably morose paintings of *The Ring* fill the feast-hall-style interior, sculptures of Fasolt and Fafner, a Jugendstil curtain showing the Norns measuring fate. An anxious sign explains that the swastika motif in the windows has an ancient and blameless origin. The hall itself has kept its purity, but things get somewhat miscellaneous alongside it, with a jaunty life-size Siegfried's Dragon put in for the fiftieth anniversary of Wagner's death in 1933 – a statue which I think would have made the Master very angry indeed – and a vivarium specializing at the moment in albino anacondas, oddly.

Bad Godesberg itself is a superbly arrogant Wilhelmine suburb, little bombed, with as its central focus the great tower which was blown up in the painfully silly sixteenth-century Cologne War discussed earlier. The Hotel Dreesen remains famous for hosting the Chamberlain–Hitler talks in September 1938 at which the future of Czechoslovakia hung in the balance. The Wagnerian flavour was ideal for Hitler, and the Norns were busy at work as the two men tried to gauge each other's intentions. The jittery, fearful atmosphere of those days has been overlaid by so many later disasters. The Soviet Union and France had guaranteed Czechoslovakia's borders, but Britain refused to join them. Through arrogance, narrowness, contempt for Hitler but also a genuine horror of what war might mean, Chamberlain made it clear to Hitler that he could do as he wished. The Munich Conference later in the month broke up the Czechoslovak state, removing the key bastion that hemmed in the Third Reich. The Soviets in total disgust at Western weakness began to make other plans. It is possible to stand in the same lightly remodelled entrance to the Hotel Dreesen that Hitler and Chamberlain stood in for their famous picture together, but it is not fun to do so.

The fighting that eventually broke out in the West ran along the same divide as in the First World War. The region described in this book was swept over twice, in 1940 and then in 1944. In the nightmarish interlude terror, genocide, forced labour, aerial bombing and the collapse of almost all social and economic norms wracked the occupied zones. Of course, for those living there it seemed in late 1940 to be a permanent future and the compelling shape we give the Second World War, ending with the Liberation, was not available to those who lived through it.

Every actor in 1939 was almost immobilized with self-consciousness. The Low Countries remained anxiously and even despairingly neutral. The Swiss mobilized some 400,000 troops and adopted their traditional 'Porcupine Principle'. The French and British, with no plan as to how they might invade the Third Reich, hoped that a fresh blockade would smother the German economy and topple Hitler – but, with the Nazi–Soviet Pact, this was like staking out the front of a house and pretending not to notice the convoys of trucks delivering all the world's goods through the back garden. The Allied commanders were reduced to near paralysis by their memories of the First World War. The scale of what was achieved was nonetheless extraordinary. French society was entirely reshaped and over two million men sent to the front. With the declaration of war and the activation of the Maginot Line, a 'red zone' was declared along the borders which shifted some two million civilians west and south-west, clearing the Nord, Ardennes, Alsace, Lorraine and the Franche-Comté of most of their population.

Within weeks of the war's outbreak it was fair to say that France was a different country, its pre-war shape gone whatever the outcome.

For the Germans the self-consciousness around 1914–18 was quite different. The plan, motivating even the most secretly anti-Hitler officer in the German armed forces, was to remove the shame of 1918. Hitler imagined a great, immediate, bludgeoning encounter in 1939 which might perhaps reach the Somme by winter, the immense German casualties forming the blood sacrifice that would awe future generations, with 1940 finishing the job. A bit less *nibelungentreu*, most generals focused on the disastrous failure to secure the Channel ports in 1914. France could be defeated in due course, but this time Britain would be the primary focus, with an invasion of Belgium and the Netherlands giving Germany the string of great docks and harbours from Rotterdam to Boulogne, closing the Channel and allowing for as long a time as needed to grind away at British seapower and bomb London flat. Unfortunately for the Germans, this plan fell into Allied hands in the January 1940 'Mechelen incident' when a German plane crashed in Belgium. The Allies were sure it was a fake, but the Germans did not know this and felt obliged to rethink.

One oddity in 1940 was that the Maginot Line worked really well, securing a huge chunk of the frontier. This so reduced the Germans' strategic options that all they could do really was invade through central Belgium or the Ardennes or both. This should have simplified life for the Allies too, keeping their main forces back to respond to whatever the Germans did. Instead, the French dogmatically insisted that the Ardennes were impassable and that Belgium was therefore the only real theatre. The French have always been blamed for this, but the underestimated Belgian angle of Germany's eventual attack plan would prove just as brilliant as the Ardennes one. The Germans knew that the French were aghast at the idea of a second war again devastating French soil. They knew that their eagerness to rush out of their fortified positions to encounter the Germans in Belgian territory would lead them to catastrophe, just as much as the 'left hook' through the Ardennes.

The campaign was a disaster for the Allies and the scale of

German success was so dizzying that it can never really be fully understood (9th May, quiet confidence; 15th May, despair). It could be argued that the French and British generals reflected their countries in their timorous enfeeblement: they had all fought in 1914–18 and were terrified of a repeat. The many months spent waiting for the German onslaught had drained away any élan they might once have had, the British commander Lord Gort deteriorating into a sort of glazed scout-master, obsessing about tiny details of uniform and supply. The Allies understood that each month they were themselves getting stronger and began to see the Germans as having hesitated too long (Chamberlain's unfortunate April claim that Hitler had 'missed the bus'). But, of course, the Germans were getting stronger too and re-equipping, retraining and absorbing the lessons of their heavy, real combat experience from Poland, the last factor perhaps the single most important difference between the two sides.

The disaster was universal and barely recordable in conventional newspaper terms. New technology (gliders and concrete-shattering explosives) destroyed Eben-Emael in a few minutes. Rotterdam was bombed with nearly 900 civilian dead, also in a few minutes. Having spent their time since the previous autumn building fortifications, the Allies indeed then left them behind to march into Belgium to crash into what they assumed to be the main German army in open fields, a strategy that would have been viewed as suicidal within weeks of the beginning of the previous war. French troops rushed up into Zeeland for just long enough accidentally to destroy much of Middelburg, where the town seems to have been evacuated with nobody turning off the gas supply, with shocking results. Meanwhile, the main attack came through the Ardennes and, as usual, the towns of Bouillon, Dinant and Sedan became the focus of the world, with the Meuse again failing to provide any real barrier. In a particular piece of hydrographic absurdity, a key lock outside Dinant could not be destroyed without making the Meuse water-level drop so much that it could be waded elsewhere. In other words, the Meuse was only a real barrier to people who liked gesturing at maps. Having broken through, the Germans raced all the way to the coast, refuelling their vehicles from abandoned French petrol stations.

The British were hustled backwards, almost as though running the historical gauntlet, in a humiliating scramble, through towns that had a generation before been bywords for resolute sacrifice – Le Cateau, Ypres, St-Quentin, Amiens. I was really disturbed that through my own ignorance at the time, I had mucked around in Cassel, enjoying its quirky hilltop location and endives, without realizing that it had been flattened in an almost forgotten British rearguard action. The defenders had the grim experience of seeing the German army arrive at the hill's foot and then pour round it towards the coast.

Lord Gort was a terrible commander but he correctly embraced defeat and evacuation via Dunkirk, the single most important British decision of the war. The Channel ports became infernos. At night burning Calais could be seen from Dover. It could be argued that this showed the original 'Mechelen' German plan had been correct: first cut off Britain and then defeat France. As it turned out, the Germans had in fact committed simply a variant on the same mistake of 1914 – and, again, it would prove irreparable.

France had become what Léon Werth called, in his great account of the defeat *33 Days*, 'a kingdom of mattresses' as cars and wagons festooned with them blocked roads everywhere, one stalled car backing up miles of traffic randomly strafed.* Some eight million French eventually took to the road, deranged with terror from the stories of what had happened to the frozen Nord in 1914–18. One and a half million French soldiers went into POW camps. Ninety thousand French troops had been killed. Everyone was improvising as neither Germans nor French had begun to imagine such an outcome. The Germans set up an occupation regime in the Netherlands, took back Alsace-Lorraine (Alsace becoming part of Gau Westmark with Baden), absorbed Luxembourg (as part of Gau Moselland) and accidentally recreated much of the old Spanish

---

* Werth says so many startling things: 'Could what we call history be anything more than men's vainest illusions? What we attribute to history in wartime and to the powerful in peacetime, isn't it a sign of our own incapacity? We make history as the sick make sickness.'

Netherlands, clumping together Belgium, the Nord and the ports under military rule from Brussels. Coastal France and the country's top half were occupied and a painfully illegitimate collaborationist government based in Vichy came into existence.

Vichy was meant to represent a victory for common sense, sharing with Britain a realistic end to the war, conceding the inevitable after such a total defeat. Its officials ranted about France's military failure being the result of 'the nation's pacifist schoolteachers'. When the war in fact carried on, Vichy was suddenly left as an embarrassment to itself, clung to by exhausted and demoralized French citizens, but with none of the panoply of Catholic quietism it had been intended to embody: merely collaborationist rather than realistic. In Belgium, Leopold III had taken the same disastrous decision – assuming that he was falling in with a new sensibleness but, as it proved, instead trapping himself on the collaborationist side of the lines. Vichy printed banknotes with the compelling slogan *Industrial labour and farm labour: the two breasts of the republic* and experimented with the idea that Pétain's France would be Ceres to Hitler's Germany's Vulcan, a metaphor that does not bear thinking about further. It never stabilized but perhaps marginally shielded some of its citizens sometimes from the unfolding horrors across the new Empire.

With German failure to win the Battle of Britain, almost the entire region covered by this book became a prisoner of events it could not control, even the German areas. The one exception was Switzerland, where in July 1940 a solemn parade was held by General Guisan in the same meadow where in 1291 the cantons of Uri, Schwyz and Unterwalden had formed their historic association, at which he declared that Switzerland would resist invasion and would never surrender. The Swiss were probably lucky – with Britain undefeated and the invasion of the USSR the following summer, there was never an opportunity for Hitler to focus on Switzerland. Swiss seriousness remains impressive and maintained a justly less tainted form of 'Germandom', despite some grim compromises.

The whole of the rest of the Third Reich's existence became from late 1940 onwards, as we can now see, a series of chaotic improvisations, vicious lashings out and gigantic labour squads. It was only consistent in its relentless hunt for Jews, who hid as best they could, but with each twenty-four hours, over weeks, months and years, bringing a chance of betrayal. The Nazi Empire remained squarely German and unable to convince more than fringe figures in the western occupied areas to collaborate wholeheartedly, although there was plenty of opportunistic *ratisme*. But for the rest of 1940 and 1941 and perhaps later, the Third Reich seemed to be the permanent future and most lost hope.

The road to Strasbourg

I was once flying from London's City Airport to the clumsily named Basle-Mulhouse-Freiburg Airport, a frequent occurrence while researching this book. It was summer and cloudless and the small plane kept at a height where the landscape was almost hallucinatorily clear below. It was like one of Louis XIV's map tables in Lille. Almost the whole of Kent could be seen in one go, as a sort of fine matting of fields with the towns as black, sparkling bits of crust (black I assume as a side effect of each building's shadow). I could see the town where I grew up in west Kent and the town in east Kent where some close relatives lived. Several times a year we used to drive over there, along seemingly endless hilly, winding little roads, snaking through hop fields and orchards, in a car that was a wheeled prison cell of bickering, recrimination and occasional actual fights between the three of us children on the back seat, curses from the front and the invariable, stylish flourish of either me or my younger sister vomiting everywhere. And there, from the aeroplane, this Winder family Anabasis was shown as door-to-door a journey of about three feet.

As the plane droned on though, the scene became much more serious. I could see the coastal towns, Deal, Dover and Folkestone, and the Strait of Dover (the Pas de Calais). On the far side, the distinctive shapes of Dunkirk, Calais and Boulogne eerily complied with their appearance on maps. It was a genuinely frightening sight – the strait is just not very wide and, thinking about the summer of 1940, the history of the world hung on its existence and on the decisions and balances in technology, shipping, foresight, accident that kept it an effective barrier.

The Anglo-French military catastrophe doomed Europe to a new Dark Age – millions of lives ended under previously unimaginable circumstances as a result of the pitiful Anglo-French bungling and timidity that ended the one serious opportunity to defeat the Third Reich before it got far worse. All over northern France innumerable, mostly unrecorded acts of defiance or determination by small groups of French and British troops slowed up the Germans sufficiently to allow some 340,000 Allied soldiers to get out of Dunkirk and make it possible for the war to continue, but victory would now take another nearly five years and come at a staggering cost.

In his chilling autobiographical novel *Flight to Arras*, Antoine de Saint-Exupéry described flying over northern France three days before the evacuation at Dunkirk began. He was on a reconnaissance mission, but he understood it to be wholly quixotic – the French air force had been destroyed, the army beaten and there was nothing therefore to reconnoitre. He flew in a spirit of stoicism and self-mockery, assuming he would be killed. He describes Arras and the region around it as all on fire, 'dark red like iron on an anvil', and has the terrible idea that the flames are being fed by 'the sweat of men, the inventions of men, the art of men, the memories and heritage of men'. He made it back to his base and gave his report:

> 'Well, I . . . Ah! Fires. I saw fires. Is that of interest . . .?'
> 'No. Everything's on fire. What else?'

Some 800 ships were involved in getting the troops out of Dunkirk, but during the summer the entire coast was a mass of activity. Everywhere British demolition teams were destroying docks and blowing up oil tanks. From Brest to the Hook of Holland there were miserable arguments between soldiers who had been allies only days before as the British tried to damage and block everything they could. A specialized British ship went along the Channel lifting up and cutting all the communication cables between Britain and France. The Dutch royal family was got across, as was forty tons of gold from Rotterdam. In extraordinary scenes at Antwerp, a huge fleet was able to escape just ahead of the Germans: 26 merchantmen, 50 tugs and some 600 barges, dredgers and floating cranes: yet again, one of the world's greatest ports seized up.

Both sides were improvising like mad as, weeks before, every part of what happened at the end of May and in early June would have been inconceivable to any of the combatants. It is easy now to see that the Germans should have thrown everything at Dunkirk, but they were both dazed by their success and aware that much of France was still protected by a rapidly organizing Anglo-French force along the Somme. These days of indecision doomed them: France was defeated but, because of Dunkirk, Britain did not need to feel defeated, and the Germans were now obliged to cross the Strait. To do this they had to defeat the British air force, as a preliminary to defeating the British navy, as a preliminary to sending across a highly vulnerable flotilla of small ships filled with an expeditionary force to defeat a rearmed and much larger British army. As it was, even the first part of this sequence failed. Germany remained a regional power, boxed in by Britain's global resources, as in 1914–18. The Germans could see the White Cliffs, but they could not reach them. Admiral Raeder despaired – the German navy had only two, damaged battleships and ten destroyers, whereas the British navy had thirteen battleships and battlecruisers and a hundred and sixty-nine destroyers.

It is striking that the three key figures in the future of France all came from the far north. Pétain was born a few miles west of Lille, de Gaulle in Lille. The latter's birthplace in the city's northern suburbs is today maintained as an almost religious museum.* De Gaulle was married in Calais, a fact now marked there by huge, excruciatingly banal statues of Mr and Mrs de Gaulle walking along like a concrete Darby and Joan. Pétain gained his reputation fight-

---

* It is a wonderful place, preserving perfectly the genteel, ticking-clock, bluebottle-dying-slowly-behind-lace-curtains atmosphere of pre-1914 French bourgeois life.

ing on the Artois front. He and de Gaulle knew each other very well between the wars in the garrison at the Arras citadel.

Both Pétain and de Gaulle are, of course, still interesting figures, but perhaps the most astonishing of the three men who decided France's future was Philippe Leclerc de Hautecloque, born just south of the Somme, schooled in Amiens (home now to another truly crummy monument). He came from a grand and hyper-military family – direct ancestors had fought in two crusades, the Hundred Years War, the War of the Austrian Succession and Napoleon's campaigns, including Russia. One had fought in the war with Samory Touré, mentioned in chapter twelve, both his uncles had died in the First World War and his father had been strikingly heroic. He had himself been in the occupation force in Trier in the 1920s. He fought in 1940 at the Battle of Lille – a crucial action in holding the Germans away from Dunkirk – and was captured. He escaped twice, eventually getting over the Pyrenees to Lisbon and taking a neutral ship to London to join de Gaulle. De Gaulle appointed him ruler of French Cameroon. De Gaulle announced this with no authority whatsoever – but it was one of those acts, effectively pretending Pétain's France did not exist, that began the process of France's political and intellectual rescue. Leclerc (he adopted this name rather than calling himself de Hautecloque to protect his family from reprisals by the Germans) then set about pushing pro-Vichy forces out of Africa and securing the Central African colonies for the Free French. With an extraordinarily mixed bag of lightly armed flotsam and jetsam, Leclerc in early 1941 set out to invade Axis territory – the remote Italian Libyan oasis of Kufra.

The battle was a tiny one (300 to 400 men on either side) but won by the French. Leclerc then set out to redeem his country. At a time when the Germans seemed universally triumphant and their handful of surviving opponents struggled to imagine how they could be defeated, Leclerc simply announced to his ragtag group in the far depths of the Sahara that they would not stop fighting until the tricolour flew again on Strasbourg Cathedral. They took an oath to this effect and set off. It is unknown how many of those present were privately incredulous at the idea, but Leclerc did exactly as he had said. With delays and setbacks, Leclerc fought his way all the way to the Libyan coast; retrained and reorganized his vastly expanded army in Britain; landed at Utah Beach, fought his way east, liberated Paris, taking the German surrender there, repeatedly defeated German forces in eastern France, liberated Strasbourg on 23 November 1944 and raised the tricolour on the cathedral.

The long years of the war bored, terrified but also infantilized almost everyone. Individuals such as Leclerc, who were genuinely able to create their own freedom of action, were rare. What had been normal life before the summer of 1914, and glimpsed briefly again in the late 1920s and late 1930s (the latter, admittedly, in the context of the boom created by rearming), vanished. The British blockade and German U-boat counter-blockade paralysed commerce. Western coasts became military zones. It was a world substantially without men – almost two million French troops were captured in 1940 and the majority of them stayed captive in Germany for the duration (re-emerging as a shunned and humiliated reminder of defeat in 1945).* Some 600,000 young Frenchmen were forced to work in Germany, many in the Rhineland or Ruhr. They were often obliged to go there by their communities (sometimes in return for POWs being freed by the Germans) and the survivors were again often viewed with terrible lack of justice as tainted on their return. In some respects there was an odd congruence with the Rhineland Germans. There too normal life was lost sight of, most young men had vanished (and were, for the first time, being killed in the same huge numbers as in 1914–18 from autumn 1941 onwards). The brief, euphoric promise of June 1940, that through Hitler's genius a new, peaceful German Europe had been created at a minimal cost in lives, faded away.

The Low Countries found their great ports reduced mostly to military use and were themselves reduced to a state of near

---

* Much of France's future spent time in this captivity, none a great military loss to the Allies: Messaien, Althusser, Sartre, Mitterrand. Braudel began writing his masterpiece *The Mediterranean and the Mediterranean World in the Age of Philip II* in a camp at Mainz, mostly from memory.

inanition. In Belgium Jews were rounded up and placed in camps in Mechelen and elsewhere before transportation to the east. Of ninety thousand Jews only forty thousand survived. As in France, this was largely carried out by local collaborators. The Germans during the First World War had stirred up Flemish dislike of the francophone elite and did the same again now. There were many competing geographical fantasies. Some Flemish fascists wanted to recreate the Spanish/Burgundian state, incorporating the Netherlands, Belgium and the old Flemish areas of northern France which were now under German military rule from Brussels, including Lille and Arras. Himmler wanted something grander: an SS-run Reichsgau of Burgundy with its capital at Nanzig (Nancy), which would have recreated something like Charles the Bold's state plus much of Champagne. Kaiser Wilhelm had thought along similar lines, and once, before 1914, proposed this to Leopold II in return for Belgium allying with Germany. In both cases the idea was to tear off such a large piece of France that it could never recover as a great power – a fearful possibility that would have been entirely familiar to Louis XI and his predecessors. The permanent emergency of the war impeded such map-drawing fantasies until it was too late.

Armageddon

Perhaps the most disturbing aspect of writing this book was an intermittent sense of walking through urban spaces which had once been filled with absolute terror. What is now expressed as cheaply built, gloomy shopping streets or rows of identikit housing is the scar tissue left from in many cases just a few moments of devastation. A handful of cities were bombed repeatedly, but years could go by in nerve-racked safety, with futile air-raid drills and messing about with fire engines – and then catastrophe would hit. In the years between the fall of France and the landings in Sicily, the Western Allies realistically had only aerial bombing with which to threaten German Europe. The experience of the Blitz in Britain had shown both that people were strikingly resilient in the face of bombing and that dispersal of people and factories over thousands of square miles made bombing horrible, but militarily ineffective. Over the enormously greater area of Occupied Europe, it was vaguely assumed that the result would be different. In the end, bombing was crucial for unintended reasons: because it diverted huge German resources (the vast arrays of anti-aircraft guns alone could have won entire battles in the East) and ultimately ended the German air force as thousands of its planes and pilots were destroyed defending German air space: by D-Day the weapon that had terrified the Anglo-French forces in 1940 had more or less disappeared.

The sense of doom – that something irreparable once happened in a place – makes some famous historical towns more or less unvisit-able. Kleve is one of the most shocking. Eradicated by the RAF in a few minutes to allow the British army to march into Germany, it lost some 90 per cent of its buildings. Still you can walk along Duke Street and Castle Street and Swans Street, but the old processional way to the castle (itself rebuilt) is a grim parody of what was once there, with spaces which once contained fountains or markets just left blank or uneasily filled with modern replacements. The Rhine and Ruhr were deluged in incendiaries and high explosive because they were important centres of industry, but also because they were close by: it was easy to hit Cologne rather than important to do so. Some towns survived until very late in the fighting. As the Allies advanced in the final months of the war, the features which had once, centuries ago, given these Rhineland towns importance (a bit of high land for a cathedral or ramparts, control of a river crossing) allowed some random German officer to think of them again as strongpoints. The Allies could also, staring at their maps, make any town into a potential junction or concentration point, and so in a few hours or even minutes blameless spots like Worms, Freiburg or Colmar found themselves destroyed.

Both sides were aghast at the artistic and historical damage being done whereas the human cost was the point, but military necessity, added to a sense that the towns represented a historic

Germandom which had fed Nazism, won. The Swiss border created strange problems. The German enclave of Konstanz had no blackout, blazing with light throughout the war so that Allied bombers would assume it was part of Switzerland, rather than a prosperous, arms-producing German city. This worked very well. By sheer bad luck, the matching Swiss enclave in the German territory of Schaffhausen was mistaken by American bombers for Freiburg and devastated, with a hundred dead. I have spent some ten years off and on walking around these towns and it is impossible not to flinch at what the shoddy 1950s town centres of places such as Koblenz or Essen permanently memorialize. Towns were destroyed for different reasons. It is routine for anyone driving off the Dover ferry to shake their heads about what a dump Calais is as they drive through it, but there are serious reasons for this. It was flattened by the Germans in 1940, partly rebuilt, but then flattened by the Allies in 1944 simply as part of their plan to make the Germans think that the Allied invasion would land there.

One shocking surprise comes with the two Dutch cities just west of Kleve, Nijmegen and Arnhem. I was visiting Nijmegen to see the tiny remains of the Carolingian Palace (which had survived, tantalizingly, as a wonderfully gnarled pile until mostly knocked down in 1798) but this ancient, history-steeped place felt as bad as Koblenz. This surprise simply came from my own ignorance, as the town centre, it turned out, had been eradicated by American bombers in 1944, mistaking it for Kleve. Some 750 people were killed. Arnhem was, famously, the focus of the disastrous Operation Market Garden. In film and popular memory, this was about the seizure of the Rhine bridge there. But the fighting was all over the western suburbs, with countless houses destroyed (some of the rebuilt ones have plaques on them describing their specific fates). After the Allies were defeated, the city's population were expelled by the Germans and it became a military zone. When finally liberated by the First Canadian Army in April 1945 Arnhem had effectively ceased to exist.

Everywhere liberation by the Allies was part of a terrifyingly random pattern, with some towns spared and others fought for. The French, Belgian and Dutch citizens were already living in overwhelmingly distorted communities, riven with distrust, black-marketeering, hunger, violence and ideological and familial ruin. The sequence in which the Allied armies landed at the five D-Day beaches (from west to east: US, US, UK, UK, Canada) dictated the final eleven months of the war, with the US forces liberating most of France and the British and Canadians heading north-east. Each town or village was either eradicated or swept through with cheers and flowers, depending on whether or not the Germans decided to defend it. The Canadians found themselves entangled in particularly horrible fighting along western canals, clearing the defenders from the opposite shore with flame-thrower tanks. Some ninety thousand German troops defended Zeeland, blocking Allied use of the Scheldt and the opening up of Antwerp. This was probably the most effective part of the Germans' Atlantic Wall and is still today littered with freakish chunks of metal and concrete left from the fighting. In the same place where the hopeless Walcheren expedition of 1809 had floundered, the Canadians and British took some thirteen thousand casualties to defeat the fanatical (and completely pointless) defence. In a horrific coda to the fighting, it turned out that various dykes had been damaged and subtly weakened. In the Great North Sea Storm of 1953 this proved fatal as they gave way, drowning fifteen hundred Zeelanders.

Everywhere the Allies liberated, a divide opened up between those who had collaborated and those who had resisted. In the post-war period many towns had different cafes for those who had been on either side. Families were split, administrations turned upside down. Released POWs would find themselves in places they no longer recognized, sometimes with wives who had long settled down with someone else. One final collaborationist flourish was the SS Charlemagne Division of French Fascist volunteers. The number of men actively fighting with the Germans was never huge – the 'Rexist' Belgian leader Léon Degrelle's Walloon Legion was only a few thousand men, mostly killed on the Eastern Front.* The Char-

---

* Degrelle, Bouillon's most contemptible citizen, managed to get to Spain and live there unrepentantly and unpunished to a great age.

lemagne Division was almost self-consciously set up to perform a last stand in 1944, filled with brutalized scrapings from the collapsing Vichy regime, while the senior political leaders escaped to the Swabian castle of Sigmaringen to await their fates. Members of the Charlemagne Division found a sort of martyrdom as the very last defenders of Hitler's bunker. I mention it here because of its curious badge. It was split down the middle – on one half there were fleurs-de-lys, and on the other the old Imperial eagle: in other words it was expressing the union of West Francia and East Francia, with the Third Reich finally crushing within the line that ran down the badge's middle the now cowed and absorbed territory of Lotharingia. But yet again – as the division's last members were shot or went into many years of Soviet captivity – this turned out to be premature.

Charlemagne comes home

I once spent a few days in the small Ardennes town of Saint-Hubert, north-east of Sedan. It is an absurdly interesting place, built around a huge shrine to St Hubert, the patron saint of hunters, who saw a vision of a stag with Christ crucified shining between its antlers, with the church as a result stuffed with stag motifs. It is a serious Catholic site, but also somewhere with fun ceremonies in the church involving woodsmen in special uniforms blowing horns. An unimprovable woodland park filled with groinking and rooting wild boar completes the picture, plus a superb restaurant that converts the boar into small, succulent slices, cooked with forest fruit. I felt myself becoming ever more bluff, reactionary, devout, muddy-booted as the days went by, thinking about buying a serge cloak and perhaps a small knife with which to whittle wooden duck-calls. Nowhere could really be more harmless or local, a summa of the hedgehog-like manner of so many of the places I have been to. I was just visiting a small church on the town's outskirts, cheerfully regretting that I did not have a hat which I could doff, when I realized there was something wrong with the building. Far from being ancient, it was oddly new. With a sinking heart I realized that my silly idyll was, as usual, going to be invaded by the twentieth century. It turned out that during the Battle of the Bulge a random V-1 killed an family living next to the church and destroyed its west end.

The Ardennes region drifts around between Dinant and Aachen, Prüm and Bouillon, Luxembourg City and Sedan. It is a seemingly endless sequence of wooded valleys, with the logic of bus routes and roads incomprehensible from ground level. At its heart lies the wonderful town of Stavelot, an ancient abbey, famous for centuries, but chiefly for its abbot having been the great Wibold, counsellor to three emperors, compulsive letter-writer and ambassador to Byzantium. Stavelot is also the home of an inn which the young Apollinaire had to abscond from because his mother could not pay the bill. This slightly thin link has been enough to create a superb Apollinaire study room, with many editions of his poems, and packed with photos of this enchanting, heavy-drinking man (when he was in Stavelot he still had his original Polish name of Albert Kostrowicki – he was known to his friends as Albert Cointreau-Whiskey).

The Battle of the Bulge raged throughout the area but Stavelot was as far as the Germans got. They made it into the main square, massacred civilians and were in turn massacred by American troops as they tried to wade across the river. After the initial shock of the German attack the Americans realized that tanks on these narrow roads could be made helpless by using dynamite and artillery to bring down trees – each winding route becoming choked with trunks and each small bridge blown up. The original German plan was to punch through to Dinant, cross the Meuse and race through Brussels to Antwerp, splitting the Allied armies and then destroying them to the north and south at leisure. The plan was ludicrous and the Germans came nowhere near Antwerp, but it was a last frenzy of staggering violence. German casualties and loss of equipment were so huge that it made the rest of the Allied advance east relatively straightforward.

Hitler was obsessed with Antwerp. The enormous number of

troops bottled up in Zeeland were there to prevent the port opening to supply the Allies. V-weapons rained down on the town.
Some twelve thousand V-1s (cruise missiles) were fired from Holland and Germany into Belgium from October 1944 onwards, and
sixteen hundred V-2s (rockets). Many of the former were shot
down, but enough got through – enough to pointlessly kill a family
in Saint-Hubert, for example. The worst disaster was when a rocket
hit the Rex Cinema in Antwerp, during a Gary Cooper film, and
killed 271 Belgians and 300 Allied soldiers.

This miserable, futile fighting against overwhelming Allied
strength was, of course, happening in exactly the same place where
everything had begun back in May 1940, a moral world away. The
technological changes were great but the place was the same – and
with the terrible thought that back then, more imaginative Allied
planning could have just as easily destroyed the German tanks lumbering along these tiny roads through these same woods. But
instead, the under-strength French reserve units had sat on the
Meuse and awaited their fate. I have not been able to find out, but
presumably there must have been a number of German officers and
soldiers during the Battle of the Bulge who had been there also in
1940 and wondered if the fate of the world really was doomed to
be repeatedly played out in these obscure valleys.

Once Hitler had killed himself and Germany surrendered, the
Western Allies divided western Germany, still following the logic
of where their armies had been positioned back at Normandy – so
the British took the north, the Americans the south. Belgium
quickly grabbed back Malmédy and Eupen, just to ensure that they
remained a needlessly tri-lingual state. The French took back
Alsace-Lorraine again and were given two great blocks of territory
along the Rhine which happily revived Ludovican and Napoleonic
fantasies, with Freiburg becoming a major French military base (the
by now President de Gaulle would fly there when he panicked
about his safety during the 1968 uprising). In a miracle of geographical obscurantism the tiny German enclave of Büsingen, a
piece of land on the Rhine surrounded by the Swiss canton of
Schaffhausen, fell under French control. Special arrangements had

to be made to allow the transit of French troops through Swiss territory to Büsingen to give its handful of inhabitants a taste of firm Allied government. The French also indulged in an appealingly retro way in their traditional activity of trying to prise off the Saarland. Despite initial American support, this went nowhere for the traditional reason that the German-speaking inhabitants wanted to be part of Germany. This was part of a wider plan by Jean Monnet to restart the French economy by absorbing much of the left bank of the Rhine and the Ruhr, using a million or so German prisoners to do much of the work. As in 1918–20, but over an even wider area, large parts of Europe were simply an enormous mess of rubble, toxins and dislocation – it would take years just to make them safe and (where they still existed) to get their populations back in the right places. As late as August 2017, sixty thousand people were evacuated from Frankfurt when an unexploded RAF Blockbuster bomb was found at a building site.

I was once walking south of Dinant along the Meuse. It is impossible on such a walk not to think about this patch of land's role in 1914 and in 1940 and in winter 1944 as, once Antwerp became clearly too far away, Dinant became the goal of the last German dash (it failed – and what would they have done when they reached it?). The Meuse has always been a grand river, but as a military obstacle just not very helpful. The high hills on either side were militarily ideal though, and it was possible to see on a map that once these hills were broken through the rolling farmland beyond was indefensible. To the north of where I was walking was the now tiny town of Bouvignes, with which Dinant had once had its ruinous feud in the late Middle Ages, as well as the fatal lock which allowed the Germans over in 1940. As I headed south though, leaving behind me the Charles de Gaulle Bridge (where he was shot and nearly killed in 1914), I was amazed to find a colossal motorway bridge soaring high over the Meuse canyon. Given the dozy, riverine atmosphere it seemed to have landed from a different movie. I felt I was staring witlessly at something I could not understand, like someone transported from an earlier century. One moment I was thinking of Patinir's landscapes of Dinant and its medieval

metalwork and unpleasant hard cookies, and then here I was gawping at this clean-lined fantasy in reinforced concrete. It turned out
that it is called the Charlemagne Viaduct and is the highest in Belgium. The viaduct is strangely named as, if asked out of the blue,
you would associate Charlemagne more with chopping up pagan
Saxons or lying in a pile of Avar gold than with this engineering
marvel, but in other ways, of course, it is an inspired name.

This refreshed and overhauled symbolism around Charlemagne
came together in the early 1950s. It turned out that the future did
not lie in France trying to pinch places like the Saarland, but in the
pooling of resources and sovereignty. Rather than thinking puni-
tively again, Monnet and others decided that, starting with steel
and coal, there was a potentially serious gain from progressively
crossing out the ways in which countries had always been nation-
ally aggressive. It helped to be operating under a combination of
the fairly benign aegis of the US and of the very malign threat of
the USSR. It will not be a surprise to the reader that I think of this
in terms of Lotharingia. The six Lotharingian or part-Lotharingian
successor states – the Netherlands, Belgium, Luxembourg, France,
Germany and Italy – having been beaten to the ground by the horrors of nationalism and ideology decided to stop any further enmity
by joining together. They would go on to make three core Lotharingian cities into their capitals: Brussels, Luxembourg and
Strasbourg. In addition the Charlemagne Prize was set up by the
City of Aachen to be awarded to whoever its judges viewed as
contributing most to the promotion of unity in Europe. And that is
probably as good a place as any to end.

Postscript

More than with any of my previous books I have felt constrained by format – *Lotharingia* could both have been twice the length and, indeed, made the opposite arguments to the ones made here, and still I would not have used up the material in my ever more incoherent heaps of notes. I wanted to write a lot more on the Emperors and the 'sacred landscape' of the Rhine; on the wonderful Clara Peeters, a great Antwerp painter of still-lifes from the early seventeenth century, who fell victim to the whole book already ballooning helplessly in its coverage of that period; I had assumed that at the centre of the book would sit Pieter Brueghel the Elder and Hans Holbein the Younger, both of whom I have venerated ever since I can remember, but about whom in both cases it turned out, to my own horror, I had nothing of any originality to say. The Dreyfus Affair, the Field of the Cloth of Gold, abortive English invasions, nothing really about Namur despite loving the town, the drift of gamelan into the West, Lorelei, the statue in Heidelberg showing Prometheus and the Eagle in a clearly and uniquely erotic context, Alpinism, how Freddie Mercury and Vladimir Nabokov just missed each other in Montreux: it's hopeless really.

I most regret failing to give space (because the twentieth century was already stuffed to the ceiling) to the four great Belgians who have at different times influenced me and who were all born within a few years of one another at the turn of the century: Henri Michaux, Georges Simenon, René Magritte and Georges Rémy (Hergé). Michaux and Simenon simply frighten me – in their very different ways their obsession with isolation and fear seems (to me at any rate) entangled in Belgian neutralism, occupation and terror. Simenon grew up in Liège and once, somewhat feverish, I came to realize that his books somehow expressed the spirit of the anomalous old

Prince-Bishopric of Liège. With his characters all oddly isolated and free-floating and doing the most nihilistic things, I cannot read his novels without thinking of the strange, crushed broken-up shape of the bishopric on old maps. Aside from his more famous Maigret novels, Simenon also managed to write perhaps the greatest novels both of the Exodus of 1940 (*The Train*) and of the Occupation (*The Snow is Dirty*). Michaux is one of the most alarming figures of the twentieth century – equally brilliant as a poet and painter, he wanted to create in both mediums 'a nervous projection screen': 'I wish I could paint man when out of himself, paint his space'. He could also be funny about Belgium in a ranting, Thomas Bernhard sort of way: 'This sad, over-peopled land . . . muddy countryside squelching underfoot, terrain for frogs . . . no wildness. What is wild in this country? Wherever you thrust your hand you come upon beets or potatoes, or a turnip, or a rutabaga . . . A few dirty, sluggish, devastated rivers with no place to go.' Having spent so long hypnotized by and over-reliant on him, it was a little confusing to take the pilgrimage to his birthplace in Namur and find it was now a branch of the Spanish clothing chain Mango.

Magritte was easy to miss out as I don't understand now why I used to think he was a good painter. Hergé though is a quite different story, with the *Tintin* books deeply entangled in every stage of my life and my relationship with my father and with my own sons – indeed I have written this paragraph just after spending a happy afternoon with one adult son discussing the respective merits of *The Cigars of the Pharaoh* and *The Red Sea Sharks*, the latest instalment in a critical process which has for me been fairly continuous over half a century. In our household these books are something like sacred texts, with that famous crux lurking in *The Black Island* where Tintin hops on a ferry to get to England. To notice this was, for all young readers in the United Kingdom, a faith-crisis of a kind familiar to any number of Rhineland sects over the centuries, forcing a haggard reassessment of their lives, as the boy journalist blows his universalism: in a single frame revealing himself not to be a plucky, if oddly dressed, British youth but a mere, dubious Continental.

I was reading *The Crab with the Golden Claws* to our eldest child when he was so small he had difficulty sitting upright, or even looking in the right direction. I had always wanted to write an entire book about Tintin and the essential Belgianness crucial to his work, only to find that Tom McCarthy and Michael Parr had written such excellent books about him that mine would have been filled merely with limp paraphrases of their work. His publisher, Casterman, being based in Tournai was my own key recent realization, making Hergé and Tintin (and Snowy) perhaps Lotharingia's leading honorary citizens.

I ended the writing of *Lotharingia* under a variety of glum circumstances, with two uncles – idols of my childhood and beyond – dying in quick succession, followed by my father, who died after a long and debilitating illness. These events – combined with children leaving home who, when I started writing this trilogy many years ago, used to hop up and down in their pyjamas to mark my return from some far-flung bit of Swabia – have put me in a somewhat introspective mood. The preoccupation in this book with the instability of dynastic change turns out to be the universal human experience: with everyone going through the same dismay as the seemingly permanent protective familial roofs and walls are randomly dismantled.

My father's death took me back to many things, not least the family Alsatian holiday with which the first of these books, *Germania*, started – a trip on a barge down a murky, vermin-filled canal which was meant to take us to Strasbourg, but which ended prematurely at a tunnel blocked up with ancient planking and rather *Scooby-Doo* warning signs. The journey managed to be a trial for us all, with my mother finally reduced to a truly frightening silence by my father's various planning failures. But in the end it was fascinating, and I always date my own serious interest in history and art to at last getting to Strasbourg, the car retrieved, the barge abandoned. These family holidays, to Brittany, to Normandy, to Alsace, were always brilliantly stage-managed (albeit with setbacks), with my mother responsible for choosing the books we read and the food we ate and both parents collaborating in a series of historical coups (spooky castles, grand palaces, funny-smelling old streets) which have formed the basis for my entire adult life.

One small story about my father on this Alsatian trip: one of the highlights was a visit to the Maginot Line. Only one section was then open to the public and only with a guide and with written permission from the military. My father, an officer in the Royal Naval Reserve, was in ecstasies about this process. He found the name of the relevant French colonel and the combination of military protocol and the opportunity of writing in 'official' French over several drafts made him a pig in clover. I remember his reading out various versions in an exaggerated French accent. *Mon colonel? – Mon cher colonel? – Je vous prie d'agréer, monsieur le colonel, mes salutations distinguées? – Ils ne passeront pas, Christopher Winder, lieutenant de vaisseau?** The process of writing the letter drew on my father's interest in military matters, protocol, foreign customs and his happy ability both to respect such things and lampoon them at the same time. My father may only have been in the Reserve but, after all, a French officer charged with answering letters from tourists would be no Joffre. My parents had a lifelong enthusiasm for France which was, as so often for the English, mixed in with incredulity and scepticism and I can still remember their cheerful laughter at receiving the official letter back from the colonel's office, which had a formal camp floridity they had not dared to dream of.

The Maginot fort was predictably macabre – an underground railway, the smell of cold damp and mossy concrete, rust, the empty gun emplacements, a mess hall decorated at some point with now fading paintings of Disney cartoon characters. But, as with the centre of Strasbourg, it was for me a great gift: a lifetime's supply of things to think about loaded up in a couple of hours.

During the protracted period leading to my father's death, I felt for the first time a wish to wander around the part of south London I had spent the first five years of my life, in Norwood Junction. I was

---

* He ended up as Commander (*capitaine de frégate!*), with a devastating uniform.

able always to point to an exact time I had left as I never went to school there and we must therefore have moved just before this unwelcome innovation in my circumstances. Walking around Norwood now it was all strangely unchanged, particularly the silhouettes of the streets around our old house, where the relationship between different towers, fences and roofs were exactly fitted to my memory. I was even able to notice that the huge cross on a Methodist Church which had been neon when we were there, blazing down into the valley, had been carried over into a replacement building but in more discreet stone. I came to Norwood now with more cultural knowledge than I had then access to. It was exciting to walk again to Crystal Palace to see the great Victorian dinosaur sculptures, no less peculiar and inspiring than then. Clearly my lifelong love affair with ichthyosaurs was already cemented at a tiny age. At the time I could not, of course, fully appreciate just how Lotharingian a spot Norwood Junction was: with the exiled Zola living just up the road, Apollinaire zooming through in pursuit of an English girl and Pissarro escaping there from the Franco-Prussian War, improbably immortalizing Norwood in a sequence of understandably slightly boring paintings.

I had a recurring image of the hill from Norwood Junction station to our house as being long and arduous, but of course this was only in relation to my then much smaller legs. I also remembered the library, which must then have been brand new, and which is still there, in the street between the railway line and our own flat. Part of this memory of labouring up the hill was a clear image of holding a library copy of *Tintin in Tibet*. I wondered about false memory – why did I think I had a copy of *Tintin in Tibet* when I had not gone to school yet and so could not read it? But, of course, I realized with a sudden, happy lift, my father had read it *to* me.

Bibliography

David Abrams and others, *The Rough Guide to France, fourteenth edition* (London, 2016)

Willem Aerts and others, *From Quinten Metsyijs to Peter Paul Rubens* (Antwerp, 2009)

Hugh Aldersey-Williams, *The Adventures of Sir Thomas Browne in the 21st Century* (London, 2015)

Robert Bartlett, *The Making of Europe: Conquest, Colonization and Cultural Change, 950–1350* (Harmondsworth, 1993)

Robert Bartlett, *Why Can the Dead Do Such Great Things?: Saints and Worshippers from the Martyrs to the Reformation* (Princeton, 2013)

Antony Beevor, *Ardennes 1944* (London, 2015)

David Bell, *The First Total War: Napoleon's Europe and the Birth of Modern Warfare* (London, 2005)

Marina Belozerskaya, *The Medici Giraffe and other Tales of Exotic Animals and Power* (London, 2006)

The Rule of St Benedict, trans. Carolinne White (London, 2008)

John Berger, *Albrecht Dürer* (London, 1995)

Florence Bertrand and others, *Le Territoire Contesté de Moresnet-Neutre, 1816–1919* (La Calamine, no date)

Jeremy Black, *Eighteenth Century Europe, 1700–1789* (Basingstoke, 1990)

Jeremy Black, *European Warfare, 1660–1815* (London, 1994)

David Blackbourn, *The Conquest of Nature: Water, Landscape and the Making of Modern Germany* (New York, 2006)

David Blackbourn, *Marpingen: Apparitions of the Virgin Mary in Nineteenth Century Germany* (New York, 1993)

T. C. W. Blanning, *The Culture of Power and the Power of Culture: Old Regime Europe, 1660–1789* (Oxford, 2002)

T. C. W. Blanning, *Joseph II* (Harlow, 1994)

Tim Blanning, *The Pursuit of Glory: Europe, 1648–1815* (London, 2007)

T. C. W. Blanning, *Reform and Revolution in Mainz, 1743–1803* (Cambridge, 1974)

Gerold Bönnen and others, *Schrei nach Gerechtigkeit: Leben am Mittelrhein am Vorabend der Reformation* (Mainz, 2015)

Shirley Harrold Bonner, *Fortune, Misfortune, Fortifies One: Margaret of Austria, Ruler of the Low Countries, 1507–1530* (CreateSpace reprint, 2015)

C. L. R. Boxer, *The Dutch Seaborne Empire, 1600–1800* (Harmondsworth, 1965)

Fernand Braudel, *Civilization and Capitalism, fifteenth–eighteenth century: The Structures of Everyday Life*, trans. Siân Reynolds (London, 1982)

Fernand Braudel, *Civilization and Capitalism, fifteenth–eighteenth century: The Wheels of Commerce*, trans. revised by Siân Reynolds (London, 1981)

Michael Broers, *Europe under Napoleon, 1799–1815* (London, 1996)

Sir Thomas Browne, *Selected Writings* (Chicago, 1968)

Yves Buffetaut and Maud Dagmay-Lacment, *Le Nord en Guerre* (Louviers, 2014)

Malcolm Bull, *The Mirror of the Gods: Classical Mythology in Renaissance Art* (London, 2005)

Benedikt Burkard and Céline Lebret, *Gefangene Bilder: Wissenschaft und Propaganda im Ersten Weltkrieg* (Petersberg, 2014)

G. J. Caesar, *The Conquest of Gaul*, trans. S. A. Hanford and Jane F. Gardner (Harmondsworth, 1982)

Rachel Chrastil, *Organizing for War: France 1870–1914* (Baton Rouge, 2010)

Rachel Chrastil, *The Siege of Strasbourg* (Cambridge, MA, 2014)

Christopher Clark, *Iron Kingdom: The Rise and Downfall of Prussia* (London, 2006)

Richard Cobb, *French and Germans, Germans and French* (Hanover, NH, 1983)

Alexander Cockburn, *Corruptions of Empire* (New York, 1988)

Roger Collins, *Charlemagne* (Basingstoke, 1998)

Philippe de Commynes, *Memoirs: The Reign of Louis XI, 1461–83*, trans. Michael Jones (Harmondsworth, 1972)

Philip Conisbee (ed.), *Georges de la Tour and His World* (Washington, DC, 1996)

David Crane, *Empires of the Dead* (London, 2013)

Charles D. Cuttler, *Northern Painting: From Pucelle to Brueghel* (New York, no date)

The Poems of John Dryden, ed. John Sargeaunt (London, 1910)

Martin Dunford, Phil Lee and Suzanne Morton-Taylor, *The Rough Guide to the Netherlands, 6th edition* (London, 2013)

Martin Dunford, Phil Lee and Emma Thomson, *The Rough Guide to Belgium, 6th edition* (London, 2015)

Catharine Tatiana Dunlop, *Cartophilia: Maps and the Search for Identity in the French-German Borderland* (Chicago, 2015)

Robert S. Duplessis, *Transitions to Capitalism in Early Modern Europe* (Cambridge, 1997)

Albrecht Dürer, *Diary of His Journey to the Netherlands*, introduced by J.-A. Goris and G. Marlier (London, 1971)

Einhard and Notker the Stammerer, *Two Lives of Charlemagne*, trans. David Ganz (London, 2008)

Carlos M. N. Eire, *Reformations: The Early Modern World, 1450–1650* (New Haven, 2016)

Amos Elon, *The Pity of It All: A Portrait of Jews in Germany, 1743–1933* (London, 2003)

Richard J. Evans, *The Pursuit of Power: Europe, 1815–1914* (London, 2016)

James Farr, *Artisans in Europe, 1300–1914* (Cambridge, 2000)

Stefan Fischer, *Hieronymus Bosch* (Köln, 2016)

John B. Freed, *Frederick Barbarossa: The Prince and the Myth* (New Haven, 2016)

Johannes Fried, *Charlemagne* (Cambridge, MA, 2016)

Robert Gerwarth, *The Vanquished: Why the First World War Failed to End, 1917–1923* (London, 2016)

Robert Gildea, *Children of the Revolution: The French, 1799–1914* (London, 2008)

Johann Wolfgang von Goethe, *Campaign in France* and *Siege of Mainz*, trans. Ricardo Cunha Mattos Portella (Amazon, 2012)

Lionel Gossman, *Basel in the Age of Burckhardt: A Study in Unseasonable Ideas* (Chicago, 2000)

Ruth Harris, *The Man on Devil's Island: Alfred Dreyfus and the Affair that Divided France* (London, 2010)

Marjolein 't Hart, *The Dutch Wars of Independence* (Abingdon, 2014)

Holger H. Herwig, *The First World War: Germany and Austria-Hungary, 1914–1918* (London, 1997)

Hildegard von Bingen, *Selected Writings*, trans. Mark Atherton (London, 2001)

Hans Holbein, *The Dance of Death*, ed. Ulinka Rublack (London, 2016)

Alistair Horne, *The Price of Glory: Verdun 1916* (London, 1962)

J. Huizinga, *The Waning of the Middle Ages* (Harmondsworth, 1990)

Samuel Humes, *Belgium: Long United, Long Divided* (London, 2014)

Jonathan Israel, *The Dutch Republic* (Oxford, 1998)

Jonathan Israel, *Revolutionary Ideas* (Princeton, 2014)

Emilia Jamroziak, *The Cistercian Order in Medieval Europe* (Abingdon, 2013)

Lisa Jardine, *The Awful End of Prince William the Silent* (London, 2005)

Mark Jarrett, *The Congress of Vienna and Its Legacy* (London, 2013)

Maya Jasanoff, *The Dawn Patrol: Joseph Conrad in a Global World* (London, 2017)

William Chester Jordan, *The Great Famine: Northern Europe in the Early Fourteenth Century* (Princeton, 1996)

Rod Kedward, *La vie en bleu: France and the French Since 1900* (London, 2005)

Maurice Keen, *The Penguin History of Medieval Europe* (Harmondsworth, 1969)

Thomas à Kempis, *The Imitation of Christ*, trans. Robert Jeffery (London, 2013)

Paul Kennedy, *The Rise and Fall of British Naval Mastery* (Harmondsworth, 1976)

Joseph Leo Koerner, *Bosch and Bruegel: From Enemy Painting to Everyday Life* (Princeton, 2016)

Henk Leenaers (ed.), *The Water Atlas of the Netherlands* (Groningen, 2012)

Herta Lepie and Georg Minkenberg, *The Cathedral Treasury of Aachen* (Regensburg, 2013)

David Lowenthal, *The Past Is a Foreign Country – Revisited* (Cambridge, 2015)

John A. Lynn, *The Wars of Louis XIV, 1667–1714* (Harlow, 1999)

Thomas Babington Macaulay, *The History of England*, vol. 1 (London, 1906)

Diarmaid MacCulloch, *Reformation: Europe's House Divided, 1490–1700* (London, 2004)

Patrick McGuinness, *Other People's Countries: A Journey into Memory* (London, 2014)

Leo McKinstry, *Operation Sealion* (London, 2014)

Gordon McLachlan, *The Rough Guide to Germany, 6th edition* (London, 2004)

Helen McPhail, *The Long Silence: The Tragedy of Occupied France in World War I* (London, 2014)

Fiona Maddocks, *Hildegard of Bingen: The Woman of Her Age* (London, 2001)

Lauro Martines, *Furies: War in Europe, 1450–1700* (New York, 2013)

Laurent Martino, *Histoire chronologique de la Lorraine* (Nancy, 2010)

Yair Mintzker, *The Defortification of the German City, 1689–1866* (Cambridge, 2012)

Pankaj Mishra, *From the Ruins of Empire* (London, 2012)

James M. Murray, *Bruges, Cradle of Capitalism, 1280–1390* (Cambridge, 2005)

Susie Nash, *Northern Renaissance Art* (Oxford, 2008)

The Nibelungenlied, trans. A. T. Hatto (Harmondsworth, 1965)

Philip Nord, *France 1940: Defending the Republic* (New Haven and London, 2015)

Eljas Oksanen, *Flanders and the Anglo-Norman World, 1066–1216* (Cambridge, 2012)

Jürgen Osterhammel, *The Transformation of the World*, trans. Patrick Camiller (Princeton and London, 2014)

Richard Overy, *The Bombing War: Europe 1939–1945* (London, 2013)

Geoffrey Parker, *The Army of Flanders and the Spanish Road, 1567–1659,* 2nd edition (Cambridge, 2004)

Geoffrey Parker, *Global Crisis: War, Climate Change and Catastrophe in the Seventeenth Century* (New Haven, 2013)

Geoffrey Parker, *The Grand Strategy of Philip II* (New Haven, 1998)

David Parrott, *The Business of War: Military Enterprise and Military Revolution in Early Modern Europe* (Cambridge, 2012)

Matthias de Poorter and others, *L'odyssée des animaux: Les peintres animaliers flamands du XVIIᵉ siècle* (Ghent, 2016)

David Potter, *War and Government in the French Provinces: Picardy, 1470–1560* (Cambridge, 1993)

Timothy Reuter, *Germany in the Early Middle Ages, 800–1056* (Harlow, 1991)

John Richards, *Landsknecht Soldier, 1486–1560* (Oxford, 2002)

John C. G. Röhl, *Wilhelm II: Into the Abyss of War and Exile, 1900–1941* (Cambridge, 2014)

Ulinka Rublack, *Dressing Up: Cultural Identity in Renaissance Europe* (Oxford, 2010)

Ulinka Rublack, *Reformation Europe* (Cambridge, 2005)

Steven Runciman, *A History of the Crusades: 1: The First Crusade* (Cambridge, 1951)

Steven Runciman, *A History of the Crusades: 2: The Kingdom of Jerusalem* (Cambridge, 1952)

Antione de Saint-Exupéry, *Flight to Arras,* trans. William Rees (London, 1995)

Simon Schama, *Patriots and Liberators: Revolution in the Netherlands, 1780–1813* (London, 1992)

Russell Shorto, *Amsterdam* (London, 2013)

Larry Silver, *Marketing Maximilian: The Visual Ideology of a Holy Roman Emperor* (Princeton, 2008)

Brendan Simms, *Britain's Europe* (London, 2016)

Brendan Simms, *The Struggle for Mastery in Germany, 1779–1850* (Basingstoke, 1998)

Brendan Simms, *Three Victories and a Defeat: The Rise and Fall of the First British Empire* (London, 2007)

Jeffrey Chipps Smith, *The Northern Renaissance* (London, 2004)

Julia M. H. Smith, *Europe after Rome: A New Cultural History, 500–1000* (Oxford, 2005)

Peter C. Smith, *Hold the Narrow Sea: Naval Warfare in the English Channel, 1939–1945* (Annapolis, 1984)

Tobias Smollett, *Travels Through France and Italy* (Oxford, 1981)

The Song of Roland, trans. Glyn S. Burgess (Harmondsworth, 1990)

Marie-Isabelle Soupart and Philippe Hiegel, *Metz Cathedral*, trans. Ray Beaumont-Craggs (Metz, 2010)

Jonathan Steinberg, *Why Switzerland?* (Cambridge, 1996)

Laurence Sterne, *A Sentimental Journey* (London, 2005)

Laurence Sterne, *Tristram Shandy* (Harmondsworth, 1997)

James Stewart, Neville Walker and Christian Williams, *The Rough Guide to Germany, 2nd edition* (London, 2012)

R. C. Strong and J. A. Van Dorsten, *Leicester's Triumph* (Leiden, 1962)

Jonathan Sumption, *Edward III* (London, 2016)

Michael Tanner, *Wagner* (London, 1996)

A. J. P. Taylor, *The First World War* (London, 1954)

A. J. P. Taylor, *The Struggle for Mastery in Europe, 1848–1918* (Oxford, 1954)

Matthew Teller, *The Rough Guide to Switzerland, 4th edition* (London, 2010)

Ann Thwaite, *Glimpses of the Wonderful: The Life of Philip Henry Gosse* (London, 2002)

Daniel Todman, *Britain's War: Into Battle 1937–1941* (London, 2016)

James D. Tracy, *Emperor Charles V, Impresario of War* (Cambridge, 2002)

Jenny Uglow, *Hogarth* (London, 1997)

Richard Vaughan, *Charles the Bold* (Woodbridge, 2002)

Richard Vaughan, *John the Fearless* (Woodbridge, 2002)

Richard Vaughan, *Philip the Bold* (Woodbridge, 2002)

Richard Vaughan, *Philip the Good* (Woodbridge, 2002)

Richard Vaughan, *Valois Burgundy* (Harmondsworth, 1975)

Richard Vinen, *The Unfree French: Life under the Occupation* (London, 2006)

David Vital, *A People Apart: The Jews in Europe, 1789–1939* (Oxford, 1999)

Alexander Watson, *Ring of Steel: Germany and Austria-Hungary at War, 1914–1918* (London, 2014)

Geoffrey Wawro, *The Franco-Prussian War* (Cambridge, 2003)

C. V. Wedgwood, *The Thirty Years War* (London, 1999)

Volker Weidermann, trans. Carol Brown Janeway, *Summer Before the Dark* (London, 2016)

Peter S. Wells, *Barbarians to Angels: The Dark Ages Reconsidered* (New York, 2008)

Charles West, *Reframing the Feudal Revolution: Political and Social Transformation between Marne and Moselle, c.800–c.1100* (Cambridge, 2013)

Joachim Whaley, *Germany and the Holy Roman Empire*, two vols (Cambridge, 2012)

Niels Wilcken, *Metz et Guillaume II* (Metz, 2013)

Peter H. Wilson, *War, State and Society in Württemberg, 1677–1793*

Adam Zamoyski, *Phantom Terror: The Threat of Revolution and the Repression of Liberty, 1789–1848* (London, 2014)

Émile Zola, *La Débâcle*, trans. Elinor Dorday (Oxford, 2000)

I must also acknowledge the superb 1:410 000 map created by the Institut National de l'Information Géographique et Forestière to mark the centenary of the First World War, showing the Western Front in remarkable detail, which I have referred to over and over again, not just in relation to the fighting but also for Lotharingian issues of many kinds.

Illustrations

The endpapers show a detail from Pieter Bruegel the Elder's *The Bee-keepers and the Birdnester*, 1565. See 'Life in 'The Garden' in Chapter seven. (© *2018 Scala, Florence. bpk / Kupferstichkabinett, Berlin / Jörg P. Anders*) The title page shows a detail from the funeral of Archduke Albert, engraved by Cornelis Galle after Jacques Franckaert, 1623 (*Rijksmuseum, Amsterdam*). The image following the contents page is a medieval miniature from the *Croniques des rois de France* somewhat schematically showing Louis the Pious (right) posthumously blessing the Empire's split into West Francia (Charles the Bald), Lotharingia (Lothair I) and East Francia (Louis the German) (*Alamy*). Chapter one: Objects recovered from the tomb of Childeric I in Tournai. From Jean-Jacques Chifflet's *Anastasis Childerici I. Francorum Regis, siue Thesaurus Sepulchralis Tornaci Nerviorum . . . (The Resurrection of Childeric the First, King of the Franks, or the Funerary Treasure of Tournai of the Nervians)*, published in Antwerp in 1655 by Moretus (the family that inherited the Plantin business – see chapter seven). Chapter two: A somewhat conjectural image of Godfrey de Bouillon at the Siege of Jerusalem. From *Hutchinson's History of the Nations*, published 1915. (*Design Pics Inc/REX/Shutterstock*). Chapter three: An illustration from Hildegard von Bingen's *Scivias* showing the Trinity (Jesus at the centre and the two circles representing unillustratable God and the Holy Ghost), from the *Rupertsberg Codex* – the twelfth-century original disappeared, probably destroyed during the bombing of Dresden, but fortunately the nuns of the abbey of Eibingen painted accurate copies in the 1920s and early 1930s (*akg-images*). Chapter four: Jan van Eyck's *Saint Barbara*, 1437 (*Royal Fine Arts Museum, Antwerp / Alamy*). Chapter five: Niklas Reiser's portrait of Mary the Rich, c. 1500 (*Ambras Castle, Innsbruck / Alamy*). Chapter six: Hans Holbein's *Dance of Death*, c. 1526 – the old man being helped to his grave. Chapter seven: sketches of dodos by

Roelandt Savery, c. 1626 (*Crocker Art Museum, Sacramento/Alamy*). Chapter eight: mid-eighteenth-century engraving of different forms of fortification by Blaise François Pagan and Sébastian Le Prestre de Vauban (*akg-images*). Chapter nine: drawing of Anton van Leeuwenhoek and tiny friends by Gaetano Gandolfi, eighteenth century (*Metropolitan Museum of Art, New York*). Chapter ten: Detail from an engraving, c. 1801, showing how Napoleon might attack England using a Channel tunnel and an armada of hot-air balloons (*Pictorial Press/Alamy*). Chapter eleven: A still of Bruno S. in Werner Herzog's *The Enigma of Kaspar Hauser (Jeder für sich und Gott gegen alle)*, 1974. Chapter twelve: The Strasbourg Statue in the Place de la Concorde draped in mourning, May 1871 (*Roger-Viollet/TopFoto*). Chapter thirteen: British tanks from the Allied occupation forces by the west front of Cologne Cathedral, c. 1919 (*The Tank Museum, Bovington*). Chapter fourteen: the ruins of St Laurentius Church and the inner city of Rotterdam after the aerial bombing of the city, 14/15 May 1940 (*akg-images/ullstein bild*).

Acknowledgements

As ever I must acknowledge the extraordinary patience and kindness of various receptionists, guides, guards, academics, waiters, librarians, taxi drivers, a ski instructor and a croupier for putting up with me in various ways. I am extremely grateful to Tim Blanning, Paul Baggaley, Christine Jones and Jonathan Galassi for sternly corrective readings of the text; and for many conversations, for help and for advice to: John Seaton, Pankaj Mishra, Ulinka Rublack, Barend Wallet, Maria Bedford, Christopher Clark, the ever missed Carol Janeway and David Miller, Mark Allinson, Tom Penn, Gillian Fitzgerald-Kelly, Richard Barber, Adam Phillips, Ellen Davies, Henrika Lähnemann, Patrick McGuinness, Lieutenant General Ben Hodges, Richard Duguid and Brendan Simms. As ever, I am very much indebted to Stefan McGrath and Tom Weldon; to Andrew Wylie, Sarah Chalfant and Tracy Bohan; and to Nicholas Blake. I would like to acknowledge the critical role played in the writing of this book by the makers of the Belgian liqueur *Mandarine Napoléon*, a sickly chaos of macerated fruit, green tea, cinnamon, eau-de-vie and cloves ('complexe, riche et généreuse, idéale pour les dames et les messieurs exigeants'). Glasses of *Mandarine Napoléon* drove along the writing of this book as much as printer ink and pencils. I would also like to thank Penny and David Edgar, James and Sandra Jones, Stephanie Poirier, Elizabeth Winder (for a great deal) and the various members of the Winder and Perrett clans.

Above all I have to thank my own family, who slightly unfortunately have grown up while I have been staring at a computer screen or been ill in Lille. It is hard to imagine a more entertaining and cheerful bunch and I am endlessly in the debt of Barnaby, Felix and Martha for many years of affection and comedy. This book is dedicated to Christine Jones, to whom I am myself totally dedicated.

Simon Winder
Sequim, Wandsworth Town 2014–18

Index